NIGHTMARE
ON
33RD STREET

ALSO BY RICK CARPINELLO

Messier: Hockey's Dragon Slayer
McGregor Publishing

NIGHTMARE
ON
33RD STREET

A LONG SEASON WITH
THE NEW YORK RANGERS

Rick Carpiniello

ALBION PRESS • TAMPA, FLORIDA

NIGHTMARE ON 33RD STREET
Copyright © 2001 by Rick Carpiniello

Albion Press
4532 West Kennedy Blvd., Suite 233
Tampa, FL 33609

Cover photo by Bruce Bennett
Cover design by Antler Designworks
Book design and composition by John Reinhardt Book Design

Library of Congress Cataloging-in-Publication Data

Carpiniello, Rick, 1956–
Nightmare on 33rd Street : a long season with the New York Rangers / Rick Carpiniello.
p. cm.
ISBN 0-9709170-0-7
1. New York Rangers (Hockey Team) I. Title: Nightmare on Thirty-Third Street. II. Title.

GV848.N43 C37 2001
796.962'64'097471—dc21

2001053671

Printed in Canada

To the author's favorite athlete of all-time, Adam Graves. What a wonderful planet this would be if there were even only a few more like him.

———

To the courageous heroes, the survivors and the victims of the World Trade Center horror on 9-11-01.

———

And, finally, to the memory of a friend, Glenn Super, whose life was all about making people laugh.

NIGHTMARE

Acknowledgments

SPECIAL THANKS to the Rangers organization, especially to coach Ron Low for his often-brutal honesty, and to the players who made an otherwise miserable season nevertheless interesting and worth writing about.

Thanks are due to John Rosasco and his public relations staff, including Jason Vogel, Keith Soutar and Jennifer Schoenfeld. Also to Darren Blake, who moves the team from city to city and occasionally helps out a lost or troubled reporter, too.

I appreciate the help from the editor of this book, Ken Samelson. Finally, gratitude goes to my fellow beat writers who make these seemingly endless seasons bearable. To them, this inside message: WDTTFGCF.

NIGHTMARE

Contents

NIGHTMARE
ON
33RD STREET

ME

I Hope I Won't Leave
With a Blindfold On

HOW DOES A TEAM get to this point?

Well, the most obvious way is to mortgage the future, to sell an organization's soul, for a Stanley Cup it hadn't won in 54 years.

From 1993 through 1994, the New York Rangers, and their president/ general manager Neil Smith, traded the likes of star players Doug Weight and Tony Amonte, and solid checker Todd Marchant for bigger, grittier, more experienced playoff performers Esa Tikkanen, Brian Noonan, Stephane Matteau, and Craig MacTavish.

Those trades helped end the 54-year-old hex, and brought the Stanley Cup to the Garden for the first time since 1940. That June 14, 1994 night, a fan raised a placard that summed up the feeling of all long-time sufferers: "Now I can die in peace."

Then the Rangers, under multiple, changing ownership groups, and Smith, did what anybody would have done. They tried to win it again.

The core of that team was intact, and a good part of it was just hitting its prime.

So Smith dealt a first-rounder in a deal to pick up Pat Verbeek. He dealt away Sergei Zubov and Petr Nedved, two highly skilled players, for Ulf Samuelsson and Luc Robitaille, choosing those two instead of Teemu Selanne, who could have been had. Selanne had just flipped over a car

1

racing in his native Finland, a rumor said, and Robitaille and Samuelsson seemed a safer bet, bringing a big-time scorer and a big-time nasty presence on defense.

And if Robitaille had done what he has done every year of his career except the ones he spent in New York—score goals like the future Hall of Famer he is—that trade might have worked out fine.

Smith had two shots at Brendan Shanahan, a power winger. One missed because, while Smith was trying to get the financial green light from ownership, then-St. Louis GM Mike Keenan traded Shanahan to Hartford. Another time, Smith was working on a deal that would have sent Alexei Kovalev for Shanahan, but had it vetoed by captain Mark Messier, who loved Kovalev, and by Wayne Gretzky, who disliked Shanahan.

While trolling for Gretzky, who was about to be traded by Los Angeles in 1996, Smith learned that also available were another bunch of former Edmonton Oilers. Gretzky, on the verge of his first trip to unrestricted free agency, didn't want to sign a new contract before being traded, so the Rangers backed away from him, figuring they could take a crack at The Great One as a free agent that summer.

Instead, with Messier urging him, Smith obtained Jari Kurri, Marty McSorley, and Shane Churla—a lot of muscle and a lot of experience with a lot of mileage—for young players Mattias Norstrom, Ian Laperriere, and veteran Ray Ferraro.

Meanwhile, the Rangers' drafts under Smith provided little in the first round from 1989 through 1996—including busts Michael Stewart, Peter Ferraro and Jeff Brown, and Stefan Cherneski, whose promising career was cut short by a major knee injury. They did come up with future NHL players Kovalev, Niklas Sundstrom and Dan Cloutier in other first rounds, but did rather well in the second round and later drafting the likes of Weight, Zubov, Sergei Nemchinov, Norstrom, Marchant, Kim Johnsson (with the last pick of the '94 draft), Marc Savard and Mike York.

SMITH'S LEGACY SHOULD ALWAYS be that he brought Mark Messier to New York in 1991, with this fierce hunger to finally win a Cup for the Rangers, and that it all worked that magical 1993–94 season. And that he fleeced Glen Sather in the trade, sending Bernie Nicholls, Louie DeBrusk and Steven Rice (and a big bag of money) to Edmonton for Messier and future considerations that brought big Jeff Beukeboom later on. He also ripped off Sather in signing Adam Graves, and giving up forgettable Troy Mallette in the compensation/arbitration case.

Unfortunately for Smith, though, he will always be remembered for the Messier fiasco in 1997, a year in which the Rangers made an unexpected run to the Eastern Conference finals with both Messier and Gretzky on the team. That would be the Rangers' last playoff appearance.

The Garden—then-chairman Rand Araskog, Garden president Dave Checketts, even Smith—had become infatuated with Gretzky, and chose to keep him as the anchor of the franchise over Messier.

The captain, the best player to ever wear the uniform, the Messiah, was shown the door. Oh, there was an ugly negotiation of a low-ball contract, and the parting was made out in a lot of corners to have been over money. It wasn't. Messier was unwanted and made to feel unwanted, and so he left, to Vancouver on a contract worth a minimum of $20 million for three years, with options for two more years.

It was a disaster of the first order. For three seasons the Rangers failed to make the playoffs, failed to even come close in three miserable, aimless seasons, while Messier was in Vancouver, also missing the playoffs for three straight years.

WHILE THAT MAY GO DOWN as Smith's biggest gaffe ever, or at least his worst miscalculation, the organization was further set on its ear the following season, when Smith fired coach Colin Campbell and replaced him with John Muckler.

Muckler came with a reputation as being good with young players, a reputation that he wore proudly from his days as the coach, then the GM, in Buffalo.

But it was a reputation built on a lie.

The Rangers were just starting a rebuilding program, one ordered during the 1997–98 season by Checketts and bought by Smith. Muckler had a complete free pass to lose, to miss the playoffs, and all he had to do was bring along some young players. He couldn't do it. He wouldn't do it.

At the end of the season in which Muckler was hired, with the Rangers woefully out of the race, Muckler nevertheless refused to play some of the team's young players. He buried guys like big Eric Cairns, skilled Maxim Galanov, defensemen Stan Neckar and Jason Doig. He called them nice things like "garbage." Some turned out to be, at the worst, NHL-caliber players. Some didn't. But this was a time when they had to play, if for no other reason that to try to drive up their value so that they could be traded for something. Instead, Galanov, a bust, and the enormous Cairns, who played the physical defense role well for the Islanders, were lost for nothing.

Muckler's biggest sin was his treatment of Manny Malhotra, the centerpiece of the Rangers' budding rebuilding program as their first-round pick in the 1998 draft.

Muckler refused to play him, called him overrated, stunted his development and wasted more than a full year of his career. Malhotra went to the World Junior Championships in Sweden in January and was scheduled to rejoin the team for a game in Toronto. The day before, however, when asked what his plans were for the 19-year-old, Muckler said he didn't even know when he was coming back. Nobody told him, he claimed, even though every other coach, every player, every member of the media, and every fan knew when Malhotra was due back.

It was disgraceful, and became the focal point for the dysfunction of the relationship between Smith and Muckler.

THE 1999–2000 SEASON was the undoing. Smith's rebuilding plan was moving along. Smith had refused to empty the vault to get Pavel Bure from Vancouver in 1998–99; and there was evidence later that the Canucks just weren't willing to trade him to New York.

But Gretzky, without top-level linemates and seeing the direction the Rangers were headed, retired at the end of that season, leaving a hole.

Then, on draft day, Smith made a series of calculated moves—his safety net being the Garden checkbook and unrestricted free agency in July. Smith traded young players Nicklas Sundstrom and goalie Dan Cloutier and a first-round 2000 draft pick to obtain the fourth pick overall. With that he plucked junior sniper Pavel Brendl. Smith then made another deal with Calgary, sending small center Marc Savard (whom Muckler didn't want around) to the Flames for Jan Hlavac and a swap of picks. With Calgary's pick, Smith chose Jamie Lundmark. He would have been unable to do any of those things if he had traded Sundstrom, Cloutier and a first-round pick for Bure.

The rebuilding was on.

To fill the holes left by the departures of Gretzky, Sundstrom, Cloutier and Savard, and to build a bridge that they hoped would carry the Rangers until their new prospects were ready in a few years, Smith and Checketts went on a spending spree. It wasn't completely their idea. Jim Dolan, the de facto owner as the chairman of MSG, had gone into the locker room at the end of Gretzky's career to promise the team would be spending millions upon millions on free agents that summer. Dolan had promised as much to Gretzky in an attempt to get him to change his mind and play one more season.

So off went Checketts and Smith, in the company jet, to woo every free agent on their list. They came away with wingers Theo Fleury and Valeri Kamensky, center Tim Taylor, defensemen Sylvain Lefebvre and Stephane Quintal and goalie Kirk McLean.

What that did was raise expectations ridiculously high. Checketts lauded Smith for having as good a summer as could possibly have been imagined. But what Smith and Checketts had bought was one star—Fleury—and a bunch of second tier players. There was no way money was going to make Taylor, Lefebvre, Quintal or McLean anything but that. Kamensky had the skill to be better, but he also had the chance to be the biggest bust of the lot.

Sure enough, with Muckler whipping the horse to win, the rebuilding process was retarded again.

Smith made a brilliant trade in mid-season, dealing Todd Harvey to San Jose in a three-way deal that brought back Radek Dvorak from Florida. But the remainder of the season was a disaster.

MUCKLER HAD DONE THINGS than angered the team, such as taking them to Edmonton a couple of days early for their season opener, because he wanted to be up there for all sorts of Oilers reunions that were ongoing with Gretzky's uniform retirement ceremony. He had family members on the team bus to the game—a no-no. When the wheels were falling off, he told captain Brian Leetch to take the players to dinner on the road, Muckler's treat. Then he handed the bill to a member of the organization. His treat, indeed.

Mostly, they hated his practices, filled with five-against-none, a lot of standing around, then exhausting sprints, even on days before games. They hated his lack of a system, particularly for protecting leads late in games.

But what killed the season was that Smith wanted to fire Muckler in November, and the Garden ownership wouldn't let him. The Garden was gun-shy after having fired Knicks GM Ernie Grunfeld late the season before and seeing Grunfeld's team go to the NBA finals. Anyway, when Smith had fired Campbell, he dried up that option on Muckler. It got bad. The players wanted Muckler out, and Smith had to go in and tell them that Muckler wasn't going anywhere.

The 1999–2000 season turned worse with two events in January. Adam Graves, the team's heart and soul, lost one of his prematurely-born twin sons. Then Kevin Stevens, on his way to being traded away, went out on the town following a game in St. Louis and got himself arrested in a sordid evening that involved crack cocaine and a prostitute.

The Rangers seemed to bond and rally around the two troubled teammates, and they won seven in a row somehow. But even then Muckler ticked off players. Leetch, who was Stevens' roommate on the road and was out with a broken forearm, wanted to go with Smith and Checketts from Atlanta to St. Louis to see Stevens. Muckler wouldn't let him.

The irony was that, while Smith and Mike Keenan couldn't stand one another, they worked perfectly well together until their separation a month after the Stanley Cup parade. Keenan would want something, and Smith would find a way to get it. Keenan, of course, would have given up a lot more than Smith ultimately would give up to get the coach what he needed. They bickered and stabbed each other in the back, but everything they did worked.

On the other hand, Smith and Muckler liked and even respected one another, or at least they kept that appearance to the last days. But they couldn't agree philosophically on the direction of the team, of what should or shouldn't be happening on the ice, and with which players. Malhotra was unfairly painted as the poster boy for the Smith-Muckler relationship, but that was only because the Malhotra situation was the one that got public.

The clock was ticking. Muckler knew he was a goner, and his assistants began to bicker, too. The team completely quit down the stretch, and lost consecutive games to Detroit by a combined 14-2 score. Checketts and Dolan were in the coaches' room after the second game, at home, and the next morning Muckler and Smith were fired. Muckler had taken down the GM, too.

John Tortorella, who would be the interim head coach for the final four games, told someone that, "as a coaching staff, we all deserved to be fired."

Ultimately, they all were, too.

"The bottom line is the results here," Checketts said the day of the Smith/Muckler firings.

"The results should have been better. We should have had more scoring. We should have had more defense. We should have had more wins. We should have had more leadership. And we should have had more pride in being a Ranger."

DOLAN AND CHECKETTS, two non-hockey men who think they know more about hockey than they do—Checketts was a basketball guy, who was a wonderful president of the Garden when it came to all the other things, like running Radio City Music Hall and bringing back Garden boxing—set out to find a new hockey boss.

They didn't look far or hard. After quickly checking out whether Lou Lamoriello, the president and general manager of the Devils, might be willing to jump over the Hudson River to Manhattan once the New Jersey team was sold, and finding out that he wouldn't, Dolan and Checketts chose one man.

He was believed to have come highly recommended from Gary Bettman, the NHL commissioner; and perhaps by Gretzky, who certainly

JIM MCISAAC, BRUCE BENNETT STUDIOS

John Muckler, who was dismissed as Ranger coach after the 1999–2000 season after once again failing to get them into the playoffs.

had Dolan's ear and admiration when he left. Checketts conducted his interview process on a golf course.

The only man considered for the job was Glen Sather. The Rangers first had to pry him out of Edmonton, which they did without a problem. The Oilers' large ownership group was willing to let him go, especially knowing that later in the summer his contract contained a window by which he could escape anyway. So Checketts got permission to talk to Sather in May, and by June 1, the deal was done.

And what a deal it was. Sather's contract has never been exactly nailed down because, for one thing, Dolan had issued a company-wide gag order on such things to go along with a general order against accessibility with the media.

But it was believed to be for as many as seven years, with clauses and such that could bring the total to as much as $5 million per year—or about $4 million a year more than any other NHL executive.

How could Sather say no? That, however, brought the natural question about whether Sather, age 57, actually came for the challenge and dirty job of running and reviving the Rangers, or whether he came for the bag of dollars.

Sather had gone eight consecutive seasons without a winning record. He had the built-in excuse of the minuscule Oilers budget. But his

Glen Sather, the architect of the Edmonton Oilers dynasty in the 1980s, faced the daunting task of restoring the Rangers' glory.

draft record was terrible, far worse than that of Smith, since the 1980s. Also, Sather failed to get anything close to equal value for his future Hall of Famers. The enormous package he got for Gretzky, and the one he got for Messier, were both bombs. He got decent value for Paul Coffey, but nothing for Grant Fuhr, Kevin Lowe, Glenn Anderson or Jari Kurri. His best trade was the one that sent Tikkanen to New York for Weight.

Sather was in his glory on the day he was introduced as the new president/GM of the Rangers, the first new one in 11 years. With the Stanley Cup finals just a river away in New Jersey on that June 1 day, the mass of media from all over Canada, the U.S. and Europe made its way in buses and cabs to the Garden. The giant room known as the Rotunda, where they keep the elephants during the circus, was used for the press conference, and many of the reporters in attendance were Sather's old buddies from Edmonton and other parts north.

He was peppered with questions about Edmonton, about the small-market Canadian teams (and the cheapskate teams like Boston), for whom Sather always championed a fight; about financial responsibility. He had little time for specific questions about his plans to turn the Rangers around, and few answers for those questions. He said he didn't know a lot about what went on the last three years, and that he wasn't going to judge. He and Checketts and Dolan all said that, if the decision to buy out some expensive contracts was made, the money would be there to do so.

Immediately, Sather began plotting the Garden's lofty goal of retooling the Rangers, a team that has missed the playoffs three straight seasons, into a powerhouse.

"We spent a lot of time together talking about the organizatioin, what he thought it might take to get it turned around," Checketts said. "We don't want to just have a great year or win the Cup as a flash. We want to build a dynasty."

That's a long way from the recent history of the Rangers.

Sather accepted the challenge, but he admitted there's a lot of work to be done.

"I know there are going to be a lot of people looking for me to fail," Sather said. "But there's ying and yang in just about anything in life. If you're not ready to accept the challenge you shouldn't be in professional sports.

"I have plenty of things to prove. There's a challenge every day in hockey. It's not something like if you build a building on Madison Avenue; it's up and it's over with. There's a challenge every day to be successful, and I enjoy the challenge."

Not surprisingly, Sather defines success the way his proteges, Messier, Lowe, and Gretzky did:

"I don't think there is success unless you win the Stanley Cup," he said. "That's what our goal is, to win the Stanley Cup."

So first, Sather needs some answers. He said he hasn't had time to "delve into why people didn't live up to expectations." He will poll the players, some of them at his summer home in Banff, Alberta, in hopes of finding those answers. Checketts has already been through that process.

"I think in my end-of-the-season interviews, (Rangers goalie) Mike Richter said something very important," Checketts said. "He said, 'Look, this isn't a one-year phenomenon. This is now a three-year phenomenon. We haven't made the playoffs, and we should be making the playoffs.' I thought that was a very important comment that a change in (management) leadership was necessary, and I think there will be other changes. I don't think we can go in with the same group of people and say we're going to get different results. It's deeper than that."

Sather did say he knows Theo Fleury better than most from the old Edmonton-Calgary days, and he suspects that Fleury, who scored a career-worst 15 goals in his first season as a Ranger, "can be a great player again."

And Checketts said that Sather will have autonomy on hockey decisions, even if he decides that a player needs to be bought out of a contract (Valeri Kamensky? Stephane Quintal?).

Checketts said the plan isn't to make the playoffs, or to win the Stanley Cup, but to build a dynasty, which is a pretty hefty goal. But he feels strongly about Sather.

"I wanted somebody who played here, who understands what it meant to pull on a Rangers sweater," Checketts said. "I felt very strongly when Quintal, at the end of the year, made the comments about not wanting to be here. I think that was part of our problem. A lot of new free agents, a lot of new transplants, and not enough respect of what it meant to be a Ranger. I think Glen will help bring that back."

This, they hoped, was a start.

IN ONE OF HIS SMILING MOMENTS, Sather told a story of his days s a tough-as-nails penalty-killer and third-line who got the nickname "Slats" from spending so much time on the bench.

Emile Francis was then the team's general manager and coach, and Jean Ratelle the team's No. 1 center. It was the 1972 Stanley Cup finals against Boston and the Rangers' trainer Jimmy "Rip" Young was hit in the head with a puck and had to go for stitches.

At about the same time, Ratelle lost the edge on his skate blade.

Francis hollered to Sather, "Slats, get over here."

Thinking he was going to take Ratelle's shift between Rod Gilbert and Vic Hadfield, Sather jumped onto the ice.

To which Francis shouted, "No, no, come on down here and sharpen (Ratelle's) skates."

"Two minutes later," Sather proudly recalled, "I was out there killing a penalty."

THEN, WHEN IT GOT DOWN to Sather and a smaller group of reporters, mostly from New York, Dolan butted in.

"Can we please have lunch now?" Dolan asked loudly. Sather followed him away from the podium. The conference was over.

SATHER'S FIRST PRIORITY was the draft, then the July 8 wedding of his son, an event at which some of the Edmonton writers would be attending. Also on the invitation list was Ron Low, the former goalie, and former head coach of the Oilers, who was forced out by a low-ball contract offer from Sather a few years earlier.

Sather and Low denied it for a month, but at the wedding it was clinched that Low would be the Rangers' next coach, since Kevin Lowe, the former Rangers and Oilers defenseman and a six-time Stanley Cup champ and Sather's No. 1 choice, would make the move from Edmonton coach and succeed Sather as the second-ever Oilers GM.

That wasn't an easy decision for Lowe. Coaching was in his blood now, but the owners of the Oilers wanted him to become the GM, replacing Sather. That would leave Craig MacTavish as the Oilers' coach. MacTavish didn't want to leave Lowe to come to New York to coach, but that would have been an option, too. Lowe wrestled and wrestled with the decision, and finally accepted the GM's job in Edmonton, a decision over which, he told Sather later, he had some regret.

In the meantime, Sather had some decisions to make, and the decision he made most often was that everything here before him was wrong. So every player whose contract was up, who could be a free agent, was let go without even consideration given to his re-signing. That included Mathieu Schneider, who not only played well in 1999-2000, but also played with grit that his teammates admired. Schneider had a terrific year, despite a coach who disliked him. Sather let him walk away. Sather also left unprotected a number of veterans for the expansion draft –free for the picking by the league's two new teams in Minnesota and Columbus.

They included defenseman Rich Pilon, wingers Valeri Kamensky and John MacLean, and goalie Kirk McLean, plus Schneider and fellow free agents Kevin Stevens, Kevin Hatcher, Alexandre Daigle, and popular minor-leaguer P.J. Stock. (Also getting the boot were assistant coaches John Tortorella, Keith Acton and Charlie Huddy; Tortorella wound up a Tampa Bay assistant, Acton a Toronto assistant and Huddy an Edmonton assistant.)

"At some point in time, this organization has to get younger and get some enthusiasm," Sather said. "I'm trying to send out a wakeup call to the entire team. If you're not going to work and sacrifice yourself, then there's no room for you. If you're just along for the ride, this is not a retirement process here."

Sather kept one key guy around, Don Maloney, who was the assistant GM to Smith, and held the organization together during the transition to Sather's team. Sather brought in guys like Tom Renney and Al Coates and scout Harry Howell, surrounding himself with layers of experienced executives who could do part of his work.

He needed a coach, though, and that would be his most important decision. Whomever he got would have to be better than Muckler. People all around the league agreed that the Rangers were, in the words of more than one GM "pitifully" coached the year before. The Rangers desperately needed a coach who would instill some sort of defensive system, or at least teach defensive responsibility and positioning in their own end, all of which escaped Muckler.

In the coming weeks, as Sather was denying he had decided on Ron Low as a coach, he mentioned the name of Mike Keenan, the coach who drove the Rangers to their championship in 1994. Keenan and Sather had spoken once. Now the unemployed Keenan was led to believe, through the media, that Sather was considering him. But Keenan couldn't get Sather to return a single call thereafter.

When the free agency period began, Sather signed defenseman Vladimir Malakhov, a career underachiever, to a laughable four-year, $14 million contract. And, of course, Sather denied having signed Malakhov for more than a week before the official announcement.

Then there was the biggest denial, and the sorriest attempt to hide the organizational move that everybody on the planet knew was coming— the re-signing of Messier, whose option year was not picked up by Vancouver. Messier had permission from the Canucks to talk to Sather before the free agency period began July 1, and they did speak, and it became just a matter of the contract, and how and when they would make the announcement. It made sense that the naming of Low as coach should come first, but that was delayed until mid-July.

THEN, ON BACK-TO-BACK DAYS, the Rangers leadership was completed. Low was officially named coach, and Messier was signed to a two-year, $11 million contract.

Low took over as Oilers coach from Ted Green with 13 games remaining in 1994-95, after two seasons of coaching in the AHL, ran the Oilers for the next four seasons, compiling a 139-162-40 record in 341 games. His Oilers made the playoffs three times, advancing to the second round twice via upsets.

But, after being swept by eventual champ Dallas in four one-goal games in the first round in 1999, Low had a contract skirmish with Sather, turned down a low-ball offer around $450,000 and was replaced by Kevin Lowe.

Low spent last season as the GM/coach of the Houston Aeros of the IHL, a team he guided to a 44-29-9 record. The Aeros reached the playoff semifinals before losing to the eventual champ Chicago Wolves in six games.

A goalie by trade, Low played for six teams, including the Oilers and the original Devils, in an 11-year NHL career.

As a Devil, Low was partly responsible for one of the most infamous moments of Wayne Gretzky's career. The powerhouse Oilers routed the Devils 13-4, and Gretzky, feeling sorry for his former teammate and pal Low, called the Devils "a Mickey Mouse organization."

Low, who brought along assistant coaches Green and Walt Kyle, will become the 18th and 19th members of the Edmonton 1984-90 dynasty to join the Rangers organization in some capacity. They are: Messier, Kevin Lowe, Adam Graves, Jeff Beukeboom, MacTavish, Esa Tikkanen, Glenn Anderson, Gretzky, Jari Kurri, Marty McSorley, Charlie Huddy, Geoff Smith, Muckler, Acton, Joe Murphy, Dave Brown, Sather, and now Low and Green. Scout Harry Howell will make it 20.

LOW IS A GOOD GUY, with a sense of humor and the respect of his players. His buddies, especially the assistant coaches, call him "Low Tide," which is hardly attractive. Or in the case of the high-pitched, dragged-out whines that come out of the mouth of Kyle, "Tiiiiide."

Low came to the Rangers well aware of the task he faces. In his own words, he isn't "coming in with a blindfold on."

Then realizing the words he chose, added, "I hope I won't leave with a blindfold on."

Coaches can be chewed up and spit out, or placed before a firing squad, in a city, and with an organization, such as this. The Rangers have had 34 coaching changes in the last 60 years, and only one of those men has won a Stanley Cup here.

As if that weren't a daunting enough task, Low is being asked by Cablevision boss Jim Dolan, by Garden president Dave Checketts, by Rangers president/GM Glen Sather, to restore order to a team that hasn't made the playoffs three years running. He is being asked, no ordered, to make the playoffs while trying to rebuild on the fly.

"It is not acceptable for this team not to make the playoffs," Sather said.

"I definitely agree with that," Low, 50, said. "That's a step that has to be taken. I don't think it's going to be an easy one. In fact, I know it isn't going to be an easy one.

"I think it's going to be imperative that there is an (attitude) adjustment. Obviously, it wasn't good. It couldn't have been good. There were too many underachievers."

Low, who is believed to have received a deal for more than the two-year limit Sather normally tries to stick on his coaches, noted that there had to be other factors, that it's ridiculous to assume all those Rangers fell past their primes at once last year. He has spoken to departed coach John Muckler several times. He and his assistants will rotate 15 game tapes among them.

He has spoken to his Manitoba neighbor, Theo Fleury, and he is gathering as much information as possible without looking back, but instead trying to find solutions.

Low's hat landed in the ring by accident, he claimed. Having been lowballed out as Edmonton coach in 1999 by Sather, who said he simply didn't have enough money to give Low a raise, the two stayed friends. In early June, Low called Sather's wife to decline the invitation to the wedding of the Sathers's son. Low, instead, would have to attend IHL meetings as the GM/coach of the Houston Aeros.

They got to talking, and Low quickly went to the top of the list. So, not only did he get the job, but he was able to attend the wedding, too.

The hiring of Green, the salty 60-year-old ex-Boston Bruin and long-time Edmonton executive/coach/assistant coach and Kyle, who ran Edmonton's top farm club, gives Sather a team he can immediately trust and know, so "we won't have to go through a honeymoon" period.

The Rangers still need some parts—certainly more size and toughness.

Talk about toughness. The knowledgeable rising-star Kyle has survived two bouts with cancer—had part of his ribcage removed, then part of a lung, and has now been cancer free for 12 years.

And Green, best known for an infamous 1969 stick-swinging incident with Wayne Maki of Chicago (Green was suspended 13 games, Maki a month), was such a mean customer with Boston that one-time Rangers president William Jennings is alleged by both Sather and Green to have put a bounty on Green's head after a couple of, as Green put it, "donnybrooks".

"Really, I came here with trepidation," Green said. "I was a little nervous walking down the streets and coming into the building because at one time there was a bounty on my head. I wasn't sure if it was still in effect or not.

"Mr. Jennings said he'd rather have my head on his desk than the Stanley Cup."

NEXT UP WAS THE MAN who would rather have the Stanley Cup on his desk than anything in the world, and who had done so six times, once with the Rangers.

When Glen Sather traded Messier to the Rangers in 1991, he told then-Rangers president/GM Neil Smith that Messier "will fix every problem you have on your team and in your locker room."

Now Sather has replaced Smith, and the problems that need to be fixed are many. On the day he named Low the Rangers' new coach, Sather spoke about the problems that crop up on every team, and how those problems have to stay inside the team, and be solved by the team.

"Mark was brought up in that same system," Sather said, maintaining his silence on the completed contract. "Mark's great for those kinds of things. He's a great guy, and if we get to that step, I'll be as happy as anyone."

The only question left was whether Messier will accept the captaincy from his close friend and successor Brian Leetch.

Low said that Messier wasn't mentioned to him until the past weekend, when it came up at Sather's son's wedding.

"Excitement is something that immediately crossed my mind," said Low, the first NHL roommate of Messier. "I'd like to have everything dotted before we talk about him, but I know what Mark brings to the table. He's an incredible leader and people rally around him. He'd be a great guy to coach.

"He's one of a handful of people in the last few decades that has been that consummate leader."

He came and he conquered here once. Now, a day later, he'd be back to try to do it again.

THAT MARK MESSIER CRIED at his re-introductory press conference is not news.

Messier always cries. He did when he won his first Conn Smythe Trophy as playoff MVP and his first Stanley Cup in 1984. He wept when the Rangers honored him for playing in his 1,000th game in 1994 by bringing his family onto the ice. He bawled when he signed his new contract in 1995. He spent a summer sobbing when the Rangers let him, or forced him to go to Vancouver as a free agent in 1997, and he broke down in his first game back at the Garden as an ex-Ranger.

But these latest tears were excessive, even by the emotional Messier's standards, and they expressed exactly how much it means to him to be back, to be wearing the blueshirt with No. 11 on the back and the "C" on the front.

That is what touched off the waterfall, when Messier's closest friend, Brian Leetch, handed over the captaincy that he had inherited when Messier left town three years earlier.

"Certainly, Mark, I have the utmost respect for," Leetch told a large crowd at the Garden news conference announcing the two-year, $11 million contract that had become a formality. "As much as anybody I've ever met, as a person, on and off the ice."

Then Leetch instructed Messier, 39, to "come up and put on the jersey that looks best on you."

Leetch unfolded the jersey with the "C" on the front, and Messier put it on and broke down.

"The people close to me know how much I think of Brian," Messier said through the tears.

"For him to turn the captaincy over to me, and for me to accept it is a real honor."

The day was not without the expected feel-good atmosphere, though, and not without some laughs.

Leetch cracked up the crowd when he said he gave up the "C" because "I was concerned Mark might become a problem in the locker room if we didn't make that move."

One of the laughs was a clever scene played out on the stage between Garden president Dave Checketts and Messier. Checketts was at least partly responsible for Messier's departure in 1997, and he badmouthed the outgoing captain for taking Vancouver's $6 million per year. At one point that summer, Checketts, who handed $18 million a year to the NBA Knicks' Patrick Ewing the same month, barked "How long to I have to keep paying for that (1994) Cup?"

So Checketts had a glass tank with dirt wheeled onto the stage, then some more dirt in a wheelbarrow, and two shovels. Checketts threw a hatchet into the dirt, and he and Messier buried it before popping flash-bulbs.

"Mark Messier has become synonymous with New York like few other modern-day athletes with any city," Checketts said. "He carried a championship on his shoulders. He has arguably meant more to the Rangers sweater than anyone who has ever worn it. I know I speak for Rangers fans everywhere—most of whom I've heard from the last three years—when I say that it's an honor that No. 11, Mark Messier has returned to New York and to the Rangers."

Checketts, who said several times, "we all make mistakes," claimed that the decision to bring back the captain was made on April 18, 1999, the day of Gretzky's last game, when Messier was introduced as a special guest and brought down the house.

"The fans' appreciation for Mark, I actually said it to a number of people that night, that 'this is the way it ought to end for him.' That night I decided we were going to get him back here, one way or another."

Surely, there was a decision made at the Garden after the just completed season that Messier would be brought back to fix the internal problems.

But if what Checketts said was even partly true, then perhaps that decision had more than a little to do with the firings of Smith and Muckler.

The coach, who had Messier in Edmonton and felt betrayed by Messier leaving to come to New York in 1991, didn't want him back.

And not only did Smith not want him back—believing that it just wasn't the right move—but it was extremely doubtful that Messier would return if Smith was still calling the shots.

Checketts said he hopes Messier, this time, finishes his career here, and that if he wants a job in hockey after his playing days, there will be one for him with the Rangers. He said nobody will ever wear No. 11 for the Rangers again.

Messier, the leading active scorer in the NHL, and the all-time leader in playoff games played, was only concerned about now and the immediate future. He guaranteed the Rangers will make the playoffs—something neither he or they have done since he left—and insisted that is not the goal. The goal, as usual, is the Stanley Cup, he said.

"Part of the allure of coming to New York is overcoming all the obstacles, all the things that make it so tough to win," Messier said. "I'm not here to retire. I'm here to win, to do the things I've done in the past.

"New York is going to be proud of this team again," Messier promised.

"Mark said he may not be able to carry a team to a Stanley Cup," said Sather, "but he can lead it."

Messier repeatedly had to stop talking at the podium because of his tears. At one point, he blurted out, "Oh, man, this is ridiculous."

Later he sat at a table with dozens of reporters and confidently answered questions. He was cooler than he had been in his first go-round, when Messier was quotable and available, comfortable and cooperative. But he felt that some around that table had betrayed him in his fight with management, leading to his departure to Vancouver.

"I still feel like I can make a difference," Messier said in a rare admission, or reference, to his age. "It's a challenge. I'm not 25 anymore. I can't walk through walls and not feel a thing like I did then. Sometimes I spend more time in bed between games resting than I used to. But I still think I know what it takes to get players around me to tick."

That is why he's here, back home.

NIGH**2**MARE

I Think Everybody Wants to Get Back to a Situation Where It's Fun again

NEW YORK

IN THE DAYS LEADING to the opening of training camp, the Rangers and goalie Mike Richter were told pretty much what they expected—that Richter won't be in goal on the first day of camp, and that he won't be in goal on opening night in Atlanta.

Richter, who underwent major reconstructive surgery on his left knee last April, said that the rehabilitation has been going better than expected, but that there is no way to beat the allotted time the new knee needs to be completely ready for the rigors of goaltending.

"It's healing beautifully," Richter said. "I haven't had much pain, and the swelling has really gone down. It's been amazing. But the doctors kind of sobered me up. They told me, 'You can give me every song and dance, but there are certain time periods I won't discuss with you.' I was surprised to hear that."

In other words, no matter how hard the workout-a-holic Richter works, he can't cut the time frame for his return. So when his teammates go onto the training-camp ice Saturday in Burlington, Vermont, Richter will be a spectator doing off-ice training.

Richter, who has been given the OK to rollerblade, and has been on ice skates only briefly, can't begin taking limited shots on goal until around October 1. If all goes well, he can begin taking shots from teammates in practice around the October 7 opener.

"I do have to get stronger," Richter said. "The surgeons told me that physical healing has to take place. No matter how strong you make it, the tissue needs a certain amount of time for it to be safe to use at a high level.

"It's 90 percent healed in six months, but it takes longer to get that last 10 percent. If I was a forward, I could play right now. But getting up and down, and really stretching it out . . . I need a little more time."

Richter and the Rangers know that he shouldn't put too much emphasis on an early return (especially since the Rangers have a soft early-season schedule).

"The only thing that keeps me reeled in is if you push it too far, the repercussions are huge," he said. "To me, that's worth another 10 days."

"He wants to get at it right now, and he's not ready right now," Rangers coach Ron Low said. "The biggest problem is keeping him away long enough."

FRIDAY, SEPTEMBER 8, 2000

BURLINGTON, VT.

The Rangers had their physicals, went through their batteries of strength and conditioning tests and made the short flight from Westchester County Airport to this lovely, green mountain city, where they will do their first business as a team on the rink at the University of Vermont, and where they have trained since 1995.

It is a terrific location for camp, just far enough away to promote bonding of teammates, just close enough to home to not be a hassle. There is enough to do in downtown Burlington—restaurants, golf courses, sights—to keep a team busy for the four or five nights it spends here.

The entire population of the state of Vermont is only about 600,000 or so. Those who drive up, as most of the reporters do, can come one of two ways. They can drive upstate through New York, then cross beautiful Lake Champlain via ferry over to Burlington, or they can drive up through Connecticut and Massachussetts and wind their way through the Green Mountains. That is the scenic route, complete with mountain-top fog—clouds, actually—and signs for moose crossings.

The city of Burlington is dominated by IBM, the University of Vermont and, of course, Ben and Jerry's ice cream.

There is also a military base, and on the first few nights of this camp, fighter jets repeatedly taking off to the Middle East break the sound barrier and awaken anybody in the area from a dead sleep.

Before the Rangers would commence skating, they came together for a team dinner at which new team president/general manager Glen Sather addressed the troops. He tried to keep it upbeat and positive, but he was also stern when it came to laying down the law.

Things were going to be different this year, he vowed.

Sather posted a private list of rules, which had to do with dress code and conduct. Some of the sillier, sophomoric rules included that any women guests in the team hotel had to first be approved by management; that alcohol was prohibited in the hotel; and that no team equipment, right down to sticks, was to be given away without permission.

The rule about women in the hotel seemed silly. These guys were here to work, and their moral reputations were pretty good anyway. There had never been any scandal, any reports of debauchery on the road. Besides, if somebody decided he was going to fool around, it would be done secretly anyway. Now it would have to be ultra-secretly. This just seemed like an unnecessary threat.

The rule about giving away sticks and things was just foolish and small-minded. Most of the guys are only too happy to give away sticks for charities—school raffles, auctions, etc. Most of them get their sticks for free, straight from the manufacturer, at no cost to the Rangers. OK, so Sather didn't want them giving away uniform jerseys, gloves, or other equipment.

(There was a player once traded by Sather from Edmonton who claimed he got a bill for a pair of "runners"—which is what hockey players call sneakers. What, was Sather was going to have another player use the sneakers that had been worn by the traded player?)

Anyway, the speech—or at least parts of it—hit home. Dave Checketts, the president of Madison Square Garden, also got up and spoke. Ron Low, the new head coach, declined to speak

"I leave that up to the master," he said.

Sather would only share bits and pieces. One thing he made clear was that this team would not tolerate some of the things that happened with last year's team—the back-biting in the media, particularly the negative, almost always anonymous griping about coach John Muckler.

When asked about the speech, Sather at first shrugged and said, "Training camp talk. Things you would say to your family."

He made a face as if he expected the discussion to turn to a different topic. That wasn't going to happen. The media on the first day of camp wanted to know more.

"Part of the message I gave them was it's pretty much a clean slate." he said. "Some of the things that were said are things that have to stay within the hockey club. I explained that to them, and I explained what a privilege and honor it is to represent the New York Rangers, and they need to honor it. If you've got a problem with anybody here, keep it on the inside.

"The other thing we talked about last night is the pressure of the expectations to win, and what happens in the initial stages if you don't win.

"I think there were a lot of expectations and pressure on these guys last year, not only from the exterior but from the interior. Internally they probably put pressure on themselves to perform and it's the old hockey cliche: 'The harder I try, the worser I get.' I told them. It's that kind of deal of putting so much pressure on themselves. I told them to relax and have fun, go enjoy themselves at training camp and make sure they don't get hurt. Get to know each other, start to become dependable."

There is probably nobody on the planet who has watched Sather more closely in his career than Mark Messier, and probably nobody he respects and trusts more.

Like Sather, Messier didn't care to elaborate in detail on the speech.

"There are some things that, quite frankly, aren't anybody's business," Messier said.

Not that he didn't want to talk about the dinner and the ramifications he hopes it might have on the team.

"You can ask anybody that was in the room," Messier said. "It was a real rallying cry. I think everybody was pretty emotional right after it, and I think everybody was ready to go to war right after that, and I think that's the kind of meeting the team needed, from the guy coming to his first training camp to guys who've been around five years to guys who've been here for 20 years. You know what's expected of you, and of the team.

"It's great to know we have people upstairs making the decisions. (Sather) is a master motivator He always has been. He knows what he wants as a team, and he knows what he wants from his players, and I think he got his message across very eloquently to everybody. I thought it was really good. I thought it was better than really good. I thought it was what everybody needed to hear."

Messier got up and spoke a bit, too.

"I didn't cry, so that was good," he laughed, taking a rare dig at himself. "I'm making progress."

BURLINGTON, VT.

Nearly 38 months after his tearful departure left the Rangers in ruins, Mark Messier went back to work, trying to rebuild a fractured team

Messier, closing in on 40, skated in the team's first training-camp workout at the University of Vermont, but more importantly, he began to attempt to remold the rubble of the three non-playoff seasons the Rangers have suffered without him.

"There's some tremendously skilled players and some building blocks," he said. "To sit here and try to foresee what is going to happen to this team after the last three years is hard to say. I mean, obviously there were big problems here the last three years to not have made the playoffs. Hopefully we can turn it around immediately. Am I expecting that? I don't think it would be fair to anybody to expect it to happen immediately. For us, right now, it's important for us to build on everything I've talked about, to really take care of the things that are important as far as being successful.

"A lot of things have to change and hopefully last night's meetings were a start to that."

Messier promised that the new Rangers will care about one another, enough so that they will no longer be pushed around. He said it will take time, that the new bonding won't happen until this team shares "trenches" together, but this is exactly the type of job for which Messier was re-hired.

Messier was asked questions about Petr Nedved, a player he scorned in their first tours as Rangers in 1995. Messier called Nedved coura-geous. He said that Nedved had been "battered from pillar to post" and still played effectively, and showed a resolve and toughness that he hadn't shown in '95.

But Messier also noted that Nedved wasn't protected from intimida-tion tactics last season. And he called for more team toughness and to-getherness.

"You can have six of the toughest guys in the league, but if you don't play as a team and you don't care for each other and genuinely feel re-sponsible for the protection of every player, it doesn't matter how many enforcers you have," Messier said. "Toughness and sticking up for each other is something that comes from within a team. It doesn't come from individuals. It never has and never will. Part of the problem last year is that the team was fragmented for whatever reason. And those things happen when a team is fragmented because other teams sense it. They

know the team isn't together, and they know you might be willing to
fight for yourself, but you're not willing to fight for each other. I know
it's not going to happen to one of Glen's teams and (coach) Ronnie (Low)
is a big believer in that and of course I've always felt that's a big part of
any team's success. So obviously, that will be one area we will try to
address."

Messier said his return to the team's captaincy, to the lead-dog role,
had evolved quickly this second time around.

"I don't think it's ever fast," he said. "There's only a few players here I
really know, that I've played with. I don't think you can take anything for
granted. We've all seen each other and played against each other, but
until you're on a team, and in the same trenches, that doesn't mean anything. You've got to build amongst the group itself, and that comes from
being around each other and getting together and becoming a team."

He was also asked what he could expect from himself in the season in
which he will hit the big Four-Oh.

"My goals have become pretty team-oriented the last few years," he
said. "That's where I get my greatest satisfaction. Winning. I never set
any individual goals other than trying to compete and trying to contribute, and that can mean anything in any different game.

"I think the most important thing for all of us—and I've been in the
same situation as this team has over the last three years—I think everybody wants to get back to a situation where it's fun again, where we're
competing and competitive and the games mean something. The last
half of last year (in Vancouver) I was finally back in that situation, and it
was a reminder of how much fun hockey can be when you're competing
for something, playing for something. That's where everybody wants to
get back to—becoming a team again, building that. We want to be competitive; we want to win again, and the sooner the better."

Messier always seems to have a way to end an interview when it starts
to become too long. A question came about what type of personnel he
thinks need to be brought in.

"That's for the big bosses," he said before starting away.

End of interview.

THERE WERE PLENTY of issues that needed resolution, left over from last
season's stench. The most obvious one involved defenseman Stephane
Quintal. One of the six free agents signed the previous summer, Quintal
had a difficult season. Expectations were probably too high on a guy
who should not have been cast as anything more than what he was—a
physical, rugged, fairly dependable NHL defenseman. He wasn't a star
before he signed, and the money wasn't going to make him a star. But he

fell into Muckler's doghouse, despite his willingness to be, on most nights, the only Ranger to do battle with the NHL's heavyweights whenever Petr Nedved or Brian Leetch would get roughed up.

Muckler never liked Quintal, because he at times like to carry the puck. Mucker wanted to play him as Leetch's partner, but in order to do so, Quintal would have to remain the defensive conscience on the pair. Whenever he turned to the offensive side, Muckler would crack about he was trying to be Leetch.

Muckler also had trouble keeping Quintal and Sylvain Lefebvre—the other French-Canadian defenseman signed that summer—straight in his own mind. He would answer questions about Lefebvre by talking about Quintal, and vice versa.

By the time the season was coming to an end, Quintal had had it. He made a big mistake with his timing, however. In the days after the firings of Muckler and Neil Smith, with the Garden's hierarchy making a grand-stand play about the need to bring back dignity and class to the frac-tured organization, Quintal was quoted in a French-language newspaper in Montreal.

He reportedly said he'd wished he never left Montreal, and that he would like to return. He said he would come back to New York only if he had no choice. He said waiting for Muckler to be fired was "hell". And that Nedved was not a No. 1 center, which wasn't a new thought. Every-body said that all season long, but now here was a player being quoted.

Checketts, reeling from the upheaval at the top of the Rangers chain of command, decided to make an example of Quintal. He had assistant GM Don Maloney and interim coach John Tortorella suspend Quintal, without pay, for the final four games of the season.

So, when camp opened, Quintal's status was in question. He met with Checketts. He met with Sather and Low. He met with Messier and Nedved. Everybody said there was no problem. Everybody said they were com-fortable with Quintal now.

"It's resolved," Sather said. "It's a brand new team."

"HE'S OKAY WITH ME," Low added. "I just said, 'you're here as far as I'm concerned. It's clean. Let's go."

Messier weighed in with his opinion: "I think the whole situation last year got to be such a downward spiral that it kind of spun out of control for everybody. Nobody really knew where to turn to, or where to go, and things like that can't happen."

Quintal admitted that he and Checketts reached an agreement by which he will recover about half of the four games' worth of pay he forfeited during his suspension.

Quintal said that, "I was really frustrated about the season, and I should have looked at myself in the mirror instead of trying to blame someone else. And I screwed up.

"We're settled."

Was all really forgiven and forgotten? Not likely. We'll see.

THE HIGHLIGHT OF THE first day of camp was a two-part series. Rugged defenseman Dale Purinton, a rookie who has made great strides from being considered a potential career minor-leaguer to now possibly getting a chance to play a limited tough-guy role in the NHL, had a terrific fight with another big, although much more anonymous rookie, Marty Melnychuk.

Melnychuk was cut and went to the trainer's room for stitches. When he got there, though, Melnychuk encountered Purinton, and Round Two was on, right in the little room down the hallway from the locker rooms. Trainer Jim Ramsay and Adam Graves were able to separate the two big guys—Purinton really didn't appear interested in off-ice fighting, fortunately, or perhaps it would have escalated.

Sather said he liked the passion and enthusiasm the two players showed, and praised Ramsay. "He separated two guys from fighting in the locker room and didn't get hurt," Sather said. "Ramsay gets my award today. He stood in there with two guys with equipment, weighing probably 260 pounds with skates on, and came out without a mark.

"I love the youthful enthusiasm a guy like Purinton showed today. Even the fact that those two guys got into it in the trainer's room. I like it. It may not be the thing everybody else likes, but it demonstrates to me that they want to be here and they want to fight for their jobs. That kind of passion is what we need. That's what I'm looking for."

THE FIRST DAY OF CAMP had, not coincidentally, Petr Nedved playing on a line with Czechmates Radek Dvorak and Jan Hlavac, and Messier on a line with Graves and Theo Fleury. Camp is built around scrimmages in which the 80 or so players are split into four squads. It was no coincidence that those two forward lines were put on the same squads, so that they could play together.

The Czechmates were, by far, the Rangers' best line last season and arguably the most positive point in the otherwise miserable year. They were put together around Christmas, two games after one of the Neil Smith's best trades ever, a three-way deal in which the Rangers sent Todd Harvey to San Jose, the Sharks sent Mike Vernon to Florida, and the Rangers got the speedster Dvorak.

In their 42 games together, the threesome combined for 42 goals and 101 points.

They also developed a chemistry on the ice and a reputation as a trio off the ice, Hlavac and Dvorak following the Pied Piper-like Nedved wherever he went, and doing as Nedved did.

They were inseparable.

The Rangers' Madison Square Garden locker room is really a number of rooms, one actual dressing room for uniforms and equipment, with benches and cubicles; a lounge, with a separate dressing area for the players' street clothes; trainers' rooms; shower rooms; etc.

One night, Dvorak was in one room and Hlavac in another, and they couldn't locate each other. So Dvorak picked up his cellphone and called the cellphone of Hlavac, who was maybe 20 feet and a couple of walls away.

THEO FLEURY APPEARS TO BE, and says he is, rededicated to being the star-level player he was prior to his embarrassing 15-goal first season as a Ranger.

But while Fleury apparently has heeded the strong advice from Glen Sather, two players who surely did are defenseman Rich Pilon and tough winger Sandy McCarthy. Pilon is not assured of a job by any stretch of the imagination, not with the mix of veterans and young prospects the Rangers have in camp. Sather told him over the summer that, if he isn't in much better physical condition, under 215 pounds, don't even bother coming to camp. Sather said Pilon will be drawing his paychecks in Hartford of the American Hockey League if he's not in top shape. Sather had a similar talk with McCarthy after acquiring him from Carolina in the summertime.

Both guys showed up in amazing shape, perhaps the best shape of either player's career. They were each down about 20 pounds or so, and looked thin and strong.

McCarthy hired a personal trainer in North Carolina this summer.

"The game's faster and I want to be able to keep up with guys," he said. "I just thought if I took some weight off I'd be a little faster."

Low wants McCarthy to be able to play a regular shift.

"Everywhere I've ever coached, my so-called enforcer or tough guy has played quite a bit," Low said. "I believe you can't just tap him on the shoulder to go out there and clean it up. You have to reward him, too, and ice time is a reward. (Fighting) is a tough job, probably the worst job in the game. Those guys, if they can skate and get in and forecheck, they become valuable pieces of the puzzle.

"We talked the day he got traded, and that day I asked him what his weight was, and what his body fat was, and I told him, 'Tell you what, if you want the wrath of (assistant coach) Teddy Green, come the way you are now. If you don't, get it down.' This guy did an unbelievable amount of work the last two months, and that's exactly what we want."

Pilon, who topped out at about 230 pounds last season, was a svelte 210.

"I've always been in 'good enough' shape," Pilon said, admitting he has never been in the condition he is now.

AND, SPEAKING OF CONDITIONS, or conditioners, Sather got a look at some of the haircuts and facial hair being worn by his new players and immediately sent out word to, among others, Fleury and Dale Purinton, that if they wanted to look like minor leaguers, they could play in the minors. Both went for new 'dos and shaves that day.

THE ONE NOTABLE PLAYER not in camp is unsigned rookie defenseman Mike Mottau.

"I've heard a lot of good things about him," Ron Low said. "You're trying to win a job on a hockey club, and not being there is one way for sure of not getting a job. It's too bad, really. I hear he's got a lot of talent."

BRIAN LEETCH, the former captain, was looking for the new captain in the hallway.

To anybody within earshot, mostly reporters and equipment guys, Leetch asked, "anybody seen a big guy, kind of thinning hair?"

When Leetch located Messier, he had to remind him about the short-cut out of the arena.

"Follow me, Mess," Leetch said, with a smile that indicated how funny it was, him leading the way and showing this "newcomer" the way around.

LOW ISN'T GOING TO PLAY anything resembling the neutral-zone trap or any of the wing-lock systems that result in passive, dull hockey by so many teams in the NHL. In Edmonton they played puck-pursuit, a skating, pressuring, gambling style, and with Sather, Low and Messier all here now, that is the style the Rangers will play. That also happens to be the way they played in 1994, when they won the franchise's only Stanley Cup since 1940.

"I can't stand that kind of hockey," Low said. "I never have and I'm not going to change. We may make some modifications, but we're going to pursue the puck and forecheck and bust our ass all over the ice."

Low's practices will be up-tempo and, usually short. They won't have the type of practices they had under John Muckler, which were summed up once by Fleury as "45 minutes of standing around, then skate our bags off."

The "bag skate," as hockey players universally call it, is simply to be ordered by a coach to skate your nuts (hence bag) off, often as punishment.

"We're trying to get as much tempo as possible, and have guys tired at the end of scrimmage and at the end of practice," Low said. "You just make sure the tempo stays high, and if it does hopefully we can carry it over into games. I mean, we're not going to be standing around very much or stopping very much.

"I don't think you want to back off. I've never been a big fan of the "bag" skate, a hard skate at the end of practice. I think if you work your tail off during practice, that should be enough."

Players love to hear that.

Low isn't about to be suckered in by any outstanding performances in the first days of low-contact scrimmages.

"It's the first day of camp," he said. "A lot of guys are going to make impressions, and a lot of guys are going to fall by the wayside as it goes along."

LOW WAS REMINISCING about his days in Edmonton, memories sparked by being together with Messier again.

"Mess was my roommate when he was 18," Low said. "He was just a raw-boned kid at that time, and obviously he's become one of the best players to ever play the game, since then."

Could Low have imagined then that one day he'd be a coach?

"Are you nuts or what?" he said. "No chance. I must have had a brain cramp."

Tim Taylor, who pretty much has been a checking center all his career, has been assigned many a night to play against Messier.

In fact, last season, when Taylor was knocked unconscious by Vancouver's Ed Jovanovski's elbow, coach John Muckler claimed that Jovanovski was sent out to get Taylor by Messier, because Messier didn't want to play against him all night.

That, of course, was ridiculous. Messier sees checking centers every night. He's not going to need any hitman to take out an opponent for him.

But Taylor said that, just about every time he has ever lined up for a faceoff against Messier as an opponent, he has either absorbed an elbow or a high stick, which is also part of Messier's legend.

So today, when they lined up for the opening faceoff of camp, Taylor asked Messier, "can we get this over with quickly?"

The two laughed about it.

WITH THE RANGERS and prospective Rangers divvied up into four teams—Red, Blue, White and Green—the camp tournament began. The players, on their own, pony up $20 apiece to make the tournament "interesting".

The teams are coached by scouts, so that the coaches and front office folks can sit up in the seats and watch the players play.

Dick Todd, the team's former assistant coach and currently a scout, was coaching the Red team, and he quickly noticed that one of the players. No. 20, was just awful.

"Who the fuck is that?" Todd said to anybody and everybody on the bench. "Who the fuck drafted him?"

He wasn't drafted at all. He was Guy Lawson, a reporter for "GQ" doing a first-person, George Plimpton-type of story for the magazine. Lawson, 37, had trained with some of the players in Westchester prior to camp and got permission from the team to participate in camp and in the preseason, although he wouldn't actually get into a preseason game.

But if Lawson was going to be part of the program, he had to be part of the whole program. That meant the punishing laps and sprints after the tournament games, with assistant coach Walt Kyle's pitched voice screaming, "Skate it out. Finish the fucking drill."

BURLINGTON, VT. -

It remains entirely possible that the Rangers' six defensemen on opening night will include not a single rookie. But the rookie defensemen are getting noticed, some for what they're doing at training camp and one—unsigned Mike Mottau—for not being here.

The one who has stolen the most notice has done so with all the subtlety of an earthquake. Big Dale Purinton, he of the 502 minor-league penalty minutes last season at Hartford, has had four fights. One of those occurred in the trainer's room on Saturday. Two of them today were against the Rangers' newly acquired muscle man, Sandy McCarthy.

While it appears that Purinton has a solid chance to make the team—he almost has to make it, because the Rangers would probably lose him on waivers if they try to send him to Hartford—he probably won't turn out to be the one guy for which they're searching. That would be Brian Leetch's steady partner, a partner he didn't have all of last season.

Leetch's right-hand man will likely come from the slimmed-down Rich Pilon, Stephane Quintal or Sylvain Lefebvre. Yet Purinton has at least drawn comparisons to Leetch's long-time ex-partner, Jeff Beukeboom.

Not only is Purinton big and tough like Beukeboom, but he has shown steady improvement. On Leetch's right side, all that is necessary is a stay-at-home guy who can keep it simple; and a bonus would be a physical protector for Leetch.

"He has to play however he has to play," Rangers coach Ron Low said after the Purinton-McCarthy bouts yesterday. "He has improved immensely year-to-year. Remember Beukeboom? The first couple years you'd swear he'd never play the game. But he ended up being a 13–14-year pro. He just kept getting better. Dale has to work his game, and he has to keep getting better. Lots of times, when you're as physical as he is, you end up getting a little more room, and more time."

Leetch has said that, ideally, he will find a partner soon, but insisted it's not a concern or a distraction.

"It was very easy (with Beukeboom)," Leetch said. "There was no decision making at all. We moved the puck together, get it up the ice, and if there was an opening, I was the one to get up there. There was no decision at all. It was easy."

Leetch has also seen Purinton in six training camps, the last three as a pro.

"That's as much as I've seen any player develop skill-wise," Leetch said. "He was intimidated when he first came here, but each year he's gotten calmer, and he's very much at ease right now. He's just so big and strong. But he wants to do it. He wants to stick around, and he wants to play here."

"I must be getting better every time or I wouldn't be here," Purinton said of his five previous training camps, in which he never had any shot at sticking.

Purinton is being pushed, too, by Jason Doig and rookie Tomas Kloucek, and even Drew Bannister, a player with a bit of NHL experience, who played for Low in Edmonton. Then there's smooth rookie Filip Novak, who was Sather's first draft pick in June. He's likely headed back to junior hockey, but already considered a top prospect, and so far he's looked fine in scrimmages.

Ironically, Purinton's NHL debut last winter was derailed by the acquisition of Pilon. While Pilon has opened eyes with his new fitness level, it has been Purinton who has gotten everyone's attention, particularly since the Rangers so badly need muscle.

"Well, we know they're both tough," Low said about the bouts Purinton instigated with McCarthy. "Dale went out and said, 'I want to be on your hockey club,' and went after the toughest guy on the club.

"I don't think you can just have one. I think if you have a couple of guys that are really big people, who can do the job, that makes the rest of your team tougher, too. The whole key is for those people to make the rest of your team team-tough."

LOW HAS ALSO BEEN impressed with the work of rookie sniper Pavel Brendl, even though the newly-conditioned Brendl has had only two scoring chances and no goals in two days of scrimmages.

"You have to base it on last year's training camp, when he was abysmal," Low said. "He did nothing. He was in terrible shape. This year he had to have a lot of things better, and I haven't seen the offensive flashes, but I've seen a bunch of things he's done defensively that make me feel a lot better about Pavel.

"He's worked very hard in the summertime, his conditioning is better."

LOW ISN'T SURE if Manny Malhotra is a winger or a center, but surely he has a better chance to make this team on the wing with Mark Messier, Petr Nedved, Mike York, and Tim Taylor up the middle.

"I think in the middle of the rink he does a lot of things as far as the checking end of it," Low said. "He angles people really well from the wing, and he moves people toward the walls from the middle of the rink. So I'm not sure what's best for him yet."

MIKE RICHTER SKATED on his own and reported no difficulty, as he is still three weeks away from taking shots in goal.

MONDAY, SEPTEMBER 11, 2000
BURLINGTON, VT.

He was a top prospect before the names Manny Malhotra, Pavel Brendl and Jamie Lundmark were ever spoken by the Rangers. But, in a flash, Stefan Cherneski's career changed.

"One shift . . . tragedy," he said.

Cherneski, a power right winger, nearly made the Rangers out of training camp in 1998. When he was finally assigned to Hartford, he lasted only 11 games. He slid into the boards in a November 13, 1998 game, and shattered his right kneecap into six pieces. It got worse when the original reconstruction didn't heal properly and doctors had to do another reconstruction on the knee in April of that season. The following summer, he had an arthroscopic procedure performed, and in December of 1999 a fourth surgery to remove the screws that had been inserted, along with a calcium deposit that was affecting the new kneecap.

He went from the top of the prospects list to the forgotten pile.

Well, surprise, surprise. Cherneski, now 21, has worked his way back into the picture. He might not make the Rangers in training camp this year; he may need to get his hockey legs back under him in the minors after playing only one game since that frightening crash—last year's AHL regular-season finale with the Wolf Pack

But, eventually, he might make it to the NHL.

"I like Cherneski," Low said after seeing Cherneski score a goal in scrimmage.

"He's skating really well, and he's getting better as play goes on. He's played only, what, 14 games in two years so it's incredible that he's as far advanced as he is now. I wouldn't mind seeing him in a (preseason) game or two, because he has some qualities. He certainly hasn't embarrassed himself out there. The kid has obviously done a lot of work.

"He's very good without the puck, too. He's a guy who winds up with eight or shots on net, and in order to do that, he has to get himself open. And he's got a heckuva release, a really good release. He's a tough kid, too. Very seldom do you see him pass up the chance to take the body on a forecheck situation."

Just that he is in camp and competing for a job is stunning.

"I've come a long ways from where I started," Cherneski said.

One of the side benefits for the Rangers is that Cherneski spent the summer working under team strength and conditioning coordinator Scott Livingston, and his training partner was Brendl. The feeling in the organization is that Cherneski's work ethic rubbed off on the young sniper, who flunked last year's camp by reporting in terrible condition. Cherneski, who began the summer working with a power-skating instructor and hasn't stopped skating since, feels that his overall strength, and the strength of the right knee, is close to 100 percent.

"I wouldn't be here right now if I didn't feel I could make a full recovery from this injury," he said. "The way things have been going this summer, there's no doubt in my mind that I'll be able to."

Cherneski, who scored 82 goals and had 210 penalty minutes in his last two junior seasons with Brandon (WHL), hasn't had a lot of discussion about his future with the Rangers' new management team, but he knows what they know.

"Just the fact that I'm still around here makes them aware that I still want to play and it's possible to do that," he said.

Low is well aware.

WITH MIKE RICHTER OUT at least for the first week or so of the season, the last thing the Rangers need is an injury to backup goalie Kirk McLean.

But McLean went out of today's workout with back spasms that had Low concerned.

"Very much so," Low said. "I guess they're going to assess it kind of daily, but the back is not something you want to have at this point in time. If he has any symptoms at all tomorrow, he won't be on the rink."

McLean said he didn't think the injury was serious, and that he'd be back in the next two days.

During camp scrimmages, there are always two teams on the ice and two teams in the locker rooms and/or workout room. So reporters spend their time either watching the game, or lurking about downstairs to talk to players. McLean's injury caused a ruckus because people were scurrying to get one of the goalies from one of the other teams to come out to the rink as a substitute. So some of the reporters didn't immediately know that it was McLean who was hurt.

When one reporter asked Ted Green who got hurt, he repeatedly said, "Curt."

THE LINE OF MESSIER, Graves, and Fleury was dismantled by Nedved, Dvorak, and Hlavac in today's scrimmage. Messier's "Red Team" is winless in three games.

"We've talked about that a couple of times as coaches," Low said. "You're looking at a 40-year-old guy who's in his 22nd training camp, and Theo is whatever he is, and Graves is whatever he is. I think it's hard to get excited about the fact you're playing in a scrimmage. I would say you'd like to see something in the exhibition games, and I'm sure you're going to.

"And they may not be able to play together. Who knows? That's why we have training camp."

SYLVAIN LEFEBVRE HAS BEEN playing right defense, a switch from last year when John Muckler refused to move him from his natural left position in order to try him with Brian Leetch.

"Don't read anything (into it)," Low said. "The pairs will all get set."

GLEN SATHER HAD DINNER with some of the reporters covering the team at one of Burlington's best restaurants. The subject got around to tipping. Sather, who is in the process of finding a home in New York City, was told that in the big city, 20 percent is the expected tip and that the gratuity in Manhattan is normally calculated on the entire bill, not the sub-total before tax. Sather laughed and waved his hand and said something snide about how New Yorkers think they're the center of the universe. He said 15 percent, on the pre-tax amount, was more than enough, and that if the service wasn't outstanding, less than 15 percent is acceptable.

At that point, it seemed, Sather was just being argumentative, trying to evoke a reaction from the New Yorkers. But Sather does have a cheap side, no doubt. He treats his organization's money as if it were coming out of his own wallet. His best buddy in hockey, Harry Sinden of the Boston Bruins, is the skinflint of all skinflints.

So there was definitely a grain of truth in Sather's pledge to frugality.

TUESDAY, SEPTEMBER 12, 2000

BURLINGTON, VT. -

Most general managers and coaches play favorites when it comes to players they've acquired or drafted, as opposed to players they inherited. It was nonetheless astounding when Sather was quoted in a *Newsday* story as calling Vladimir Malakhov "the best defenseman we have."

Sather apparently forgot about two-time Norris Trophy winner and Conn Smythe winner Brian Leetch.

Naturally, Sather defends his signing of Malakhov to a four-year, $14 million contract this summer, while letting go of Mathieu Schneider, who would have cost half as much. Not only will people debate whether Malakhov is better than Schneider, but also whether Malakhov is even the second best defenseman the Rangers have.

OF COURSE, ANY TIME Mark Messier gets hurt now, it will be blamed on his age. The 39-year-old captain left the Rangers' training-camp scrimmage after one period due to tightness in his left groin.

Messier said his removal from the scrimmage was "precautionary" and called the injury typical of the tightness players feel in the early stages of camp, particularly on a soft ice surface such as the one at the University of Vermont's Gutterson Field House. Indeed, several players, including Messier's linemate Adam Graves, have felt groin tightness in the first four days of camp. Only one, Jason Dawe, has had to miss time because of a groin pull.

Messier may not play in tomorrow's Blue-White game, featuring the top 40 players of camp.

Neither may Radek Dvorak, who left the same scrimmage with back spasms he deemed not serious.

Goalie Kirk McLean did a mini-version of a Willis Reed yesterday, coming back from his own back spasms to lead his team to the scrimmage tournament title. Mike York, who has had a stellar camp, scored the tournament-winning goal in OT.

DALE PURINTON HAD TO make a stop in the trainer's room today, but before he did, he stopped short of the door and peeked into the room, feigning fear—as if he might get into another loud altercation in there.

MESSIER WAS TALKING ABOUT his linemates, and raving about Theo Fleury's vision and ability to play the give-and-go game Messier thrives on.

He smiled when somebody asked him if he was familiar at all with his other winger. Messier played his first six years as a Ranger with Adam Graves on his left wing for virtually every shift.

"That will take some time, yeah," Messier smiled. "I don't know where he's going to be. Somebody told me he likes to go to the front of the net."

Graves was already out of the building, on his way to a local hospital to visit sick kids.

Somebody said to Messier, "that Graves is a bad guy."

"Yeah, we'll have to work on his people skills," Messier said.

One year here in Burlington, a kid asked Graves for his autograph, then asked for another one for his brother. Graves asked the kid where his brother was, and when the kid told Graves his brother was in a hospital recovering from an auto accident, Graves jotted down the hospital name and room number, and visited the brother that day.

WEDNESDAY, SEPTEMBER 13, 2000

BURLINGTON, VT.

Manny Malhotra has always had the support of his Rangers teammates.

Now, though, he's getting strong support from his coaches, too, and that is something new.

That could make the difference in the 20-year-old center's progress, even if it does include a possible assignment to Hartford (AHL) for some playing-time and experience.

Mark Messier can relate. He turned pro at 17 in the old World Hockey Association, then went right into the NHL with Edmonton, one of the teams absorbed by the NHL when the WHA folded.

"I never really had a chance to develop in any league for a long time," he said. "I was always playing against guys much older than I was, and never skated in a league long enough to figure whether if I could excel until I finally got, basically, doing it. When I was 17, I developed in a professional league, so it took me a while to kind of catch up.

"Manny's a player in that respect, coming in when he was 18 and not really having the opportunity to hone his skills against players his own age, in his own league, his developmental stage," Messier said. "Then, of course, having not played much in the last two years, kind of set him back in that regard. At the same time, you look at him now and he's 20 and he's already three years into the league, so that's got to be a plus.

"Like anything, he needs confidence to know he can do the things he's done in the past. And you have to know that the team and the coach and everybody behind you have confidence in you; that everybody's in your corner and they're going to give you the opportunity to succeed and be successful. All those things play an important part in anybody's development, let alone a guy who's 18 and expected to play and do things as well. So once he starts to feel more comfortable that the team is behind him, the management, the coaching staff, everybody is giving him every opportunity, and he feels confident what he can do for the team, that will really help him a great deal. It will give him the confidence to settle down and play his game."

LOW SAID HE WOULD LOVE to see Pavel Brendl make the team, but that it doesn't make sense for him to stay as a fourth-line player. Brendl has played very well at camp, and is in good physical shape, but he hasn't scored goals. Likewise, Jamie Lundmark has had a decent camp, but hasn't jumped out from the pack, either.

"(Brendl) has got all the tools," Low said. "He's got to prove that he's ready to come right now and play."

Low added that he will find roster spots if any of the young players prove to be ready.

"If they make it, if we feel they're ready to help the hockey club, then we'll have to move some older guys. If they're not ready to help the hockey club, why would we make ourselves worse?"

Glen Sather feels the same way,

"I've said before, I'd like to have 23 guys age 20 and younger, on this hockey club," Sather said. "I know it isn't going to happen. But wouldn't it be wonderful if you had six guys in camp who could beat out Leetch for his job, and five centers who could beat out Messier for his. Just think of the depth you'd have in the organization. Then I woke up."

THURSDAY, SEPTEMBER 14, 2000

BURLINGTON, VT.

Before Low trimmed his roster to 36 players for the start of the preseason, he and his assistant coaches were putting names on a blackboard and figuring which would stay and which would either go to Hartford (the minor-league Wolf Pack has its own preseason) or return to junior hockey.

One of the names on the blackboard was that of Filip Novak, who has been outstanding in camp.

Sather walked into the room, circled Novak's name, and jotted in capital letters "KEEP" right next to it.

LOW WILL BE INTERESTED to see how well, or how poorly, the team plays in its own end after last year's disaster.

"A lot of the tapes I watched, there was a lot of times it had nothing to do with the defensemen," Low said. "It was the forwards breaking down and leaving gaps where guys were driving Mack trucks through."

DEFENSEMAN BRIAN LEETCH, when notified of Sather's remark earlier in the week that Vladmir Malakhov is "the best defefenseman we have," simply and typically laughed. "That's good," Leetch said. "That means we'll have a great defense."

3

The Captain is Back

RYE. N.Y.

THE RANGERS BEGIN their always-excessive preseason tomorrow in Philadelphia. They will play nine exhibition games, which will be far too many for everybody but those who need the additional opportunities to make the team.

Some teams play as few as five or six exhibitions, believing that to be a sufficient number to get everything in order, get everybody ready for the regular season, which in itself is dreadfully long. But the Rangers are the Rangers. They are in demand, even when they stink. So every year, it seems, the Rangers are off to play some preseason game in a brand new NHL city—this year, it's Columbus, Ohio, which will have an expansion team, the Blue Jackets. Last year they played a game in Minneapolis, against Phoenix, because the state of Minnesota was a year away from expansion (the Wild, also debuting this season, in St. Paul). They regularly play in places like Dallas and Atlanta. They have played at neutral sites such as Las Vegas, where tough guy Tie Domi once claimed to have tripped over a giant grasshopper while on a breakaway on the outdoor rink. They played a two-game tournament against Toronto in London, England in 1993, a sponsored event for which NHL commissioner Gary Bettman walked into a flea market and bought a trophy. They have regularly played games in Detroit, some of which are rumored to have been the "future considerations" of a past trade.

All this travel, all these unnecessary games, some have concluded, contributed to the Rangers' annual slow starts.

The Rangers' preseasons have also been notable for whom they didn't play. For years they didn't play the Philadelphia Flyers after a game at the Garden in 1985, a game which featured more than 500 penalty minutes—a total which would be an NHL record if it had been piled up in a regular-season or playoff game. The highlight of that contest came late in the third period, when just about everybody had been kicked out of the game, until both teams had nine skaters left. Yet Philadelphia coach Mike Keenan, who ordered and orchestrated most of the mayhem, was called somehow for having too many men on the ice. The Rangers were coached by Ted Sator, a former Keenan assistant in Philadelphia. So impressed was Sator that every player in a Rangers uniform that night, including unknown rookie goalie Terry Kleisinger—who skated the length of the ice and fought Flyers goalie Bob Froese—made Sator's opening-night roster.

The Rangers also refused to schedule the Islanders for an exhibition game for several seasons because of what happened in 1997. That season, the Rangers were unveiling their throw-back- style blue jerseys, with the laces in the collar, an idea hatched by always-nostalgic president/GM Neil Smith.

Smith wanted the Rangers to wear his pride-and-joy jerseys on opening night at home against the Islanders. But Islanders GM Mike Milbury, who would never pass up a chance to annoy and anger his archrivals, refused to have his team wear its home white uniforms on the road. So the Rangers had to wait to debut their new blues, and Smith vowed to make the Islanders pay by refusing to schedule them in the preseason.

The Rangers also stick to the dramatic. So, for example, in the 1996 preseason newly-acquired Wayne Gretzky didn't play a single home exhibition game so that the Rangers could unveil him for the first time on Garden ice as a Ranger at the home opener. The same will happen for Mark Messier this season. He may play three games or so on the road, but he won't play at the Garden until the home opener, October 11, so that the organization can officially welcome him back and re-introduce him as captain with all the bells, whistles, smoke and lasers his return deserves.

THE PRESEASON MEANS MOST to some of the Rangers' top prospects, who have some proving to do. Jamie Lundmark, a center, and winger Pavel Brendl, both 19 years old, will have to be brilliant in their exhibition opportunities or face starting the season back in junior hockey. Center Manny Malhotra, 20, who had his sophomore season wasted by the misuse by coach John Muckler, faces the fate of starting the season in the minors, at Hartford of the American Hockey League, unless he can beat out Tim Taylor for a center job, or unless Low changes his mind and tries Malhotra on the wing.

Lundmark in particular has to be better than he was in the training-camp scrimmages in Burlington. While he wasn't bad, Lundmark certainly didn't stand out enough to earn a job. The Rangers' coaches and front office still think he will be a big-time player, but at 19 and coming off a wrist injury that cost him the second half of last season, he probably isn't ready at the moment. In camp, he has even been outplayed by centers Derek Armstrong and Francois Fortier.

Brendl, a super sniper in junior hockey, has impressed everybody with the work he's done to improve two crucial parts of his game—his conditioning and his work away from the puck. But Brendl didn't score in Burlington. Last year, he scored but couldn't do anything else, including keeping up with his teammates.

Low said it is possible, but unlikely, that a player like Brendl would be kept around as a fourth-line player and power-play specialist. And when it was brought up that Brendl has nothing else to prove in junior hockey, where he scored a league-leading 59 goals and 111 points in 61 games, Low said, "The one thing that can't happen if he goes back is to go back with that attitude."

If, however, Brendl lights it up in the preseason—Muckler wouldn't even let him play a single game at the Garden last year—the Rangers will find a spot for him.

Malhotra's cause is different, and this year he will benefit from being eligible to go back and forth from Hartford if he needs playing time. Last season, with a year of junior eligibility left, the choices were that the Rangers had to keep Malhotra around, or send him back to junior, but he couldn't go to Hartford for anything but a conditioning assignment.

Low said that Malhotra was "a dominant figure" at times in Burlington, and he has to continue to show the aggressive style that is his ticket to the NHL. Low and the Rangers love his size, his speed, and his attitude. Trouble is, there's no center spot available behind Messier, Nedved, York and Taylor, and Low hasn't even considered a move or Malhotra to the wing yet.

The other positions open are on defense, where two young players could make the jump. Among them are favorites Dale Purinton, Tomas

Kloucek and still unsigned Mike Mottau, as well as Drew Bannister, Jason Doig, 2000 draftee Filip Novak, and Terry Virtue.

PHILADELPHIA

In addition to across-the-board improvement, the Rangers want to play a more physical, tougher brand of hockey this season.

But if the NHL is going to crack down on penalties as it has promised to do, the Rangers will have to figure out two things. One, they will have to be more disciplined than they were in their preseason opener and, two, they will have to kill penalties a lot better than they did today.

The Philadelphia Flyers scored four power-play goals in a 5-1 victory over a Rangers team missing most of its firepower at First Union Center. The penalty killing should get better; the Rangers haven't yet worked on it.

"They knew it before the game," Low said. "We talked about it (Friday) with (NHL VP of hockey operations) Mike Murphy. They're going to call second penalties, they're going to call slashes, and anything that hits hands is going to be called. We've got to be smarter, that's for sure. We took some dumb penalties."

The Rangers tried to be aggressive physically, and some—Dale Purinton and Manny Malhotra in particular—were.

"Really, slashing isn't part of being aggressive," Low said about the eight power plays they handed the Flyers. "You're not going to get away with slashing. You can forget it. So throw it out of the repertoire completely and get into the hits."

TIM TAYLOR, the always-battered checking center, suffered an eight-stitch cut above his left eye when rocked into the boards by Flyers defenseman Dan McGillis. Taylor has a history of concussions—the Rangers aren't immediately calling this a concussion—and he has had nothing but injuries since coming to the Rangers in the summer of 1999 as one of the six big-ticket free agents they signed. Some of Taylor's more odd injuries last season included appendicitis the first day of training camp and drop foot—a nerve injury to the leg which prevents one from being able to lift his foot. Taylor also had a bizarre injury when, right off a faceoff, an enormous splinter from his own stick went through his glove and deep into his hand, requiring emergency surgery.

NEW YORK

Back to the Garden. The Rangers played their first home preseason game, a rematch with the Flyers tonight. First they held a practice yesterday, open to the public, which is rare at their Playland practice facility, and unheard-of at the Garden.

The locker room has undergone a reconstruction, with more built-in comforts for the players, including a high-density television in the lounge.

The most noticeable difference, though, is typically Messier. The team photo from the 1994 Stanley Cup championship, which used to hang a few yards down the hall, is now front and center as you leave the new locker room. You can't leave the room without seeing it.

When Messier first arrived in 1991, he and then GM Neil Smith made sure the team's history was celebrated, not ridiculed. Photos of the great players and teams in franchise history were hung, as well as plaques commemorating achievements. Also, when Messier first played as a Ranger at the Garden, he had a huge table—on which sat water buckets, hockey tape, boxes of gum, etc.—moved. The reason? When Messier speaks before games, between periods and after games, he wanted to be able to look each guy in the eyes.

BEFORE THE GAME, Theo Fleury ran into his old buddy, Kevin Stevens, now with the Flyers. They shook hands in the doorway between the locker rooms.

"How is it over there?" Stevens asked.

"Night and day," Fleury said. "Night and day."

Stevens, the ex-Ranger, is happy as a Flyer. Stevens still faces a possession charge for his arrest in an Illinois suburb of St. Louis in January, and still goes to an alcohol-rehab program two or three times a week. "My every day life is tough," he said. "It's changed because all that happened. But it's not like I crave alcohol. It's just that I can't drink." Stevens said he hopes to have his case settled without going to court. "They tell me the longer it goes, the better it is," he said. "I try not to think about it too much."

MIKE MOTTAU, who won the Hobey Baker Award (college hockey's Heisman Trophy) made a surprise appearance at the Garden. Mottau signed a tryout contract, which will at least allow him to play some preseason games and work out for the coaching staff while they try to hammer out a contract. He's a couple of weeks behind.

PHILADELPHIA'S YOUNG TOUGH GUY Todd Fedoruk, trying to make a name for himself in the NHL, challenged Sandy McCarthy at center ice. Dale Purinton, trying to make his own name, leaped into the fray before McCarthy could get involved. He and Fedoruk threw bombs at one another.

Funny thing is, Purinton and Fedoruk are old buddies from junior hockey. They are so close that they share a bizarre trait. They both got their names tattooed on their backs, in gothic print, across their shoulders, just as their names now sit on the backs of their jerseys.

MARK MESSIER'S RETURN is expected to spell good news for most of the Rangers.

But one of them figures to lose his linemates and some ice time—Calder Trophy finalist Mike York.

York doesn't see it that way.

"No, not at all," said the 22-year-old center. "Just having a chance to play with a guy like that is totally awesome, especially with all the success he's had in the past.

"You never really know what's going to happen, that's up to the coaches. And I'm ready to start winning some games this year."

Last season, spent mostly between Adam Graves and Theo Fleury, York led the Rangers in goals with 26 as a freshman. Now Messier figures to skate between Graves and Fleury.

But, because York can do so many things so well, because his game is so well-rounded despite his 5-foot-10 frame, Low —who compared York to Edmonton's valuable Todd Marchant—doesn't see much about York's role changing.

"I would imagine it will change to a degree," Low allowed. "He's a pretty solid hockey player in both ends

BRUCE BENNETT STUDIOS

Coming off a strong rookie season, Mike York drew raves from his teammates for his gritty play.

of the rink. There's not too many things he does wrong. You can watch him on TV, and you don't really appreciate him as much as when you watch him go through a scrimmage, where it's maybe not ultra important that you're always in great position, yet very seldom is he out of position. He's a really solid player. So, is his role going to change? I don't know. He's going to be pretty much counted on to score points like he did last year and be the great defensive player he was last year, as well. So maybe his role isn't going to change."

Added Fleury, "That just makes our team all that much better now, now that we've got Mess, Petr (Nedved) and him. Now we've got three solid veterans, and instead of a two-line team it's three. Then you throw Tim Taylor's line in the mix, and it's a pretty good team."

York scored the only goal in Saturday's 5-1 loss in Philadelphia. He also scored the title-winning goal in OT during the Rangers preseason tournament in Vermont.

He has caught Messier's eye.

When some of the Rangers began arriving in Rye, N.Y. for informal pre-camp skates, Brian Leetch told Messier to watch York.

"Mark didn't know anything about him," said Leetch, "and we were skating with him and Mark goes, 'He's a pretty shifty guy, huh?' I said, 'Oh, yeah, you're going to love him. He's an old-time guy.' "

Messier noted the coincidence of York's timely goal-scoring.

"There's a little bit of a pattern developing there with this kid," Messier said. "Watching him last year, he really seems to have a knack for concentrating the puck on the net, and that's a gift in itself. On top of that, he's really gifted. He's quicker than he looks out there, he's stronger than he looks out there and he handles the puck. His stick skills are very, very good. He handles the stick as well as everybody. So many times last year he scored a nice goal, a big goal, he seems to have that knack for scoring at a big time, at the right time. In today's game, anybody who gets things directed at the net is very valuable."

York got a lot of attention at the very end of last season, when just about everybody else had packed it in. He was still playing his tail off.

"I really wanted to keep going," York said. "The season's not over until you play all 82 games. So you have to try to stay focused, and it's pretty tough when you're out of the playoffs, to stay focused. I hate losing, no matter what the circumstances are."

"I can't really remember the last four or five games, to tell you the truth," Leetch said, perhaps fibbing a bit. "He played great the whole year. He never quit."

He just earned the admiration of his teammates, none more than his linemates.

"You look at his play all year, and he played really well," Fleury added. "He's got great speed, and when you're a smaller player that's what you need. Not only that, he's gritty, too. You have to survive, absolutely."

That grittiness is something Fleury understands first-hand.

"Maybe it's from being shorter than everybody else," York said. "You can't take a shift off, or you'll get hurt."

"I think the thing that surprised a lot of people last year, especially coming out of college where you play 36-40 games, was his ability to play consistently over 82 games," said Graves. "To play at a high level and consistently score big goals for us, it was obviously a surprise for some of us, but the more you get to see him, and the more you get to see him play, the more you realize he's the real thing. He's a very skilled player and he excels in a lot of areas: He's good defensively, he's good on draws, strong on the puck, and he really understands the game. He's smart. When he can't beat you with muscle, he'll beat you with finesse. For a smaller guy, or for anyone for that matter, to have that kind of skill and instincts, it will make you an excellent player. With his work ethic, it wasn't a fluke, that's for sure, and I would expect he'd do as much if not more this year."

WEDNESDAY, SEPTEMBER 20, 2000

RYE, N.Y.

It appears that Mike Mottau will have just four exhibition games, or fewer, to prove he belongs in the NHL to start the season. The Rangers' unsigned rookie, and the Hobey Baker winner as college hockey's best player last season at Boston College practiced with the Rangers for the first time today. Because he is not in game condition—having been working out at B.C. for half an hour a day—he is unlikely to play either of the next two exhibitions, on the road in Atlanta and Dallas. There will then be four preseason games remaining for Mottau to convince Rangers president/GM Glen Sather he is worth more than the approximate $1.5 million, including signing bonus, two-year offer on the table.

Sather grinned when asked if he'd improve the offer should Mottau look good in camp.

"If he looks like Bobby Orr," Sather said.

"It's completely up to me, how I play," Mottau said. "Glen Sather said he'd reevaluate our situation when the exhibition games are done, and we'll go from there.

"It was really tough, being a rookie and not really being proven and missing some of training camp, but I just wanted to make sure the deal I was going to sign, or could sign, was the right deal for me. There's a deal on the table right now, but it's been pretty similar to the one that was offered at the beginning with some simple revisions. It depends on how well I play to see if anything can be done to increase or sweeten the deal for me. So it's up to me and how well I play."

Mottau might not make the team to start the season, anyway, since Dale Purinton has probably (literally) fought his way into a spot and, barring a trade, the Rangers have six other shoo-ins.

Mottau joined the team on the two-game trip.

TIM TAYLOR DOES INDEED have a concussion. He remained at home.

THURSDAY, SEPTEMBER 21, 2000

ATLANTA

It was 1994 again. Or at least 1997. Messier played his first game with the Rangers since his tearful departure to Vancouver. Early in the game against the Thrashers, Brian Leetch put the puck behind the net, and Messier saucered a pass—that is, he elevated off the ice, over a defenseman's stick, and had it land flat before it reached its destination—right onto the stick of Adam Graves, who slammed it into the net.

The goal was announced as so many from 1991-97 were announced: Graves, from Messier and Leetch. From the pressbox way up on top of the Philips Arena, you could see the enormous grins on the faces of all three old friends. Graves wound up scoring three goals in the game, and there isn't much that would delight the rest of the Rangers than for the immensely popular and admired Graves to bounce back from a season of personal tragedy.

For all of the Rangers, 1999–2000 was a professional disaster. For Graves, though, it was worse.

No Ranger is looking forward to 2000–01 more than Graves, for a number of reasons. One of those is the most obvious—the return of Graves's favorite center, Messier. The other is simply the chance to getting back to playing hockey, having a chance to win, and having fun again.

"When we signed Mark, Adam and I talked that day and he said, 'This year's going to be different,' " Low said. "He's a committed guy. He's a solid guy, a solid athlete, and he's one of those guys who took last year as hard as anybody. He's a helluva player, solid around the net, stands in front on the power play, gets those rebounds, he does a lot of things really well. He's a bull."

He was a tower of strength last year, when one of his infant twin boys,

Jaxon, died only a few weeks after being born in January. Right on top of that was a fatal illness diagnosed in Graves' father—Adam's idol, role model and best friend—who died over the summer, barely four months after his cancer was discovered.

"I think, the way I look at it in the end is that everyone goes through different times in their life where they have to deal with different situations and you just try to become stronger because of it," Graves said. "You count on your family and your friends, and you work together. I know all my strength and perseverance comes from my family, my wife and three children. You just move out from there and have fun. I get to play a game I love to play, and I get to play it with my family. That's what it is, my family."

He found the strength to persevere through his father's illness. The two spent loads of time together over his final months, got to say all the things that needed to be said, exchanged all the feelings for on another.

"Unfortunately, there are things you can't control," Graves said. "I think you just do the best you can, be as honest as you can and work as hard as you can, and the things you can control will fall into place. It doesn't matter what you do, and it's a lesson my dad always taught me, regardless of what you're doing, you give it your all and you'll never have to question anything when you do that."

There was nobody happier than Graves when Messier signed in July to return to New York after three playoff-less seasons for both the Rangers and Messier's Vancouver Canucks.

"Selfishly, I'm thrilled to have him back, not only as a player but as a friend," Graves said.

Graves knew Messier was coming back when Messier attended the memorial services for his father in Toronto.

"It's not easy for anybody to go through that; that was something nobody wishes on anybody," Messier said about Graves's personal tribulations.

"You know, he's a real solid guy. He's been able to deal with it in the best way that he could. I think he had some time with his father, and they were able to talk a lot before he passed away and say a lot of things, perhaps, he wouldn't have had a chance to say. I think that relieved a lot of the pain after his father passed away, or as much as possible anyway. There were a couple of situations there that were really tough, and you hate to see it on anybody, but if anybody could have dealt with it very well, it's Adam."

When Graves made his promise to Low, that this season would be better than last, that things will be different, Low figured he was referring to the team. Graves doesn't talk about himself that way.

"But, you know, Gravy never really thinks about him(self)," Low said. "He's the ultimate team player, and I think if it's good for him, it's good for us. That's the thing we have to get across to a lot of players, that there's a lot of things we can do better, and it's going to be better for all of us."

It will be better if Graves buries the type of saucer pass Messier put on his stick early in the game.

Graves, from Messier and Leetch.

Graves said it "felt like old times."

"I asked Gravy if he had scored a few like that," Leetch said. "He said, "Oh yeah, quite a few like that. Empty netters. Saucers right onto the stick, and just knock it into the net."

Messier is back. He hasn't officially made his debut at the Garden yet, but he's back.

The Garden is Messier's house. It was from 1991–97. It was still his when he was introduced on the day of Wayne Gretzky's retirement party. And now it is, officially, again.

That is why, when the Rangers play their home opener Wednesday, T-shirts will be handed out, reading, simply: "The Captain is Back."

He is back. Back where he orchestrated the most famous hockey night in Garden history, in 1994. Back where, in the 1997 Eastern Conference finals, he and the Rangers last played a playoff game.

Three fruitless years later, barreling toward age 40 in January, he is back home.

How much he has left, and how much he can mean to a team that otherwise has done little else, if anything, to improve, are still questions to be answered from here until April. The other way to look at it is that Messier's return certainly can't hurt, and that the Rangers can't get any worse.

"I just think that after the three years the team had, and then they went ahead and made all the changes they did, I think it's just like when you open the garage door the first time in springtime," Messier said. "You get a woosh of fresh air for everybody. I think everybody kind of came to camp with a renewal of feeling, and with kind of a fresh start for every-body."

But especially so for the three who welcomed him back with open arms, the only three still here from the Cup year—Leetch, Graves and Mike Richter.

"Obvioulsy, it was tougher for the guys that were here for the six years that I was here, because things were pretty good here," Messier said. "We were playing well, and obviously the Cup. For those guys to see the team kind of regress and miss the playoffs for three years was really tough on them, because they know how good it can be in New York. They're looking forward to having a fun year again.

"That's what we have to establish again. You've got to work hard and play hard, but in doing that, you have to make it fun again. You've got to enjoy coming the rink. You have to look forward to coming to the rink, whether it's for a game or practice."

Richter has time and again said, "Does he fix all our problems? No. Does he help us greatly? Absolutely."

How much? That is the million-dollar question.

ANOTHER KEY MOMENT WHEN, after a power-play goal scored with Petr Nedved on the point, Messier went over to Nedved on the bench and enthusiastically tapped him on top of the helmet. Messier didn't care for Nedved in Nedved's first go-round as a Ranger in 1995, and in fairness, Nedved was in a tough spot. He was acquired in the compensation deal handed down by commissioner Gary Bettman for St. Louis' signing of coach Mike Keenan. Also in the deal, the popular and gritty Esa Tikkanen went to St. Louis, and Nedved wore Tikkanen's No. 10. He was the new-comer to a championship team, and a finesse player on a team of grit, a team that had battled and bled together. He was a run-and-gun, fancy player under a coach, Colin Campbell, who wanted a bunch of guys with broken noses.

Nedved was run out of town, to Pittsburgh, and Messier skewered him when they met in the regular season and again in the playoffs. So, naturally, everybody later put two and two together and concluded that Messier hated Nedved. In fact, Messier hated the way the kid played.

But last year, with Messier in Vancouver, Nedved earned his badges of honor by playing well, playing hard, playing with courage.

Now, through two ridiculously different paths, they are teammates again, and Messier was tapping the top of Nedved's helmet. Making peace. Making amends.

PAVEL BRENDL GOT AS GOOD a chance as he is going to get to make the Rangers' roster this season.

The 19-year-old sniper, who had played just 10 shotless shifts in the Rangers' win over Philadelphia on Tuesday, was on the left side of fellow Czechs Petr Nedved and Radek Dvorak in the Rangers 5-3 comeback win over the Atlanta Thrashers. The Rangers need to know if Brendl is ready to play on a top NHL line, or if he needs to spend another year in junior hockey.

So far, Brendl has shown the Rangers coaches his work ethic is greatly improved. He has shown that he has a clue without the puck. But he hasn't scored, either in the training camp tournament, or in two pre-season games. With the Flyers getting 11 power plays Tuesday, there wasn't much chance for Brendl, playing on a fourth line, to get off the bench, much less score.

"It was a hard game to judge anybody but your penalty killers," Low said. "Brendl was as cold as ice sitting on the bench as much as he did. It almost seemed like it was going to be anti-productive."

So tonight, Low decided to see what Brendl's got. Actually, Low knows what Brendl's got. He just needs to see him do it. Low needs to see Brendl beat out somebody for a job by scoring, or at least getting chances.

"When I saw him play in junior he was very dynamic," Low said. "He scored goals for fun."

Brendl showed a couple of flashes in his 11:31 of ice time in Atlanta, had two shots om goal, and was crashing the net when Nedved scored the winning goal.

Throughout the roster, and through just two preseason games, things are starting to become apparent as far as who is making a bid to stay and who isn't. Dale Purinton has punched his way to a job, and hasn't looked terribly out of place on defense, either. He could turn out to be one of the Rangers' top six defensemen. That would mean that, barring a trade or losing a defenseman in the waiver draft, Mike Mottau, Jason Doig, Tomas Kloucek, Drew Bannister and Terry Virtue would probably start the season in Hartford. Bannister has done enough to warrant a call-up if and when the Rangers need a defenseman.

Manny Malhotra is certainly at least challenging Tim Taylor for a job, and with Taylor out until early next week or later with a concussion, the door is wide open for him.

An interesting addition could be Johan Witehall. He could displace John MacLean on a fourth line. Witehall is faster, more physical and a lot younger. What remains to be seen, though, is if he can match the dependable MacLean's offensive expectations of 15 goals or so. Witehall, like Purinton and Doig, would have to go through waivers to be assigned to Hartford. That's another reason why the Rangers will probably keep him (and Purinton).

MESSIER, PERHAPS A TAD GROUCHY while playing with the flu, handed out a signature stick sandwich to a rookie Atlanta player who probably wasn't aware of his reputation. Andrei Skopintsev tried to blindside Messier, whose peripheral vision can make that a hazardous gamble by an opponent. Messier's stick came up just in time, and the kid went back to the bench bleeding from the mouth. The Rangers, and their coaches, had a couple of chuckles about it on the bench and later in the room.

DALLAS

Brian Leetch may finally have a partner, but the Rangers aren't committing to anything yet. Still, Leetch teamed effectively with Sylvain Lefebvre on the two-game preseason trip through Atlanta and Dallas.

"It felt good," said Leetch, who has been without a steady partner since Ulf Samuelsson left, and who has had only one other regular partner, Jeff Beukeboom, in the last 10 years. "But, anyone you're playing with, you need to put time in. We did a lot of talking, and we just tried to start learning tendencies, what he likes to do, what I like to do. Basically, it's putting in time so you can start playing off each other.'

Low wouldn't say that Lefebvre and Leetch will start the season together, but he liked what he saw.

"I thought Syl played really well," Low said. "I thought he played outstanding. He was physical, and took the body. He chose to move the puck to Brian a lot of times to get the puck out of trouble, but when he wasn't there, he made good outlet passes up the wing. He was solid. I thought he was really solid. He's always been a very, very solid defenseman.'

Lefebvre didn't get a chance to play with Leetch last year, because coach John Muckler didn't feel he could make the switch from his natural left side to the right of Leetch. But Lefebvre said that, while he hasn't played on the right the last few years, he was used on either side for about five or six of his NHL seasons.

"It's a little bit of an adjustment, but I felt pretty good," Lefebvre said. "The coaches make that decision. I just want to play, and if I play with Brian it would be an honor. I'll just do my job and let Brian do his stuff."

ROOKIE DEFENSEMAN MIKE MOTTAU, still unsigned but with the team on a tryout contract, was to make his Rangers debut in a game that was played with a lot more emotion and nastiness than most exhibitions, and with the powerful Dallas Stars fielding almost a full roster. It was 1-1 until Dallas' Ted Donato scored with 1.8 seconds remaining in sudden-death overtime.

AFTER THE GAME, a reporter asked Leetch rather casually, "How are you doing?"
"I'll be right back," Leetch said.
He emerged from the trainer's room a few minutes later. Leetch, it turned out, had injured his groin on the slushy ice at Reunion Arena on this 97-degree day in Dallas. The reporter didn't know that, but Leetch thought

the "How are you doing?" question was feuled by the fact that he had missed the entire OT. So Leetch, who is ultra-aware of his responsibilities with the media, came clean and volunteered the information.

STEPHANE QUINTAL DIDN'T PLAY, so he sat in the press box. In the back of the box is a table with coffee and popcorn, and Quintal ran into a few reporters between periods. He asked if the writers were going to fly home on the charter flight with the team. He was told that the writers rarely fly on the charter, mostly because they have to write after games while the team is long gone, but also because it's an uncomfortable situation. Where do you draw the line between "on the record" and "off the record?" Quintal was asked.

He immediately had a question himself: "There is such a thing as off the record?"

Quintal was jokingly referring to the firestorm he started last season with remarks he felt were off the record, which showed up in the newspaper in Montreal and got him suspended.

THE WAIVER DRAFT is coming up, and a reporter had a question for Glen Sather during the game. It was simply a clarification.

"If a player makes it through the waiver draft unclaimed, and you want to send him to Hartford, he doesn't have to go through waivers again, right?" Sather was asked.

"You can put a guy on waivers any time," Sather barked, completely misunderstanding the question and trying to avoid answering anything, in typical blustery fashion. So the question was reworded, in hopes of being answered. Again, Sather said, "You can put a guy on waivers any time." This time his voice gave away his annoyance.

It might be a long year with this guy.

SATHER WASN'T FLYING BACK with the team. He was going to Vancouver to be a character witness in the Marty McSorley trial. McSorley, who played for Sather in Edmonton, is facing assault charges for clubbing the Canucks' Donald Brashear in the head with his stick last season.

Rangers assistant coach Ted Green knows all about such incidents. He was involved in perhaps the ugliest stick swinging in NHL history in 1969, when he and Chicago's Wayne Maki clubbed each other. Green was suspended for 13 games, then the third-longest suspension in league history. Maki got a month.

MESSIER, STILL SICK, was kind of grumpy to a Dallas reporter after the morning skate. It's understandable. He has to hear same questions over and over, and will all year, in every city. There will be questions about his return to New York, about his age, about his career. After the game, Messier sent John Rosasco, the Rangers' public relations guy, to find the reporter and apologize for him.

NEW YORK

Following an 8-2 loss to the Devils, the Rangers players, coaches and staff were running for the bus parked inside the Garden, on a ramp. They would take the bus to Newark Airport, and fly immediately on the team jet to Columbus, Ohio, for tomorrow's game.

One by one, or in small groups, the Rangers exited the locker room and turned right to catch the bus. Among the last out were Messier, and staffers John Rosasco and Darren Blake, who handles all the travel arrangements. Messier waved for them to turn left out of the room. Rosasco and Blake looked at one another, then looked at Messier. "Come on," Messier said, wearing a very cool suit and those blue shades that are becoming his off-ice trademark. "This is a shortcut."

Now, picture this: Two guys who have been working at the Garden for years, and the captain, who had been gone three years. And Messier knows the shortcut to the bus.

THE NO-TRADE ROSTER freeze for Friday's waiver draft went into effect at 2 p.m. today, with protected lists to be submitted by 4 P.M.

MIKE RICHTER EXPECTS to begin taking shots in goal by the end of the week, and if all goes well, could practice with the team by the end of next week.

COLUMBUS OHIO

A brand new team will play in a beautiful new arena, in this neat city. The Blue Jackets will make their NHL debut this season, along with the Minnesota Wild in St. Paul. The Jackets' new Nationwide Arena, which sits in the shadow of a cool little skyline, sparkles. It also includes the team's practice facility right there on the premises. Downtown is also just a short drive to Ohio State University's campus.

The fans will have to be educated, though. They were pretty well behaved when Rich Pilon twice fought Jean-Luc Grand-Pierre tonight, but in the Jackets' first preseason game, when a fight broke out in the third period, the good citizens littered the ice with garbage and beer bottles.

WITH THE RANGERS MAKING this good-will stop in Columbus, public relations man John Rosasco explained to Mark Messier that it was only natural the local media would want to talk to him. Messier knows this. He knows he will face the same things in every stop, all the questions about being back in New York, about closing in on 40 years of age, etc.

So Messier, who was grouchy to a reporter in Dallas earlier in the week, happily greeted the Columbus media with a big smile and the first question: "What can I do for you today?"

PAVEL BRENDL FINALLY BROKE out with three assists in the game.

Low needs to see his offense if Brendl is to make the team this year, but doesn't need to see it to know Brendl will eventually be an NHL sniper.

"I think his offense is a given," Low said. "Pavel Brendl is going to score in this league. I don't think there's any doubt about that, and I don't think anybody else doubts it either. You look at Brendl and his numbers in junior, and it says he's going to score. He's improved a lot of ways. I'd like to see him get the puck more and chances to score."

THURSDAY, SEPTEMBER 28

EAST RUTHERFORD, N.J.

Theo Fleury finally got a little taste of success in New York last night. Wrong sport, though.

Fleury, the Rangers' right winger looking to rebound from a nightmarish first season in New York, took batting practice with the Mets at Shea Stadium prior to a National League playoff-clinching win over Atlanta.

Fleury batted in a group with Mike Piazza, Robin Ventura and Todd Zeile, and said he came within 10 feet of hitting a batting practice homer. The fans didn't know who the 5-foot-6 guy in the cage was at first, but most caught on by the time Fleury was finished hitting.

"It was awesome," Fleury said.

Now he has to find a way to have success, both on a personal level, and with a playoff team, in New York.

If training camp and the preseason are any indication, Fleury appears to be ready to reverse his fortunes and get back to the sniper he was his entire career before becoming a Ranger and scoring an embarrassing total of 15 goals.

The Rangers played their seventh preseason game tonight against the Stanley Cup champion Devils, and Fleury was in the lineup for the sixth time. He was right on top of the Rangers' scoring list with three goals and five points in his first five games.

Fleury says he worked hard this summer to be faster and stronger and in better overall condition.

He knows that last year was his own fault to a large degree. He has switched sticks, too, to a hollow, Kevlar, one-piece stick as opposed to the old metal stick with the wooden blade that fit into the shaft. When somebody asked him how he was going to snap the one-piece stick, as he so often did in fits of anger and frustration last year, Fleury quickly answered, "I won't have to."

The insinuation was that he intends to score more and be frustrated a lot less this season.

"I feel good, yeah," he said. "I think I'm going to the net again, skating better. There've been a lot of power plays, and that kind of fits right into my game, too."

Where Fleury fits is still to be determined. The obvious spot for him would be on the right of Mark Messier and Adam Graves, where he played during the Rangers' camp tournament in Burlington.

But in recent preseason games, Low has had Fleury playing with his center from last season, Mike York, and they have clicked. York was tied with Fleury for the team scoring lead, and their chemistry has been undeniable.

"I really like playing with him," Fleury said of York.

But he left a pause, because Fleury would love to play with Messier, too. And if Fleury plays with York, then who plays with Messier? John MacLean? Messier probably would be best suited to play with a faster winger than MacLean, and said he enjoys playing with a give-and-go type like Fleury. Since the Czechmates aren't likely to be broken up, there aren't many options for Messier's line if Fleury plays with York.

Fleury said he will be happy wherever Low puts him.

"It doesn't matter," he said. "They're both such good centermen, as long as I do my job and skate and keep my feet moving, I'll be fine."

He'll be fine if the puck goes in the net this year. The fans at the Garden can be very forgiving when you produce.

"It doesn't really matter to me," he said about the anticipated reception he'll get at the Garden.

"As long as I work hard and do the things I'm expected to do, you know? . . ."

Those expectations are high.

FLEURY WAS JOKING before the game about being in the lineup for six of the first seven preseason games, as if he were some sort of rookie. When a veteran plays a bunch of preseason games, the other guys start calling him "Ironman."

Somebody stepped past Fleury and asked him if he made the team. "I don't know. I have a meeting tomorrow," he said. "I hope so. If not, I'll collect my 5.5 in Hartford."

ON GAME DAYS, the Rangers have optional practices. Low wants guys to exercise their option if they're tired or sore. "It's optional," Low said. "You don't have to fuckin' go."

LOW WAS HOLDING HIS POST-GAME press briefing right against the door to the coaches' room at the Meadowlands, when assistant Walt Kyle barged through the door. Kyle didn't have time to hide the can of beer in his hand.

Low: "Where did you get that?"

Kyle: "I found it. I'm trying to find who it belongs to."

DEFENSEMAN RICH PILON, unprotected for Friday's waiver draft, was the likely object of the scouts from Columbus, Los Angeles, Chicago, St. Louis, Atlanta, Tampa Bay and probably a few other teams at tonight's game. Pilon had fought Jean-Luc Grand-Pierre twice in Columbus, and tonight he fought the Devils' Ed Ward. He's never been one to back off an altercation, but even for Pilon this seems excessive.

"I have to. It sucks, but I feel like I'm fighting for a job," he said.

MESSIER PLAYED HIS LAST GAME until opening night.

FRIDAY, SEPTEMBER 29, 2000

NEW YORK

The season begins a week from tomorrow and for Low, there aren't really many difficult decisions that still need to be made.

"Not really," Low said. "I mean, there's decisions to make yet. But the guys who are going to end up playing are making them not difficult, really." A couple of decisions that could have been made for Low didn't materialize today, when defenseman Rich Pilon and right winger John MacLean went unclaimed through the waiver draft. That could mean that defensemen Mike Mottau or Dale Purinton, or winger Johan Witehall, are sent to Hartford at the conclusion of the preseason simply because the Rangers have so many veterans around. Purinton and

Witehall would then have to go through waivers, which would be a risky proposition.

Of course, MacLean might start the season on injured reserve with his sore back, and I.R. is always a route around the 23-man roster limit.

One job still wide open is that of backup goalie to Kirk McLean to start the season, at least until Mike Richter is ready to play. Jason LaBarbera was called up from Hartford Thursday, and played so well in a 2-2 tie with the Devils that Low nixed his plan to split the game and let LaBarbera go the distance.

"Yeah, it's a job we want somebody to grab, to take it," Low said. "Nobody has yet."

Low raved about LaBarbera in Burlington, but had to send at least one of his goalies to Hartford immediately. There simply wouldn't be enough practice time to keep them all around. But neither J.F. Labbe nor Johan Holmqvist, played well enough in their chances. So LaBarbera got his opportunity.

"He's big, pretty solid, and he certainly didn't look intimidated," Low said. "He certainly played well."

Meanwhile the Rangers claimed forward Andreas Johansson from Calgary in the waiver draft. Johansson, 27, originally was drafted by the Islanders in 1991, and has bounced around in the minors and in NHL stops in Pittsburgh, Ottawa, Tampa Bay, and Calgary. He will spend this season playing in Europe.

Smooth defenseman Filip Novak, who has been reassigned to his junior team in Regina (WHL), was named the winner of the Lars-Erik Sjoberg Award as the top rookie in training camp. Sjoberg, a former NHL/WHA defenseman, was the Rangers' European scout who died of cancer in the late 1980s.

Jamie Lundmark and Pavel Brendl likely played their final game tonight. Both are probably headed back to juniors although both made themselves noticed this week. Brendl showed some flashes, finally, in his three-assist game in Columbus. Low said that Lundmark has "been really good the last week and a half; I thought he was pretty average at the start."

SUNDAY, OCTOBER 1, 2000
HARTFORD, CONN.

Low was pacing the corridors of the Hartford Civic Center, where the Rangers' farm club, the Wolf Pack, plays its games and where, today, the Rangers will close the preseason against the archrival Islanders.

Low, in between searches for places to sneak a smoke, was asked what he has learned about his new team.

"It's a really receptive team," Low said. "If you throw any ideas out, you tell them and they pretty much do it."

Then Low paused and got honest.

"I still don't know if we work hard enough," he said. "I don't think we can ever think it's going to be easy. Sometimes you get that feeling, that we kind of cross over the line, that your skill thinks it's going to be better than the opposition's.

"Well, that ain't happening without outworking them. No way. I think there's good skill here, lots of skill. If skill doesn't get outworked, skill wins a lot of the time. I think the key is going to be to try to get that to a team-oriented thing, where it's not, 'I'm a skilled guy.' But, 'We're a skilled team.' This way there's not one splinter here and one splinter over there. It's got to be together."

Suddenly, Low's face lit up.

"Wait a minute, let me say hello to this little son of a bitch," he said.

It was Butch Goring, Low's best friend and the Islanders coach. Low and Goring became friends as teenagers in Manitoba. They played junior hockey together, were in each other's wedding party, have cottages 50 feet apart on Lake Dauphin in Manitoba. They have dinner together four times a week in the off-season, and play golf together almost daily, and often fish together the same day.

Imagine these two buddies going at it in the regular season.

THE RANGERS BEAT THE ISLANDERS 2-1 and closed their preseason 3-3-2-1 (that fourth column is something new; when a team loses in overtime it gets a point, credited as an OL. So the standings read: wins, losses, ties, overtime losses. It will take some getting used to, and losses in OT will still feel like losses. But, in truth, an OT loss is a tie).

They will be off skates tomorrow for the team's alumni golf tournament, held at two private clubs in Westchester. The Rangers will then have a lot of systems work to do the rest of the week to get ready for the opener Saturday in Atlanta.

Once again, the nine preseason games proved to be too long, and the Rangers' penchant for making unnecessary road trips proved costly when Brian Leetch suffered a groin pull on the slush at Reunion Arena in Dallas.

And the job hunt didn't need to be nine games long.

Realistically, there were only three jobs for grabs, with two goalies and 18 skaters all locked into the 23-man roster, to be submitted Tuesday. That means that Manny Malhotra, Jason Doig, Johan Witehall, Dale

Purinton, and Mike Mottau were battling for three spots, and since Doig, Witehall, and Purinton all must clear waivers in order to go to Hartford, the logical and almost certain losers, for the moment, are Malhotra and Mottau. They were more victims of their own waiver status—they can go to the minors and back without being claimed—than of their performances. Mottau is still unsigned, as well, but said he will sit down with his agent and make a decision in the next two days.

The other two prized prospects, Jamie Lundmark and Pavel Brendl, didn't even get uniforms today, and are surely headed back to their junior teams for the entire season.

Low said he has made up his mind which goalie—Jason LaBarbera or J.F. Labbe—would win the job of backing up Kirk McLean until Mike Richter is ready (he took some light shots on goal Saturday and could practice by the end of the week), but wouldn't say which. That race might also have been made moot since Labbe has a bad shoulder, and since neither is likely to play a minute unless there's an emergency.

The Rangers are also shopping around for a trade, and one veteran who certainly is available is defenseman Stephane Quintal, who may not be among the top six on opening night if Purinton, Rich Pilon and Leetch are all in the lineup. Purinton didn't hurt his chances by leaping in to fight enormous Zdeno Chara of the Islanders after Chara kneed Radek Dvorak today.

Low didn't mind that Purinton took an instigator penalty and a 10-minute misconduct in a one-goal game.

"I don't think you have to worry about it if it's a hit, but it's a knee," Low said. "Dale took it upon himself and, no, I don't think that's a bad time. Dale has to do what he has to do. Too many times last year, that was let go. He's willing, and likely one of the things that was missing last year was for people stepping up to be counted when guys were mauling our skilled players.

He's a great team guy."

RYE, N.Y.

Glen Sather was up to a dirty trick and word leaked out before he could finish it.

Sather secretly, he thought, placed Stephane Quintal on waivers and worked out a deal with the Chicago Blackhawks to sidestep a clause in Quintal's contract.

The agreement was that Chicago will have claimed Quintal off waivers when the 48-hour waiver period expires, and once the Blackhawks have their man, they will send two unwanted players to the Rangers. Those are expected to be winger Michal Grosek and defenseman Brad Brown.

That agreement allows both teams to get around the clause in Quintal's contract that calls for him to receive an extra year, the 2003-2004 season at $3 million, if he is traded. In addition, it is believed the Rangers will pay $1 million of the $7.45 million Quintal is owed for the next three seasons.

When the report appeared, Sather flipped. The report came from a source outside the organization, but Sather combed his own office trying to find the leak. He was livid. He denied the deal, wouldn't even acknowledge that Quintal was on waivers.

The Rangers have been trying to trade Quintal since the end of last season, when he was suspended for the final four games after making remarks to a French-language newspaper in Montreal.

Before training camp opened, Quintal apologized to all parties and reached a deal by which he recovered some of the four games' worth of lost salary. Realizing that Quintal was too valuable to let go for nothing, and that they were having trouble trading him due to the fifth-year clause, the Rangers said all was forgiven, and even protected Quintal for the waiver draft last Friday.

The Blackhawks need a strong, veteran defenseman, having traded Bryan McCabe to Toronto for unsigned ex-Ranger Alexander Karpovtsev on Monday. As a non-playoff team, the Blackhawks will be one of the first eligible to put in a claim on Quintal. And the Hawks are likely also looking to shed some salary, which they will do when they complete the "trade" by sending two players to New York.

BY PUTTING QUINTAL ON WAIVERS, the Rangers also left themselves one under the maximum 23-man roster yesterday. That leaves them room to sign rookie defenseman Mike Mottau and add him to the roster.

While that signing could be done by tomorrow, however, Low said that Mottau probably won't stay with the team unless Brian Leetch can't play in Saturday's opener due to a groin strain. Low thinks Mottau would be better off playing 30 minutes a night at Hartford than six or seven minutes on the third defense pair.

Leetch, who skipped practice today, hopes to skate today. If he can't play Saturday, the schedule might work in his favor in that the Rangers are then off until their home opener a week from tomorrow.

OF THE SIX PLAYERS the Rangers assigned elsewhere today, none was a surprise.

However, the move of one player they kept was unexpected, as was the instructions given to demoted center Manny Malhotra.

Low told Malhotra to go down to Hartford and learn to play left wing, and moved career left winger Valeri Kamensky to the right wing on a line with Mark Messier and Adam Graves.

Neither move is stunning, but it is curious that neither experiment was carried out during a month of training camp and nine preseason games. Malhotra played one preseason game on the wing, after Low said in Burlington that he thought Malhotra would be more effective in the middle.

In addition to Malhotra, winger Jeff Ulmer, center Derek Armstrong, and goalie J.F. Labbe were all sent to Hartford; while 19-year-old prospects Jamie Lundmark and Pavel Brendl were returned to their WHL junior teams, Moose Jaw and Calgary, respectively, where they will remain all season.

The assignment of Malhotra was understandable because he did not have to go through waivers in order to go to Hartford as would all of the Rangers who remained with the big club—including defensemen Dale Purinton and Jason Doig and winger Johan Witehall. Rookie goalie Jason LaBarbera won the job of backing up Kirk McLean until Mike Richter's knee is ready, and defenseman Mike Mottau is still around, but unsigned.

Malhotra, wasted under coach John Muckler the previous two years, was unhappy with the demotion.

"I have no problem going to the left wing, but I'd rather learn that up here," Malhotra said. "I don't like the feeling of going there ... out of sight, out of mind . . . I don't like that. If I was here, I could impress him right away, or he could see the way I'm improving, or the way I'm handling left wing right away.

"He obviously knows I'm not thrilled with the situation, but if that's what he thinks it's going to take, I'm going to do it. He said, depending on how I play there, I could be back within a month."

Low said, "I don't think him missing the whole damn year last year helped him any."

LOW SAID HE "wouldn't bet on" Brian Leetch being ready opening night, but Leetch historically doesn't miss games unless he's seriously hurt.

RICHTER TOOK SOME SHOTS on goal today, and skated briefly with the team for the first time since his major knee surgery. He hopes to practice by the end of the week, and be back playing by October 20–29.

AFTER YESTERDAY'S ALUMNI golf outing at the Fenway and Century Country Clubs in Westchester, Sather addressed the group from the dais following dinner.

"Next year," he promised the former and current members of the organization, "I'll bring the Stanley Cup here."

RYE, N.Y.

Stephane Quintal's one-year stint as a Ranger will end tomorrow at noon when he is claimed on waivers, either by design by the Chicago Blackhawks, or by another NHL team.

The only thing that could trump the planned deal is a claim by one of the six teams that finished behind Chicago in the standings last season, or by expansion Minnesota or Columbus, before noon tomorrow, the end of the 48-hour waiver period on Quintal. If another team claims Quintal, it will have to pay his entire remaining salary.

Quintal skated with the Rangers today, but did not speak to reporters, and Sather would not comment on the situation, although he would not deny that Quintal was placed on waivers.

"Whatever you've read is just a rumor," Sather said about the scheme.

THE RANGERS' ROSTER was further shaped yesterday when rookie Mike Mottau signed a two-year contract and the team added the defenseman to its 23-man roster. To make room for Mottau (Quintal remains on the roster until he is claimed), the Rangers put Brian Leetch on injured reserve retroactive to September 23, the date he suffered a groin strain in Dallas.

RYE, N.Y.

Surprise, surprise. Chicago claimed Quintal off waivers at noon, then announced a trade of winger Michal Grosek and defenseman Brad Brown to the Rangers for "future considerations."

Sather denied that his acquisitions were part of a pre-arranged trade for Quintal.

This agreement is headed to the NHL Players Association for an investigation and a grievance. Sather claimed that he would have been able to acquire Grosek and Brown for future considerations even if another team had claimed Quintal.

"Yes," Sather said. "But I'm not sure the future considerations would the same as what they are today."

And what, exactly, are they today? Sather wouldn't say, for obvious reasons. He also wouldn't confirm or deny that the Rangers will pay $1 million of the $7.45 million left on Quintal's contract for the next three seasons.

The players union, according to spokesman Tim Wharnsby, will not get involved unless Quintal or agent Pat Brisson request an investigation.

"We're looking into that," Brisson said. "We've got to analyze the process a little bit."

Brisson said that the Rangers originally came to him and Quintal and asked them to waive the clause. They declined.

"They were interested in doing a trade with Chicago, and since Stephane had a fifth year activated if he gets traded in the first two years of his contract, we didn't want to waive that," Brisson said. "So they decided to put him on waivers. But an hour later, Grosek and Brown end up in New York."

Brisson said that Quintal, who was called out of practice today and didn't speak to reporters, took the news well before heading to Buffalo for tonight's Blackhawks opener.

"As far as Stephane is concerned, and as far as his career is concerned, this might not be a bad thing," Brisson said. "It was their decision, and we respect that."

Sather said he saw in Quintal's play a "stigma" left over from last season. Sather said Quintal looked "scared" when he played his one pre-season game at the Garden and that the Rangers didn't want to "wait around for three months" for Quintal to get straightened out.

Grosek and Brown, both 25, will report to the Rangers tomorrow and are both expected to play in the opener at Atlanta. The big and talented Grosek (6-2, 216), who was traded from Buffalo in the Doug Gilmour deal last March, figures to play on a line with Mike York and Theo Fleury; while the pugilistic Brown (6-3, 206) is penciled into the top six on defense. Brown had 134 penalty minutes in 57 games last season; while Grosek had 13 goals and 40 points in 75 games. Grosek is a rare combination of size, speed, skill and aggressiveness, but rarely has put it all together.

ASKED IF ANY OTHER RANGERS are on waivers, Sather said, "That's privileged information." Sather also cornered a reporter who had been critical of him and the team and told him, "We're all in this together." The reporter had to keep himself from laughing at such a notion. This ain't Edmonton.

JAMIE LUNDMARK, assigned to his junior team, Moose Jaw (WHL) has refused to report and demanded to be traded from Moose Jaw, one of the worst teams in the league, to a contender. Sather said he was shocked at

Lundmark's demand. Lundmark doesn't want to be dealt from the Rangers, just from Moose Jaw to a top team like Kootenay or Regina.

THE RANGERS WERE LOUNGING around in front of a giant-screen TV in a room outside their locker room, killing time while awaiting their flight to Atlanta. On the screen came the image of Marty McSorley clubbing Donald Brashear last season, as the trial continued in Vancouver.

Just as McSorley was taking his two-handed chop, which has been played to death on television outlets everywhere, wise-cracking assistant coach Walt Kyle strode past the TV.

"It was a fuckin' accident," Kyle said without facial expression. Then Kyle disappeared into the next room.

LOW WAS CHATTING with reporters when he was asked if he felt there were any negative feelings lingering from last season.

"If there are," he said, "We're in deep shit.

"It can't be lingering in the room right now. We haven't played a regular-season game yet. We've had negative things come from being negative. But right now, everybody's positive. Everybody's starting off. So if we're thinking negative thoughts at this point in time, we're in deep shit."

COLORADO AND DALLAS, two superpowers out West, opened the season last night. It was a war of a 2-2 tie between two hungry, talented teams.

Messier had seen the game.

"We'll kick their ass," he said, grinning. Messier knew darn well that the Rangers aren't anywhere near that class of team.

FRIDAY, OCTOBER 6, 2000

ATLANTA

The Rangers are what they are. They are a team that has managed the near impossible, missing the playoffs three years in a row. They are a team that could be much better without making many personnel changes; or a team that could be worse because it didn't.

But, because the record says they are 0-0-0-0, we don't know much about them yet.

The new coaching staff and management team are trying to figure that out, too, after a 3-3-2-1 preseason that declared nothing definitive.

The Rangers will have to be going in one direction together, because they will be going in that direction at a faster pace. Unlike last year, when the Rangers' system was, at best, inconsistently implemented, and when practices often featured a lot of standing around followed by pun-ishment-like skating; Low's team will practice hard, keep the tempo fast, and the system will be well-defined.

"Our system's certainly different, trying to pressure and skate more," Brian Leetch said.

"Ron's idea of practicing is fast paced, and every drill you're going fast. There's not a lot of teaching. They do most of the teaching off the ice, beforehand, or after games."

Leetch, however, has been through too much to be blindly optimistic.

"Camp is always so positive and full of energy anyway, especially after the last few years coming off miserable endings where it's fun to get back and start," he said. "This year's not a lot different. It's hard to judge, because I'm sure last year I was just as excited as I was this year, with the new players coming in and not making the playoffs two years in a row. Now it's three years in a row, and Mark's back, with Glen (Sather) and the new coaches, for me to judge is difficult. It's hard to remember all the way back to last training camp."

The Rangers won't go anywhere at all if: Theo Fleury, and Valeri Kamensky can't play better than their dreadful 1999–2000 seasons; if goalie Mike Richter's knee doesn't hold up; if Messier gets hurt for a significant length of time; or if the defense doesn't improve (the person-nel hasn't improved).

The Rangers can make big strides if: Messier makes Leetch and Adam Graves, Fleury and Kamensky play better; if Low proves to be a far bet-ter tactician and motivator than John Muckler; if having Messier around makes the Rangers deeper with Petr Nedved on a top scoring line and Mike York providing top quality scoring on a third line.

There are many more "ifs." But right now, we know very little about these Rangers.

RON LOW HAS A CHANCE to do what no Rangers coach has done for seven years. Mike Keenan, Colin Campbell, and John Muckler never won an opening night game, going a cumulative 0-4-3 in season-openers, since Roger Neilson's 1992–93 team beat Washington in its opener.

What that proves is that opening night doesn't mean much, since Keenan's 1993–94 team won the Stanley Cup and Campbell's 1996–97 team went to the conference finals, while Neilson's 1992–93 team missed the playoffs.

But, whatever the opening-night record says, the Rangers know this: They need to get off to a good start under Low after three straight non-playoff seasons. The Rangers are notoriously slow starters—they have needed at least four games in each of the last four years to get their first win—and have not been able to dig out of the early holes in the last three seasons.

"I don't know about expect it, but I think it's something we feel we have to have," Low said about a fast start. "We have to get ourselves out of the gate. Everybody says it every year, the first day, and we have to walk the walk, I guess. It's really important that the hockey club gets out of whatever funk it's in and tries to make as much as possible as early as possible because, no matter what anybody says, they don't get any easier to win in March."

The Rangers, who begin their second Mark Messier era, have a cup-cake of a schedule, starting with the second-year Thrashers and including five of their first six against fellow non-playoff teams from last season.

Low is happy with the way the past week shook out, with the way the roster was finalized—Brian Leetch will be activated from injured reserve tomorrow and play in the opener, as winger Johan Witehall cleared waivers and was assigned to Hartford to put them at the 23-man limit.

Low was happy with the system details the Rangers worked on in four practices, and that they will get three more days of work before Game 2, the home opener Wednesday.

Low said he has spoken to the team for a month about what it has to do, and he will continue to hammer away at it.

"It's going to get repetitive," he said. "There's a lot of things you say over and over again because one of the reasons, I think, these guys didn't win last year is the things they didn't do nightly that they have to do to win. They'll hear those things 82 times. And they're not big things."

RICHTER HAS STEPPED UP his practice regimen, and could go through a full practice for the first time Monday.

NIGHTMARE 4

The Mix Isn't Quite Right

ATLANTA

Opening night is always exciting, even when a team celebrating its 75th season has to open against a team celebrating its second season. And a win on opening night, even over the infant Atlanta Thrashers, is a win is a win is a win for the Rangers.

That is what new coach Ron Low and returning captain Mark Messier got tonight.

The Rangers hung on for a 2-1 victory over the Thrashers. Nobody seemed to care that it was a death struggle, right down to the final buzzer.

Low did what no Rangers coach since Roger Neilson did in 1992—get an opening-night victory. The Rangers had been 0-4-3 on opening night the last seven seasons.

Now Low, Messier and the Rangers will have a chance, on Wednesday against Montreal, to do something else the Rangers haven't done since Messier departed in 1997—go two games over .500. They have been a single game over .500 only five times since 1996–97, and they lost their next game all five times.

And get this: They won a 2-1 game, which is rare indeed. The Rangers were 1-33-8 when scoring two goals or fewer last season.

There was a black mark on this win, though. Expensive free-agent defenseman Vladimir Malakhov injured his left knee—his good knee—in the first period. Malakhov missed most of last season after major reconstructive surgery on his right knee. Malakhov's injury was diagnosed as a sprain. He is to be reevaluated today, but Malakhov insisted "everything's fine; nothing serious."

But this was reminiscent, if it turns out to be serious, of Valeri Kamensky's opener last season. He re-broke a forearm that had sidelined him the previous year, and that injury was blamed for the disaster the Kamensky signing had become. And, by the way, there were rumors that one of the reasons the Rangers signed Malakhov was a feeling that Kamensky might perform better if he had another Russian teammate.

As FOR MESSIER'S RETURN, it was somewhat less dramatic than the 2-1 OT win in Montreal in his first game as a Ranger in 1991, the Thrashers having had an 0-4 all-time record against the Rangers, compared to the decades of despair the Rangers had been having at the Montreal Forum. That 1991 win also was the first in a Presidents' Trophy season, which ended up with Messier holding the league MVP trophy. None of those things will happen this time around.

But tonight will count just the same in the standings, maybe more considering how important it is for this fragile team to have a good start.

"I think it's important to get off to a good start just because of the way things have gone the last few years," Messier said. "You know, confidence and momentum is a big thing, whether you're a team that's played well for a long time, or a team that's just coming together, or an experienced team or a young team. Confidence and momentum play a big role in any season."

Messier admitted that he got a few "chuckles," particularly when he lined up at the blue line for the National Anthem with old friends Brian Leetch and Adam Graves.

"But there are so many more things on the forefront as far as the team's concerned right now, it just seems so overwhelming with the amount of work to be done and things to accomplish the next little while, I really haven't had time to reminisce too long."

SATHER LABELED "totally false" a rumor out of Canada that the Rangers were talking a blockbuster with Phoenix: Mike Richter, Theo Fleury, Jamie Lundmark and Pavel Brendl for Keith Tkachuk and unsigned goalie Nikolai Khabibulin.

THE RANGERS' 23-MAN PAYROLL, unofficially, was "only" at about $54.66 million including the injured Richter in place of rookie goalie Jason LaBarbera, who will be in the minors once Richter is healthy. The payroll topped out at about $61 million last season.

EARLIER IN THE DAY, Sandy McCarthy and Jason Doig got into a taxi from the Ritz Carlton to go to the morning skate at Philips Arena. The cab driver started to take them to Turner Field, where the Atlanta Braves were hosting a National League Division Series playoff game against St. Louis. Both McCarthy and Doig are black.

McCarthy laughed as he related the story. "You see two well-dressed brothers getting into a cab, you assume they're ballplayers," he said.

Doig didn't think it was so funny, didn't even crack a smile.

THE TWO NEWCOMERS, Brad Brown and Michal Grosek, had an immediate impact. Brown played a lot more minutes than planned after Malakhov got hurt. Grosek, who at his best can be an annoying guy to play against, was on a line with Mike York and Theo Fleury.

"He's got a little bit of everything," Fleury said. "Plus he plays like an asshole. Now we have three assholes on our line."

Understand that Fleury thinks that is a high form of flattery.

But some of Grosek's former teammates in Buffalo and Chicago called him "Two guys." Why? Because, they say, one guy can't be that stupid.

SATHER SAID HIS TESTIMONY in the McSorley trial consisted only of answers to generic questions on the role of a hockey "enforcer."

BY THE WAY, when the new GM speaks to the media, he rarely says anything worth printing. Yet a reporter from the *Atlanta Journal-Constitution* caught him in a chatty mood about the problems the Rangers had last season.

"The locker room was fractured because of internal problems with the general manager and the coaching staff," Sather said, referring to Neil Smith and John Muckler. "John and Neil are both real good people, but it's like when there are two really good people in a marriage. They get married but something happens and they get divorced. It changed the internal workings of the hockey team because some players were in the Muckler camp and some were in the Smith camp."

RYE, N.Y.

In all the hoopla of the new Rangers front office, the new coaching staff, the new (old) captain, and some of the other new faces, it was easy to lose sight of one fact.

The most important Ranger in the first part of this season is Kirk McLean, no doubt about it.

With the Rangers desperate to get off to a flying start against some pretty soft competition, and with No. 1 goalie Mike Richter still on the shelf for a dozen more days or so, it is up to McLean to earn results.

It is his chance to run with an opportunity he rarely got last year.

"Yeah, I'm excited, but everybody is with the new look to the squad," he said. "But I'm not going to overplay my role. I'm just going to go out and do what I do best and use my experience as much as I can."

On Saturday in Atlanta, in a game the Rangers could have embarrassingly lost to the second-year Thrashers, McLean allowed just one goal— and he got a big piece of that shot—in stopping 27 shots for a 2-1 victory. When Atlanta scored that goal, the game turned for quite a stretch, and McLean was superb in preserving the lead built on two late first-period power-play goals. Late in the game, too, McLean was as good as the Rangers needed him to be.

It shouldn't be stunning that McLean was able to step in and perform. After all, he had a terrific preseason, finishing with a 39-save, 2-1 win over the Islanders. He has been an NHL regular for 14 seasons. And, it can be forgotten that he nearly stole the Stanley Cup from the Rangers in 1994 when, as Vancouver's No. 1 goalie, he single-handedly won Game 1 and very nearly pilfered Games 2 and 7.

But McLean, now 34, was forgotten under Rangers coach John Muckler last year.

McLean, signed as a free agent before last season, started five straight October games as Richter recovered from a back injury. In the first four of those, McLean stopped 88 of 95 shots and went 3-1 with a 1.76 goals-against average.

Once Richter came back, though, McLean collected dust. He started just five of the next 46 games, until Richter hurt his knee at the All-Star weekend skills competition. Even then, Muckler rode Richter, who on one leg started nine straight late-February, early-March games. By then, McLean was so rusty, it was ridiculous to expect him to be able to be effective.

It was just a terribly difficult season.

"It's difficult, sure," he said. "Everybody wants to play. I really worked hard to contribute in other aspects of my game, leadership-wise. It was a different role for me last year as far as showing it on the ice. I had to be more (vocal) in the locker room; more vocal than I was in the past, which, with my age and my experience, it was a good thing and it felt good.

"We have a great bunch of guys here and they made me feel as much a part of the team as anybody. I think sometimes when you're not playing a lot you get a feeling of alienation, but again, I think the experience in our locker room helps a lot in that situation."

Richter's knee has given no indication that he can't be a workhorse again once he gets started playing games. Low, who was a backup goalie himself for much of his career, said he hasn't "a clue right now" on how much he'd expect McLean to play.

"I don't like to have a guy sit for too long, but on the other hand, you want to get as much mileage out of Mike, too," Low said. "Obviously, he's in a group of four or five guys in the league who can win you games by himself, so we'll cross that when we get there, I guess. It would be nice to have him play 60, realistically, if his knee can handle it."

McLean said he will take it as it comes, although he has so far been impressed with Low and his staff.

"Their up-tempo practices have been really upbeat and really positive," McLean said. "It's a no-B.S. type of coaching staff. They let you know the way it really is, and as a player, that's what you ask for. You don't want to get the runaround and have your mind somewhere else trying to figure out what's going on. What I like about the coaching staff is they tell you the way it is, what your role is going to be, and this is what we want out of you and if you don't do it, we'll find somebody else."

VLADIMIR MALAKHOV'S LEFT KNEE was examined by team doctor Tony Maddalo today, and it was determined he suffered only a mild sprain. A knee sprain, though, is actually a tear. A mild sprain is a slight tear. He's day to day and doubtful for the home opener.

WEDNESDAY, OCTOBER 11, 2000

NEW YORK

The home opener was a hoopla-filled event, centered on the 75th anniversary of the franchise, its history, and the return of the captain. New York City mayor Rudy Giuliani hosted a small group representing the team at City Hall the day before the opener.

Then, on opening night at the Garden, they brought out the lasers and the smoke. There were numerous signs welcoming back Messier during warm-ups. The pregame ceremony lasted more than half an hour. Emcee John Davidson, the unparalleled MSG Network analyst, announced the invited members of the Rangers' past, from Clint Smith, who played on the 1940 championship team, to Mike Keenan, who coached the 1994 Cup winner. Even Keenan, who was reviled upon bolting the team a month after its victory parade, was loudly cheered. Then, too, it may have been that the folks who fill the Garden were just pining for the good old days.

Also introduced and brought out onto the ice were former GM/coach Emile Francis, and ex-Rangers stars Rod Gilbert, Eddie Giacomin, Jean Ratelle, Andy Bathgate, Gump Worsley, Chuck Rayner, Vic Hadfield, Brad Park, Ron Greschner, Dave Maloney, Steve Vickers, and Walt Tkaczuk.

Then the current players were brought out, one by one, with Messier last. Of course, the returning captain received a thunderous roar from the sold-out crowd and, of course, he cried tears of joy. Messier then presented Smith, the oldest living Ranger, with a gold Rangers logo shield.

During the crescendo of the National Anthem by Garden staple John Amirante, Messier cracked up. He had looked at Amirante and just broke into laughter.

"He was up on his toes," Messier said later. "I know from experience that when John gets up on his toes like that, it must be a big game."

Messier isn't Superman anymore. His return to Madison Square Garden as a Ranger, after a three-year mistake sent him to Vancouver, wasn't exactly magical.

But still, completely by accident, Messier scored what turned out to be the game-winning goal in a 3-1 victory over Montreal, a win that kept the Rangers—get this!—undefeated.

Their 2-0 record marks the first time since Messier left town that the Rangers are two games over .500, and even if their two victims don't have a prayer of being in the playoffs, Messier has the Rangers playing with a bit of the swagger that's been missing.

The Rangers are 2-0 for the first time since 1989.

Radek Dvorak scored twice in another effective, but overshadowed, game by the Czechmates line, and by goalie Kirk McLean, who has stopped 55 of 57 shots in two games. Dvorak got the game's first goal on a power play (the Rangers have scored four times with the man-advantage in two games) and the clincher with the team's first even-strength goal of the season. In fact, McLean's pass to Theo Fleury started the play on which Dvorak scored the first goal.

In between, Messier clunked in the winner.

Twenty-four seconds into the third, Messier had broken in around Eric Weinrich, and had his snap from the right circle stopped by goalie Jeff Hackett. Weinrich broke his stick over Messier's forearms, and Messier retrieved the puck from behind the net. Weinrich grabbed a teammate's stick, and as Messier attempted to thread a pass to Adam Graves, the puck caromed off Weinrich and into the net. Messier looked to the roof and laughed as he celebrated his first Rangers goal since the 1997 playoffs.

"It would have been nicer if I had came down the right side and threw it in the bottom corner," Messier said, referring to his signature off-wing, wrong-footed snap shot. "It doesn't matter how they go in."

At this point, it also doesn't matter how the Rangers win, or whom they beat.

"We're not running on all cylinders," Messier said. "I think everybody's aware of that, but I think we can make up some of that with some heart and some hard work and some talent."

Messier has played better games. Much better. Still, he rose to an occasion again. And still, he seems to have the ability to push others to play better. Valeri Kamensky and Fleury, who had nightmarish 1999–2000 seasons, look like different players. Fleury played an aggressive, aggravating game and had a breakaway, although he fired wide.

"It's deja vu," Fleury laughed. "I'm getting closer, though."

Messier had cried and laughed before the game. He also showed another emotion, one that was rare as could be—nervousness.

"I thought he was very nervous in the first," said Low. "He handled the puck a couple of times and it was bouncing off his stick. That's not like Mark at all. For him to be nervous says an awful lot about the way he plays the game, and the emotion he brings."

"I was a little nervous," Messier admitted. "I couldn't believe it. I've played in a lot of big games, in a lot of different situations. I don't know if I was putting too much pressure on myself to play a good game, or to do too much too early, but I felt better as the game went on."

The Rangers took command of the tired 1-3 Canadiens, who played their home opener Tuesday, and never looked in danger of losing the lead.

"In order to be successful in any team sport, players have to be able to do more than perhaps they've ever done at certain times in their career," Messier said. "I think you have to be overachievers, whether you're a supserstar on the team or a guy who plays five minutes a game. Everybody has to have that kind of mindset, every time we go out there, that on this particular night perhaps I might have to do something I don't normally do. I think that's a little bit of a learned skill. We have to find a way to become overachievers."

THE RANGERS WHO WERE members of the AHL champion Hartford Wolf Pack last season, got their rings today. P.J. Stock, now with the Canadiens, got his, too. He also lost a scrap to a much-bigger Sandy McCarthy, who celebrated his first fight as a Ranger by waving his fingers. It didn't really sit well with the Garden crowd, particularly those who weren't terribly familiar with Stock. They just saw McCarthy beat up this tiny guy, and didn't think he should be celebrating it.

McCarthy did make his presence known in the desired way, however, when big Montreal center Trevor Linden hit Leetch. Linden was Vancouver's captain in 1994, when the Canucks' strategy in the Stanley Cup finals was to rub out and wear down Leetch and the Rangers' other puck-moving defenseman Sergei Zubov. Leetch was belted around throughout the seven-game series, and still managed to take apart the Canucks. More to the point, the last few years Leetch had been banged and run over with little retribution, since his big partner, Jeff Beukeboom retired. So now Linden was taking a shot at Leetch. Immediately, McCarthy skated to Linden, got his shoulder right in Linden's chest and his goatee right in Linden's face, and said, "You fuck with Leetchie, you fuck with me."

That's what he was brought here to do.

THURSDAY, OCTOBER 12, 2000

RYE, N.Y.

The Rangers' second-biggest catch from the free-agent market this past summer won't be playing for the next month or so.

Defenseman Vladimir Malakhov had an MRI on his left knee today, and a partial tear of the anterior cruciate ligament was discovered. Malakhov, who suffered the injury on opening night Saturday in Atlanta when he stepped in a rut, originally believed the injury was minor. He had hoped to play Saturday in Pittsburgh.

However, the result of the MRI will sideline Malakhov for about four weeks.

Malakhov was signed to a four-year, $14 million contract on July 11, with options for a fifth season.

Malakhov missed the first 54 games of last season while recovering from surgery to reconstruct the ACL in his right knee. When he returned, Malakhov was traded from Montreal to the Devils, where he won a Stanley Cup ring.

With an extra roster spot open due to Malakhov's placement on injured reserve, the Rangers chose to call up David Wilkie from Houston

(IHL) rather than rookie Mike Mottau, who has been unimpressive in his initial week at Hartford.

CHARITY STORIES ABOUND in hockey, and there are several players among the Rangers whose charity work rivals, perhaps even exceeds, that of Mark Messier. But this is a special story. The Hackensack (N.J) Medical Center has named a facility for the Rangers captain. The Mark Messier Skyway to Tomorrows Children links the Women's Pavilion and the Children's Pavilion of the Don Imus Pediatric Center for Tomorrows Children. The glass enclosed skyway will include an indoor playground, and will also house some of Messier's personal career memorabilia in an interactive showcase.

Nobody in the New York area was happier about Messier's return to New York than the Tomorrows kids and their families. Messier held a $1,000-a-plate dinner to kick off the hockey season, and though the place only held 100 people, he said he easily could have sold another 100–200 tickets.

Messier raised some $245,000 for the kickoff of the new building that night.

He auctioned off his opening-night jersey and two tickets for $13,500 on an internet auction and when there was some confusion about the winning bid, Messier agreed to add two more tickets, an autographed stick and a post-game, locker room meeting for another $6,500. He also auctioned five golf packages for $10,000 each. The Rangers donated $20,000 out of the money raised by their 75th anniversary book, and the NHL added another $10,000.

Now Messier is beginning his points club, in which he donates money for every point he scores and asked corporations and fans alike to donate what they can on a per-point basis, too.

"He gets a lot of satisfaction out of it, as does our whole family," said Messier's sister, Mary-Kay, who is also extremely active in the charity. "Over the years it's been really rewarding, and it was the ultimate honor to have the building named after him."

FRIDAY, OCTOBER 13, 2000

RYE, N.Y.

Hockey players spend a lot of time just killing time. For example, on days like today, when they are traveling (in this case, flying to Pittsburgh) there is time from the end of practice until the bus to the airport departs. Normally, guys will work out, shower, get massages, and have lunch. Most times, a catered meal is delivered to the players' lounge.

And they sit around, eat, talk, and watch TV. Sometimes they watch video tapes, and one of the favorites among hockey players are these underground fight tapes. They are generally poor-quality, grainy videos of the bad-old-days of hockey, the days of bench-clearing brawls and melees; even of mayhem off the ice.

So the Rangers today were spread around couches and chairs and watching some classics. The Big Bad Boston Bruins of the late 1960s and early 1970s. The Broad Street Bullies, the Philadelphia Flyers of the 1970s. They watched the night in the early '80s when the Bruins went into the stands at Madison Square Garden, after a fan had reached over the glass and grabbed a Boston stick during a post-game fracas. In that unforgettable incident, Mike Milbury of the Bruins was seen beating a fan with his own shoe.

They watched a bout between heavyweights Steve Durbano of St. Louis and the Rangers' ever-popular, Staten Island-born Nick Fotiu, a fight that carried over into the hallway between the locker rooms, where a steel door was kicked open. The door still bears a dent witnesses insist was created by Durbano. They watched the Islanders' Clark Gillies, Bobby Nystrom and Gary Howatt gleefully punch-out opponents. They watched noted enforcers like Dave Schultz, Ed Hospodar, Dave Brown (now a Rangers scout), Paul Holmgren, Dave Semenko, and so many more.

Jan Hlavac and Radek Dvorak and some of the other young guys were laughing along with everybody else, but their eyes were wide open, as if they couldn't believe these fights were real, that this is the way hockey used to be.

Messier was providing running commentary, having come in at the end of that era when he and a bunch of 18–20 year-olds were growing into a dynasty in Edmonton.

"Can you imagine all of us, 18 years old, playing against these guys," Messier asked. "When we played at the Spectrum (in Philadelphia) we never stopped skating. Although we did have the great equalizer— Semenko."

PETR NEDVED WAS TALKING about a play he made in the home opener. He held onto the puck and kept going forward, using his reach and all his strength. He knew that, if he could delay just a bit longer, Radek Dvorak would beat his man to the net.

Nedved was right. By holding off the two Montreal Canadiens who were trying to knock him off the puck, Nedved gave Dvorak the time he needed to streak in on right wing and bang in Nedved's pass for the clinching goal Wednesday night.

Dvorak, whom John Muckler predicted would be a 40-goal scorer one day, is off to a flying start.

He has two goals and an assist in two games—matching his output for all of October last season, while he was having his minutes limited in Florida—and those numbers truly could be better for all the chances Dvorak's remarkable speed have created.

"He's definitely the fastest guy on our team," Nedved said. He added that what separates Dvorak from other fast skaters is his first few strides, and that maybe only Florida's Pavel Bure could catch him in a race.

"Those first couple of steps, you have to pull him down, or he's by you," Nedved said.

The addition of Mark Messier, and the resulting move of Mike York to a third line, has given the Rangers more depth up front. So much so that Nedved, Dvorak, and Jan Hlavac, the Czechmates and the Rangers' No. 1 line last season, have more room. Teams still focus on stopping Nedved's line, but now that focus is spread around. Atlanta, for example, started the opener using its best defense pair against Messier's line, before switching the attention to Nedved's line.

And if Nedved's line is checked tightly, as Montreal tried to do, that leaves more room for Messier's line, and York's line.

"For sure," Nedved said. "Other teams are going to have to juggle their defense."

As for his own fast start, Dvorak said, "We're winning, and that's what's fun. That's what matters. We need every point we can get."

THEO FLEURY WANTS EVERYBODY to know that the Mets are 10-1 since he took batting practice with them at Shea Stadium last month. "I'd better get a ring if they win it all," Fleury said.

STILL NO TARGET DATE has been set for Mike Richter's return, but Richter has said he feels he'll be able to jump right in, rather than go to the minors for a start or two first. Low said he hasn't planned on asking Richter to go down to Hartford before making his first NHL start.

SATURDAY, OCTOBER 14, 2000

PITTSBURGH

You knew the Rangers weren't going to keep on winning forever. But you probably didn't figure they'd revert to their March, 2000 form so quickly.

Playing for the first time this season against an opponent that qualified for the playoffs, the Rangers unraveled against the exhausted Pittsburgh Penguins and got what they deserved, their first loss of the season, 8-6 at Mellon Arena.

The Rangers, who now go back on a diet of three more non-playoff teams, wasted two more goals from Mark Messier and four more power-play goals. They did it by laying out a red carpet for Jaromir Jagr, who had as easy a four-goal night as any player could have. The last time the Rangers played this poorly, Garden boss Jim Dolan started firing people.

For a team still getting its legs back after opening the season in Tokyo, and a team that just played its home opener the night before, the Penguins sure had a lot of jump. Some of that, of course, had to do with the Rangers' defensive-zone play. Several times the Rangers completely forgot about that big No. 68 guy—you know, the NHL scoring champ, that Jagr fella.

The Rangers treated him the same way they treated unknown Roman Simicek, and Jagr showed his appreciation with his seventh career hat trick, and first four-goal game in the wild affair.

Kirk McLean's 1.00 goals-against average took a beating.

The bottom fell out for the Rangers, though, after Robert Lang tied the game 4-4 with 52.5 seconds left in the second period. Just 53 seconds into the third, Sylvain Lefebvre lobbed the puck toward the Pittsburgh zone, and all five Rangers on ice went for a change. The puck never got to the Penguins blue line, as Michal Rozsival bunted it out of the air. Complicating mattters, Brad Brown, one of the Rangers coming onto the ice, fell.

That left Kip Miller and Jagr all alone. Miller dropped it off to the wide-open Jagr, who made it 5-4. Martin Straka made it 6-4. Simicek made it 7-4. And Jagr made it 8-4 by the 9:15 mark of the third.

"Everyone anticipated it going deep instead of making sure," said Brian Leetch, one of those who went off the ice. "They were coming, we were going and we got caught in between."

"They got us running around on the rush, and in our own zone."

"That line change that put us down 5-4 was just horrific," said Low. "The third period, we started trying to pick pockets instead of finishing checks. You can't do that, especially against a team with the amount of skill those guys have. If you don't finish them off, they're going to stick it to you."

Low added that "we stunk defensively" and put most of the blame for that on the Rangers' forwards.

Jagr was laughing later. He said he still doesn't feel right, that his hands aren't where he wants them to be. And he insisted that he had five goals, since he accidentally tipped Theo Fleury's second goal past Pittsburgh goalie Jean-Sebastien Aubin.

"We've got a lot of work to do still," Messier said. "We made some mistakes as a team and they have enough skill to make you pay. There were some good things tonight, but obviously there are things we need to address."

And quickly. Paul Kariya and Teemu Selanne of Anaheim come to the Garden Monday

ART COULTER, the captain of the Rangers' 1940 Stanley Cup championship team, died today in Mobile, Alabama. The Hall of Fame defenseman, a punishing hitter and shot-blocker in his day, was 92.

MONDAY, OCTOBER 16, 2000

NEW YORK

So much for the cupcake schedule and the fast start.

The Rangers are now 2-2 after another sloppy loss, this one to the Anaheim Mighty Ducks, 4-3 at the Garden tonight. The Rangers were only moderately better defensively than they were in their football-score loss in Pittsburgh Saturday, but they were also not nearly as good offensively or on the power play, and they paid again for their mistakes.

They lost to a team whose only other win was on opening night, in the first-ever game of the Minnesota Wild.

After their home opener against the Montreal Mighty Canadiens, the Rangers talked about how important it is to establish home-ice as an advantage again. Well, the worst way to do that is to come out and fail to get a single shot on goal for the first 15:23 of the game, and that's what the Rangers did tonight.

In addition to their inability to create anything offensively, the Rangers looked much as they did in that 8-6 nightmare in Pittsburgh Saturday, playing a bungling defensive game. Or where they left off last season.

"I don't know," Low said. "It looked like we were back on our heels, kind of watching what they were doing instead of playing like we were supposed to be. I guess it's something that has to be addressed. I know last year, they said every first period here was a bit of a bummer; that they started behind the eight-ball every night. That can't happen. We have to get ourselves going."

"Obviously, that's not the way we can start hockey games," Theo Fleury said. "We picked up where we left off in Pittsburgh when, hopefully, we would have learned a lesson from the game before."

Low said he got no indication of what was coming either in the morning skate, the warmup, or in the locker room, which is pretty much what John Muckler often said last year.

RICH PILON TKO'D big Jim Cummins with a left hook, and Pilon simultaneously had his nose broken for the seventh time in a second-period scrap.

THE RANGERS' POWER PLAY is a league-leading 9 for 25 (tied with Phoenix) through four games. The Rangers didn't score their ninth PPG last season until Game No. 27, on their 110th opportunity.

WEDNESDAY, OCTOBER 18, 2000

CHICAGO

If tonight was any indication, the Rangers have a ton of work to do. They beat the sorry Chicago Blackhawks, 4-2 in a half-filled United Center, but they didn't look very convincing in doing so.

Still, it beat by a mile the two sloppy losses which preceded this game. You just have to wonder how these Rangers will hold up when they start facing some real competition—and next week's home-and-home with a banged-up Philadelphia team barely qualifies.

As Mark Messier explained it, the Rangers were "good at the right times" as opposed to the game against Anaheim Monday, when the Rangers were good longer, but bad at the wrong times.

The Blackhawks, a team made up almost exclusively of ex-Rangers and ex-Devils, a team that had beaten only Columbus (twice) this season, gave the Rangers all they could handle.

This time, McLean bailed them out in what was the end of his tenure as the team's No. 1 goalie. With Mike Richter coming back to start Sunday against Tampa Bay, McLean's playing time will shrink dramatically.

But the Rangers saw to it that McLean went out with a flurry—a flurry he could have done without. He called them "a couple of oopses."

Key players made several frightening defensive decisions, including a whiff on a body check by Brian Leetch that resulted in the first Hawks goal, by Steve Sullivan, to make it 1-1; and passes right in front of the net by Messier and Petr Nedved that had McLean scrambling madly to stop the likes of Tony Amonte point-blank. McLean also had, while it was 2-1 in the third, a shot that hit the post, hit him in the mask, bounced off his blocker and into his glove.

So it was a big, collective "Whew!" when Jan Hlavac scored the clincher and Theo Fleury fired a 180-footer into an empty net "Hang that one on him," said Low. "That was Kirk's win. He's done a great job for us."

How does this happen? How do veteran players make such gaffes with the puck in the defensive zone?

"I don't know if it's nerves or what," Low said. "It seems we're gripping the stick awful tight. A lot of pucks went under our sticks when we were trying to pass it. If we were nervous, uptight, I don't know what it is. But a veteran hockey club shouldn't be nervous or uptight. I guess we're going to have to battle our way through whatever it is.

"In the third period, Mark threw one right in the middle, they nearly scored on. Petr Nedved . . . right in the middle, for no reason. We had the wall open. . . . The place you can't throw it is in the middle."

MOST OF THE RANGERS were shocked by the small crowd (12,806 was the announced attendance) at United Center. The Blackhawks, an organization still living in the 1950s—home games are not shown on television—drew about half that for a game against Columbus last week.

RON LOW HAS GOTTEN good reports recently about rookie defenseman Mike Mottau from Hartford coach John Paddock. And while Low feels Mottau will benefit from more AHL experience, he allows that, given the parade of defensemen auditioning for the Rangers' third pair, "Mike Mottau might not be ready for us right now, but we're ready for him." David Wilkie was returned to Houston after the game.

NEW YORK CITY is just nuts with the Yankees playing the Mets in the Subway Series and the Rangers have a scheduling conflict. The Rangers want to move their Sunday game against Tampa Bay from 7 p.m. to an afternoon start, because the World Series is going on that night. Tampa Bay is playing the Devils in New Jersey Saturday night, and NHL bylaws don't allow afternoon games after night games. The Devils won't (or claim they can't) move their game to the afternoon to accomdate the Rangers. So the Garden will be half-filled Sunday, and those there will be watching TVs or listening to radios.

The league offices wouldn't step in. And the NHL wonders why everybody thinks it's a third-class pro league. Interestingly, the Devils are now owned by a group headed by George Steinbrenner, who owns the Yankees.

RYE, N.Y.

The Rangers jumped upon the Subway Series bandwagon during an open practice at Playland. Before a couple of thousand fans, the Rangers practiced wearing Yankees and Mets jerseys. Brian Leetch, an enormous life-long Yankees fan, had no trouble picking his jersey. Mark Messier decided to be more political. He had a jersey made up that was Yankees on one side and Mets on the other.

Seven of the Rangers attended Game 1 of the World Series later tonight—Messier, Leetch, Petr Nedved, Val Kamensky, Theo Fleury, Sandy McCarthy, and Dale Purinton. Most stayed to the end early in the morning, but McCarthy, Fleury and Kamensky got up and left as the Yankees came to bat in the bottom of the 12th inning. They could hear the winning run score from outside the stadium.

"We knew exactly what happened," McCarthy said. "It sounded like a bomb exploded."

Messier has attended games with Leetch in the past. In fact , in 1994 they carried the Stanley Cup onto the field in Yankees uniforms, and before the game they took batting practice under the stands; they were scheduled to take regular BP, but couldn't because of bad weather.

Messier loves going with Leetch. "He knows everything about the game. I'm just looking around. He's going, 'now they're going to throw him three straight curveballs and get him to hit into a double play.' And he's always right."

NEW YORK

There were two silver linings for the Rangers in tonight's otherwise miserable 4-2 loss to the Tampa Bay Lightning at the Garden.

One, goalie Mike Richter made his first start of the season and looked pretty darn good for a guy who hasn't had two healthy knees since the All-Star skills competition last February. Two, most of New York didn't see this performance, although the turnout at the Garden was a surprisingly good one, about 12,000 or so.

Other than that, it was pretty dark for the Rangers. Having played five of their first six games against non-playoff teams, the Rangers' 3-3 split is less than acceptable, especially since they opened the season 2-0.

"No, it isn't (acceptable)," said Theo Fleury, who was called for a game-turning retaliation penalty at the second-period buzzer.

"Losing isn't something we can't accept easily," said Mark Messier, who had two more assists and has eight points in six games. "We do some good things in the game, then hurt ourselves by doing some things at the wrong times in the game. We're obviously aware of some things, but our game awareness right now is lacking. I think we're not aware of the timing of things on the ice and we're making mistakes at the wrong times of games.

"There's reasons why you win and reasons why you lose. We have to look at the game tonight and understand why we lost the game tonight and continue to improve and continue to preach the things we think are necessary to win and try to do them better."

The Lightning, bombed by the Devils Saturday night, came in 1-4-1 and got a hat trick by Fredrik Modin and the usual stellar evening's work from goalie and Rangers-killer Kevin Weekes to wreck Richter's return. But they also got a gift first goal, a Modin rebound off the crossbar which was accidentally kicked into his own net by Rich Pilon.

After Brian Leetch tied it, the Lightning got a gift 5-on-3 advantage to open the third period. Fleury, who claimed that Weekes speared him, took a tiny slash at the goalie, touching off a mini melee. The Rangers, already a man short, wound up two down.

And the Lightning got a goal from Mike Johnson 5-on-3, and another from Modin 28 seconds later, 13 seconds after the second penalty expired. A 1-1 game was then 3-1 early in the third, and pretty much over.

Richter was making his first start since March 27, the fateful night on which the Rangers completed a home-and-home disaster against Detroit, which cost both coach John Muckler and team president/GM Neil Smith their jobs. Richter hadn't won since March 8, when he stole a victory at Anaheim on one leg.

He had to shut it down for the final four games of last season, and on April 5 had major reconstructive surgery on his left knee. After the game, Richter said the knee "was fine" and "I'll continue to get my timing back, but I'm really disappointed we didn't win."

Last season, because of a back injury that cost him five games, Richter didn't get his first win until game No. 8.

Richter's first loss last season came in game two, in Vancouver, and that was significant not only because Messier was an opponent that night, but also because the Canucks' goalie was Weekes.

Weekes beat the Rangers for his first NHL victory, after starting his career 0-13-2, and just like that he became a nemesis. While splitting the season between Vancouver and the Islanders, Weekes piled up a 4-1 record against the Rangers, including his first NHL shutout. Over the summer he was dealt to Tampa Bay, and tonight he was frustrating the Rangers again.

The easiest part of the schedule is over. The Rangers wasted it.

The good part is that most of New York's attention was in the Bronx.

MONDAY, OCTOBER 23, 2000

RYE, N.Y.

Ron Low had just found a positive, and only a few words into it, it had already turned into a negative.

Low, after all, is an honest guy.

"I liked the play out of Mark Messier again," Low said after Sunday's horrid 4-2 loss to Tampa Bay at the Garden. "I mean, I think he's been our best player almost game in and game out. And we should be responding to that and we aren't, I don't think, as a group, nearly enough. This guy's leading us unbelievably so. We have to start getting into the things he's doing out there. Right now, he's playing great."

You can read it right there, the positive (Messier's play) and the negative (the guy is closing in on his 40th birthday, and he shouldn't be their best player). And more negative (where is everybody else?).

Actually, if you look at the Rangers' 3-3 record and the quality of the play of some of their players, it doesn't add up. They have wasted terrific starts by Messier, Leetch, and Fleury.

More to the point, they have wasted a schedule as easy as could be. Their first six games included five against teams that didn't make the playoffs last season. The Rangers didn't play a single set of back-to-back nights. They played three times against teams that had played the night before, and lost two of those. Two of the Rangers' wins were down-to-the-wire battles with dreadful Atlanta and Chicago (combined record: 2-8-6, or 0-8-6 if you take out Chicago's two victories over expansion Columbus).

And now it gets tougher. Much tougher. The Rangers open a home-and-home against Philadelphia tomorrow, and no matter what injury troubles the Flyers have had—John LeClair, Eric Lindros and Mark Recchi have all been out—it will still be a step up from the soft competition the Rangers have so far faced.

Also, tomorrow's Garden game starts a stretch in which the Rangers will play four times in the next six nights. Included in that is Thursday (at Philadelphia) and Friday (against Pittsburgh) games which will be the first of seven sets of back-to-back games the Rangers will play in the next eight weeks, a chunk of schedule that will have the Rangers travel out West twice, and will bring such contenders as Ottawa (twice), Phoenix, Toronto (twice), the Devils, Colorado and Los Angeles (twice).

That is why the Rangers could not afford to waste their first six gimmes. They needed to go 4-2 or 5-1. But they went 3-3, and that wasn't good enough.

Low claimed to not be unhappy with being .500, saying that the Rangers aren't in a hurry, and noting that this is a work in progress with a new coaching staff, new system, new captain and some new players.

Still, Low is absolutely unhappy with at least three aspects of the Rangers' game: The aforementioned inability to follow Messier's lead; the inexplicable shoddy, panicky play in the defensive zone, where opponents are regularly left alone in prime scoring areas; and what the coach called an "East to West" game in the offensive zone, rather than "North to South."

Given that, Low has some changes planned. Michal Grosek, who doesn't kill penalties and therefore found himself benched for a lengthy stretch of Sunday's game, is out.

John MacLean, who can kill penalties and score goals, is in. Adam Graves, removed from Messier's line late in Sunday's game, is back with Mike York, and Fleury takes his place with Messier and Kamensky.

Kirk McLean will be in goal, too, and he will play one of the back-to-back games Thursday or Friday, which likely means Mike Richter gets one of those two games and Sunday's against Boston.

The Rangers need to be better than they've been. A lot better. And soon.

"The game is 60 minutes long, but there are four or five moments in the game, normally, that are ultimately turning points,' Messier said. "We have to be aware of the game situations better and react better and execute better at those crucial times. In our losses this year, I don't think we've been good enough in that area, in those four or five crucial times in every game."

NEW YORK

Nothing has changed. The Rangers have a new general manager, a new coaching staff, a new captain, some new players.

Yet they are the same Rangers. The same ill-prepared, poorly-motivated Rangers. The same soft team making the same mistakes as they made all of last year. And the year before. And the year before that.

The Rangers made a team in a woeful downward spiral look like champs tonight in a 5-4 loss to the banged-up Philadelphia Flyers at the Garden. Ron Low's Rangers have now lost four of their last five, the only win being a hang-on-for-dear-life victory over pitiful Chicago. They tried to sugar-coat this loss because they came close at the end, after falling behind 3-0 then, after getting it to 3-2, falling behind again by 5-2.

Low broke up Mark Messier and Adam Graves—something several Rangers coaches have tried to do, something that has bombed every time— and the Rangers fell under .500 for the first time this season.

But surely not the last.

The only bright note for the Rangers was Graves's power-play goal in the third, which pushed him into a tie with Andy Bathgate for third on the franchise list with 272 goals.

Once again the Rangers got off to a dreadful start, which was made far, far worse by a Messier giveaway that Keith Primeau quickly turned into a 1-0 lead 12 seconds into the game.

Soon it was 2-0, then 3-0, and the Rangers, who went 12:25 without a shot on goal, were looking a lot like they did last year.

"We can't be that fragile," Low said when it was suggested that the Rangers were reeling from that early punch. "If we're that fragile, we're not going to go anywhere anyway."

"It's a simple bank off the boards," said Messier, who played with a stomach virus but didn't duck the blame for his boneheaded play. "But it was a big play in the game. When a leader of your team makes a mistake early in the game, it really seemed to rattle us a little bit, and we couldn't really regroup. It was a tough play for all of us, especially knowing we were ready to play the game, and everybody was looking for a big game. To have them come out and score right off the bat, it was a tough break for us."

Last year the Flyers came to the Garden with an 0-5-1 record and the charitable Rangers fixed Philadelphia's season by going down twice in a home-and-home series without a fight, and without a goal. Tonight, the Flyers (minus unsigned Eric Lindros, and injured John LeClair and Mark Recchi) came into another home-and-home with the Rangers with an 0-5-2 mark since an opening-night win, having been outscored 31-15 in those seven games.

So when the Rangers cut it to 3-2 on goals by Jan Hlavac and Brian Leetch, the Flyers should have been fragile and vulnerable.

Instead, the Rangers threw them a rope. Petr Nedved coughed one up and two Rangers left their men, and with 1:06 left in the second period, the Flyers' Justin Williams scored a gift goal, a killer goal.

"Unforgivable," Low said. "That was one of our brain lapses, and it cost us the hockey game."

Another sitting duck, and the Rangers misfired again. They are 3-4, despite the opportunities afforded by the schedule to be 4-3 or 5-2 or 6-1.

"For us I don't think it really matters who we're playing, or where we're playing, or the schedule or anything," Messier said, using a line he would repeat over and over again during the season. "We're in a position now where we have to look at there's 20-something teams that finished ahead of us last year, the last two years. We have to look at every game as if it's a tough game and we have to play desperate hockey. We have to play with a fear of losing."

"Are we any better than anybody right now?" Low asked. "Right now we are not. I read it all the time, that we're playing teams that are under .500 and teams that haven't made the playoffs.

"Well, guess what, fellas, neither have we. And the only way we're getting out of it is to put our butts in gear a lot earlier than we are now."

It is past that time. Otherwise, these will be the same old Rangers, and this will be the same season as the last one, and the one before it, and the one before that.

WEDNESDAY, OCTOBER 25, 2000

RYE, N.Y.

The Rangers' defensemen weren't to blame for Messier's cough-up that led to Keith Primeau's goal 12 seconds into Tuesday's game. The defensemen weren't to blame for the bad-angle goal that Kirk McLean let slip between his legs. And the defensemen weren't to blame for Petr Nedved's giveaway and for two forwards leaving the zone on the crushing fourth Philadelphia goal after the Rangers had dug their way back from 3-0, to within 3-2.

Still, the Rangers' defense has been a very weak link in the early part of this already bad 3-4 season.

New president/GM Glen Sather came in and tried to put a stamp on this team over the summer, when he made the decision to not even consider re-signing free agents Mathieu Schneider (who went instead to Los Angeles) or Kevin Hatcher (Carolina). And he made the decision to trade Stephane Quintal to Chicago for Brad Brown and Michal Grosek, who was a healthy scratch Tuesday. The housecleaning was supposed to create some room for one or two of the Rangers' young defensemen to make the team.

Sather's lone upgrade, if you can call it that, was to sign Vladimir Malakhov to a stunning four-year, $14 million contract with an option for a fifth year. While many, including some of those in the Rangers locker room, doubt that Malakhov is better than Schneider, Malakhov never made it through his first game, suffering a partially torn left ACL.

As for the kids, well Jason Doig got two games of "don't dare make a mistake" and naturally failed. Dale Purinton hasn't played a second. Mike Mottau, Tomas Kloucek and others have spent the entire season in Hartford. Instead, the Rangers have tried to plug holes with career minor-leaguers David Wilkie and Drew Bannister.

With the exception of the Brian Leetch-Sylvain Lefebvre pair, the Rangers defense has been in flux, and ineffective. Leetch, with 10 points in his last six games, is playing ridiculous loads of ice time. In five of the seven games, he has played more than 30 of the 60 minutes, including 32:25 Tuesday.

"I don't think we can keep playing Brian that much or he's going to be dead by Christmas," Low said.

In an attempt to fix part of the problem, the Rangers today called up Mottau, the club's top prospect and a puck-moving, play-making defenseman, who should make his NHL debut tomorrow in a rematch at Philadelphia. Bannister was assigned to Hartford.

NEDVED WON'T USE IT as an excuse for his giveaway, but twice in Tuesday's game he went to the boards and was blasted by Dan McGillis. The first time, the Rangers bench didn't see it, according to Low. But Brown, the rugged defenseman, saw it and didn't do a thing about it.

Brown is now unsure of what he can and can't do on the ice. He intervened when big Luke Richardson was getting tough with little Mike York, and got a penalty and an additional misconduct for complaining. Brown also put a perfectly legal hit on Tampa Bay's Martin St. Louis Sunday, and was called for a boarding penalty by veteran referee Bill McCreary. That call prompted the league to put out the word to officials to be more careful. The league fears that hitting will disappear if clean hits start getting penalized.

THURSDAY, OCTOBER 26, 2000
PHILADELPHIA

In hockey tradition, the coach sits in the front seat on the team bus. In this case, the Rangers didn't take a bus to Philadelphia, they took a train.

Still, from the hotel to the arena, they were back aboard a bus, and therefore Ron Low was in the front seat. And because of that configuration, the coach is always first off the bus, first into the arena, first to the locker room. As such, Low led the parade around the corridors in the First Union Center this afternoon.

He was spotted by a reporter who had this simple, innocuous greeting: "How ya doin'?"

"Don't ask me how I'm doin'," Low snapped good naturedly. "Ask those fuckin' guys behind me how they're doin'."

YOU KNOW THINGS ARE BAD when you go out and lose, even get shut out, and it's an improvement.

The Rangers lost for the fifth time in their last six games, 3-0 by struggling goalie Brian Boucher and the Philadelphia Flyers. And, yes, it was better.

Better than any of their four previous losses in terms of sloppiness, readiness and effort.

But that's a sad state of affairs for the Rangers.

The Rangers face Pittsburgh tomorrow at the Garden, then play Mike Keenan and the Boston Bruins Sunday, and Low may take some interesting steps to shake up his sleeping offense.

He may break up the Czechmates—Petr Nedved, Radek Dvorak, and Jan Hlavac—who were briefly separated tonight, and who haven't been apart since Dvorak arrived last New Year's Eve.

"That's Ronnie's decision," Nedved said. "Obviously we're not scoring goals. We are generating some chances, but the puck's not going in. Sometimes a coach is going to make those changes. It's just the way it is. The bottom line is we're not scoring goals."

Hlavac has three, Dvorak two and Nedved one. In fairness, their ice time has been reduced, especially their power-play time, by Mark Messier's arrival. But they aren't creating much at even-strength, either. Nobody is. The Rangers have 12 goals in 5-on-5 situations in eight games.

Low saw his team play better, create more, but fail to get to rebounds, fail to get to the net, fail to score against a goalie whose confidence was shot and whose 4.52 goals-against average ranked 37th among regular NHL goalies.

So Low moved people around, and the Czechmates infuriated him most because rather than use their speed wide on the slow-footed Flyers defense, they played a fancy, drop-passing, cut to the middle game that resulted in zero offense.

"I thought Dvorak was going outside a lot, and it seemed like (Hlavac and Nedved) were drop-passing the blue line, so I wanted to switch that up," Low said.

"We're cutting to the middle too much. We've got guys that can fly down the wing like those guys can, and we keep cutting to the middle, it seems like we're just letting guys catch up to us from behind, and that's not what we want to do."

Now there will probably be more changes, and Low has tried a number of things already.

"Nothing is written in stone," Messier said. "Nothing says anybody has to play anywhere. So what you try to do is find a way to manufacture some goals."

"We've got to snap ourselves out of this thing," Low said. "It's not going to get any easier with Pittsburgh. We've got to keep grinding and see if we can find a way out."

MIKE RICHTER MADE HIS second start of the season and was saddled with his second loss. He had no chance on Michal Sykora's first NHL goal in the first, although Richter looked awkward trying to get across the crease. He had no chance on Rick Tocchet's dunk in the third. The last goal was an empty-netter.

Low wouldn't completely rule out the possibility of Richter playing again tomorrow although the original plan, and suggestion of team doctors, was that he not play on back-to-back nights in the early going. Richter noted that November is a very busy month, and he doesn't think it would be a good idea to push himself to play tomorrow.

MESSIER HAS BEEN PLAYING with a horrid stomach flu that has been going through the team. It's been an unpleasant thing, to say the least.

Before the game, Messier was asked of he was feeling any better.

"Better?" he asked. "That's where I'm going right now." As he said it, he was running toward the bathroom.

THE RANGERS MADE THEIR TREK to Philly via Amtrak. They chartered three cars of first-class accommodations, and enjoyed the ride down. Normally, it's a bus trip. But the Rangers were escorted by cops through both train stations, onto and off of each train. They had catered food, and televisions on the train.

On the way home they were able to watch the Yankees' World Series clincher. But they were going into the tunnel under the Hudson River just as Luis Sojo's winning single bounced up the middle. The train pulled into Penn Station, directly beneath Madison Square Garden, in time for some members of the staff to run up to their offices to see the end of the game.

Low was one of the few people rooting for the Yankees who wanted them to lose Game 5. He had tickets and a night off for Game 6.

NEW YORK

This was like Billy Martin pulling a lineup out of the hat. Except it worked for Billy Martin.

Ron Low, because of a series of circumstances, wound up with the No. 4 or No. 5 goalie on the organizational depth chart starting in a 4-1 loss to the Pittsburgh Penguins tonight at the Garden.

Low also shook up his lineup so dramatically that every defenseman had a new partner, and every line was different. Among the oddities were Adam Graves, virtually wasting on the bench as the fourth-line center until the third period, and Tim Taylor moving from center to wing on a line with Mike York and Michal Grosek as a makeshift checking unit assigned to handle Jaromir Jagr.

Well, they couldn't. Neither could goalie Johan Holmqvist, 22, a top prospect who did himself proud in his first NHL appearance, as the Rangers went down for the sixth time in the last seven games.

Low's button-pushing had some positive effects. It certainly got Graves stoked, and the Rangers played one of their more fiery games . . . after it got to 3-0 and too late.

But there may have been a defining moment when the Rangers' captain decided enough was enough, and it was time the Rangers stopped taking and did some giving.

Messier had a couple of run-ins with an old nemesis, aggravating ex-Islanders defenseman Darius Kasparaitis. Messier, celebrating his 1,488th game (sixth all-time, one ahead of Wayne Gretzky), dropped his gloves and punched out Kasparaitis in a rough second period. Messier also scored a goal in the third, and Rich Pilon had a couple of smackdowns with Jaromir Jagr. The Penguins, annoyed with all of this, got some revenge at the end of the game. Tough defenseman Bob Boughner in obvious retaliation for the Pilon-Jagr incidents, jumped the unsuspecting Petr Nedved, who had his nose broken at the final buzzer.

Late in the game, Low benched Theo Fleury, who, despite his terrific play in the early part of the season, continues to take dumb penalties, and a lot of them. Low said he will sit Fleury more often if the penalties continue, or that he will demote him and cut down his ice time.

A SITUATION THE RANGERS have known about for weeks, maybe months, still managed to sneak up on them in the last two days. With the knowledge that Mike Richter's reconstructed left knee would not allow him to play on back-to-back nights for about a month, the Rangers were not prepared for the first back-to-backs on the schedule.

When Kirk McLean came down with back spasms (which he had in training camp, as well) on Thursday, the Rangers had to recall not one, but two minor-league goalies for their game against Pittsburgh.

Before the game, Low admitted that Richter was so stiff after his first start Sunday—not just his knee, but his entire body, after playing for the first time since March—that he would have been unable to play if Low had pulled McLean when it got to 3-0 against Philadelphia. So Richter should not have even been on the bench for that game. And, with the Rangers playing the first of seven back-to-back situations in the next eight weeks, they will probably have to recall at least one goalie every time the schedule brings games on consecutive nights.

Low said the plan was to bring up Holmqvist tonight, anyway, to back up McLean, and that the plan now is to not have Richter on the bench on a night he isn't supposed to play.

This begs the question, though, why wasn't Holmqvist, J.F. Labbe or Jason LaBarbera on the bench instead of Richter Tuesday? And why wasn't LaBarbera, Low's first choice, called up today?

Low said LaBarbera, who has been transferred to Charlotte of the ECHL, wasn't recalled because he hadn't played this week. Actually, LaBarbera did play in Charlotte.

More important, if LaBarbera is their first choice, why don't the Rangers put him in Hartford and make sure he plays a lot between callups?

Low said he "will not play Richter in back-to-backs for a month."

As for McLean's back, Low said, "I'm sure we'll end up getting him looked at one way or the other, because it's something we have to be fully aware of in the situation we're in. It's not a comfortable situation, first of all, to have to bring a guy to back up somebody for games. I didn't want, to be honest with you, to take the chance of having a game go like the other night (Tuesday) and say, I need somebody to go in there right now, and I can't go to my backup.

"That's awful. Three goals in the first period, generally for me that's a cue where I'm going to start saying, "Well, it's about time.' And I couldn't play (Richter) so it's a situation I don't feel comfortable with."

MIKE MOTTAU, in his second NHL game, got roasted on a move by Jagr, who then beat Holmqvist (combined NHL experience: one game).

"You don't see that (move) in college," Mottau managed to smile.

RANGERS PROSPECT JAMIE LUNDMARK got his wish yesterday, when he was traded from Moose Jaw to Seattle in a WHL deal. All it means is that Lundmark will play for a better team while he's in juniors. This trade has nothing to do with his NHL rights, which the Rangers own.

Lundmark has no desire to leave the Rangers' organization.

MEANWHILE, an *Edmonton Sun* reporter with long-time ties with Glen Sather, was in town covering the World Series. He was invited up to Sather's office for the afternoon, and came out with a story.

"The mix isn't quite right," Sather said in the Edmonton paper the next day. "And some guys can't play. John MacLean has played two games. He's making $2.5 million and he can't get up and down the ice anymore. His giddy-up doesn't giddy-up anymore.

"That's the problem here. They have guys signed to long-term contracts not living up to expectations."

It didn't sound like a ringing endorsement of the team, and certainly not of MacLean.

SUNDAY, OCTOBER 29, 2000

NEW YORK

A victory of any kind would have been good enough. A really solid, aggressive team-tough victory, albeit over a struggling opponent and a pair of mediocre goalies, was even better.

And a near-shutout by Mike Richter made it a fairly fabulous evening.

Now, let's see the Rangers do it again. They beat Mike Keenan's Boston Bruins 5-1 at the Garden tonight to snap a four-game losing streak, their second win in the last eight games. Richter got his first win of this season, the first with his new left knee.

Afterwards, Low was asked if this win might have a catapult effect.

"I don't catapult on one game," Low said. "We've got a long ways to go before we jump on any catapult."

Messages have been sent in many different forms, from Sather's published rantings that the team is an unfixable mess, to Low's constant player shuffling.

Whether tonight was a result of any of those attempts at motivation, or whether it was just the law of averages catching up to the Rangers, we won't know until the next few games are played out.

But the Rangers looked like a different team against the tired Bruins, who played a tough OT loss to Toronto the night before. For the first time in five games, a span of 250 minutes and six seconds, the Rangers took a lead, and for the first time since the second game of the season, they upped it to 2-0.

Low's machinations included the demotion, as promised, of Theo Fleury to the fourth line, and the new defense pair of Brian Leetch and Rich Pilon, who has played his best, toughest hockey as a Ranger in recent games, and has now had six different partners in 10 games.

Low said he "liked the mix a lot" and felt it was the Rangers' best game, at 5-on-5, this season.

Low got a fiery game out of Fleury, who scored a short-handed goal, and another terrific outing from Leetch, one of the few bright spots this season, who had two assists on the first three goals.

And the Rangers got the most important ingredient—strong goaltending from Richter in his third start. Richter came within 3:15 of his first shutout in 82 games, when a Jason Allison shot/pass banked in off the Rangers' Sylvain Lefebvre.

Sather's comments included "It's going to be a process to try to fix it" and "so far it's gone pretty much the way I thought it would go. It won't be easy," in addition to remarks about too many players being too slow, too old and too expensive to move.

"I can't answer for everybody," said Richter, who heard of the story second-hand. "There's no question, whether you're mentioned by name or not. It's our organization and yeah, it does hurt, and you have to respond to those things, depending on who's saying it. Glen knows an awful lot about the game and he's our GM, so you should respond when it's coming from within your own organization. I thought the guys, for the most part, did a darn good job of that tonight."

"We're trying to challenge ourselves," Leetch said. "We don't need any outside criticism in the position we're in right now. It's not a fun spot to be in, coming to the rink and losing. We need wins, and this was something to stop the slide. But we need to climb a hill. We've got a long ways to go."

Fleury scored the Rangers' first short-handed goal of the season (they scored just 14 of them in the 246 games Messier spent in Vancouver) early in the second. Messier tacked on his fifth and sixth goals, the second on a signature wrong-foot, right-circle snap shot in the third.

SATHER HAS TOLD John MacLean and his agent Rick Curran to try to find a team willing to take him. The Rangers will be willing to pay part of his salary. Sather told them he can't find a taker.

PILON, PERHAPS IN THE best shape of his life and now with the opportunity of a lifetime playing with Leetch, has been mean, nasty (41 penalty minutes already) and solid on defense.

"I want to prove, not to myself but to everybody that I can still play the game," he said. "People were counting me out that I can't play this game anymore. You know, screw them all. I can still play."

He was washed up. Done. Thirty-two years old. Out of shape. Way too injury-prone.

That was last year. This year, the Rangers supposedly had a bunch of kids ready to replace Pilon, who was available to Minnesota and Columbus in the expansion draft and to every other NHL team in the waiver draft.

Now, Pilon, slimmed down by almost 20 pounds from last year's high with the prodding of Sather's threats to let him play in the minors, and playing again with that nasty edge that made him one of the Rangers' most hated opponents for 11 years as an Islander, is a key guy.

Pilon knows being Leetch's partner means "More ice time," he said, relishing the thought.

"Well, when your body's feeling good . . . my body, knock on wood, is feeling a lot better and that's making things a lot easier, to go out there and bang and finish your checks a lot harder. You get into a couple of fights here and there, trying to get the team going every now and then."

Last year, not only could he not have handled the minutes, but he played passively, because of his conditioning and a bad shoulder.

"You've got to pick your spots a lot better," Pilon said. "When your body's healthy, you don't have to pick your spots."

The Rangers' coaches felt Leetch's partner, Sylvain Lefebvre was uncomfortable switching to the right side, and/or that Lefebvre was having trouble handling the minutes.

Leetch plays half of every game, more than 30 minutes a night. A lot of that is on the power play, when Pilon will be resting up on the bench. So perhaps he can handle it.

"We'll see how many minutes he can take," Low said. "We're still in the experimental stage here and Vlad (Malakhov) is still at least a couple of weeks away. If Richie can, it's fantastic for us. He's been physical, and that's one thing he has been the whole year. He played against (Boston's) big guys and he did fine."

But Pilon isn't getting comfortable with his new assignment or his renewed status.

"Nothing's solidified," he said. "You come to the game and every day is a grind. I'm here to play and win. I'm not looking for another contract. I'm not looking for anything. I'm looking just to be here and win."

Pilon doesn't want anybody to expect him to pile up points now, however. Yet it was pointed out to him that he might get a few assists just by giving the puck to Leetch.

"I thought of that, too," Pilon said. "He's getting it all the time."

RYE, N.Y.

Valeri Kamensky has what the Rangers suspect is a bruised kidney after taking a cross-check in Sunday's win over Boston. Kamensky is listed as day-to-day and his status will be reexamined today. He's peeing blood, which can't be much fun.

Malakhov has resumed skating on his own, but still has pain in his left knee when he goes side to side. He remains hopeful that he can play in a couple of weeks, but he clearly won't be ready in the four weeks (next weekend) originally forecast.

The Rangers defense is taking a beating. Kim Johnsson was hit on the right hand by a Paul Coffey shot, then sprained his left wrist along the boards. Brad Brown, who looked "wobbly," according to Low, after being run into the glass by Boston's Ken Belanger, lost his footing later on, and lost a fight to Belanger later still, insisted he did not suffer a concussion. But he sure looked like he had a concussion.

RYE, N.Y.

Low started practice normally, but he didn't like what he was seeing. So he split up the teams for a scrimmage, and he wanted to see some spirit.

"You're going to fuckin' skate this way, or fuckin' skate the other way," he hollered at the players, the other way being skating them till they drop. Low admitted it was an "awful practice," and said he had to sit down because it was so draining to watch.

LOW WAS A TEAMMATE of John MacLean with the Devils once upon a time. Now Low can at least sympathize with MacLean's limbo. They spoke today.

"He was very much a professional guy," Low said. "I guess this is more about coaching, and there are points in time when the hardest part may be players and how you handle them, and basically, I'm going to be truthful with Johnny and likewise, him with me. There comes a point where Johnny MacLean and myself were really good friends, and what's happening right now isn't going to have any bearing whether we depart here and leave here friends or not. I just consider the guy to be a great pro, and he has been a fantastic pro, and I still think he can play somewhere else. Our conversation went deeper than that, but that's all we need to talk about."

A reporter asked Low if he thought Sather made a mistake by going public with his criticism of MacLean.

"I'm not going to go there," Low said, smiling. "You guys can start all the fuckin' shit you want, but I'm not going there. 'Did Glen make a big mistake?' Oh yeah. I'll get on the fuckin' trampoline and jump up in the air. This happened last year, fellas, and I'm not going there."

WHILE HE WAS AT IT, Low said he wasn't at all surprised at the strong start by Messier.

"I told you guys, at the end of last year I thought he was one of the top five, six centermen in the league in Vancouver. He was unbelievable down the stretch drive and if he stays healthy he'll be fine. Mark Messier doesn't play like a guy who's 39 years old. He skates better than most 25-year olds for God sakes. He can still get down the ice, which is what this game's about. And with the head he's got, he's smarter than most. He can play the game."

THE RANGERS HELD THEIR annual team Halloween party tonight. This one didn't produce the classics of some of the parties of the past. The best all-time costume was once donned by Scott Fraser, an overpaid, unproductive winger the Rangers signed from Edmonton.

Fraser dressed up in a burglar's outfit. Who was he supposed to be?

"My agent," Fraser said.

That's The Kind Of Game We Would Have Lost Last Year

NEW YORK

If there was one thing the Rangers absolutely needed to change from last year, it was No. 14. There was no way they were going to make the step up to playoff contender if Theo Fleury didn't vastly improve his offensive output from his career-worst 15 goals last season.

Of course, it would be almost impossible to imagine Fleury not surpassing that wicked number this season. The Rangers still have a ton of work to do to get back to the playoffs, but Fleury is holding up his end of the bargain.

The diminutive, annoying winger scored his seventh, eighth and ninth goals of the season, plus an assist tonight in a 6-1 victory over the Tampa Bay Lightning at the Garden. The Rangers closed to within a game of .500 heading into their most stern test of the season tomorrow at East-leading Ottawa.

The Rangers also got three goals from players who hadn't scored this season—Eric Lacroix and Fleury's two linemates, Tim Taylor and Sandy McCarthy.

Fleury needed 34 games to get his ninth goal last season, on December 26. Not only is he scoring again, but he is playing with the edge that made him a perennial all-star in Calgary. He is making the Rangers' fourth line go, but he has been a powder keg on special teams. Tonight he scored twice on the power play (he has four PPGs, three more than last year) and his second short-handed goal in two games. His 15th career hat trick gives him 398 goals for his career.

"I think Theo's working pretty hard right now," Low said. "He's been really feisty, which I likely didn't see that much of in the films (of) last year. He's had some huge hits. I mean, he's playing a lot like the Theo Fleury I saw for all those years out on the other side. He's a great hockey player, I'm telling you. What you saw last year was an abberation. He's a really sound hockey player."

Fleury hit some bad luck last year, no doubt. He hit a pile of goalposts early in the season, and continued to hit them as his luck refused to change and his confidence waned. His sticks were broken regularly in anger and frustration. And he wasn't in shape. And he wasn't working this hard.

"The best thing I like now is, like, the second goal was a perfect example," Fleury said.

"The puck came across. It was rolling. I took my time, let it settle down, looked up, saw the five-hole and put it right there. Maybe last year, when I started struggle, I started to squeeze the stick, I probably would have buried it right in his chest."

Then he would have broken the stick. Now he's using a one-piece Kevlar stick, virtually unbreakable. He insisted, though, that he never lost confidence.

"No, to be honest with you, when you're sitting there on the bike in the summertime, you're thinking about all the things that happened the year before, and you have to just chalk it up to bad luck or whatever. Obviously, I wanted to come back this year to prove, once again, that I can still play, that I can still do the things I've always done.

"When you play for a long time, you're going to have years where things aren't necessarily going to go the way you wanted them to go, and it's how you rebound after those kinds of things that really makes a difference."

Mike Richter made a difference, too. He was terrific in keeping it 0-0 until the second, when the Rangers scored four, including two in 24 seconds by Fleury (a long slapper, with Adam Graves crashing goalie Kevin Weekes's crease) and by Taylor (on a rebound, Mike Mottau's first NHL point).

After Ryan Johnson cut it to 2-1, Mark Messier and Mike York worked the wall and Messier made a fancy pass to Brian Leetch, who made an even better pass to Fleury on the other side of the ice. That was the one Fleury settled down before firing through Weekes's pads. McCarthy and Lacroix each added great individual-effort goals, and Fleury finished off York's short-handed 2-on-1 break, which was also started by Leetch.

Fleury, who had been relegated to the third line as punishment for his silly penalties, is still getting plenty of ice time because he and York are the No. 1 penalty killing twosome, and because he and Leetch are the No. 1 power-play point tandem.

Low said he had some concern bit when he demoted Fleury on the basis of repeated offensive-zone penalties, concern that he didn't want Fleury playing without that nasty edge.

"Yeah, there was, because it depended on how he took it," Low said. "We had a talk that next morning, and it was a really good talk. It was based on the thought process that he can't take those kind of penalties because every time he did, we ended up getting scored on, with him in the penalty box. That was, in essence, the message, that he was my first-unit penalty killer and we can't afford to have him in the box."

Nor could they afford to have him not scoring.

AFTER THE GAME, John MacLean, who isn't playing, nevertheless joined the team on the trip to Ottawa. But his Rangers days are just about over.

The 35-year-old right winger is in the process of negotiating a buyout of his contract, and it hasn't been, or won't be, a pleasant negotiation.

Glen Sather, who negotiates everything, won't simply buy out MacLean for the standard two-thirds of the $2.5 million he is to make this season. Instead, Sather has told MacLean's agent, Rick Curran, to come up with an acceptable number or MacLean will have to earn his money playing in the minor leagues. And, Sather said, it won't necessarily be their top farm club, either. Which means MacLean is being threatened with the prospect of playing in some hockey outpost if he doesn't negotiate his buyout to a nice, low number.

"He offered me one today that was unacceptable," Sather said.

"What I told him was that 'I don't want to do anything that's going to be embarrassing, but I told you there's a sense of urgency about this almost six weeks ago,' and it just sort of went along being ignored. So I want to get it resolved."

Sather insisted he was trying to treat MacLean with "as much respect as possible" but that "with this team he just doesn't fit right now, so we want to come to some conclusion."

As for whether MacLean could be sent to the Rangers' AHL affilliate in Hartford, Sather said, "If he can't play here, he's going to have to play someplace. And I'm not saying it's going to be Hartford, either, because we're doing the same thing down there. I want to develop kids.

"And besides, I made a promise to all these guys in training camp, that it doesn't matter what your contract is. If you can't play on this team, it doesn't matter what you make. Maybe that's why Theo (Fleury) has got nine goals."

KANATA, ONTARIO

The best team in the East (at the moment) is such because of its ability to play any way, any night and win. The Ottawa Senators can even play badly and find a way, and that is why they have lost just once in 12 games.

The Senators came from behind to beat the Rangers in a game that turned wild late, 6-5 at Corel Centre tonight. It was a game that, for a while, was going to be the Rangers' best of the season, and instead turned into a painful loss, snapping a two-game winning streak.

"I thought we deserved a better fate," Low said. "It was an unbelievable battle by our hockey club. We worked hard from the beginning to the end of the game. By the end we were down to four defensemen, and they still battled."

For a second game in two nights, against the best team, by far, that they've faced this season, the Rangers sure had some hop. Some of that may have to do with the way Low has deployed all four lines lately, saving some legs for the next period and the next game every night.

The Rangers dictated the first period, were at least as good as Ottawa in the second, and throughout the night they finished more checks than they would have finished in a month last season. They matched Ottawa's speed, forced turnovers, and created plenty of opportunities against the stingy Ottawa defensive system.

And on all those fronts, the Rangers made progress. They weren't just singing songs when they talked about the positives that came out of this game.

"It could have gone either way," said Adam Graves. "It was pretty even the whole night, and they have a heckuva hockey team, so you have to play fairly well to play them even. Even though it wasn't good enough, and it isn't acceptable, we have to build off everything, wins and losses. If we play hard like that game in and game out, we're going to win a lot of games."

As Mark Messier added, "You're never happy when you lose, but I think we're making steps as we go along."

This is a far cry from the first nine games of the season. If the Rangers had played nearly as well as they did last night, their record would be shining instead of the dull 5-7 it is.

The game got away from the Rangers when rookie goalie Johan Holmqvist, playing in place of less-than-100 percent Kirk McLean (upper back spasms), made a big mistake in the third. The Rangers had just taken a 4-3 lead on a high-speed Radek Dvorak-to-Jan Hlavac 2-on-1 goal. Play was headed the other way when Holmqvist punched Rob Zamuner, who was in his crease.

Ten seconds into the power play, Sami Salo's shot not only took out Rich Pilon (bruised right ankle), but it caromed right to Marian Hossa, who buried it.

"That's a bad penalty," Holmqvist said. "It's easy to say now."

Holmqvist, who was remarkable at times, especially against the dominant Alexei Yashin, then gave up a pair in 33 seconds.

There is a bad pattern setting in here, though. The Rangers are just 3-3 when scoring four goals or more. They were 21-1-1 when scoring four or more last year. Offense doesn't look like it will be a problem with this team. Defense might be a different story.

"You get five in this building, you should walk out with a point, at least," Low said. "It was tough to lose that point.

"To be really honest with you, this might have been the best we've played as far as everything was involved. We had a lot of body checks, really good ones and thrown by everybody. This is a tough opponent, a really tough opponent, and I thought we responded exceptionally well."

Compared to where the Rangers were a week ago—passive losers of four straight and six of seven—this was as good as a loss could be.

"In the long run, this will turn into points," Graves said.

FLEURY, WHO SCORED his 10th goal of the season (and 399th of his career) is getting tired of the constant comparisons to last season, and how long it took him to get to each goal. He's tired of being told, and of reading that he "didn't score his 11th goal last season until January 19" or "his 12th goal until January 27."

"When did I get my 10th last year?" he asked sarcastically. "When I get to 16, can we please stop?"

Fleury's hot streak isn't only benefiting him. Linemate Sandy McCarthy, known for his fists more than his hands, is on a career-high three-game point streak.

KANATA SITS OUT in the middle of nowhere, in the suburbs of beautiful Ottawa, the capital of Canada. It's too early in the season to appreciate

Ottawa, a city built around the winding Rideau Canal. In the dead of winter, when the canal freezes, everybody skates on it. Businessmen and women can be seen skating to work, briefcases in hand. Downtown is dotted with ancient government buildings that look like castles and fortresses. But the Corel Centre is out in God's Country. There is one road to the arena and in the evening, everybody is going that way. They are also driving directly into the sun, which snarls traffic terribly.

AFTER THE GAME, Mark Messier commandeered the team bus, dropped off the staff at the elegant Chateau Laurier hotel and took the team to dinner.

"That's what a leader does and that's how he unites them," Sather said in *Newsday*. "That's what's happening right now. They're becoming a team."

THE RANGERS HAVE A rare day off in Montreal tomorrow. Usually, Montreal is not part of a trip. Most times the Rangers fly in there Friday afternoon, play Saturday night, and fly right home. But this time they are Montreal-bound right after the game, and they won't even have to practice tomorrow.

"We don't have enough fuckin' (healthy) players to practice," Low snarled.

FRIDAY, NOVEMBER 3, 2000

MONTREAL

John MacLean has, in his own words, "a strong, supportive family."

He needs it these days, probably the worst days of his 18-year NHL career.

Sather has publicly torn into MacLean, painting him as an old, tired, slow guy who can't keep up anymore, all the while insisting that he is "respectful" of MacLean. Sather has also, publicly, threatened to send MacLean to some minor-league outpost like Charlotte of the ECHL or Manitoba of the IHL unless MacLean and his agent, Rick Curran, can come up with an acceptable (read: cheap) buyout.

MacLean and Sather met tonight, but there was no resolution to his situation.

MacLean clarified that, had the Rangers wanted to buy him out early in the summer, they could have done so for two-thirds of his salary. Once July 1 arrived, though, any buyout has to be bargained, and the player can refuse anything less than 100 percent of his salary, in this case $2.5 million.

"It's within the framework of whatever can be done," MacLean said. "Can they buy me out?

"Yes they can. Do I have to agree to a buyout? Yes. But I mean, still, my job is to play. Yeah, they could buy me out. I have to agree to what the terms are, too."

So MacLean, while standing his ground apparently on the money issue, doesn't know what will happen or how or when.

He said it's no fun. He said he will continue to work hard and practice with the team and be ready if he is ever called upon to play.

Being around the team during this fiasco, he said, isn't difficult.

"No, why would it be hard?" he asked. "You practice. It's not hard to be around. The guys are all good guys here. They understand. They know the situation, and I have nothing to say, or hide from, or apologize for.

"My job is to play. I don't know what's going to happen. I have done everything that's asked of me. I don't know what else to do. I don't know how to handle anything else. I'm a professional hockey player. That's what I do. I play. If they need me to play hockey, I'll be in the lineup."

That isn't likely to happen. What's next?

"I don't know," MacLean said.

THE OLD MONTREAL FORUM ghosts still live at the Molson Centre for the Rangers. Consider: The Rangers were 1-10-4 in their 15 regular-season visits before Mark Messier became a Ranger the first time, at a Forum press conference, October 4, 1991. Messier's first game as a Ranger was the next night, a 2-1 OT win at the Forum. The Rangers are 1-12-5 in Montreal since that night, for a not-so-grand total of 3-22-9 in 34 regular-season visits since 1983–84. There is an unbelievable caveat, however. The Rangers inexplicably went 3-0 at Molson Centre in their 1996 playoff series, which they captured with four straight wins after dropping the first two games at home.

TONIGHT WAS ONE of those rare nights when the visiting team is in town, but the home team isn't. The Rangers arrived in Montreal this afternoon; the Canadiens were in Buffalo tonight.

SATURDAY, NOVEMBER 4, 2000

MONTREAL

The Rangers are now doing what they are supposed to do.

They are establishing themselves as a cut above the bottom teams in the league, and piling up important points at the same time.

They won for the third time in four games with a 5-2 victory over the Canadiens at Molson Centre.

The Rangers have finally figured it out, that by simply beating the abundant bad teams in the NHL, you can make a pretty good living. And the Rangers have beaten and beaten up some of those bad teams lately—with romps over Boston, Tampa Bay and Montreal. Plus they played probably their best game of the year in a 6-5 loss in Ottawa Thursday.

"I think we're playing an awful lot better hockey," Low said. "First of all, there are a balanced four lines, which is what I really like to play with. And the energy level's been a lot higher because of it. But I also think a lot of guys have committed themselves to not being mercenaries, but to being New York Rangers. That, to me, is the key.

"The whole key is they have to believe it in the room, and they've got to believe in themselves, and I think that belief is slowly creeping in. It's baby steps, and we're not going anywhere too fast, but they're starting to believe in themselves."

In order to beat those lesser teams, or anybody, the Rangers had to get their own house in order, and they have done that. Low, remarkably, found that the best solution to spreading out the scoring is to put Theo Fleury on the fourth line, and Fleury has taken off. After scoring his 11th of the season, his sixth in four games and the 400th of his career, Fleury is on pace for 70 goals . . . as a third-liner.

"If this was last year," Fleury said, "I think around 2010 I was expected to get my 400th goal."

Fleury's first-period milestone goal, created by Sandy McCarthy, touched off the Rangers' first three-goal third period of the season, with Adam Graves and Mike York getting into the act.

Mark Messier added a power-play goal in the second. Perhaps the best news for the Rangers is that Petr Nedved is getting off his skid, with his second goal in two games—a rocket that flew under the crossbar so fast it had to be video-reviewed.

Low reiterated and admitted it was almost an accident that Fleury is on that line simply because he was taking bad penalties, and Low demoted him as punishment.

"That stroke of genius," Low laughed, "would not have taken place. It's worked out great, I think we've gotten the absolute utmost out of Sandy and Timmy (Taylor) because they've got a guy on that line that's just snapping the puck around. The other three lines are playing really solid. It's just dumb luck, and I'll settle for it."

It is also not coincidence that this little streak of strong play immediately followed Messier's punch-out of Darius Kasparaitis of Pittsburgh. Since then, they have adopted a chip-on-the-shoulder attitude they also haven't had in years.

"Our confidence is definitely growing, and that's a big part of any team," Messier said.

Tonight, Dale Purinton provided most of the fireworks in his first game of the year and second NHL game of his career. He fought big Enrico Ciccone twice, the second time because Ciccone bumped Brian Leetch. That reaction hadn't happened nearly enough the last three years.

"That was a no-brainer," Low said appreciatively. "You knew it was coming, and that was a great play by Dale."

The Rangers' aggressiveness also caused turnovers.

"That's the style of game we want to play," Fleury said. "We want to cause mistakes and capitalize on them."

The Rangers don't want to get too excited about this little run of success.

"I do think we should have the highest expectations you should have," Richter said. "But at the same time you have to be realistic about the needs that have to be addressed and where we have some deficits and what we have to improve upon. We are not going to walk in and overwhelm any team unless we're working as hard as we can. Every night's going to be a dogfight. We're a team that has to continue to build and develop our confidence and our identity.

"But we have a long, long way to go."

RICHTER'S SHUTOUT BID ended with Trevor Linden's goal in the third. Richter hasn't had a shutout since Feb. 26, 1999, a stretch of 85 starts; and the Rangers have gone 118 games without a shutout.

NEDVED SCORED AGAIN, and showed that, when he's on, his wrist shot is as dangerous as any in the NHL.

"What a shot that was," Low said. "There wasn't much room there, but that was a vintage Petr Nedved shot. Under the bar, short side, almost unstoppable."

MONDAY, NOVEMBER 6, 2000

RYE, N.Y.

Okay, here is tomorrow's Rangers-Edmonton Oilers reunion in a nutshell:

All the former Oilers are here. All the former Rangers are there. The former president/GM/coach of the Oilers is the president/GM of the Rangers. A former Oilers and Rangers Stanley Cup champ, who was the Oilers' head coach last year, is now the Oilers' GM. The coach he had replaced as

Oilers' coach is now the Rangers coach, and the guy who replaced him as Oilers coach is another former Oilers and Rangers Stanley Cup champ who was previously an assistant coach for the Rangers and the Oilers. The Oilers' two assistant coaches were both Rangers' assistant coaches before that, although one of them played for the Oilers and never for the Rangers. One of the Rangers' new assistant coaches was the Oilers' assistant coach, but also once was the Oilers' head coach, replacing John Muckler, who also coached both teams. The other Rangers assistant coach was coaching Edmonton's top far club last year. And the current Rangers head coach, when he was the Oilers coach, was fired by, or quit under the pressure of the Rangers president/GM, who was then the Oilers president/GM.

Exhale. And that's not to mention players like Mark Messier and Adam Graves, who have achieved glory and fame in both places.

The names and new positions, to simplify, are: Glen Sather (Rangers president/GM), Ron Low (Rangers coach), Ted Green and Walt Kyle (Rangers assistant coaches), Kevin Lowe (Oilers GM), Craig MacTavish (Oilers coach), Charlie Huddy and Bill Moores (Edmonton assistants).

Tomorrow, they get together at the Garden.

The person who will surely be most affected, emotionally, is Sather, who built and ran the team that won five Stanley Cups in seven years and featured some of the greatest names in the history of the sport, most of whom have since passed through New York.

Sather, however, was unwilling to comment on his feelings today.

The other Rangers participants downplayed it.

Low talked about how there's no rivalry, since the teams played once last year, and will just once this year. He admitted that it might have been more poignant for himself and Sather, etc., to play in Edmonton this year, one city the Rangers won't visit.

He said he "kicked" himself a bit after quitting as Oilers coach in the summer of 1999, after Sather made an insulting contract offer.

"Yeah, you question yourself, but don't do it for long," he said. "You might find out you're an idiot."

"I think, yeah, once you've said what you had to say, you end up thinking you shouldn't have done it, you shouldn't have left at that point in time. But the year in Houston (IHL) was great and if I had to stay there three years it wouldn't have mattered to me. It was a situation that came up and I felt like that was the right thing for me to do at the time. After it was done, you likely kicked your butt around at mid-summer, but after that, after the year that was taking place in Houston, I was pretty happy with the decision no matter what happened.

"It was also good to get interviewed by more than one person for jobs this year.

"It's the same wherever you are. The pressure to win is no different here than it is in Edmonton. Your pressure as a coach is to win. It doesn't matter what your payroll is. It doesn't matter what anything else is, you're pressured to win. And that pressure comes from yourself, not (the media). It comes from me. You guys can say whatever you want, and that's fine. The only pressure that's ever been there is from the people that run the thing up top, and yourself. The rest of it's irrelevant. There's just more of it here than in Edmonton, but it doesn't change anything at all."

Low was asked if he's looking forward to seeing his old pals from the Edmonton media.

"Yeah, except for one fat prick," Low said. He was talking about the one writer be believes tried to get him fired.

Low, in fact, was more talkative about a story in an Edmonton paper over the weekend, one that concluded the Oilers were on a fairly easy road trip—Columbus, New York, Philadelphia, Pittsburgh and Minnesota. "Hardly Murderers' Row" the story said.

But the most inflammatory comment made by Edmonton players was that the schedule was "favorable."

"They're sitting, in the papers there, saying this is going to be the easiest road trip they've had for a long time . . . and they should come back with at least four wins out of five games," Low said. "Easily-beaten Rangers or something.

"I don't know if somebody gave them that line or not. It's likely going to be on our wall as one of their guys saying it."

Nobody would say that there's any additional fuel for tonight's game.

"No, I've made the crossover," Green said. "My heart and soul are in New York. You know, there was a lot of history and lot of success in Edmonton. A lot of that was very enjoyable years.

"There's a new challenge now, and that challenge is here."

THE PRACTICE AROUND the NHL is that, for every game, anybody who has ties as a former player or former coach with the opponent puts a dollar figure on the chalkboard. Whatever money is up there goes to anybody who scores the game-winning goal that night.

So there will be plenty of people putting money up on both sides tomorrow.

"If I start doing that, it would be about 18 teams in the league that I played for or coached, and that would get expensive," Low said. "But there might be a couple hundred on the wall."

Speaking of which, Sather took a bunch of his old cronies out to dinner in Manhattan tonight. They ran up a bill of $660, then stiffed the waiter on the tip, leaving $80 (about 12 percent).

Two-time Norris Trophy winner Brian Leetch mixes it up with former Ranger mate Alexi Kovalev of the Pittsburgh Penguins.

BRIAN LEETCH IS ONE of the all-time Rangers simply because of his two Norris Trophies, his Stanley Cup, and the Conn Smythe Trophy he won as the first Amercan player named playoff MVP in 1994.

Now, though, Leetch is starting to get to the top of the ladder on the all-time franchise lists.

Leetch goes into tomorrow's game against Edmonton three assists short of Hall of Famer Rod Gilbert's franchise record of 615 assists. And the way Leetch is piling up points (he leads the NHL with 15 assists), that record could be his any day now.

Leetch, one of those rare great players who have spent their entire career with one team, just thinks it's funny when he sees the lists he's climbing. His 870 games played are fifth among all-time Rangers; and he's only 19 points shy of Jean Ratelle's total of 817 points, second to Gilbert's team record of 1,021.

"It's fun to see when they have it set up there, that your name keeps moving up," Leetch said.

"It's kind of funny to me. I always get a kick out of it, because I've always been here and you always assume that the players who were here before you have done so much. You know, you come and try to make your little mark but it's funny to be up there in the top five in a lot of different categories and know you've played as long as these guys you've heard about, and gotten as many points as these players.

"I mean, Rod's number (7) is retired. He's around the rink all the time. It does make me laugh.

"I never look at myself as being in that position."

NEW YORK

Ron Low did what the 18,200 wanted to do after the Rangers' breath-taking 4-3 victory over the Oilers at the Garden.

The Rangers coach went through the locker room and shook hands with every player on his team after a game that was on-the-edge hockey, played the way it should be played.

The fans left the building with a collective "Wow" following this up-and-down, physical, fast-paced game that never once reminded anybody about the neutral-zone trap or any of the other game-slowing, fan-numbing defenses so many coaches deploy today. This could have been cut into clips to be used as TV advertisements for hockey.

"I wish we could play every game like that," said Petr Nedved, whose razzle-dazzle, behind-the-back pass to Radek Dvorak turned into the game-winning goal with 5:15 to play. "It was a fun game for us to play and fun for the fans. Unfortunately, that's not the way hockey's played the last couple of years. That's too bad."

The Rangers served some notice, too. Not just that they've won four of their last five and reached the .500 mark at 7-7, or that they beat a team on a four-game winning streak. The Rangers did some talking with their feet, to all those who simply look at the number of over-30s on their team and more simply, make the assumption that these Rangers are slow.

"I know what I felt," Low said. "We were fine. We were fine in Ottawa the other night, with a team that can fly. I also think we matched up physically with them, with a lot of hits in this hockey game, which is what we've been looking for in this building."

Low deserves full marks for unleashing the speed the Rangers have, for giving Brian Leetch what he called "the green light" to go up ice all the time (John Muckler had the caution flag out for Leetch last season), for coming up with and finding crucial ice time for four lines.

Leetch was spectacular, playing a season-high 35:22 and joining the play to score two goals from the back side, which gave him 800 NHL points. And while Nedved's Czechmates line provided the plays that led to three goals, the best line Low had was that of Mike York, Michal Grosek and Eric Lacroix.

Of course, the Rangers had to spot the Oilers two in a span of 49 seconds, goals by Bill Guerin and Eric Brewer that made it 2-0 before the game was two minutes old. That has become so common, Low said, that the Rangers barely flinched. In fact, he said, their resolve was very good.

Mike Richter, first and foremost, gave the Rangers a chance by keeping it right there. Then Sandy McCarthy took on huge Georges Laraque in a fight that got the crowd going.

"That's not an easy opponent," Low said. "If you want to set a tone for the hockey club, taking on Georges Laraque is doing it for the team and not because you like doing it."

Lacroix drew a penalty and Leetch scored a power-play goal that cut it to 2-1. Thirteen seconds after a Lacroix goal was disallowed because he kicked it in, York tied it in the second. Jan Hlavac started a power-play sequence that led to Leetch's power-play goal for the lead in the third.

But Todd Marchant beat Messier to a loose puck on a faceoff, then went around Theo Fleury at the point and gave the puck to Mike Grier for a short-hander to tie at 3-3. The Rangers' power play got it back, though, on the back end of a 5-on-3. Hlavac outmuscled Janne Niinimaa behind the net, and Nedved whipped the puck backward to Dvorak while being slashed on the back of the leg by Tom Poti. Dvorak slammed it past goalie Tommy Salo, and Low and the Rangers had their win against all their old friends from Edmonton.

"We outworked a hockey club that's pretty hard to outwork," Low said.

As impressive as it was, the Rangers' speed was what really opened eyes against the speedy Oilers.

"It starts in practice, a lot of high-speed practice," Leetch said. "Our system's very similar to Edmonton's and forces us to move our feet."

They're moving their feet now.

BEFORE THE GAME, McCarthy was egging on Low to get in there and put some money on the board. Low, the moment McCarthy left, acted as if he'd already put up his money and gave Ted Green a hard time about putting some up, too. Low also wondered, kiddingly, when Sather might make his way down and nail a nice big bill to the board.

WEDNESDAY, NOVEMBER 8, 2000

RYE, N.Y.

Offense doesn't always necessarily win, but in hockey, it sure is better to watch than defense.

The Rangers, who have been Strangers to offense for a long time, are suddenly finding the net often, and the result, at least in the short term, has been not only goals but wins.

The Rangers have scored 25 goals in their last five games, going 4-1, and only losing their best game of the year, 6-5 in Ottawa a week ago.

The reasons the goals are coming are many, not the least of which is the potent power play which ranks second in the NHL and has provided at least two goals in seven of the first 14 games.

But the power play doesn't work without the players, and the Rangers' offensive players are now playing their best hockey in years. Brian Leetch is the ring-leader, moving the puck from the defensive zone on out, then joining the play from behind. That's how he scored two goals in Tuesday's 4-3 win over Edmonton, and that's how he shares the league-lead with 15 assists.

Leetch has been freed from the shackles of previous coach John Muckler, who told Leetch to gamble less . . . then refused to admit having done so.

"He's an amazing guy," Low said. "I don't know how you do that when you're getting the kind of ice time he's getting, but he's been up ice a lot this year, and been getting the green light to go whenever he feels he can make it an out-manned rush."

With youngsters Dale Purinton and Mike Mottau in Tuesday's lineup against the speedy Oilers, Low was careful to limit their playing time. So he depended even more on Leetch, who played a season-high 35:22 at high speed.

The Rangers have also gotten plenty of offense from Mark Messier, who wasn't a Ranger last year, and from Theo Fleury, who had only 15 goals last year and already has 11 this season. Now they are starting to get it from Mike York, whose role and ice time have changed.

Most notably, they are getting offense from the Czechmates again.

Petr Nedved snapped out of a goal slump with two in his previous two games, then had a terrific night against Edmonton, setting up the game-winner. His hard times appear to be over.

"Definitely," Low said. "He's shooting the puck without thinking about it now. He's not aiming it. He's just letting it go, and that, to me, is what Petr Nedved's all about. If he hits corners with that shot, nobody stops him. I don't care what goaltender it is."

Radek Dvorak scored his first goal since the second game of the season on Tuesday, the winner, and Jan Hlavac, who still doesn't shoot enough, has been solid all along.

"I thought they really played well," Low said. "They drove the puck wide, with the exception of a couple of plays in the third period. And the one Leetch scored on, I was just about to scream at Hlavac for not taking it wide when they had the 3-on-2. Then they make an unbelievable play to

Brian. That's what we talked about at the beginning of the year. I guess we can't take, or we're not going to take creativity away from them. If that would have created a 2-on-1 the other way, I would have been pretty ticked off. We'll let it slide at this point in time because it was an unbelievable goal."

MIKE RICHTER, who starts tomorrow in Washington, has won four starts in a row, and has stopped 144 of the last 153 shots he has faced.

WASHINGTON, D.C.

Another game on the Eastern Corridor, so the Rangers took the Amtrak train again. This time, though, the trip took longer than expected.

So Mark Messier sought out Darren Blake, the team's director of operations who makes all the travel arrangements, and had this simple statement: "Hey boss, we'll be flying back."

That is as good as an executive order. So Blake immediately arranged for a plane.

THE GAME SURE LOOKS EASY when the puck is going into the net, and the Rangers are making it look easy now.

They dictated the pace against a team that normally doesn't allow visitors to dictate, and beat the Washington Capitals 5-3 at MCI Center for their third win in a row and fifth in six games.

They have scored 30 goals in those six games.

And get this, for what it's worth, the Rangers are in first place in the Atlantic Division with an 8-7 record. They knew it, too. Low said they talked about it before the game, and that the guys were excited about it.

"It's a stepping stone," Low said.

Messier said it's one of those little motivating factors that help get a team through the 82-game grind.

It has also made a difference that in those five victories, the Rangers have gotten superlative goaltending from Mike Richter.

Richter, who has won five starts in a row, made enough big saves to allow the Rangers to play their get-it-and-go transition game. Indeed, some of their best offensive rushes came off scrambling saves by Richter.

"That's part and parcel," said Low, a former goalie himself. "It's going to have to be that way, and Ricky knows that. The saves he made in the third period, he made two of them when we broke down badly. He made two key saves sliding across. He was great."

Five goals. Nothing makes a team look as good, or as confident, as a big number on the scoreboard.

"It covers up mistakes," said Brian Leetch, who played a mammoth 36:18 and crept to within one of Rod Gilbert's team record of 615 assists. "We couldn't afford mistakes in the past. We'd make a couple and they would end up in our net, and that was enough to lose.

"Now we make a mistake, and if it ends up in, we've got an opportunity to go back and get a couple, win the game and move on. Instead of focusing on a couple of negatives in the game, the goal-scoring can cover up for that. And, obviously, the goaltending, too. Mike's allowed us to make a couple of mistakes."

"We've got a lot of offensive ability in this room and everybody's been taking turns," said Fleury, who scored again. "It's been fun.

"We're building something really good here. Obviously, I think things are probably happening a lot quicker than everybody thought they would, but we're not doing anything flashy. We're just playing really hard, and playing really smart."

"I also think that keeps the other team on edge,' Richter said, "because they can't throw everything at you offensively, even when they're down, because we're apt to come back with our transition game so quickly, that any chance they take, we can come right back."

The Rangers have come back, from a wretched 3-6 start against the dregs of the league, to first place, for however long it lasts. It's amazing what 30 well-placed goals can do.

VLADIMIR MALAKHOV has made enough progress while rehabbing his injured left knee that the target date for his return is now Sunday against Phoenix.

THE RANGERS MADE a minor-league trade to lighten their goaltending glut, when they dealt goalie J.F. Labbe to Columbus for defenseman/winger Bert Robertsson. The 26-year-old agitator played in the Edmonton organization and will remain with the Houston Aeros of the IHL. The Rangers have a bunch of younger goalies who need to play instead of Labbe—Johan Holmqvist and Jason LaBarbera among them.

PRIOR TO THE GAME, the players were getting a big kick out of the Bush-Gore election saga, this being the nation's capital. The Canadian guys were especially rough on the Americans.

Richter, an American, had about enough.

"All I know is the last time they had an vote (in Canada) it was to keep the country together," he said.

Low got a kick out of the whole scene, and was giggling as he walked down the hallway trying to find a place to sneak a smoke in the newish arena.

RYE, N.Y.

It seems funny to say, when a team scores 30 goals in a six-game span, but the key to the Rangers' success in those six games has been Mike Richter.

Richter said he no longer even thinks about his reconstructed left knee once he steps out onto the rink and he appears to be playing at least as well, if not better than he was playing just before he suffered the injury at All-Star weekend in February.

Richter has been in goal for five of the six games, and won all five. The only loss in that span was a 6-5 decision in Ottawa (with rookie Holmqvist in goal), perhaps the Rangers' best game of the season. Maybe they would have won that game, too, if Richter had been in goal.

The Rangers' style of play leaves Richter with some fires to put out, and he has their confidence that he will do so. Nor does he mind it.

Yet Richter disagrees that the Rangers have been playing strictly run-and-gun.

"I still say, we've been working so hard in the defensive zone, that's allowed us to break out as a group," Richter said. "And we're controlling the neutral zone pretty well, so we're creating offensive chances because we're working so hard in each zone. It's not a matter of just hanging high and hoping the chances come.

"I think it goes hand-in-hand. We're playing so well defensively because we're working so hard, that that's creating offensive chances. A lot of people pay lip service to that and say if you take care of your own zone it will set you up in the offensive zone, but it really is happening for us, and I think that's why the games we've won, we've been able to fill the net. It just wasn't a one-side thing. We're playing well in all three zones."

Low has repeatedly called Richter one of the top five goalies in the league, and his long-time teammates Brian Leetch, Adam Graves and Mark Messier, can no longer come up with enough superlatives because they are so used to his high level of play.

"He's one of the best goalies in the league and any team that wins the Stanley Cup has great goaltending," Theo Fleury said. "Mike's been there before, and he's playing great right now."

Richter and the Rangers will get a stern test Sunday when Phoenix comes to the Garden. The Coyotes had their 12-game unbeaten streak (7-0-5) snapped by Detroit Wednesday, their first loss since October 12, when they were beaten 2-1 in San Jose, only their second loss of the season (9-2-5). The Coyotes are in Columbus tomorrow, looking to start a new streak.

After that, the Rangers head to the Northwest for three games—in Minnesota, Vancouver and Calgary—in four nights. The latter two games are on consecutive nights, Friday and Saturday, and Richter has yet to play back-to-back games, so that could be a new test. Or, Low might wait until the following week, when the Rangers play Toronto and the Islanders on consecutive nights, to push Richter into a back-to-back situations.

SUNDAY, NOVEMBER 12, 2000

NEW YORK

The balloon popped. Not only could the Rangers not score a lot, they couldn't score at all, in a 2-0 Garden loss to the Coyotes.

As well as the Rangers played, some saw this as a setback.

Brian Leetch noted that here was the chance for the Rangers to carve a notch in their belts by beating a top team, and they didn't do it. Their only other loss in the last seven games was against the only other top team they played, Ottawa.

"They certainly played a different game than the teams we played the last five or seven games," Leetch said. "The teams we faced, we were able to get into a good skating game, and forecheck and defend.

"They're a top team and we need to find ways to beat the top teams. Those are the type of games that feel good to win because you work hard to come out on top. You know, there's a lot of positives to where we've gotten. We've got to take the next step, and that's winning games like this."

THE RANGERS DID GET to see two new defensemen at work. Vladimir Malakhov, the Rangers' $14 million free agent, played his second game of the season, managing 24:10 of ice time. He returned from a partial tear in his left ACL, suffered on opening night in Atlanta. Rookie Tomas Kloucek, 20, was also inserted into the lineup and made his first NHL appearance a solid one on defense.

Another defenseman, Kim Johnsson, will make the trip and could be back from a broken bone in his right hand by the weekend or some time next week.

RYE, N.Y.

John MacLean's tenure as a Ranger probably ended today, and his future as an NHL player became more cloudy.

But his resolve remained strong, even as Glen Sather turned up the heat on the 18-year NHL veteran who turns 36 next week.

MacLean left the team upon being put on waivers for the second time this season, and if he clears waivers at noon Wednesday, as expected, MacLean has been told by the Rangers that he will be assigned to the IHL. That could mean the Houston Aeros, the former team of Rangers coach Ron Low and current team of another ex-Devils teammate of MacLean, Dave Barr.

Or it could mean Manitoba—a worst-case scenario for MacLean, but the ultimate bargaining chip for Sather.

Sather wants to buy out MacLean, but he failed to do so over the summer, when the league bylaws stipulate a player can be bought out for two-thirds of his remaining salary. Sather told MacLean early this season that he would be bought out of the final year of his contract (worth $2.5 million) if the team was unable to trade him. Sather advised MacLean and his agent, Rick Curran, to negotiate a buyout at less than $2.5 million.

That, of course, is a demand Sather has no right to make. So Sather strong-armed MacLean, threatening him with an assignment to the minor leagues, and worse, to an outpost other than the Rangers' AHL affilliate in Hartford, where he could collect his $2.5 million and miss his family terribly.

Well, MacLean apparently is calling Sather's bluff.

MacLean and Curran thought that they had negotiated an acceptable buyout at more than two-thirds of his salary for 2000–01, but less than the 100 percent the Rangers will have to pay him if he simply plays out the year in the minors.

But Sather tightened the screws further by trying to get MacLean to agree to taking his buyoutover two years. Understandably, MacLean wants it this year.

"Sure I'm angry, upset," MacLean said from his New Jersey home. "I'm all those things. I think it was the wrong way to have been handled. But that seems to be the way he handles his business. I can't do anything but go from there.

"I have great support on the family front and we'll make the most of it. I'm prepared as I'm ever going to be. It'll be tough if and when I have to do it, but I'll get through it, and we'll get through it."

Sather was attending GM meetings in Toronto and was unavailable for comment.

MacLean was asked what he thought about the tactics, and said, "It doesn't seem to matter what I think anyway."

MacLean also thinks, as do the Rangers, that another NHL club would be happy to have him once the buyout is completed and he can be signed for a lesser salary.

"We felt I probably might have hooked on," MacLean, who has played in just two games this season, said. "Now I have to go this way. I need to play, too."

Wasn't it just April, then June, when Madison Square Garden president Dave Checketts was spouting off repeatedly about how he and his new general manager would bring the dignity back to the Rangers organization, and about wanting players to be proud to have the privilege of wearing the Rangers uniform?

And wasn't it just September when Sather spoke to his players at training camp, then to the media the next day, about how this year, whenever there is a problem it should be kept inside the team, that the dirty laundry should not be aired outside?

So, it's difficult to reconcile why Sather felt it so necessary to treat MacLean—who has been nothing but a classy professional his entire career—as if he were dirt. How is that dignified, or how is that supposed to make players proud to wear the Rangers' uniform?

And why it was necessary to play out this whole classless situation in the newspapers?

Can anybody explain that?

TUESDAY, NOVEMBER 14, 2000

RYE, N.Y.

Mark Messier knew it was coming, but probably wished it might pass. Before flying to snow-buried Minnesota to start a three-game western trip, Messier was surrounded by reporters.

A simple question brought a puzzling answer.

"Are you looking forward to going back to Vancouver?"

"In what sense?" he said.

Messier has done the going-back thing before: Back to Edmonton as a Ranger, back to New York as a Canuck. The Rangers are in Minnesota tomorrow, then Messier goes back to Vancouver as a Ranger. It won't be quite the same. He will probably be booed.

"I don't think it can compare because we never had the chance to complete the task at hand in Vancouver," Messier said. "In Edmonton and New York we went the whole distance and won the Stanley Cup in both places, which makes a feeling of (being) more complete. It was a different set of circumstances in Vancouver in my three years there. At the same time, I was proud with the way the team came together and played well that third year after a tough couple of years there."

Some fans in Vancouver, and some members of the media, felt Messier was there for the money (he made $20 million, including his buyout, over three seasons). Some felt he was responsible for the upheaval in the front office and coaching staff, and responsible for the trades of popular players like Trevor Linden, Gino Odjick and even Pavel Bure.

"Winning is a large part of it," Messier said. "The team in Vancouver there was a pretty tight-knit team. They had some success, had gone to the Stanley Cup finals (in 1994), they were together a long time, they had a good relationship with their coach, Pat Quinn, they were entrenched in the community for doing a lot of good things.

"The only thing that wasn't happening was they weren't winning. So when I came in there and all that was broken up, I was largely viewed as the guy who was breaking up a good thing, so to speak. But it would have been happening whether I was there or not because the bottom line is winning, and when you're not winning, changes are going to be made. That, along with the fact that we struggled the first two years, a lot of very popular players were moved, and only until last year could you see any real headway."

Last year, the Canucks nearly made the playoffs with a strong finish, and Messier refused to bail out, even though he knew the team would not pick up the option year on his contract and he would be leaving in the summer. He could have asked for a trade to a contender, a short-term move, then become a free agent in the summer. He decided to stick it out; said he never even considered going anywhere else until his contract ran out.

And this year, with the Canucks off to a terrific start, a number of Messier's former teammates credit him with teaching them how to win, most notably Ed Jovanovski.

"We played well last year, and I think we got a little taste of success, and how hard you had to work to get success," Messier said. "I think last year filtered over to this year. You could see it starting to turn the corner last year.

"I can take a lot of satisfaction out of it, particularly since they're not in our conference."

RICHTER WILL START the next two games in goal, and said he is sure he's ready to play back-to-back games for the first time, if Low decides to go that way Friday in Vancouver and Saturday in Calgary.

SPEAKING OF RETURNS, Theo Fleury will make his second trip to Calgary as an ex-Flame. He went back with Colorado after being traded late in 1998–99. "I thought I changed my name to Lou," Fleury recalled about the reception he got from the fans that time.

WEDNESDAY, NOVEMBER 15, 2000

ST. PAUL, MINN.

As expected, John MacLean cleared NHL waivers and was assigned to the Manitoba Moose of the IHL as punishment for not agreeing to take an 80 percent buyout.

So MacLean will receive 100 percent of his $2.5 million salary while playing in the Winnipeg-based outpost.

Sather said he ran out of options when no other team was interested in taking MacLean off his hands.

Sather said he offered to pay 80 percent of MacLean's salary in trade talks, leaving other teams on the hook for just $500,000. That was the same 80 percent Sather and MacLean's agent, Rick Curran, had agreed upon as a buyout ($2 million). Sather, however, said there was never an agreement that the buyout would be paid out over one year. Sather insisted it be paid over two years, an offer MacLean refused.

"It gets to a point where you just can't go any farther," Sather said. "It doesn't make sense from a business point of view."

Sather did say he had become uncomfortable with the whole situation.

"Uncomfortable from the point that here's a guy that's played 16 years and I wish we could have kept him in the league with somebody, but there just wasn't anybody that was interested," Sather said.

Sather said he expects MacLean will report to Grand Rapids, Michigan, today, where he will join Manitoba on a road trip. MacLean must report to collect his salary.

If he plays well in the IHL, that could also spark some interest later on, especially as teams try to bulk up for the playoffs. A team needing a veteran two-way winger could get MacLean almost for free down the stretch.

Sather said he had considered buying out MacLean over the summer, at which time it would have only cost the Rangers two-thirds of MacLean's salary as per the collective bargaining agreement.

"Yeah, but I hadn't seen what he could do at training camp, and I didn't think it was fair to do anything of that type just coming in," said Sather, who was hired June 1, and thus had only a month to decide on buyouts. "He could have come to camp and lit it up, and would have been fine. I don't think 36 is old."

THE RANGERS DID WHAT they had to do, although they will get no points for style. A win over a team in its infancy, after all, is never nearly as notable as a loss to that team.

So the Rangers will take their 3-2 win over the Minnesota Wild at Xcel Energy Center and flee to Vancouver for the middle game of their three-game trip. The victory, the Rangers' sixth in eight games and third straight on the road, will not be on the highlight film. It will not be remembered at the end of the season.

But it would have been a terrible game to lose.

"Yeah, it would have," said Petr Nedved, who scored the middle goal of three in a span of 2:29 late in the second period. "Those are two points you might need down the road."

Instead, the Rangers only have to be concerned about Vladimir Malakhov, who late in the game twisted the left knee that kept him out for six weeks earlier in the season. It was not immediately known if it was a serious re-injury or, as they call it, a "tweak"

SATHER SAID HE HAS no idea if his team will be in the running for Eric Lindros. "I haven't spoken to him since the draft in Calgary. I told him, when he's feeling better and he's ready to go, give me a call and let me know," Sather said. Lindros, an unsigned restricted free agent, has said he won't play in Philadelphia again. At the draft, Sather and Flyers GM Bobby Clarke spoke in generalities about a deal that would include the Rangers sending draft picks which would be based on how much Lindros played. Sather vehemently called "absolutely untrue" a story in Ottawa that had the Rangers offering Petr Nedved straight up for Lindros last week.

If Sather offered Nedved for Lindros then he should be fired. And Clarke should be fired for not taking it.

Sather also said that the Rangers would "take the steps necessary" as far as getting their own medical people to test Lindros, only once Lindros is ready to play.

FORMER RANGERS COACH Herb Brooks, who lives in nearby Shoreview, Minnesota, and will coach the U.S. Olympic team at Salt Lake City in 2002, attended the game. He will have Brian Leetch, Mike Richter and maybe Mike York on his roster for the 2002 Games.

ALL EXPANSION TEAMS and teams moving to new arenas would do well to follow Minnesota's blueprint. And just about every team in the NHL could take some pointers with the way the Wild exercises its sound system during stoppages. The music is good, not ear-splitting loud, and not overwhelming. Washington's noise machine, for example, is like a nail in the head. No wonder nobody goes there.

Another thing, the Wild p.a. announcer takes the time to learn the pronunciation of the visitors names, unlike most announcers, who regularly bungle the names of foreign players.

FRIDAY, NOVEMBER 17, 2000

VANCOUVER, BRITISH COLUMBIA

This one won't go into Mark Messier's memory scrapbook, and the Rangers will be happy to forget about it quickly, too.

Messier's return to Vancouver was an out-and-out disaster for himself and his teammates, who fell apart in a 4-3 loss to the Canucks at GM Place.

Messier was booed every time he touched the puck, and his line, with Adam Graves and Valeri Kamensky, continued its string of awful games, which is now at least five in a row. That streak coincides with the return of Kamensky from a bruised kidney, although Messier and Graves have done less than their share in that stretch.

Messier thus failed to do what he did the first time he went back to Edmonton as a Ranger, and the first time he went back to New York as a Canuck—win.

Messier shrugged off the booing—to a giant horde of Canadian media members, both electronic and print—as the home fans supporting their team. He spoke in clichés, careful to not say anything worthwhile to the crowd of cameras and microphones.

He had been mobbed by TV cameras and reporters after the morning skate, and the front of the *Vancouver Sun* sports section featured a huge photo of Messier and three stories about his return.

But, while there were some who cheered him, those who didn't were vile.

One sign read: "Mark Messier is a great player . . . For me to poop on."

For three years every little slump, every bad play, was analyzed as simply the fall of an old player. Or worse, a player who was there for the money.

That annoyed some of the Rangers who know better.

"Fans want to win," Leetch. "They want to win the game, and it helped them get into the game to pick Mark out.

"They didn't obviously have a good understanding of what they had here in Vancouver. He's a unique individual and he means a lot to the players in the locker room. No one wants to win more than him. He doesn't come to just show up. He's there to help the team win and do whatever he can off the ice, and on the ice his actions speak for themselves. I feel very lucky to have played with him before, and I feel lucky that he's back again."

This was the first really bad game the Rangers played in the last nine (6-3), and it turned in a terrible second period.

"We lost our composure," said Ron Low, who thought his team got carried away hollering at the officials in the second period. "And it was a game we couldn't afford to lose our composure."

Low added that "penalties changed the hockey game" and that "I didn't think the refereeing was very good at all." He specifically pointed out that Theo Fleury, who was called twice for penalties, had his pinky finger slashed. Fleury had to have the finger frozen and stitched, and it may be broken, although Fleury said that won't keep him out of his return to Calgary tomorrow.

That game will now make or break this three-game trip.

"We lost our focus of the game," said Tim Taylor. "We got mad at the referees, and we weren't really playing like we did in the first period."

"That's the disappointing part about this," Fleury said. "We beat ourselves, and that's something we should never do."

They probably won't forget this as soon as they'd like.

GLEN SATHER'S PRIZED free-agent signee might be finished, after playing three games and completing only one.

Defenseman Vladimir Malakhov, who missed 15 games with a partial tear of the ACL in his left knee suffered on opening night, reinjured the knee Wednesday in Minnesota and might need season-ending reconstructive surgery.

That decision hasn't been made yet, and it probably won't be made as long as Malakhov feels he can and wants to play. In fact Malakhov went to Ron Low this morning and wanted to play in Vancouver, but trainer Jim Ramsay told him he couldn't.

Low said Malakhov won't play in Calgary, and probably not in either of the games Tuesday or Wednesday. Then a determination will be made at some point—the options being Malakhov continuing to play on a knee that is sore, stiff and not completely stable, as Mike Richter did last year; or having the complete reconstruction surgery, which means five-to-seven months of rehab.

Malakhov will be examined by Dr. Barton Nisonson upon the team's return home Sunday or Monday.

"I hope it's not (surgery), but I've got a lot of swelling in the knee," Malakhov said. "Fuck, I hope not. It won't make me happy. Very sad."

That would be a disaster for Malakhov, who missed the first 54 games of last season after reconstructive surgery on his right ACL. And it would be a disaster for Sather and the Rangers, who signed Malakhov to a four-year, $14 million free-agent contract over the summer.

"I went last year with the same surgery," Malakhov said. "It's very hard to come back. I missed a lot of games. I'm having bad luck lately."

He said that one option is to try to rehab the knee and its surrounding muscles through exercise, but didn't sound optimistic since that is what he did during the 15 games he missed between opening night, when he was first hurt, and last Sunday, when he finally returned.

The rehab after surgery is daunting.

"It's long," Malakhov said. "I don't want to do surgery. But if I have to . . . I want to talk to the doctors and we'll see."

In Malakhov's place was the returning Kim Johnsson, who missed five games with a broken bone in his right hand. Johnsson had soreness in the hand when he tried to shoot the puck but said that stick-handling wasn't a problem. He wore extra padding to protect the hand from re-injury by a slash.

The Malakhov injury, however, puts a crimp in the plan to reduce some of Brian Leetch's massive ice time. Low had planned to use Malakhov and Johnsson, perhaps as a pair, against the opposition's top forward lines to free up Leetch from so much defensive responsibility. The benefits, Low said, would be two-fold in that Leetch not only would play fewer minutes, but he would also be given more opportunity to go on the offense.

Now that plan may have to be scrapped since Low isn't likely to trust Brad Brown or rookie Tomas Kloucek with the responsibility of taking on the opponents' top forwards and the required ice time.

On the positive side, Low likes what he has gotten out of Kloucek, who doesn't look out of place at all in his first NHL week. The 6-3, 220-pound, 20-year-old has been physical and steady defensively and appears able to handle the faster NHL game.

Kloucek is one of several defensemen among the Rangers' top prospects, including Mike Mottau, Dale Purinton and second-round pick Filip Novak, who is having an outstanding season (9-16-25 in 21 games) with Regina of the WHL.

LAST WEEK, Wayne Gretzky was named executive director of the Canadian Olympic hockey team for the 2002 games in Salt Lake City. So the speculation began about whether Mark Messier would be selected to play on the team, when he's 41 years old. Messier was terribly disappointed and hurt to be passed over in 1998, the first Olympics to feature NHL players. He said, prior to the selection of the team for the Nagano, Japan, games, that in addition to winning more Stanley Cups, his remaining goal was to represent Canada in the Olympics. It didn't work out, as Messier wasn't called.

Now Messier would love another shot, but only if Gretzky and his assistant, Messier's long-time close friend Kevin Lowe, think he can still compete and contribute.

"I've told Wayne and Kevin not to feel obligated because of what we've been through in the past," Messier said in the *Toronto Globe and Mail*. "It's important to really concentrate on the team and who can help and who can contribute, no matter what's gone on in the past.

"There's some tough decisions. Nobody's ever going to be totally happy with the selections. You have to have a vision, the ability to be confident in your ideas of how you want the team to look an dact and skate and play."

Messier added that it's important to "not waver because of outside reactions and public response."

FLEURY IS LOOKING FORWARD to his return to Calgary tomorrow, partially because his son lives there, and it is his 13th birthday. Fleury realizes the Rangers haven't won in Calgary since 1987, too. "Yeah, we used to always beat them," he said.

IN *THE VANCOUVER PROVINCE*, Low admitted that the turning point of this season was when Messier punched out Pittsburgh's Darius Kasparaitis in the game before they won six of eight.

"Up until that point we didn't touch a soul," Low said.

LOST IN THE CRAZINESS: Leetch tied Rod Gilbert's team record with his 615th assist.

THE BEST MOMENT OF Messier's return came after the game, when Messier took a little time to emerge from the shower. Sylvain Lefebvre, who shaves his head just as Messier does, bent down in his stall to tie a shoe. With only the top of his head visible, in a flash, Lefebvre was surrounded by the media. They thought it was Messier. The entire group sheepishly shuffled away once they realized it wasn't the ex-Canucks captain.

AS THE RANGERS PILED off their bus, one-by-one, at the players entrance at GM Place this afternoon, they had to walk through a large group of fans that had lined both sides of the door, and were being held back by security guards. Messier was obviously the most noticeable of the Rangers, but the rest pretty much snuck through. Brian Leetch, Mike Richter, Theo Fleury and so many others barely received a reaction. Then one of the security guards and a number of fans began yelling to one of the players: "Bert, Bert Robertsson!"

The Rangers' extra had played his minor-league hockey in Vancouver.

SATURDAY, NOVEMBER 18, 2000

CALGARY, ALBERTA

Now it was Theo Fleury's turn to hear the booing that Mark Messier heard the night before.

Fleury returned to Calgary for the first time as a Ranger and the second time as an ex-Flame, hoping for two things. One, he was hoping that the Rangers could get a different result out of the Saddledome than they had gotten for Messier in his return to Vancouver Friday.

Two, he was hoping that the booing wouldn't be as severe as the last time he came back to Calgary, shortly after his trade to Colorado at the end of 1999, and that some of the emotional wounds would have healed.

Fleury, on a turn-around mission with 14 goals, one short of his output for the entire 1999–2000 season, has spoken this week about the bad feelings that surrounded his leaving Calgary, where he spent the first 11 years of his career. The Flames didn't want to give him anything close to market value, so they traded him for prospects and young players rather than lose him for nothing as a free agent.

What bothered Fleury was that it was rumored, and reported, that the Flames offered Fleury $5 million to stay, and that he rejected it. Fleury denounced that as a lie, saying that Calgary's best offer was never anywhere near $5 million, and claimed the story was planted, although he wouldn't identify who did the planting.

Neverethless, Fleury wishes he could have parted on better terms with the fans who adored his feisty style. He had about 70 friends and family members at the game, and a post-game birthday celebration for his son, Josh, who turned 13 today.

"I still have the Flames logo tattooed on my chest," Fleury was quoted as saying in the *Calgary Herald*, "and no matter how much soap you have or how hard you scrub, it'll never completely come off."

THEY WERE ONE SHOT away from their three-game trip becoming a disaster. Except that the Rangers got the shot that mattered, Valeri Kamensky's game-winning slapper at 3:44 of sudden death that gave them a 5-4 win over Calgary at the Saddledome.

So the Rangers come home with four points on the trip, even if they nearly tossed away two of them. The Rangers had a 3-1 lead on the Flames late in the second period and leads of 3-2 and 4-3 in the third.

"It's fun when you win those, and if you lose those you're certainly disappointed," said Brian Leetch, who set a team record for career assists and matched his point total for all of last season (26). "We needed a win like that, not playing our best and still finding a way to win."

Fleury and Leetch put on a show, as they have all season long. Leetch scored the game's first goal, on a play started by Fleury. Leetch then broke Rod Gilbert's team record with his 616th assist. Fittingly, the record-breaker was a beauty of a pass for a Petr Nedved dunk, on the power play.

And Fleury scored a short-handed goal that not only tied the team record of five in a season, but also matched his entire goal total for 1999–2000 with his league-leading 15th overall.

But Fleury could have cost the Rangers the game. He wasn't around at the end, taking a roughing penalty with 5.7 seconds left in regulation, then adding a misconduct in his aggressive, theatrical argument that Toni Lydman had stolen Fleury's stick before Fleury punched him.

Mike Richter, starting on back-to-back nights for the first time since undergoing reconstructive left knee surgery, was outstanding early with four tough saves in the first three minutes.

THE FLAMES GOT a controversial power-play goal during a Dale Purinton double minor.

Ex-Ranger Marc Savard ripped a shot from the top of the left circle, and it appeared the puck went through the net. The puck tore the top off the water bottle atop the net, and crashed into the backboards as play continued for a few moments. After video replays, it was ruled the puck went up under the crossbar and through the mesh, although replays surely did not definitively show that. It is rare when the NHL's video replay rule isn't 100 percent certain in its ruling. This was one such case.

BRIAN LEETCH, off to a marvelous start with 26 points—seven more than any other defenseman—and averaging a league-leading 30 minutes a game, is getting very premature notice as a candidate not just for the Norris Trophy (best defenseman) but also for the Hart Trophy (MVP). Chris Pronger of St. Louis accomplished the rare feat just a year ago.

Leetch laughed at the November date, but said it's nice to be recognized.

"I guess it's better than being the biggest bust of the year," he said.

RYE, N.Y.

The Rangers made the cross-continent trip back to New York—those in the media had the additional nightmares of changes in Toronto or Montreal or Minnesota, plus the considerable lines at Customs, while the Rangers fly direct in comfort and have the Customs agents come onto the plane, to them—and there was plenty to think about.

Their top two MVPs to this point in the season are, unquestionably, Brian Leetch and Theo Fleury. Or Fleury and Leetch.

They have done it game after game for the Rangers. Lately, and without much fanfare, the Czechmates have been heating up, too. Petr Nedved (4-7-11), Radek Dvorak (1-9-10) and Jan Hlavac (3-3-6) have combined for 27 points in the last eight games, and also combined for six of the Rangers' first nine game-winning goals (three by Hlavac). And all of that, along with solid performances from a bunch of others—Mike Richter, Rich Pilon, Kim Johnsson, Mike York, to name a few—had the Rangers in decent position.

But, there was this gnawing fact. The Rangers' big-name line centered by Mark Messier was struggling.

Struggling mightily. Until Saturday night in Calgary, that is.

That night, Messier had a goal and an assist, and Valeri Kamensky an assist and the game-winner in OT, while winger Adam Graves played one of his more physical, more involved games in a while.

The Rangers coaches never lost faith. Indeed, after a 4-3 loss in Vancouver Friday, in which Kamensky scored a fluke goal, Low was asked if he was concerned about that threesome.

"No I'm not. Not at all," Low said. End of answer.

Low, a guy who says what he feels, didn't have to say any more. His assistant coaches spent time doing extra work with Graves in practice, and on Saturday, that line helped win a game the Rangers nearly blew and couldn't afford to lose.

They were the difference late in the Rangers' third game in four nights in three different time zones, all on the road.

Not bad for a bunch of old guys.

"One thing about it," Low said, "they had a lot left in the third."

Low has limited Messier's minutes by letting others kill penalties, and by using a fourth line regularly. It's a necessary step with a soon-to-be 40-year-old.

"That line was the difference in the third period and at the end. They had lots of jump. Lots.

"I'm not going to be concerned about Mark, and I'm not going to be concerned about Val and Gravy. They'll play. They'll find a way to get themselves out of whatever they're in. They're professionals and they'll play."

In the five games since Kamensky returned from a bruised kidney, though, they hadn't produced offense. Graves didn't have a point in the five and wasn't getting his expected hit quota, Messier had but two assists and wasn't clicking at all, and while Kamensky had two goals, he was being easily knocked off the puck with regularity.

Messier faced the questions after the game in Vancouver. He was asked about not killing penalties for the first time in his career.

"Whatever we need to do to win," Messier said.

Then about the lack of production.

"That's the way the season goes," Messier said. "You're going to be hot and cold at times.

"When we're not producing offensively, we want to make sure we're doing our jobs defensively, so we're not getting hurt on that side of the puck. You know, it's our job to score goals and we've got to keep at it, going and getting some rubber at the net and driving and doing the things we were doing before."

More importantly, he and his linemates are back from their little slump. Not that Low ever had any doubts they would.

RYE, N.Y.

Vladimir Malakhov had his re-injured left knee examined by Dr. Barton Nisonson today, and it was determined that he will sit out for two weeks, then decide whether he can play or undergo season-ending reconstructive surgery.

Malakhov, who had reconstructive surgery on his right knee prior to last season, originally suffered a partial tear of his left ACL on opening night in Atlanta. He missed 14 games, and twisted the knee Wednesday in Minnesota. The major surgery would end the season for Malakhov.

CENTER MIKE YORK asked the other day, "What's the record for short-handed goals in a season?" The reason York wondered is that his penalty-killing partner Theo Fleury already has tied the Rangers team record with five short-handers in the first 19 games.

Mario Lemieux had 13 short-handed goals in 1988–89, breaking Wayne Gretzky's record of 12 in 1983–84. Fleury's career high is seven short-handers in a season (in 1990–91) and he has 33 short-handers for his career. With 63 games left, he shares the Rangers' single-season record with Don Maloney, Mike Rogers, Mark Messier and Mike Gartner.

Fleury, incidentally, holds the NHL record for short-handed goals in a game, with three in an 8-4 Calgary win over St. Louis March 9, 1991.

THE RANGERS THIS MONTH HAVE: won in Montreal, where they had been 3-22-9 in 34 regular-season visits; won in Calgary, where they had been 0-11-6 since 1987; and lost to Phoenix at home, where the Coyotes had lost eight in a row since 1991. Coming up: they go to Nassau Coliseum, where, despite their recent run of four wins in five visits, they have historically had problems, and Friday they are in Buffalo to face Dominik Hasek, who shut them out five times in a six-game span from 1997–98 through 1998–99.

TUESDAY, NOVEMBER 21, 2000

NEW YORK

After a rocky start, the Rangers have learned how to beat the bounty of bad teams in the NHL. Now they have to figure a way to beat one of the good teams.

The Rangers' record against teams with winning records fell to 1-8 with a 3-1 loss to the Toronto Maple Leafs at the Garden. Their inability to beat the upper-echelon teams has the Rangers still treading water at 10-10 after the season's first 20 games.

Of course, that's a heckuva lot better than the 6-11-3 the Rangers put in the books for the first 20 games last season.

"Whether it's 1-8 against (top teams or) other teams, we need to get more wins," Mike Richter said.

Because they are so plentiful, a team can almost make the playoffs just by beating the bottom teams. But to be taken seriously, a team needs to be more than competitive, which is what the Rangers have been in games against Phoenix, Vancouver and now Toronto, each a loss which could have been a win with a bit more discipline.

But wins haven't come against Pittsburgh, Philadelphia, Ottawa or the aforementioned three above-.500 teams. The only one the Rangers have beaten was Edmonton.

"It is part of our record, but I do think we'll match up better with the top teams as we go along," Richter said. "It's got to be done. We can't wait for it to happen, we've got to find a way to do it. I think that's going to happen when we start sticking to our plan a little bit more. We get away from our game and we get in trouble.

"Part of what good teams are made of is the discipline to have a game plan and use in all circumstances. I think when the games get tighter and the competition gets better you have to be more disciplined. We are learning that, but we're not there yet."

"We're not going to make the jump until we win close games against the better teams," said Brian Leetch, who was honored prior to the game for breaking Rod Gilbert's club record for assists on Saturday. "We've improved from where we started. We still have to make the next step and start beating the better teams."

AN INTERESTING TWIST came out of the Leafs' locker room. Unbeknownst to Leetch or any of the Rangers, Toronto goalie Curtis Joseph was accusing Leetch of a spear that not only resulted in Joseph being spun around on Kamensky's goal, but also, according to the goalie, should lead to a suspension for Leetch.

"I would like to see that goal again," the normally easy-going Joseph told the Toronto media. "I was being speared and that one should be sent in to the league for review."

The goal cost Cujo a chance to become the first Maple Leaf to shut out the Rangers at the Garden since Johnny Bower on January 10, 1965.

THE RANGERS LOST a key checker and penalty killer when winger Eric Lacroix was hit by a Yanic Perreault pass in the third period and suffered a broken index finger. He is expected to be out for four weeks. Rich Pilon also was twice hit with pucks, in his right hand and right leg, but x-rays were negative and he plans to play tomorrow against his former team, the Islanders.

GILBERT WAS TELLING STORIES outside the locker room before the game, and talking about Leetch and Bobby Orr. Gilbert recalled how Orr had frustrated the Rangers in the early 1970s. One time, Gilbert said, he decided he was not going to let Orr play his game of keepaway. So Gilbert chased him. Orr went behind his own net. Gilbert, a terrific skater, went around the right post and flushed him out. Orr went up the boards, with Gilbert a step behind. Orr went behind the Rangers net. Gilbert was still chasing. Orr then continued on along the boards, until he was back where he started, behind his own net, and ready to go again.

Gilbert was out of breath as he told the story, just as he was out of breath, and out of luck, chasing Orr.

UNIONDALE, N.Y.

Oh, it's fun to watch multi-millionaires make fools of themselves. The owners of the Rangers and the Islanders did that prior to tonight's Battle of New York at Nassau Coliseum.

Nobody could laugh too hard, though, because they were doing it for charity. The Dolans, Charles and his son Jim, who run Cablevision and the Garden and all its teams, and Islanders owners Charles Wang and Sanjay Kumar of Computer Associates, announced the formation of the Pat LaFontaine Trophy. The regular-season series winner each year will get the trophy, named for LaFontaine, who played for both teams, with both sides kicking in $50,000 a year to go to the winner's favorite charities. LaFontaine also gets a donation for his charities.

During the press conference to announce the idea, the owners sat on either side of the podium, manned by Islanders play-by-play man Howie Rose—himself a former Rangers radio announcer—along with their general managers, coaches and team captains.

The owners, particularly Jim Dolan and Wang, played a lot of "nyah, nyah, nyah, nyah" with one another, each claiming the other didn't have a prayer of winning the trophy, and each barbing the other for his team's long failures to make the playoffs.

Charles Dolan and Wang grew up near one another on Long Island, and Dolan said he dreamed of having a train between their houses, which he called the "Charlie Choo-choo."

Ugh. Then, when somebody asked what would happen if the season series ended tied, Wang and Jim Dolan agreed there should be a shootout, something clearly against the collective bargaining agreement and something the players surely wouldn't be happy about doing after a hard-fought regular-season game.

Mark Messier, seated at the end of the Rangers' table, frowned at the suggestion.

The Rangers' chosen charities are: NYR SKATE, Cheering for Children, and the Lustgarten Foundation for Pancreatic Cancer. The Islanders' are: Make-A-Wish Foundation, Cancer Care of Long Island, and St. Christopher Ottilie Center for handicapped children. An additional $10,000 a year will go to LaFontaine's charity, Hockey's All-Star Kids, which benefits children's hospitals in NHL cities.

Charles Dolan also said that he still hopes that a new Garden on Manhattan's West Side will be built in the near future. However, Jim

Dolan said that the progress of such a plan rests entirely with offices of the governor of New York and the mayor of New York City.

THE WAY THEO FLEURY figures it, last year the puck "would have hit the outside of the post and stayed out."

Now it's going in, and Fleury saved the Rangers again. He fired a power-play goal just inside the post, past ex-Rangers goalie John Vanbiesbrouck with 34.2 seconds left in sudden-death overtime to give the Rangers a 4-3 Thanksgiving Eve win over the Islanders.

And the way Tim Taylor figures it, along with a bunch of others who experienced last season, "that's the kind of game we would have lost last year."

Fleury's league-leading 16th goal—topping his output for all of last season—came less than a minute after Messier rang a one-timer off the post, and seconds after Vanbiesbrouck stopped another Messier shot. The power play was created when Kevin Haller, a long-time Messier antagonist, was called for taking down Mike York, and it gave the Rangers a chance to atone for blowing a 3-2 third-period lead.

"That's the sign of a good team," Fleury said. "When you're not at your best and you win the game, same as in Calgary (Saturday), where we were badly outshot and managed to get the two points, that's important."

Ron Low beat his buddy Butch Goring in his first taste of Rangers vs. Islanders, a series now 78-77-17 in the Isles' favor after 172 regular-season meetings.

MESSIER BECAME THE SIXTH player in history to reach 1,500 games played, and also broke a tie with Leetch for 11th on the Rangers' all-time goal-scoring list. Leetch had pulled even at 191 Rangers goals in the first period, with the power-play goal that gave the Rangers the early lead, off a steal from his old buddy, Vanbiesbrouck.

ONCE IN A WHILE, something important happens in a hockey game that goes completely unnoticed. The Rangers' victory over the Isles got a big assist from equipment manager Acacio Marques. Leetch had a skate problem late in the second period of a 2-2 game. Leetch debated whether to take both skates off while Marques worked on the broken skate, since the period was about to end. Marques talked him into keeping the other skate on.

Sure enough, the Rangers went on the power play with 1:20 left, and Marques put four new rivets in the skate and got Leetch back onto the ice in the final minute. The power play turned into a 4-on-4, and Leetch played a key role in setting up Messier's go-ahead goal with 6.8 seconds left. Leetch credited Marques for his work, and called it "an Indy 500 pit stop."

AFTER 21 GAMES, roughly a quarter of a season, the Rangers are 11-10. It breaks down in ugly fashion, though. 1-8 against teams that currently have winning records; 10-2 against teams that don't.

"I guess, without having Malakhov except for three games, you've got to be satisfied with the way the hockey club has come along," Low said.

"There's a real good chance to get better. I think we will get better.

"There's a lot of talent here, an awful lot of talent here, albeit stubborn at times. There is talent. The other thing I can honestly tell you is I haven't seen them quit yet, and that's really impressed me. They work, some nights not as smart as you'd like, but they work. I have no problem with that. Coaching a hockey club that works hard, I have no problem with that."

BUFFALO, N.Y.

Another trip, another city just buried by a snowstorm.

The Rangers seem to be playing this season as if they are sometimes up to their necks in snow.

After a hard-fought 3-2 loss to the Buffalo Sabres at HSBC Arena, a game decided by a bounce one way or another, the Rangers have alternated wins and losses for eight straight games. They have crept over .500, then dipped back to .500 four times in that span, and not coincidentally, every victory has been against a team with a losing record, and every loss to a team with a winning record.

"I think, as you see our team, we're trying to stick to a system," Brian Leetch said. "We've been, I guess, less inconsistent. Our losses have been by a couple of goals, and when our power play hasn't come through for us. Our mistakes are becoming fewer and further between, and that's encouraging. Guys are working hard. So, you know, it's not what we want to do, to just continue to hang around (.500).

"But the last 10 games, we've definitely made some strides. We've got to take the next step now. We're a little bit up and down now, but it's getting better."

The need to turn that improvement into some wins, and soon, is simple. The Rangers will face five pretty fair teams in a row—Ottawa, Los

Angeles, the Devils, Toronto and Colorado, cumulative record of 28 games over .500—a major, major test. Their record against teams with winning records is 1-9.

One interesting sidelight to this game was the benching of Adam Graves in the final minutes, as Tim Taylor took his place on Mark Messier's left. Graves has struggled, in part, because his linemate, Valeri Kamensky, has the puck most of the time. Graves hasn't had a point in nine games.

The last time Low messed with Graves's ice time, Graves responded with his best hockey of the season—and the Rangers went on their best streak of the year.

The Sabres, looking like the Chicago Blackhawks in their new money-grabbing, er, alternate red-and-black jerseys, broke a 2-2 tie at 7:50 of the third, on a power-play created when they hemmed the Rangers into their own end for one of many times in the game.

Mike Richter had to stop James Patrick twice through a huge crowd in front, and in the ensuing mad scramble in and around the crease, with infractions happening everywhere, Mike York knocked agitator Vaclav Varada into the net and was singled out for interference.

"Just an awful call," said Richter, who also felt the net had been dislodged a moment before the winning goal went into the net. "They can't see everything, and they did a good job, but they missed that one. I was interfered with on the play prior to that, speared and taken out of the play, turned around. The second guy was taking me out of the play while the puck's being thrown at me, and they give York the penalty. That's amazing."

The Sabres went on the power play, and Alexei Zhitnik ripped a shot wide. Richter did the split on the shot, and was unable to get back to the other side when the puck caromed off the backboards. Jason Woolley was able to corral it and slip it off Richter into the near side for the 3-2 lead.

The Rangers, who lost for only the second time in seven road games, had to come back from a 2-0 hole against Dominik Hasek, who at one point in the last three seasons had shut them out five times in six meetings.

SUNDAY, NOVEMBER 26, 2000

NEW YORK

You open the newspaper and there are the NHL standings, and in those standings are now four columns for a team's record. W-L-T-OL. Last year, it was actually worse, when it was W-L-T-RT, because the last column was for "regulation ties," which were overtime losses, and which also counted in the L column.

This year, the NHL came up with the overtime loss column. The OL. They don't count in the regular loss column. They are what they say they are. Overtime losses. Teams get one point for OLs.

It's easy to hate the OL. Here's why:

The fourth column is just not right. It isn't natural to a sports fan. Heck, the third column—ties—is foreign to baseball and basketball, and almost never a factor in football standings. It's weird enough for hockey teams to have records that look like 11-10-6. But add to that and make it 11-10-6-3, and it just looks horrible.

The whole extra column, basically an accounting column for the point the losing team gets in overtime, became necessary when the NHL went to the terrific, 4-on-4, nothing-to-lose OT format last season. Both teams in OT get a point guaranteed, so the hockey is just frantic as teams play for the extra point without jeopardizing the point already gained.

The trouble is finding a way to make the standings and the teams' records add up.

But the OL has made it more confusing. For example, just this week:

Calgary lost four straight games, but two were OLs. Is that a four-game losing streak?

Carolina had two wins, with an OL in between. Is that a three-game unbeaten streak?

Toronto had three wins, two ties and an OL. Were the Leafs unbeaten in six?

The Canucks had four straight wins, then an OL. Is that a five-game unbeaten streak?

The Islanders lost five in a row, then had an OL. Did they snap their losing streak?

As it is now, you could LOSE every game in OT, and be unbeaten at 0-0-0-82.

One simple suggestion: Since an OL is equal to a tie, simply tag the third column in the standings: T/OL. A team that is 13-12-5 has the same number of points, afterall, as a team that is 13-12-3-2.

The winning team still gets a W, and the corresponding two points, a losing team in regulation still gets nothing, and a team that gets to OT but doesn't win gets its point, whether it loses or ties. Which, mathematically, is what happens now.

Only now, the standings are just eyesores.

YOU KEEP HEARING that Brian Leetch is headed for a third Norris Trophy, and the way he's playing, it's hard to imagine there's a better defenseman on the planet. But you have to wonder if Leetch is going to get enough votes when, it certainly seems, so many of those who vote don't have a clue about the plus/minus system. Leetch's plus/minus is never going to be high on the plus side because he plays half of every game, against the other team's best scorers, on a team that isn't very good 5-on-5. So he is on the ice for a lot of opposition goals, naturally.

All the goals the Rangers score on the power-play with Leetch on the ice don't count in plus/minus ratings.

Yet there are those writers who don't understand that comparing a player's plus/minus to that of a player on another team is ridiculous. There are also those who think a high plus rating means a player is good defensively. Not so. Great offensive players on good even-strength teams, like Jaromir Jagr, will have high plus ratings. Players who play a lot on good 5-on-5 teams, like the Devils, will have high plus ratings. Great defensive players on bad even-strength teams will have minus ratings. Got it?

And *USA Today*, for example, rates Impact Players, and weighs plus/minus ratings as if it can be applied across the board like goals and assists. So Leetch isn't one of the top Impact Players in the NHL according to that paper, which is ridiculous.

RON LOW WAITED for each Ranger to step off of the ice tonight so that he could deliver personal pats on their backs.

The Rangers coach had just seen his team play what he called "its most solid 60 minutes of the year." Not only that, but the Rangers began a stretch of five games in eight nights, all against teams around the top of the NHL standings, with a strong 3-2 victory over the Ottawa Senators before a Garden crowd that was less than two-thirds full.

The Rangers beat one of the NHL's above-.500 teams for only the second time in 11 games this season, and snapped an eight-game winless streak (0-7-1) against the Senators.

This was as good a start as Low could have hoped to have.

"He was happy with the way we played," said Theo Fleury, who had two more assists and now has a whopping 31 points in 23 games. "Obviously they had the momentum going into the third period having scored the last two goals (of the second), and we just kind of took it away from them.

"You know, we're such a better team when we have the lead because it forces the other team to open up and take some chances, and that plays right into our hands. We have so many skilled guys that can do so many things out there."

When Ottawa's Jason York put one past Mike Richter 23 seconds after Jan Hlavac's power-play goal (which turned out to his his fourth game-winner of the season), and then Daniel Alfredsson scored, it was 3-2.

"They smelled blood a little bit," Richter said.

Earlier this year, that might have been a problem. Indeed, in the Rangers' last two victories they blew third-period leads then won in OT. And last year, well, it would have been a loss.

"There were a lot of things said in the dressing room," Low said. "One of the things was that we're playing a team that's a really solid hockey club."

Low was asked if this game was extra meaningful.

"Yeah, it's two points," he said. "That's exactly what it means. We play six more of these teams in the next six, so we won't go to far unless we can repeat."

The next batch of games will tell a lot about Low's Rangers.

MONDAY, NOVEMBER 27, 2000

RYE, N.Y.

It's pretty much like breaking up Batman and Robin. Low removed Adam Graves from Mark Messier's line late in Friday's loss in Buffalo, and for the entire win over Ottawa on Sunday.

Graves, in a 10-game pointless streak, played just 7:42 of that game on an energetic line with recalled Manny Malhotra and Michal Grosek. The playing time was probably the lowest Graves has ever had as a Ranger. And his break from Messier was only one of a handful of times it has been attempted by Rangers coaches.

Most of those have been met with awful results. Low did it once earlier this season, and after two periods, Graves was back with Messier and flying, his buttons sufficiently pushed by the coach.

Low is hoping, as are all the Rangers—and the fans of the immensely popular Graves—that this is just a slump and not something more serious. And that Graves, 32, will bounce back once again.

"Adam's been a slow starter forever, and I guess at this point in time, I've seen three, four or five of the games he's played were really excellent hockey games and that's not enough for Adam," Low said. "He's a better hockey player than that, much better. He needs a change right now. If you leave it the way it is and it's not working, then somewhere down the line you're going to kick yourself because you left it, if it doesn't change around 40 games from now. So, do it now, and hopefully you'll get a result out of it."

Graves, as usual, said all the right things. He will do whatever Low asks of him, whatever is best for the team, etc. But he defiantly insisted he's not on the downslide.

"I certainly feel confident that I know I can play the game at a high level," Graves said.

That hasn't happened lately. He has been a step late on body checks, a step late getting to rebounds and loose pucks. His play has probably also suffered from the style of play of linemate Valeri Kamensky, who holds the puck a lot, and therefore loses it a lot.

"I don't know if he's going to get out of this slump playing on (that line)," Low said. "Then, yeah, I do feel he has to come off. He has to have a change of scenery. He likely has been watching Mark and Val play, and not playing his game. His game is working the corners and doing a lot of body contact, and then the other part of his game becomes really relevant. Hopefully he can get it done there."

Graves, who has spent time working with the assistant coaches after practice lately, admits he has struggled, that it isn't only his offensive production.

"At times I was in between a little bit, not reading the play, jumping in late. Those are things that have to come naturally. You have to read the play. You can't sit on the ice and say, 'I've got to do this.' You've just got to go out and play."

Messier's winger Sunday was Mike York, who brought a new energy to the line. But it was odd being away from Graves.

"Sure," Messier said. "I mean, I've been playing with Gravy ever since I've been a Ranger.

"But it's not set in stone, who plays with who or who plays where. We've got a different group and it's important to do what's best for the team at any particular time. Right now, Gravy just need to play with a little less pressure on him."

Messier explained that, by pressure, he meant the pressure to score that is, naturally, placed on Messier's linemates.

Messier was asked if he felt Graves would get back to the type of player he has always been.

"I have no doubt," the captain said.

Low likes the way York skates, and also the way he thinks and creates. It is also a chance for York, who lost a lot of his ice time to Messier's return to New York, and a lot of his offensive responsibilities.

"He's an awesome player," Messier said. "He can play anywhere. He's the kind of guy who could play defense if we needed him to. He's got so much speed and smarts. He's a guy on a team that you could put in any situation, no matter what is, and he responds to it. He's really low maintenance, he comes to play hard every night. He's got to be a coach's dream."

NEW YORK

Every one of the Rangers players who answered a question about the frantic style of play in tonight's 7-6 Garden win over the Los Angeles Kings did so with a smile or a giggle or an out-and-out laugh.

Ron Low, though, wasn't chuckling. He managed a grin that barely hid what he went through during this melee of a game, the kind you might expect to see on a pond somewhere, but not on an NHL rink. Not in this era.

"You don't want to know," Low said, when asked what it was like for him. "You do not want to know."

He used the words "crazy," "ridiculous," and "bizarre." He said the Rangers treated NHL scoring leader Ziggy Palffy, who had an easy hat trick, as if "he was a bad player the way we left him alone. It was kind of like that 8-6 game with Jagr."

Low said that after the first period, when it was 3-3, he predicted it would "be 11-10."

Or, as Rich Pilon said, "It's a fun game to watch, but a nightmare for the players and coaches.

"Especially the coaches."

Low is no stranger to games like this; as Glen Sather used to say in Edmonton, never critique the wins, and Low won't.

"I told them I'm burning the tape, and a lot of them are lucky," Low said.

They won't be so lucky if this continues to be a habit. Scoring goals is great, and can be a dangerous weapon. But allowing four, five, six is fatal. Even three a night won't get you to .500 in the NHL.

The Rangers were up 3-0 on three goals in 1:06, the last two in a 13-second span. The Kings were back in it with three quick ones, two of those in 1:01.

There also was the odd and unusual. Most unusual, the Rangers' seven goals came at even strength—they had scored just 39 goals at 5-on-5 in the first 23 games.

There were others, too. Theo Fleury, for instance, was credited with a goal when his slapper beat starter Jamie Storr at 5:50 of the first. However, Fleury corrected the scoring, noting that the shot went in off teammate Tim Taylor, who got the goal. Later on, Taylor set up Fleury's 17th.

The Rangers got two from Mike York, who replaced Adam Graves on Messier's line Sunday; and got a goal and an assist from Graves, who had gone 10 games without a point. They had a goal—temporarily—from Pilon, who hadn't scored in his previous 222 games (!), but that was later changed to Graves, who tipped it. They got two assists from Sandy McCarthy.

They got a goal from Petr Nedved, who had scored just once in his last 31 home games, and none at the Garden in 11 games this season. That one came 13 seconds after York's first goal (which made it 2-0), and after Los Angeles coach Andy Murray called a timeout designed to settle his Kings.

The Rangers' second straight win over an opponent with a winning record pushed them two games over .500 for only the second time in four seasons—the other being when they began this season 2-0.

Palffy's third goal, off a Leetch giveaway and another botched assignment, at 11:55 of the third, gave Low a little more agita.

"We got away with one," Low said. "I'll tell you right now we won't get away with one (tomorrow) like that."

For those who like thrills, the Rangers and Kings meet again December 14 in L.A.

First, things should be a tad different tomorrow, when the Rangers visit the streaking Devils, a team they have not beaten since Mark Messier's first tenure as a Ranger—January 12, 1997—a streak of 19 regular-season games (0-13-6).

GLEN SATHER WOULD NOT comment on Eric Lindros, who has been cleared to return to the NHL, but won't be playing for Philadelphia. All Sather would say is that he hasn't been contacted by Lindros, his family, or his lawyer, Gord Kirke, since the draft in June. Sather would insist on further medical assurance before attempting to make a deal with the Flyers or to negotiate a contract for Lindros who, by the way, will not be covered by the standard NHL insurance. He may be uninsurable, which means his new team will be on the hook for whatever the terms of his contract turn out to be.

THE NHL PLAYERS ASSOCIATION filed a grievance against the Rangers and the Chicago Blackhawks for their waiver deal in which the Blackhawks claimed defenseman Stephane Quintal off waivers, then traded Michal Grosek and Brad Brown to the Rangers for "future considerations" just prior to the season opener. The agreement was made to avoid a clause in Quintal's contract which would add an extra year if he was traded.

MATHIEU SCHNEIDER, who played his heart out for the Rangers last season, despite serious differences with coach John Muckler, then found himself an unwanted free agent, signed with Los Angeles and is having a terrific season so far. Glen Sather didn't even consider bringing back Schneider, having been given some bad advice by somebody outside of New York.

So the Kings defenseman summed it up perfectly when he told the *Los Angeles Times*, "If Neil Smith were still here, I'd still be a Ranger."

TIM TAYLOR SUFFERED a Grade 1 (mild) left shoulder dislocation when he was hit by Kelly Buchberger in the first period, and played the rest of the game. He was told if he's hit on that shoulder before it heals, he could miss 4-6 weeks. Taylor hopes to be reexamined Sunday.

WEDNESDAY, NOVEMBER 29, 2000

EAST RUTHERFORD, N.J.

Mark Messier had tormented the Devils in his first six years as a Ranger. Three times Messier's Rangers faced the Devils in the playoffs, and three times the Rangers eliminated them. Most memorable, of course, was Messier's guaranteed victory in Game 6 of the 1994 Eastern Conference finals. The Rangers were down three games to two, going back to the Meadowlands, when Messier promised victory. Then he scored three goals and an assist in a come-from-behind 4-2 win.

But for three seasons, while Messier was in Vancouver, the Rangers couldn't beat the Devils.

Coincidence, some said. Well, tonight, with Messier back in a Rangers uniform, the Rangers' regular-season winless streak against the Devils hit 20 games (0-14-6) with a 5-2 loss at Continental Arena.

But, it must be noted, that the game was 1-1 until Messier went down with a nerve injury in his left leg. Coincidence? Maybe.

The Rangers, who are 0-10-1 in their last 11 regular-season visits to the Meadowlands, lost their captain, the game, and their two-game winning streak very quickly. The defending champion Devils, who had taken over the game shortly before Messier left, won their sixth in a row.

In the span of about a minute, the game and perhaps the Rangers' immediate future, turned bad.

Messier was hit on the the peroneal nerve alongside his left knee with a shot by his old buddy, Sergei Nemchinov, and couldn't put weight on his left leg, suffering from a nerve malady known as "drop foot." The feeling was gone. At first, Messier thought he broke his skate. He remained on the bench until the next stop in play, then headed to the locker room. On his way, Messier went to wipe something off his skate, and fell hard. He had trouble getting back to his feet, then limped through the Zamboni entrance.

Messier was able to laugh about it later, calling it his leg-flailing backflip onto his back, an "Exit, stage left" move. He said the plan is to take the next couple of days off, and that he hopes to play Saturday.

"I've never had anything like that before," he added.

But two of his teammates have. Brian Leetch got it from sleeping awkwardly in 1997–98, and missed two games. Tim Taylor had it last year, from a slash. He missed no games, but for two weeks he had to have his foot taped pointing up, because he couldn't keep it from falling downward himself.

Sather, by the way, absolutely flipped out when he heard the term "drop foot" announced by the public relations staff.

"Right now he says the feeling is coming back," Leetch said. "He can move his foot. But he's got to be careful with it tonight and see for sure tomorrow. It definitely gets better immediately right away, but then it can stay where it's not functional for a little while."

With Messier gone, the Rangers showed how vulnerable they can be, particularly against teams with big centers.

Moments after Messier left, Petr Nedved had a 2-on-1 break and, as has become the habit of Nedved's line, overpassed. The Devils countered and Jason Arnott stepped into a lead pass from Patrik Elias and blasted it past Mike Richter's glove for a 2-1 Devils lead.

Early in the first period, Messier twice put mean-spirited cross-checks on Bobby Holik after a whistle. For the three years Messier spent in Vancouver, Holik ran roughshod over the Rangers, leaving heaps of blue shirts stewn about. But Holik has always spoken reverently of Messier, almost as if he was intimidated by the Rangers captain.

That little show of force by Messier quieted Holik physically for most of the evening. But Holik was a factor nonetheless. He scored the game's first goal late in the first, which was answered by Manny Malhotra's second in two games in the second. Then after Messier left, Holik manhandled Theo Fleury, who retaliated with a stick across the back of Holik's helmet. Just after Fleury escaped the penalty box, Scott Gomez set up Brian Rafalski for a one-timer from the high slot and a 3-1 Devils lead.

"We broke down," Low said. "When we lose somebody like Mark, we've got to have more resolve."

Low wasn't unhappy with the game as a whole, though. Or, as Fleury said, "It was a big test for us, and I thought we answered the bell."

As for the streak, which is alive and well and actually now covers parts of five seasons (the Rangers last won January 12, 1997), Messier pretended to know nothing about it, or Holik's antics.

Then he invoked the inarguable argument.

"I don't think they're dwelling on us winning three playoff series in the 90s," he said. "We're certainly not dwelling on the fact that the last three years, them beating us. History is history. It's a new year."

VLADIMIR MALAKHOV'S SEASON will end when he undergoes reconstructive surgery to rebuild the anterior cruciate ligament in his left knee.

"He hasn't been here this year so far anyway," Low said. "It's a road block and we've already been over it."

Low said that Malakhov "was likely as good as Brian (Leetch)," through training camp, and that the plan was for him to not only be Leetch's power-play partner, but that Malakhov could have eaten up some of Leetch's overload of ice time by playing 30 minutes a night himself.

"We're really lucky Theo (Fleury) has done the job he's done," Low said of the power-play pointman. "That's the job Vlad was supposed to be doing for us, besides being a big guy who could move people from the front of the net."

Team doctors Barton Nisonson and Tony Maddalo will perform the surgery at Lenox Hill Hospital Friday. The normal recovery period is five-to-seven months.

THEO FLEURY LET Bobby Holik have it after the game. Fleury called Holik an "asshole" and tore into his style of play, adding that he's an example of what the NHL is trying to rid itself of. This time, Fleury's use of the word "asshole" wasn't meant as a compliment.

"He's allowed to do whatever he wants on the ice and there are no consequences he has to pay," Fleury said. "He slashes guys, he hits guys over the head with his stick and they never, ever call it ever. It's an absolute joke. An absolute joke.

"And he doesn't fight. He never, ever fights. I don't understand how they can allow him to play whatever way he wants to play out there and never be accountable to anybody. I just think that if we're trying to clean up the extracurricular activity, well, just show a tape of the way he plays and that's a great example of all those things."

Holik said, "They called me an asshole? No. They've used that before. That's fine."

THURSDAY, NOVEMBER 30, 2000

RYE, N.Y.

The nerve injury to Mark Messier's leg apparently isn't serious.

The Rangers are calling Messier probable for Saturday's game in Toronto. Messier did not need treatment today, as the team took a day off.

MEANWHILE, the grievance filed by the NHL Players Association against the Rangers and Chicago Blackhawks for their October 5 waiver "deal" that sent Stephane Quintal to the Blackhawks while circumventing a clause that would add an extra year to Quintal's contract, is not expected to affect the Rangers. NHL chief legal officer William Daly indicated that he can't see any scenario in which the Rangers are responsible for the extra year; or any in which the "trade" is nullified.

NIGH**6**MARE

Baby Steps

RYE, N.Y.

For four of the last six periods they have played—all three against Los Angeles, and the third period against the Devils—the Rangers have been terrible defensively. Especially the forwards.

"I think it's the 'chicken with its head cut off' theory," Ron Low said. "Of the 12 forwards we likely had eight or nine who were suffering from that disease, chasing (the puck). I think, once the head's off, I don't think there's too much thinking, besides chasing. It likely separated all thoughts from their body."

Low said that trainer Jim Ramsay "started reattaching (heads) this morning."

That isn't the only reason Low believes the Rangers will be better in their own end when they play the top team in the East (in Toronto) tomorrow, and the top team in the West (Colorado) the next night.

"One of the things you can really attribute it to is we haven't had a practice in three weeks," Low said. "I mean, literally, haven't had a practice day. We've been on the ice, where we've been just having a stopover between games. Today's the first practice we've had in I don't know how long, an actual strung-out practice where we've been able to go 45–50 minutes, where guys are trying to do things that we've been poor at lately.

"Guys are back in the zone. That's not the problem. There's nothing being lazy about it. They're just doing bad things. Sometimes you wonder why you'd come all that way back to do some of the things we do when you get back there."

THE NERVE INJURY to Mark Messier's lower left leg has subsided, and he said he has complete feeling back, after skating in practice. Messier, who plans to play tomorrow in Toronto, said all that is left is similar to a bad bruise on the outside of his left knee.

"I'm lucky, I guess," Messier said. "Some guys have gotten some long-term stuff with that."

He added that the original feeling wasn't like pins and needles, but rather as if there was no feeling whatsoever. Messier, knowing that Brian Leetch had a similar injury that kept going away and coming back, said he awoke a number of times the past two nights to make sure the feeling was still there.

Messier, who will be 40 in January, was asked if he feels compelled to try to play all 82 games to answer the doubters.

"No, because age doesn't have anything to do with injuries," Messier said, pointing out that 18-year-old Marian Gaborik of Minnesota and Detroit's Chris Chelios, 39 next month, were both out injured. "There's no discriminating who gets sore. You hope you get lucky. You're going to be sore at times. You just hope you don't get anything that's going to keep you out of the lineup for any extended length of time.

"I think my durability over the years speaks for itself. It's not like I'm trying to prove something, that I can play 82 games and not get injured."

THE RANGERS' POWER PLAY has stalled (1-for-10) in the three games since Adam Graves was removed from Messier's line and, therefore, from the power-play unit. Low said the Rangers didn't get a single scoring chance in five power plays against the Devils.

"Adam being there definitely adds a different look to it. Your shots from the point are definitely being screened and tipped," he said, adding that both Theo Fleury (sore backside, flu) and Valeri Kamensky (flu) weren't 100 percent. "I don't think (Graves's absence) is the problem, and if I do think it is, believe me, he'll be back on it."

VLADIMIR MALAKHOV underwent what the team called "successful" reconstructive surgery on his left knee. He's out five-to-seven months.

TORONTO

Ron Low saw it coming. He saw it all week. He tried to cut it off in practice Friday, too.

Didn't matter. The Rangers paid for their mounting sloppiness and laziness in their own end of the rink. They paid by getting humiliated 8-2 by the Toronto Maple Leafs at Air Canada Centre.

They paid by falling back to .500, and in danger of falling below it with Colorado in town on a roll tomorrow, and with Peter Forsberg expected to return from a ribcage injury.

They paid by seeing their goals-allowed total hit 90 (after 19 in three games), which is three more than their potent offense has scored in 26 games. They paid by having goalie Mike Richter, their savior most of the season and last season, get yanked. They paid again, when Low went into the postgame locker room and gave the Rangers a well-deserved what-for. Low was asked what troubled him the most.

"What didn't? Low said. "It was abysmal. It was the worst effort by our forwards all year as far as defensive-zone coverage."

Then, asked about Friday's practice, which was supposed to stem the tide from the three miserable periods the Rangers played against Los Angeles Tuesday (a 7-6 win) and the awful third period they played in New Jersey Wednesday (a 5-2 loss), Low snapped.

"Oh, I'm sure it must have sunk in real well," he said. "I know it must have gone into everybody's heads and settled in there."

Low told the team, sarcastically, that they could blame the goaltending, and the defensemen.

"The real crux of the problem is not that," Low said, his voice rising a few decibels with each sentence. "It's forwards coming back into our zone that are doing an absolutely terrible job. In fact, four times tonight, guys were standing with guys that scored goals and never touched them.

"We were absolutely brutal in our own zone as forwards. Brutal."

Low paused.

"So what do you tell them?" he started up again. "You tell them that they were brutal. And I mean brutal. And yes, I did. That's the first time I saw anything that was even close to an effort that lacked effort. I didn't think the forwards worked hard tonight. I really didn't. That's the real problem."

The work ethic went bad, and that is one thing that a coach cannot accept.

"It can't keep going on," Low said.

Then, he could go no longer.

"I've said enough," he said. "I've said enough. I don't want to talk about it."

He turned and walked a few feet away from the assembled media, muttering and swearing.

Every single Rangers player was minus on the final stat sheet, an absurdly rare feat.

"It was not a good effort against L.A., but we got away with it," Brian Leetch said. "Tonight there was nothing good going on and we got exposed every time."

"It's hard to say you can see it coming," Messier added. "Mistakes have been compounding. We've been able to score some goals to cover them up in some of the games, but we got flat-out beat tonight. No steering around it tonight.

"That's why you have to instill a system, so when things do go bad like this, you can say, "Okay, let's go back to the drawing board; let's start from scratch and get back to basics, back to the system, back to doing things that were successful for us." So you don't go into a downward spiral. Without it, there's nothing to hang onto."

That's what their coach tried to tell them Friday.

THE PHILADELPHIA FLYERS have scouted the Rangers' games all week. The odds of Eric Lindros actually ever becoming a Ranger lay somewhere between slim and flying pigs.

It simply is going to take too much risk in order to satisfy both the Flyers' trade demands and Lindros' contract demands for it to actually happen. Besides, there are other factors.

Let's say, for argument's sake, that Glen Sather can get Flyers GM Bobby Clarke to agree to take a package of conditional first-round draft picks. For example: The Flyers would get a first-round pick for every year Lindros completes in full health, up to five first-rounders.

Now, let's say that Sather can somehow get Lindros to take a contract that will pay him per games played. For example: $2 million signing bonus, then another million bucks for every 13 games he plays, which could add up to about the $8.5 million he turned down from Philly if he plays a full season. That would put the Rangers' budget—which Sather treats as if it were his own money—at almost no risk.

Sound good so far?

Well, then, how about this? If the Rangers get Lindros, it could preclude them from being in the running for Teemu Selanne, who will probably be dealt out of Anaheim early in 2001. Then there is the super crop of potential unrestricted free agents coming up next summer—Joe Sakic,

John LeClair and Rob Blake among them. If the Rangers have Lindros at a possible $8.5 million or more on their payroll, they probably aren't going to be spending the $10 million or so it will take to reel in one of those other guys. The other guys aren't playing as if every shift, every bump, could be their last.

Clarke, though, isn't going to take a sliding scale of draft picks for Lindros, not when Toronto is offering players and picks. In Toronto, the speculation is that the Leafs are ready to part with a number of legitimate NHL players and at least one No. 1 draft pick.

If the Rangers start dangling players or prospects, or guaranteed picks, they're as nuts as Clarke is, and Clarke is nuts if he thinks he's going to get equal value. If Toronto does offer him a front-line player, he better jump at it.

Sather talks about buying a used car, and making sure you kick all the tires and take it for test rides and have the engine checked before you commit to it. He sounds intrigued, but very skeptical that Lindros can be a healthy player again, or whether it would be a gamble worth taking to get him. However, Sather will explore it. (Sather also has said he doubts that Clarke would actually trade Lindros to the Rangers.)

But this is kind of like the Pavel Bure situation in 1999. Neil Smith made the smart move then.

He decided he could get Theo Fleury, a free agent, without giving up anything in return, rather than Bure, who would have cost him his entire A-list of prospects. And Bure would have cost the Rangers $3 million more a year than Fleury in salary. If Fleury had scored last year like he's scoring now, that decision never would have been questioned by any sane person. Fleury scored 15 goals, though, and Smith was crucified in newspapers and on the radio, and ultimately fired.

So why should Sather give up value for Lindros, who might last one shift, when he can get Sakic or LeClair for nothing but dollars in the summer?

Sather asked the other night, "How long did Pat LaFontaine play here?"

Sather knew the answer was 67 games. He made his point. One hit and LaFontaine's career ended, just as everybody figured it would.

Lindros' over-under is a lot fewer than 67 games. He has suffered six concussions, four of them last year, one on an accidental bump in practice. The first time he got hit after that, he was out for seven months. The next time he gets hit, his career will likely be over.

Imagine that happening while, for example, Jamie Lundmark is a Flyer.

This isn't Eric Lindros the Flyers are peddling. This is an accident waiting to happen. Who needs it? Not the Rangers.

THE JOHN MACLEAN FIASCO included one other item that didn't become public right away.

Sather's buyout offer to MacLean included the stipulation that he couldn't sign with an Atlantic Division team once he became a free agent.

NEW YORK

For those who believe in moral victories, or that a well-played loss is a good step after a string of terrible games, the Rangers accomplished all of that tonight.

For those who believe only in the bottom line, though, the Rangers' 6-3 loss to the Colorado Avalanche at the Garden was their third in a row and dropped them back under .500 at 13-14.

And it wasn't pretty the way they lost it, either.

The Rangers' Mike York had scored what should have been a killer short-handed goal to forge a short-lived 3-2 third-period lead only to have the Avalanche answer with two quick goals for the win, then tack on two empty-netters to make it look like another blowout.

The go-ahead goal came during a dumb penalty by Theo Fleury, who kicked out Jon Klemm's skates during a behind-the-play get-together, a call that probably didn't have to be made, or could have been made against both players.

And while Low was critical of the call, Fleury took his medicine.

"I guess I let my teammates down, and let the coaching staff down," Fleury, who was fired up to face his former team, said. "It's a bad penalty to take and no one feels worse than I do. We worked as hard as we worked in a long time, and we should have gotten a better result."

Fleury was part of the reason the Rangers were even in the game at that point, sending the shot on goalie Patrick Roy on which York scored on the rebound, the Rangers' sixth short-hander of the season and the first not scored by Fleury.

It came during another questionable penalty, on which Rich Pilon was singled out even though he and Dan Hinote were going at it "like two roosters," in Pilon's words. But Peter Forsberg scored moments after Pilon got out of the box to tie it, and Joe Sakic scored during Fleury's penalty to win it.

"We deserved a better fate, than to have it decided by calls," Low said.

Another call that went Colorado's way came when Roy shot the puck over the glass at center ice, and the officials didn't call the automatic delay-of-game penalty because the puck went over the glass where it is lower than it is around the rest of the rink. Never mind that the puck was 12 rows up.

Despite the 6-3 score—which means the Rangers were outscored 25-14 for the 1-3 week—this was their best game in the last four. Petr Nedved, Jan Hlavac and Radek Dvorak were flying, and Nedved and Dvorak scored twice in 1:10 for a 2-1 lead in the second.

They did battle, they were physical, and they were miles and miles better than in Saturday's 8-2 embarrassment in Toronto. Pride had something to do with the bearing down.

"Any time you get kicked as bad as we did (Saturday) there has to be some kind of response," Low said. "And the first thing we did tonight, very well, was take the body all night, and not just one line but all four. That was the difference in the hockey game. The score, at 6-3, means nothing to me. It was how we played it, and we played it very soundly."

Low had reunited Adam Graves with Mark Messier and Valeri Kamensky, who were particularly bad Saturday.

The coach went into the lockerrom afterwards and told the Rangers "for a hockey club that's played as much as you've played for the last three weeks, you played a great hockey game." Then he walked out.

"They did," Low said. "They played very well."

"That's the best team in the league," Fleury said. "We've had a tough schedule and we played really hard, and the guys should be proud of the way we played. We battled back when we were down a couple of times. It was a good hockey game."

The Rangers' best game of the week. For what that's worth.

WEDNESDAY, DECEMBER 6, 2000
NEW YORK

Brian Leetch, Theo Fleury, Mike York, Mike Richter.

They have been the MVPs of the Rangers' season, in whatever order you might choose.

Tonight, those four were pivotal in pulling the Rangers out of their three-game losing streak with a 3-2 win over Washington at the Garden, a victory that pulled them back to .500 at 14-14.

There were plenty of others responsible, too, as there almost always are when the Rangers win or when they lose.

The Rangers scored all three goals on the power play, which was jump-started as usual by pointmen Leetch and Fleury.

Leetch had three assists to tie Jean Ratelle's total of 817 points, which is second on the all-time Rangers list behind Rod Gilbert (1,021); and

Fleury had three assists, about five great scoring chances, and now has a remarkable 39 points in 28 games.

"I hope he gets a lot more," Mark Messier said about Leetch. "I think he's just the ultimate Ranger, coming up through the system, through the draft, playing here his whole career, winning the Stanley Cup in 94. He's what being a Ranger is all about. He's playing just unbelievable hockey this year and he played an unreal game tonight."

As for the latest milestone, Leetch, who joined the top 100 NHL scorers of all-time last week, shrugged and said, "Well, I've been here a lot of years; that's the biggest thing that shows."

The Rangers' power play scored each of the three goals, and two of those were direct results of Adam Graves creating problems for the Capitals defensemen by planting himself in front of the net, something that had been missing when Graves was removed from Messier's left for four games last week.

Messier's line, with Graves put back on the left side Sunday, also got some additional life when Johan Witehall's legs replaced the struggling Valeri Kamensky—who had a recurrence of a bruised kidney that cost him three games earlier in the season—and when York replaced Kamensky on the power play.

The Rangers' power play didn't take much time in scoring its first two goals. The first power play needed just six seconds, and the second one needed just 10 seconds.

At 9:18 of the first, Messier won a draw to start a textbook, set play. Graves tapped the puck back to Fleury, who whipped it across the blue line to Leetch at the left point. Both Graves and York drove to the net, tying up two defenders and allowing Messier to pop open.

Leetch zipped a diagonal pass to Messier outside the right post, and Messier slapped it past goalie Olaf Kolzig for a 1-0 lead.

"It helps to have a guy who can make that pass," Messier said of Leetch. "It's one thing to see the play and it's another thing to execute it."

The Capitals tied it during a 4-on-4 situation, as Sergei Gonchar blasted one past Richter and in off the left post.

But, as the 4-on-4 turned into a Rangers' power play scheduled to be only 12 seconds long, the Rangers scored again. Fleury sent Leetch up the left side, and Leetch deftly one-touched a short pass to surging Petr Nedved (who had jumped onto the ice to replace Dale Purinton as he escaped the penalty box). Nedved streaked to the net and turned Kolzig inside-out, putting a pretty back-hander over the goalie's shoulder for a 2-1 lead.

Late in the period, Leetch got the point that tied Ratelle. Again Graves went to the front, and tied up Calle Johansson. That allowed Leetch's point shot to get through on a screened Kolzig, and also allowed York to get free to bury the rebound for his eighth goal and a 3-1 lead. York also made a couple of amazing defensive-zone plays to help a dazzling Richter preserve the win.

While Richter is one of those goalies who doesn't care if it's 7-6 as long as he's got the seven, it was good for him to put a two on the board for a change, after the Rangers gave up 25 goals in four games.

"For all the right reasons," Richter said. "We have to be able to compete in one-goal games that aren't shootouts as well as in shootouts. It looked like we weren't going to get more than three tonight, and you have to be able to be responsible defensively—not just sit on the lead, but be able to compete and hold the lead.

"It was a very sharp game, and we needed to have it. We had a couple of tough games in a row, and we did get better (Sunday against Colorado), but not enough to win. Tonight there were just no two ways about it. We needed to get a win."

LOW SAID KAMENSKY was passing blood Sunday but didn't tell the anybody because he wanted to play. Kamensky said he told team trainers immediately. Kamensky had an ultrasound test, which was negative, tonight.

MICHAL GROSEK has dived into Low's doghouse.

Low questioned Grosek's intensity and work ethic.

"The big thing about Mike is I'm not sure the passion for the game is there right now," he said. "That's what bothers me most. I don't see that real ferocious drive. That part of the game is a must if you're going to be in a limited ice-time role. The way to get your limited ice time up is to show that you can do that. That's what we need out of Mike.

"Do I have to tell him? I shouldn't have to."

Grosek instead pointed out his disappointment with the limited minutes. He said he thought when he came to New York he would get the ice time he got in Buffalo last year, before he was dealt to Chicago.

"I got five minutes of ice every game," he said. "It's a bad question to ask how I'm playing. I don't think I've played yet. I don't know what is my role. If you put me on the fourth line, you're only going to play six shifts a game. I don't know what you can do with six shifts a game."

Grosek went into a rant that had become typical for him. He played the martyr.

"No points. It's fuckin' terrible. Fuck it, I suck," Grosek said. "Whole fuckin' season, no points. It's a fuckin' joke."

RYE, N.Y.

Rest assured that Low will try to assure more rest for his veteran team in the next few weeks.

Low and several of his players credited a bit of rest for Wednesday's three-game losing streak-snapping win over Washington.

"We played better in our own zone, likely because we had a rest," Low said. "We didn't practice (Monday), and had a very light practice, although it was up-tempo (Tuesday). Guys seemed to get their legs back. That's the most jump Brian (Leetch) has had in a while because he did get rested, and likely the same thing with Theo (Fleury) and guys that are getting lots of ice time.

"You look at rest sometimes and wonder if you should be giving as much as you are. But every time we've had it, we've responded pretty well to it."

The Rangers haven't had much of it lately. The toughest stretch for a hockey player is the three games in four nights, and the Rangers have gone through five sets of those since November 1. Tomorrow they play the second of another three-in-four set, before heading to California for three in four nights there. Then the schedule finally spreads out a bit.

"I think it made a big difference for everybody," Leetch said of the breather Low provided this week. "When your whole team as a group can play a little better, it makes a big difference. The whole team benefited. We could force the play more."

"Just shows what kind of team we have," Fleury said. "We can bounce back when we have to.

Our schedule doesn't get any easier after this, but we have an opportunity now to get above that .500 mark and get that monkey off our backs and put some wins together and make a little bit of a run here."

IF THE RANGERS are going to make any kind of run, they will have to continue to click on the power play, which had slowed down lately before scoring all three goals against Washington.

"Geez, we could have had a lot more, too," Low said. "I mean, we had a lot of great scoring chances that didn't go in the net."

The reason it's so good is the variety of talents—from pointmen Fleury and Leetch to Mark Messier's playmaking from the wall, to Adam Graves and Mike York going to the net. Then, the second wave brings Petr Nedved, Jan Hlavac and Radek Dvorak, who don't set up in the traditional way, but use their speed and creativity. Those three continue to get chances off the rush, which is an unorthodox way to do things with a man advantage.

"Our power play's been good all year, and when you have two pointmen who can really spread the box out and make the plays it makes a huge difference," Messier said. "You know, when they've got four men on the ice, there's got to be something open and we've been able to find the open man quite a bit this year and execute our power play."

OUT OF PITTSBURGH came word that Mario Lemieux, the Penguins' owner, is coming out of his three-year retirement.

"We might see a couple of goaltenders retiring," Mike Richter said. "That is absolutely amazing. How's he going to fit himself into his own budget?

"But, honest to God, I hope he does well. He's such a great player, such a great asset to the league. . . . But I hope he trades himself to here."

What Lemieux's return likely means is that Pittsburgh is now one of the Eastern teams pretty much assured of a playoff berth. Let's see. There are the Devils, Philadelphia, Ottawa, Buffalo, Toronto. Pittsburgh makes six. The team that wins the weak Southeast Division gets in automatically. That leaves one more spot. The Rangers' job just got tougher.

FRIDAY, DECEMBER 8, 2000

NEW YORK

For the second game in a row, the Rangers faced a team that tests your patience and discipline, and for the second game in a row, the Rangers passed the test.

They beat the Buffalo Sabres 5-2 at the Garden to go back over .500 at 15-14, their first home win over the Sabres since October 27, 1996. In their previous seven visits, the Sabres had gone 4-0-3 with three shutouts and seven goals allowed.

The Rangers, however, took care of their own end of the ice and the offense followed against nemesis Dominik Hasek (8-1-4 in his previous 13 against the Rangers).

"That was a heckuva hockey game," Low said. "There was a lot of physical contact and a lot of really sound plays. Our forwards had a lot of jump tonight, a ton of jump."

Brian Leetch moved past Jean Ratelle and into second place on the Rangers' all-time scoring list with his 818th career point, a beauty of a pass to Theo Fleury, who scored his 18th and 19th goals of the season. Leetch now trails only Rod Gilbert (1,021).

The Sabres played their typical game, which is difficult to watch and difficult to play against.

They sit back, clog the middle, don't try to attack much, and hope that their goalie, Hasek, gives up fewer goals than his opponent.

Buffalo forces an opponent to play a patient game, and waits for a mistake to spring a counterattack. The Rangers didn't comply much. They were patient, and they kept their turnovers to a minimum.

"We talked about it before the game, and we thought we played really poorly in their building the last time we played," Low said. "If we could just maintain some kind of presence in our own zone—which we did for the third game in a row—we could get chances, and we did."

"At times we've been guilty of beating ourselves in these types of games this year," Mark Messier said.

The best way to play against a team like Buffalo is to play with the lead and force the Sabres to open up and take some risks.

The Rangers got the lead, but it lasted only 51 seconds. Ex-Sabre Michal Grosek, just a few short steps out of Low's doghouse, had enough jump to be moved early in the game from a checking line to Messier's right.

Grosek slammed Buffalo pest Vaclav Varada, then goalie Mike Richter made a good stick save on defenseman Jason Woolley in the right circle. The Rangers forced the play the other way, and Messier knocked defenseman Richard Smehlik off the puck in the corner. Messier sent a short pass to Grosek, who cut to the net, faked Hasek to the ice and put a shot up high for his second goal of the season and a 1-0 lead. That was Grosek's first goal in 16 games, and first point in 14.

"He hasn't been getting five minutes of ice time (as Grosek said earlier in the week), he's been averaging 11," Low said. "But by the same token, he's been getting dumped on a little bit, and he responded."

A different kind of milestone was reached early in the third as Dale Purinton pinched up the left boards to keep a puck alive, and Mike York slapped Purinton's carom past Hasek for the eventual winner and Purinton's first NHL point. Fleury immediately retrieved the puck for the rookie.

Somebody asked York if it was a big lift to win a game like that.

"It's a big lift when we beat anybody," York said. "Especially when we go on the road for the next four games."

THE SABRES HAD PLAYED on Thursday, and had to fight through one of those terrible Buffalo snowstorms this week, so Theo Fleury offered up an excuse for them: "Maybe they were tired from shoveling their driveways," he said.

THE GARDEN OFTEN HOSTS youth hockey games prior to Rangers home games. It's good for community relations, and it's good for the ice to get scraped up and repeatedly resurfaced by the Zambonies.

Anyway, in a game between two mite teams today, a youngster took an errant stick in the mouth and lost two front teeth. Adam Graves heard about it and, after the kid was treated by team doctors, Graves treated the kid to a tour of the locker room. Graves steered the kid in the direction of Dale Purinton, who cheered him up by flashing a toothless smile himself.

SATURDAY, DECEMBER 9, 2000

BOSTON

Mike Keenan was in the middle of another storm, which is nothing unexpected to those familiar with the Rangers or their former coach.

What is also not unfamiliar is a Keenan-coached team that succeeds despite all that is swirling around him. Keenan's Boston Bruins scored four third-period goals to beat the Rangers 6-4 at FleetCenter.

Keenan reportedly was facing a mutiny of some sort, and there were rumors floating around the FleetCenter that he was close to being fired after just 22 games as Boston's coach. Although details were sketchy, earlier in the day, a Boston trainer, Don DelNegro, quit because of Keenan's tough tactics. At least a few Bruins players then went over Keenan's head, to the offices of team president Harry Sinden and GM Mike O'Connell to request that Keenan be reeled in, or perhaps fired. DelNegro was back on the bench for the game.

Keenan just laughed, waved his hand, and said, "Naah," when asked about the incident. He has seen worse, he said.

Whether this is a major blowup, or just a typical day in the coaching life of Iron Mike, remains to be seen.

The Rangers may be facing a bit of a problem of their own, in addition to the sloppy loss. Petr Nedved will face a league review for a whack he put on the neck of Boston's Joe Thornton in the second period. Nedved, who was only assessed a minor penalty—Thornton got four minutes in the nasty stick exchange—retaliated by chopping his stick downward toward Thornton's shoulder, catching the Bruins center in the neck.

"We started pushing each other and I got off balance," Nedved said, trying to explain why his stick came up, then came down. Colin Campbell, who doles out NHL justice, may not see it the same way. And it might be noted that Nedved was hardly then-coach Campbell's favorite player when the two spent their one season together with the Rangers in 1995.

The tired Rangers—finishing yet another three-in-four nights—came back from a 2-0 hole on goals by Brian Leetch, Valeri Kamensky and Mark Messier, only to see their 3-2 lead disappear in the wild third period. After Jason Allison's goal tied it early in the period, Boston scored three times and the Rangers once in a span of 1:05 late in the third.

And while four of the six Boston goals went in off Rangers (the first two off Rich Pilon's skate, the third off Kim Johnsson's skate and the sixth off Brian Leetch's body) and another went in off the leg of the Bruins' Bill Guerin, the Rangers were still justifiably mad at themselves.

"It seems like if you're not doing the right things, you get fluky goals against you," said Messier, who had a goal and two assists. "After a bit of a slow start, we plowed our way back into the game, but we didn't play well enough to win, and although there might have been lucky or fluky goals, those things happen when you're not doing things correctly."

Low wasn't thrilled with any part of the game, but particularly galled with the start, in which the Rangers managed two shots on goal in the first period (one went in, by Leetch) and with the finish, when the Rangers cut it to 5-4 on Theo Fleury's 20th, and gave it right back.

"That's still not what the game was all about," Low said about the finish. "The game was that we weren't ready to jump out of the gate tonight at all. They came in here, and they got in here later than us last night (after an OT loss in Columbus). There was no excuse for what happened in the hockey game, in the first period.

"We were not ready tonight. For whatever reason, we were not. They deserved to win."

The Rangers fly to California tomorrow for three more games in four nights, starting Tuesday in San Jose, and this wasn't the start to the trip the Rangers envisioned. They are back to .500 after 30 games. Now they face life without Nedved, probably, for a little while.

"There's certain things you need to do in a game in order to win," Messier said. "We didn't do the little things well in the game. We didn't finish our checks as well as we had been. There were a number of things when you look at it.

"And I think we got a little bit of a false sense of security because we found ourselves up 3-2 after two periods. But we didn't really deserve to be up, and we didn't deserve to win the game.

"We never did."

"OBVIOUSLY WE LET a huge chance slip away," Fleury said. "We've really got to play well these next three games."

"These games," added Tim Taylor, "at the end of the year, you just pray you don't look back and hope you need the two points for something, because this was one of the games we should have won.

"We're just at a point where we keep getting closer to get that next step, above and beyond an average team, and we keep putting ourselves back. We're getting closer. We really are all pulling together, and that's the one thing we didn't have last year. We just have to get to the next level. We have to find that next step."

FUTURE HALL OF FAMER Paul Coffey, waived by the Bruins this week, is negotiating a buyout of his two-year, $4.5 million contract. Coffey has said he isn't sure if he wants to play or retire. He said he won't play hockey for a while even if opportunity arises, and instead plans to spend holidays with his family. Sather, who had Coffey in Edmonton, of course, won't rule out the chance that Coffey could be a Ranger even as he approaches 40.

If Coffey doesn't find work, Mark Messier will be the only remaining active member of the Edmonton teams that won four Cups in five years in the 1980s, although there are still plenty of survivors from the 1990 Cup team captained by Messier.

BOSTON'S BILL GUERIN jumped ex-Bruin Tim Taylor at the buzzer after Taylor hit Jonathan Girard. Guerin had him in a headlock, and Taylor was stunned to hear Guerin talking to him. "I'm sorry, but I have to do this because you-know-who is behind our bench," Guerin said.

WHILE SPEAKING WITH THE MEDIA, Mike Richter accidentally tore a button off his dress shirt.

"Jesus Christ, it's one of those days," he said. He wasn't joking.

DESPITE HIS DENIALS, Glen Sather has shopped Theo Fleury around the league, sources insist. However, it will be nearly impossible to trade Fleury, who won't waive his no-trade clause, and if the Rangers attempt a Stephane Quintal-style waiver trick, Fleury most certainly would be claimed. Then the Rangers would stand to lose him and get nothing in return, which would be the worst deal Sather's ever made. And, really, at $6.5 million and on pace for a 45-goal, 100-point season, Fleury's not overpriced.

MESSIER WON'T FLY with the team to San Jose. Instead, he flew from Boston to New York after the game to undergo root canal. He is to join the team tomorrow in San Jose.

SAN JOSE, CALIF.

For years, as he has become more and more of a target for punishment by opponents—particularly one enormous man named Eric Lindros—Petr Nedved has gotten this advice from general managers, coaches and teammates:

"You're going to have to start getting your stick up."

Nedved got his stick up in self-defense Saturday, when he whacked Boston's Joe Thornton across the neck, and late Monday night he learned it would cost him a three-game suspension (the entire West Coast trip) and $56,149.73 in lost pay. Colin Campbell, the former Rangers coach now in charge of NHL justice, handed out the penalty after a telephone hearing with Nedved and Low, among others, Monday.

Nedved began to defend himself, particularly against Lindros, in the past few seasons. Yet, when he failed to fend off an attack by Pittsburgh's Bob Boughner in the final seconds of a game earlier this season, Nedved wound up with a broken nose and Boughner wasn't punished.

"I wasn't really thinking if I'm going to have my stick up that something like this is going to come out of it," Nedved said after the morning skate at San Jose Arena. "With all fairness, sometimes there is a time that you have to do it—and I'm not saying that has anything to do with this incident—but if somebody's going to come down the boards, sometimes you're going to put your stick up and that's just the way it is. Look at the game with Pittsburgh, I'm in front of the net in the last minute and I get my nose broken because . . . I don't know why.

"I saw (Thornton) swing at me, and I tried to protect myself. Don't get me wrong, this is a tough sport. You play through, and this is not me but everybody in the dressing room. It's part of the sport and I don't have one single problem with that. It's just that sometimes you have to protect yourself."

Nedved said his explanation to Campbell was a bit different than his plea the night of the incident, that he was off-balance and his stick came down accidentally.

"I explained what went on," Nedved said. "I think what happened on that whole play, if you watch it closely from the beginning and not just the last thing—if you watch the last thing it's a different story—but what happened down the boards was I hit Thornton with a clean hit and as soon as I hit him, he whacked me in the head with the stick. He came from behind and whacked me over the head and then he gave me a crosscheck in the ribs. We skated away from the boards and he was trying to punch me.

JAMES BAKER, BRUCE BENNETT STUDIOS

Czechmate Petr Nedved, who had a difficult relationship with captain Mark Messier in their first tour of duty with the Rangers.

"I had to protect myself with the stick. I used it as a shield. It came up and I followed through and I hit him in the shoulder and neck area. That's something the league's been watching closely and the sticks can't be flying up high. That's just the way it is. In my mind, I gave him a good hit. He's a pretty big guy and should be able to take a hit, from me anyway."

Low agrees that finesse players, especially those from Europe, are always told to be meaner and tougher.

"Petr has to judge that himself," he said. "I mean, a stick over the head, a crosscheck in the back and a punch in the head, I guess you have to defend yourself at some point in time. And listen, I'll tell you one other thing. You try and get European guys to play tougher because I think they have to for us to be successful. And yet every time they hit a North American, it's a retaliation. Hey, they've been fighting through it. Give them credit, they've been working at it."

Low's plan was to move Nedved's right winger, Radek Dvorak to center, on what would still be an all-Czech line, since Michal Grosek would move up to right wing on that line.

Dvorak, who played center for almost a whole season in Florida when Rob Niedermayer was injured three seasons ago—and for a game and a half under John Muckler last season when he arrived in a trade for Todd Harvey—was looking forward to being able to use his speed in the middle.

Low was just trying to get by.

"Petr's injured," Low said, by way of reasoning. "So, let's not even worry about him for three games. Let's not even worry about it. If we do feel sorry for ourselves, we're going to get our butts kicked out here, and that's not what we came out here for. We have to come out to play hockey, whether he's out, (Mark Messier) is out, (Mike York) is out. We had the possibility of having Mike York (virus) out today, and we're lucky to have him. So look on the bright side; he's not out."

LOW, IN A SLIP of the lip, said, "Mark is a little bit hurt."
That didn't escape any of the reporters gathered around. Nobody knew Messier had an injury.
"What's wrong with him?" Low was asked.
"Nothing," he said. That was that.
Messier, typically, said "I'm okay. Just a little wear and tear. Nothing too sore."

ERIC LACROIX, an honest-to-goodness magician—he can make stuff disappear, and you truly can't figure out where it went—is also a very funny guy.
This morning he was explaining his broken finger and why it's taking long to come back from it.
Simply, he can't hold his stick.
Sandy McCarthy and Tim Taylor were listening to this, and decided enough was enough.
McCarthy piped in, "Why don't you tape your stick to your hand?"
Taylor immediately added the cruelest cut possible: "Yeah, like you tape your gloves to your hands?"
Ooooh. That's about the worst thing you can say to a player, to infer that he won't drop his gloves, that he won't fight.
Lacroix acted hurt. His head slumped and he grabbed his heart as if he'd been shot by an arrow.
Then he went on to explain how he's fought, and against some tough guys, too. He mentioned Darren McCarty of Detroit and Scott Thornton of San Jose. As he said each name, he pointed to a spot on his head, as if there was still some bump as a result, some swollen proof.
"The only fight I ever won," Lacroix said, "was against Brian Noonan. I kicked his ass twice in the same game."

GARDEN PRESIDENT DAVE CHECKETTS flew to San Jose with his public relations man Barry Watkins for tonight's game. The reason for Checketts's pop-in was a golf outing Sather organized for the writers and staff members at his place in Palm Springs tomorrow.

Out in the hallway before the game, Checketts praised Sather. He asked a couple of writers for their honest opinions about Sather, but didn't get much in return. Checketts was just bubbling about Sather's "honesty" and his work ethic, and blah, blah, blah, what a wonderful man he is and what a terrific job he's doing. It all sounded like a back-handed cheapshot at Neil Smith, Sather's predecessor whom Checketts fired last March.

"I have a lot of trust in Glen," Checketts said. "Glen's the perfect guy for this team. He's patient. And he's very realistic about what needs to be done. He's not willing to sacrifice youth to get better immediately. I feel very confident he will be successful.

"I feel very good about this organization. I feel like we have a structure between the coaching staff and the management that works very, very well together and is pointed in the right direction."

Checketts also said, "You can go out and sign every major free agent imaginable and not make the playoffs. We've tried that."

TWO DOWN, literally, two to go. The Rangers' four-game road trip has turned sour very quickly, with two games lost in the third period, including a 3-2 defeat by the Sharks at loud San Jose Arena, one of the best hockey buildings anywhere.

The Rangers again have a losing record, with games in Los Angeles and Anaheim remaining on this excursion, after which the hectic early schedule changes in their favor.

The Sharks got two goals early in the third period—the same period that killed the Rangers when they blew a 3-2 lead in a 6-4 loss in Boston Saturday—to snap a 1-1 tie in what had been a high-speed car-chase of a hockey game.

San Jose's power play got the go-ahead goal after goalie Mike Richter made two terrific stops on Vincent Damphousse. Owen Nolan, who had a big night, carried the puck around the back of the net and got it to Marcus Ragnarsson in the left circle. Ragnarsson squeezed a shot between Richter's arm and his body, and just inside the near post, for a 2-1 lead at 2:29.

The killer goal came at 6:42, and again it followed two huge stops by Richter, the second against Patrick Marleau. Brian Leetch let Marleau get around him, though, to bury the rebound for a two-goal lead.

"That's a key play," Leetch said. "I can't let my guy get to the net, regardless."

What happens when the No. 1 power play meets the No. 2 penalty-killing unit? Mayhem. The Rangers' power play was just run ragged by the Sharks, and it started in the first half minute of play when Valeri

Kamensky drew a penalty to Marcus Ragnarsson 17 seconds into the game.

Kamensky then committed a pair of turnovers, the first of which resulted in two glorious chances, by Marco Sturm and Vincent Damphousse, which were turned away by Mike Richter.

At 1:12 of the first, during the same penalty, Kamensky coughed up the puck again and the short-handed Sharks broke 3-on-1. Jeff Friesen made a perfect pass across the slot to Owen Nolan, who blasted it past the helpless Richter for a 1-0 San Jose lead.

The period, off to a roaring start, turned downright mad after that. There were 2-on-1s, breakaways, back-and-forth chances reminiscent of the 1980s. The Sharks repeatedly gave the Rangers' puck-carriers shots, and chose instead to take away the pass, and yet the Rangers continually chose pass instead of shot, and helped shut themselves out in the first period.

Up in the press box, Tampa Bay general manager Rick Dudley was doing some scouting.

"This is great," he said about the frantic pace of the game. "Do they always play like this?"

Yup, he was told. Just about every night lately. The rematch with the Kings in L.A. Thursday ought to be a beaut.

TODD HARVEY, the former Ranger who was traded to the Sharks in the deal that brought Radek Dvorak to New York last season, had tests on his head this week after slamming it into the ice at the end of a fight with Edmonton's Jason Smith.

"First and only test I've ever passed," Harvey said.

WEDNESDAY, DECEMBER 13, 2000

LOS ANGELES

It would become a familiar theme, not only the late losses or the poor defensive zone play, but also the unwillingness of the Rangers' shooters to shoot.

Nedved, suspended at the moment, and his linemates Radek Dvorak and Jan Hlavac, are the main culprits. Dvorak moved to the middle of Hlavac and Michal Grosek in the first game of Nedved's suspension, and nothing changed.

Low was happy with their play, except for their insistence to pass instead of shoot.

"I definitely know we should shoot more," Low said. "I mean, we've been talking about it all year. It's hard to get the Czechs to shoot the puck for whatever reason. They don't want to shoot it. Devo's got one of the best wrist shots in the game, likely close to Petr, and he won't shoot.

"What are you going to do? Shoot them? I don't know."

Dvorak knows. He has been told time and again to shoot.

"Yeah, we always try to make a pretty play, a nice play, make some pass," he said. "It doesn't work. We have to shoot the puck. If you don't shoot, you don't score. It's pretty simple."

Yet it doesn't get through.

"I don't have any problem with the way we competed, the way we played," Messier said.

"They're a good team. They have some guys that can make some plays and they did. But we also got a lot of chances and I thought if there's anything we could have done better is shoot the puck. We had a lot of chance in the first half of the game to shoot the puck, especially on some 2-on-1s, and we tried to make a play instead of shoot the puck."

Last week, when the Rangers beat Washington to snap a three-game losing streak, Low noted that they had a day off followed by a light practice in the two days leading up to the game, and that the Rangers have responded every time they've been rested this season. Well, today was a day off, for many a day of golf in the Southern California sun, so the Rangers should be energized when they meet the Kings tomorrow in a rematch of their ridiculous 7-6 win at the Garden November 28. That night, what saved the Rangers was their power play, and their willingness to shoot.

THURSDAY, DECEMBER 14, 2000

LOS ANGELES

If all teams played like the Rangers and Los Angeles Kings play when they get together, hockey's attendance and ratings would surely soar.

The two teams met for the second and final time and they played another game that left heads spinning on both benches and throughout the Staples Center, an almost indescribable 5-5 tie.

The game ended with Valeri Kamensky hitting the crossbar in one end, and goalie Kirk McLean, starting for only the second time since October 24, stopping Lubomir Visnovsky on a breakaway in sudden death.

"For a goaltender, it's hell," McLean said about the style of play.

"I was crying," said Petr Nedved, who sat out the second of a two-game suspension and therefore couldn't get in on the offensive action.

The Rangers snapped a two-game losing streak with their first tie of the season.

Low, who had threatened to sit out Radek Dvorak and Jan Hlavac if they didn't start shooting the puck, got three goals from that twosome, and got another shootout against the Kings in a battle of two of the four highest-scoring teams in the NHL.

The Rangers fell behind 2-0 and 3-1, went ahead 5-3 in the third, and saw that lead quickly disappear as Kings captain Rob Blake put up a five-point night (three goals and two assists).

This wasn't nearly as wild as the 7-6 game the two teams played at the Garden Nov. 28, a game that could have been 13-12. The Kings had tightened up since then, winning four of five, and had gotten back injured No. 1 goalie Stephane Fiset, who was 3-0, 1.67 before tonight.

Low didn't like this one much better than the 7-6 game.

"Seeing as we came back from 2-0 and 3-1, it was much different," Low said. "I felt we deserved better than we ended up with."

The Rangers got into trouble early. They put the high-powered Kings on the power play four times in the first period, were outshot 18-5, outscored 2-0 (on goals by NHL leader Ziggy Palffy and Blake) and it could have been worse.

Low decided it was time to shake up some things in the second, and that helped the Rangers get back into the game, then get it tied at 3-3.

Low put Theo Fleury on the Mark Messier-Adam Graves line, put Mike York in suspended Petr Nedved's spot between Dvorak and Hlavac, and demoted Valeri Kamensky.

Tht thinking behind the moves?

"The first period was behind it completely," Low said. "I did not like what I saw. It was emotionless. It had the makings of a Toronto (an embarrassing 8-2 loss) and there's no way that that's going to happen again. Whatever has to happen, if we have to sit five or six guys, you can't let that happen again."

"We've got to cut down a little bit of that erratic play in our zone," McLean said. "Up two goals with 10 minutes left, we should be able to close teams down. We shouldn't give them a sniff."

That's what they were saying last season, when third periods with leads, and third periods that were tied, turned into lost points game after game after game. It was supposed to be different this year, and so far, it really hasn't been different at all.

MIKE RICHTER got a rest after a ridiculous stretch in which he started 18 of the Rangers' last 19 games since October 24.

Last year it was on the Rangers' California swing where the season really fell apart. They were competitive, but lost 2-1 on a third-period goal in San Jose. Richter's 36 acrobatic saves then stole a victory in Anaheim (Jan Hlavac tied it with 1:20 left and Brian Leetch won it 29 seconds into OT). That would be the highlight for the rest of the season.

The Rangers were defeated in Los Angeles the next night, and closed the season with only one more win, going 1-11-2 down the finishing stretch.

This trip shouldn't be nearly as decisive, but it was still extremely important that the Rangers didn't limp home 0-4.

It also became imperative that Richter get a night off at some point, and with the Rangers finishing another three games/four nights stretch with back-to-back games against L.A. and Anaheim.

Richter has looked like he's overplaying shots lately, and has been scrambling back to his net on odd-man breaks, and on shots that sail wide and carom off the backboards. He appears to be just a bit off, which could be a sign of fatigue. Remember, this is a guy coming off major reconstructive left knee surgery, a guy who missed training camp and the first three weeks of the season, and a guy who couldn't play back-to-back games until mid-November.

WITH ERIC LACROIX BACK after missing 11 games with a badly broken finger, Manny Malhotra was scratched. Malhotra, who has been up and down from Hartford of the AHL so far, is having trouble getting meaningful minutes. Low figures to send him back now, so that Malhotra can play. This was an option the team didn't have the last two seasons. Malhotra would have had to go to junior hockey, where he had remaining eligibility, and once he went back to juniors he would not have been able to return. Now Malhotra can go back and forth, and that is best for his development.

DESPITE HIS STANDING NEAR the top of the NHL in goals and points, Theo Fleury is still sometimes burned by his reputation as a player who plays on the edge. Fleury was given a penalty for roughing his boyhood pal Kelly Buchberger late in the game, a phantom penalty Fleury and Low charged. Then, just before OT began, Luc Robitaille punched Fleury after what looked like a clean hit. Robitaille was given four minutes, and Fleury, who didn't appear to do anything, got two. The result was a Rangers power play, but Fleury, a power-play sparkplug, had to spend the two minutes in the box.

"The last, what is it, five games, I've been penalized for working too hard," Fleury said. "Two minutes for working too hard."

"I watched three replays and I still haven't seen it," Low said. "I saw Buchberger run him, and I didn't see the rough anywhere. I disagree with the call."

Low wasn't a fan of the officials at all in that game. He argued one of the Kings' goals.

"We thought it was offside, but it wasn't," Low admitted. "We looked at the replay and it wasn't. That might have been one of the ones they got right."

ANAHEIM

For the Rangers, it's not a matter of the glass being half full or half empty. For the Rangers, it's more like there are two glasses, one brimming full, the other bone dry.

One glass is the Rangers' offense. The other is their defense.

For three seasons before this one, maybe even longer, the Rangers have thirsted for the kind of offense they have now, or any offense at all. They would lose one-goal games galore, lose low-scoring games. And if an opponent got up by a couple, the game was usually over.

It's not that way for the Rangers any more. Trouble is, the game is never over, no matter what the score or who leads, because the Rangers can't stop anybody, either.

After Thursday's 5-5 tie in Los Angeles, a game in which the Rangers trailed by two goals twice, and led by two in the third period, they were back at the top of the NHL in goals scored with 109, and back at the bottom in the league in goals allowed with 114.

There is some comfort for the Rangers now that they aren't out of any game. That's how they felt after the first period Thursday, when they trailed 2-0. They know they can put up five goals on any night, which they couldn't do in recent years.

"Yeah, but we'd rather put five up and win 5-3 or 5-2," said Brian Leetch, who has always been one of those who realized how many of the Rangers' problems were created because they couldn't score. "We've got to give up a few less scoring chances. Too many scoring chances.

"Our goaltenders have played well, and we've given up the most goals."

Mike Richter, who has been fabulous at times, ranks 41st among all NHL goalies with at least 480 minutes played at 3.24 goals-against per 60 minutes. Kirk McLean, the victim/beneficiary in Thursday's game, ranks 47th and last at 3.79.

"We shouldn't have needed to score five and that's the thing in the end," Low said after coaching another heartburn-inducing game, not unlike the 7-6 game the Rangers and Kings put Low through at the Garden last month. "But yeah, it's good that we can score five goals on the road. It's not the first time we've done it, but likely the first time we scored five and walked away with what we wanted out of it."

By the way, fans have been leaving Rangers games home and away in a complete buzz over the type of game they have just witnessed. So have scouts and executives from other teams. The Rangers may or may not make the playoffs. They may or may not have a winning record. But they might be the best show in the NHL.

Low, like most of his players, thinks the own zone problems can be fixed, or at least improved.

And he thinks there can actually be more offense if and when the Czechmates learn to shoot the puck.

Low thought that Hlavac and Dvorak were much better at that in L.A., but he also couldn't help but point out a couple of instances where they tried to pass instead of shoot late in the game.

"But you know what?" Low said. "Baby steps. Thirty-one games in and we're still taking them."

THE WORST PART of the schedule is now over for the Rangers, but unless they learn to keep so many pucks out of their own net, the worst part of the season is still ahead.

The defensively-challenged Rangers, who have no problem scoring goals, closed out an 0-3-1 road trip with a 6-4 loss to the Mighty Ducks at Arrowhead Pond. The Rangers were outscored by a ridiculous 20-15 in the four games, and fell to two games under. .500 for the first time since November 2.

For the seventh time in the last 10 games, the Rangers allowed at least five goals, and this time they needed less than two periods to allow the fifth goal to the Ducks, playing their first game under new coach Guy Charron, who replaced the fired Craig Hartsburg Thursday.

The Rangers, playing a third game in four nights in three different cities, would have had a tough time even if they were able to muster a little defensive discipline. But they couldn't do that, either.

It's not just a matter of the system, or that the Rangers are simply playing run-and-gun, and Low understandably doesn't like the notion that it is.

"You know, there's been a lot of talk about that the last couple weeks, talk that, jeez, we should tighten it up defensively," Low said. "The problem I see with the hockey club is not tightening up defensively. We have our people back in the zone. It's what you do when you get there. I mean, we're forechecking with one guy a lot of times, and we have four guys back in the zone and somebody's walking up the middle and scoring.

"I don't see it being from the system. Our system's there to make guys skate and work hard in both ends of the rink. They're coming back into our zone and they're working their butts off to get there. The question is, what do you do when you get there."

For the second night in a row, they allowed their opponent 18 first-period shots and two first-period goals, and for the second night in a row, it could have been worse.

Mike Richter got off to a horrible start, allowing a goal 33 seconds into the game. Mark Messier let his man, Matt Cullen, get in behind him to score.

The Rangers couldn't even make a player change properly during a 4-on-4, as they were called for having too many men on the ice (they also took three penalties to nullify their own power plays).

AMONG THOSE IN ATTENDANCE was ex-Rangers president/GM Neil Smith, now a Mighty Ducks consultant, who is believed to have seen his first Rangers game live since being fired March 28. Smith kept a low profile, running into a coaches' room down the hallway before he could be seen by any of his former players.

AT THE MORNING SKATE today, Michal Grosek and Bert Robertsson were both acting like idiots, which they have been known to do, when somebody took something a bit too far. Then a playful wrestling match nearly broke into fisticuffs. The few players still around had to break it up, and it was frightening because Grosek was barefooted while Robertsson was still in skates.

DURING NEDVED'S SUSPENSION it became terribly apparent how valuable he is to this team. Nedved started the season slowly, which is not unlike him, but had started to come on lately. The team looks a lot weaker when he's not playing.

So Nedved was answering the inevitable question. He will be a re-stricted free agent in July, and restricted is the key word. He can't go anywhere, because other teams almost never bid on restricted free agents. It's pointless to do so, because virtually every time, the team that holds the player's rights simply matches the offer he gets.

Well, the next Nedved negotiation promises to be ugly in that Nedved—a kid with remarkable inner strength who defected from Czechoslovakia as a teenager—has already forced two trades as a restricted free agent. He missed more than half of 1993–94 in a contract stalemate with Vancouver, which ultimately dealt him to St. Louis late in the season. And in 1997–98, Nedved sat out the entire season rather than take what Pittsburgh was offering, and was traded the next November to the Rangers.

Now, Nedved's contract is due again, and he now has to deal with one of the most fierce negotiators in the game—Sather, who acts as if every penny is coming out of his pocket.

"I keep the cards at my side and I don't think about it," Nedved said. "I don't worry about it. I never negotiate my contract during the season. I would never want to do that. If that were presented I wouldn't say no, but I think it would be a distraction for myself and the team as well. I think there's a time and place when that's going to happen.

"This team, with the high payroll and everything, it's not acceptable to not be in the playoffs, so that's the main thing I'm thinking about. The rest will work itself out."

Might Sather be a potential roadblock?

"I hope not," Nedved said. "I don't see it that way. As I said, I'm not going to think about it. I hope things are going to go smooth for a change, and I don't have to negotiate a contract in October or December or January. I don't really feel like doing that. I've done it a couple of times myself and I sure don't feel like going through the same road. Those things I'm really leaving to the time when they present themselves. And in fairness we have to really see how the season goes and what's going to happen after the season. Weird things happen. I love New York and I hope I'll be playing here for another five or 10 years. But who knows, maybe in the summer I won't even be here."

MONDAY, DECEMBER 18, 2000

NEW YORK

Low said "baby steps" the other night in Los Angeles, and he has used that term a lot when talking about the process his team is undergoing while trying to break a three-year non-playoff streak.

That term would have been appropriate tonight, as well, as the Rangers desperately needed to play a better defensive game and at the same time needed a victory to snap a four-game winless streak.

Baby steps. The defense was better, and the Rangers got their win, 6-3 over the Florida Panthers at the Garden to start a three-game homestand.

"I thought some parts were still scrambly," Low said. "In our own zone we got running around a couple of times. But we created more havoc in their zone than we had on the road trip.

"We could have had a lot more goals, and we had a lot more chances 5-on-5, which was good to see."

If the Rangers are going to get help in the form of a defenseman— and no, they can't really be interested in Paul Coffey, can they?—they will have to wait. As of midnight last night, a holiday roster freeze went into effect until December 27. But one stopgap might get the chance to be a permanent, or at least longer-term fix is Tomas Kloucek, the 20-

year-old who was called up from Hartford Sunday and played an impressive game.

The first game back from a road trip is always difficult, especially so when it's a West Coast trip—except when you're playing a team that has six wins in its first 31 games, and a team that had scored 68 goals all season long.

The Panthers, in other words, were just what the Rangers needed after going 0-3-1 on the trip and after giving up five goals or more an almost unbelievable seven times in the last 10 games. The Panthers themselves were tired, closing out a four-game trip.

The Rangers came in weary, too, none more so than Mark Messier, who is suffering from a bout with the flu for the third or fourth time this season. Messier, exactly one month short of his 40th birthday, has been overtaxed and also playing through some sort of injury.

Oh, yes, he had also been one of their main culprits in the defensive zone lately.

But the Rangers benefited from the return of Petr Nedved, who sat out a three-game suspension during the California trip, and the young legs of Kloucek.

Nedved said he felt especially strong because of the workouts he was able to go through while suspended, the type of workouts a player rarely gets during the 82-game grind.

"I think something good came out of that," he said. "Under the circumstances I thought we played pretty well tonight, and personally I wanted to make things happen for the team because I felt I let the team down with my suspension. So I wanted to go out there and get things done."

Richter made some terrific stops, too, particularly those against Pavel Bure, with whom his career will always be intertwined. Bure had a single assist, and no goals on four shots.

Low was asked why the Rangers, winners in five of their last six at the Garden, play so much better at home than on the road.

"Jeez, we weren't talking about that a little while ago, were we?" he said.

No, they weren't.

TUESDAY, DECEMBER 19, 2000

RYE, N.Y.

When was the last time the Rangers needed a permanent fix for a hole in their roster and they called upon a 20-year-old?

Maybe Don Maloney in 1979?

Well, defenseman Tomas Kloucek is no lock to win a permanent spot on the Rangers defense, but Low plans to give him a chance to do so. Low, unlike his predecessors, isn't using Kloucek as a last resort. He's using Kloucek because he thinks there's a chance the kid can do the job.

Kloucek, who was with the team earlier this season, was recalled Saturday from Hartford, where he had played his way onto the AHL All-Star team. Low promised him ice time against Florida and he got it—23 shifts for 18:31—in an impressive performance.

The Rangers need to be able to play their third defense pair, and with tough-and-willing Dale Purinton on that pair, Low had pretty much pared his defense to four at crunch times in games.

Purinton, for all the progress he has made, can't play 18 minutes at this level.

If Kloucek succeeds, it might fill a void internally, rather than forcing Glen Sather to sacrifice assets in a deal for a more established defenseman like Phil Housley or to sign absolute-last-resort Paul Coffey.

Low, who has a way with young players that John Muckler lacked, would love to see that happen.

"Yes I would," he said. "I think it would be great if he could do that for us. First of all he's 20 years old. He has tons of energy. If you watched the game, he didn't drop off as the game went along. He was hitting people as hard in the third as he was in the first. And yeah, I would. I'd love to see him be able to step in and do that because he'd be a huge boost to us back there. The thing that was really good about him was the physical part."

What makes Kloucek such a top prospect is that he can do a little bit of everything on defense.

He's big (6-3, 220) and terribly strong, yet he's mobile, handles the puck well, and is smart.

Mostly, he's not rattled easily—which opened eyes last year when he debuted in the minors as a 19-year-old logging tons of ice time and earning AHL all-rookie team honors.

The Rangers are certain he will be a regular NHL defenseman. It's just a matter of when.

"I thought Kloucek was a big plus for us," Mark Messier said. "He was probably more ready to play than he was in the past. It's funny, he obviously has all the skill and size and strength and everything else. It's just, when is he going to be ready at this level? Mentally he's got to be ready, and if he is, the skill level is there. Obviously, he's physically ready to play. He just has to understand that it's playing for keeps up here, and if he plays like he did (Sunday) he can help this hockey club."

The 1998 sixth-round draft pick turned a bit shy when asked if he felt he is ready to make the jump permanently.

"Sure, I guess I feel good," he said. "It's the coach's choice."

The speed of the NHL game, he added, isn't a problem.

"I can handle the speed," Kloucek said. "It's a big difference, but it's a bigger difference when you come from juniors to the AHL. I can handle it, but the first few minutes is the worst."

Low said Kloucek was outstanding against Florida, and that the kid might have become tentative in his first stint with the Rangers after being physically beaten off the boards by Vancouver's big Todd Bertuzzi. Kloucek's passing suffered as his confidence waned, and he was sent back to Hartford after limited minutes.

"Tonight he made good passes, made good selections with the puck," Low said Sunday night.

"If there was nothing there he just flipped it up off the glass and got it out. He was just a lot more stable the second time through. And one thing we didn't do is we didn't limit his ice time. We wanted to play him and see how he was going to react to ice time. He did a very good job. He also was very strong killing penalties. Very strong."

WEDNESDAY, DECEMBER 20, 2000

NEW YORK

Okay, so the Rangers felt their 6-3 loss to the St. Louis Blues was a lot closer to the one-goal game it was for 11 seconds late in the third period than to the 4-0 score the Blues held with less than 12 minutes left.

Maybe it was. They didn't play terribly. They certainly didn't play soft. Defensively they have been much, much worse. Offensively, well, nobody does anything offensively against St. Louis, although Ron Low believes the videotape he will watch tomorrow morning will show that the scoring chances were close, if not slightly in favor of his team.

But it was 4-0, and moments after the Rangers got late goals from Petr Nedved, Michal Grosek and Mark Messier to make it 4-3 with 2:58 to go, Michal Handzus banked one in off a Ranger to put them away. Then Pavol Demitra finished off a five-point night—the second in four games by a Rangers opponent—with a hat-trick goal into an empty net.

The Rangers treated it like another one of those moral victories—not unlike the loss to Colorado at the Garden a few weeks back, or the one-goal loss in San Jose last week, or the 2-0 loss to Phoenix earlier, or the one to the Devils at the Meadowlands. They battled, yes.

Yet they played another elite team and had a chance to win the game, or tie it, for 11 seconds.

Again, there's no shame in losing to the team that now has the best record in hockey, a team that hasn't lost in 10 games (9-0-1), a team that has allowed an unbelievably stingy 59 goals in 30 games, has killed off more than 90 percent of opposition power plays and has lost four times all year (22-4-4).

"Our hockey club played fine tonight," Low said. "I don't have any fault with the way they played. None."

There may have been a few additional woes along the way. For one, Rich Pilon suffered a probable concussion—that's what it always turns out to have been when the team's official word is "he had his bell rung"—on a high hit by Dallas Drake in the first period. Pilon and Low both believed it was an elbow by Drake, and the league will surely take a look at it.

With Dale Purinton going on injured reserve yesterday with a subluxed rib suffered on a collision with Todd Harvey in San Jose last week, and aggravated in a get-together with Jim Cummins in Anaheim, and thus doubtful for Saturday's game, the Rangers might need an emergency re-call from Hartford.

Glen Sather's search for a defenseman via trade (he may have one ready to be finished, pending the end of the holiday roster freeze December 27) probably got stepped up.

The league may also review an incident involving defenseman Brad Brown in the third period. Brown, who had two mix-ups with heavy-weight Reed Low, the second of which left the St. Louis rookie bloody, got fed up with Blues superpest Tyson Nash late in the game. Nash sucker-punched Brown, and Brown chased him down and returned the favor several fold—a cross check, a punch from behind and a game miscon-duct that piled Brown's total for the game to 34 penalty minutes.

The league isn't tolerating blows to the head these days, and while Brown will probably escape,he might not.

The bigger problem is that of Mike Richter, who took responsibility for the loss. For the last two games he has been allowing big rebounds, two of which ended up in his net.

After starting for the 21st time in 23 games, he admitted fatigue.

"Maybe he's played too much," Low said. "It's something we're likely going to have to address."

"Personally I felt I just didn't play well and that's the difference in the game," Richter said. "I didn't make the saves I had to. When we battled back to make it 4-3, they got a lucky bounce, but somewhere along the way you have to save a few more.

"I was tired. I just didn't have a lot of jump in my legs. You're going to have those games and you have to play through them."

He said he never considered sitting it out last night, because all players go through tired periods and "you have to play through it. . . . you have to try to."

SEVERAL RANGERS SAID they believed Reed Low, the rookie making quite a pugilistic reputation to himself, broke his sinus bone in his fight with Brad Brown. But, even as he bled profusely into a towel in the penalty box he refused to leave, they felt, because he would draw the reaction of the 18,200 in attendance as he skated across the rink to the locker room with the bloody towel.

Also, Brown had got a few congratulatory phone calls from friends in the league for punching out Nash. There aren't many players in the game more despised, on the ice, than Nash.

FRIDAY, DECEMBER 22, 2000
RYE, N.Y.

Eddie Giacomin's team record for wins is safe, at least, until New Year's Eve. Goalie Mike Richter, just two victories shy of Giacomin's record of 266, won't play the next two games.

"I think he needs a rest," Low said simply.

As a way of making sure Richter gets that rest, the Rangers placed him on injured reserve, retroactive to Wednesday's loss to St. Louis. He will be eligible to return for Thursday's home game against Atlanta.

Until then, rookie Vitali Yeremeyev, headed for the AHL All-Star game with his 1.81 goals-against average in Hartford, will be the Rangers other goalie with Kirk McLean. Low wouldn't say whether Yeremeyev would play tomorrow's matinee against Nashville or Wednesday in Carolina, or neither.

Low said that the reason Yeremeyev wasn't called up in time for today's practice was, "because we didn't realize that Mike had a little swelling on his knee until this morning."

Richter, however, insisted it wasn't the knee, but rather the overall body fatigue, that has bothered him recently.

"My leg's fine," he said. "I have no real problem with my knee. I just think I could have been a little bit better at anticipating spots where I could have maybe taken some rest on my own, figured it out. We had a pretty grueling schedule in the last five or six weeks. ... There's times when it's smart to take rests here and there. . . . He (Low) said "It's a good time to do it. We have days off anyway. You miss two games, you get a week's rest."

Low made this decision, based on Richter's public comments Wednesday night.

"I did discuss it with him, and I'm not sure how much of it was a discussion," Richter said.

"He presented it as this is what we're thinking of doing, but he could have used past tense. But you feel pretty comfortable with somebody who . . . doesn't have an agenda other than to have the best chance of winning."

Low isn't concerned that this might be a long-term problem.

"No, I'm not at all," he said. "I'm likely worried more about, I think there's been a little mental fatigue set in here in the last 8–10 days. I saw a great game from him in San Jose. In Anaheim I thought he was not great. Against Florida he worked his way through it, and the last game I thought he was tired. That's the first time I've seen what I consider to be a tired goaltender.

"He, physically, said he felt tired that day. That's an indication that you're due for a break."

Richter has said that he would prefer to play through fatigue, because every player faces that pitfall during the season. But Low wants him to be more up-front in the future. Richter said that he has never, and will never, ask out of a game because he's tired, but that he can pick his spots for rest in the practice schedule, etc.

"I think it's something we're going to have to monitor, and it's something he's going to have to be pretty honest with us as a coaching staff and trainers," Low said. "If you feel fatigue, if you do, we're going to have to know. But he told me that that was the first day he felt that, real fatigued."

Low added that he was happy with the way Richter had come along so far.

"I swear I didn't expect anything from him before Christmas, to be honest with you, from a guy with a reconstructed knee," Low said. "I've never been around a goaltender who had it done, but I know for players, at four months after they start playing they start getting back to normal, generally. So, yeah, I was really surprised and pleasantly so."

Richter joked that he was just making sure he'd be ready for the team's skills competition (January 7), well aware that it was at the All-Star game skills event in Toronto that he tore his anterior cruciate ligament last season.

And while Richter said he'd welcome the chance to participate in an All-Star game, and another skills competition, "I seem to have, in the last few weeks, pretty stealthly, took myself out of worrying about that this year."

THEO FLEURY, whose name keeps coming up in a rumored blockbuster with Phoenix in which the Rangers allegedly get Keith Tkachuk and unsigned goalie Nikolai Khabibulin, was again asked today if he would, under any circumstances, waive his no-trade clause, even to be united with his buddy, Wayne Gretzky in Phoenix.

"No," Fleury repeated in a millisecond.

AFTER PRACTICE, Adam Graves and a few teammates (Mike Richter, Brian Leetch and others) were headed to Manhattan and a restaurant named Cronies. Graves, who seems to have a charity event or a hospital visit on his schedule every day, has headed up a Toys for Tots drive around Christmas, and it has grown. Now Graves and whatever teammates he can round up spend three days—one in Brooklyn, one in Westchester and one in Manhattan—trading their autographs for Christmas toys for underprivileged kids. Normally the lines go around the block, and Graves & Co. will stay hours longer than they were scheduled.

Today's stop brought this year's total to more than 15,000 toys collected. That's 15,000-plus smiles on December 25, and that, says Graves, "is what it's all about."

The Rangers and the Garden are a charitable bunch. They will hold a ton of events during the season, which eventually will include:

- More than $60,000 raised for Ice Hockey in Harlem benefiting inner city kids (Manny Malhotra is the Rangers' spokesman);
- More than $80,000 raised for Family Dynamics, providing support and programs for single-parent families and prevention of child abuse (Graves is the Rangers spokesman);
- More than $100,000 for the Exchange Club Child Abuse Prevention Center of Westchester;
- More than $550,000 for The Ronald McDonald House, a home for children with cancer and their families while undergoing treatment (Brian Leetch and Hall of Famer Rod Gilbert are co-spokespersons);
- More than $185,000 for NYR SKATE and The Christopher Reeve Paralysis Foundation (raised in the team's SuperSkate skills competition and celebrity game, in-house silend auctions, raffles, etc.

It was announced that four Rangers prospects, including Pavel Brendl (Czech Republic) and Jamie Lundmark (Canada) will compete in the World Junior championships in Russia December 26-January 5.

NEW YORK

Here's a new one. The Rangers lost on a penalty shot in overtime, and to the best of anybody's knowledge that had never happened before in the history of the NHL.

At least it hadn't happened since 1942—the last year overtime was used for tied regular-season games until OT was reinstituted in 1983—and it certainly has never happened in the playoffs.

The Rangers, though, weren't interested in history after their 3-2 sudden-death loss at the Garden to the Nashville Predators, on David Legwand's penalty shot back-hander past goalie Kirk McLean with 3:17 gone in OT.

They could argue that the penalty shot should not have been called by referee Terry Gregson, because rookie Tomas Kloucek didn't actually pull down Legwand, and because Legwand did send the puck toward the net on his breakaway, a puck McLean had to stop whether it was a legit shot or not.

They could lament that Mike Richter, who is 11 for 12 in stopping penalty shots in his career, was in street clothes, being rested, and that if he were in there, this wouldn't have happened. McLean has now stopped two of six. They could second-guess themselves for having Kloucek on the ice, even though it really is a no-lose situation—the losing team gets a point in the standings, just as if it had tied.

But what really pained the Rangers, the taste that will stick to their tongues as they have their holiday meals, was a blown 2-1 lead on, of all things, a short-handed goal with 1:43 left in regulation.

It should never have come down to the penalty shot.

"You wouldn't think so," Mark Messier said. "You get a power play with a 2-1 lead, with a chance to increase the lead to 3-1 or (at worst) run the clock out. That's a tough way to lose a point."

It sure made everything else that happened, or didn't happen, less important. The Predators trapped the daylights out of the game, outshot the Rangers 41-28—though most of their chances were from the outside—and, as expected, worked their fangs off. The Rangers weren't horrible, weren't simply guilty of looking past a third-year team that had never beaten them (and still the Rangers haven't officially lost to Nashville according to the silly NHL standings format which rewards overtime losses).

"A power play, with two and a half minutes left, we shouldn't give up goal," Brian Leetch said.

"Regardless of what went on the rest of the game, they shouldn't have scored there. It doesn't really matter. With two and a half minutes left, that's pretty much the game there. We're looking to get two points and go on the break, and it all boiled down to those two and a half minutes."

Ironically, it was Kloucek who drew the penalty to Marian Cisar that put the Rangers on the late third-period power play. But, even after Low warned his players that the Predators would be sending all four players up ice in the short-handed situation if the puck was turned over, in an effort to try to tie the game, that is what happened.

Valeri Kamensky stopped skating in the neutral zone and let his man, Scott Walker, walk into the circle unchecked. That is exactly where McLean kicked a Tom Fitzgerald rebound, a spot that should have been very safe. Instead, Walker ripped it through McLean to tie.

"Val started off with Walker and ended up, stopped skating a little bit in the neutral zone, and Walker kept going," Low said. "That's why they got the goal."

Then, in OT, Jan Hlavac made a dangerous pass to Kloucek at the blue line, the puck hopping over the rookie's stick. Legwand broke away, and Kloucek caught him, tied him up, and was called for the penalty shot.

"It really is irrelevant," Low said about whether the shot should have been awarded, the point being that the Rangers should never have been in OT.

Low admitted that, since the Predators are a Western team, the point they got was insignificant to the Rangers, so they were going for the point themselves, as they should. If it had been a conference foe, or a division rival, Kloucek might not have been out there in OT.

INCIDENTALLY, IN THE WAKE of Legwand's historic penalty shot goal in overtime against the Rangers, it's worth noting that all five OT penalty shots since sudden death was re-introduced in 1983 have had ties to metropolitan area teams or former New York/New Jersey. Ex-Ranger Luc Robitaille was stopped by ex-Devil Sean Burke in 1989; the Rangers' Tony Amonte was stopped by ex-Islander Kelly Hrudey in 1994; Hrudey stopped Sergei Fedorov in 1995; and the Islanders' (and ex-Ranger) John Vanbiesbrouck stopped the Devils Patrik Elias' earlier this season.

THE CLOSING OF THE SALE of the Phoenix Coyotes to Wayne Gretzky's group is expected by December 28. At that time, Gretzky and the Sather are expected to get serious about a trade which would include unsigned goalie Nikolai Khabibulin, and could include power winger Keith Tkachuk.

ADAM GRAVES, who had scored five of the Rangers' last 11 OT goals coming into this season, didn't get a shift in OT today.

GRANTED, THE RANGERS' SCHEDULE has been brutal since November 1. But the excuses should be gone now. After their trip next week through Dallas and Phoenix, the Rangers will leave the eastern time zone once, and will play just two games on the road against the Western Conference—at Nashville and Columbus. This year they will not have to visit Detroit, Edmonton, St. Louis or Colorado—four probable losses being taken off their schedule.

RALEIGH, N.C.

With Glen Sather poised to start dealing, and with Wayne Gretzky about to become, finally and officially, the guy calling the shots in Phoenix, rumors of a Sather-Gretzky swap are flying.

However, some things have become apparent in the last few days. One of those is that Chicago, very interested in acquiring both Keith Tkachuk and Nikolai Khabibulin, could be dangling Tony Amonte. That opens up the possibility that the Rangers will get involved in a three-way, or in a subsequent deal, to reacquire their former winger.

However, Gretzky may not be as willing to deal Tkachuk as he is to trade unrestricted free agent-to-be Jeremy Roenick, and he would rather see Khabibulin land somewhere besides either Chicago or New York.

Jamie Lundmark, the Rangers' top prospect, is believed to have dropped a rung or two in the eyes of the Rangers' brass, and could be available, as would be Manny Malhotra. Lundmark, however, opened some eyes with a dazzling three-assist game in Team Canada's tournament-opening 9-0 win over Belarus at the World Junior Championships in Moscow.

A LOT OF NHL TEAMS, and coaches, see the Christmas break—the NHL is closed December 24 and 25—as some sort of a benchmark in the long season.

Not Ron Low. He has set next week as the "break" in the Rangers' season.

After games tomorrow in Raleigh against Carolina, and at home the next night against Atlanta, the Rangers play four straight games against top contenders (Dallas twice, Phoenix and the Devils), and that will take them through the 41-game halfway point of the season. That set of games begins with a New Year's Eve game in Dallas, followed by four days in the desert and a game in Phoenix.

"I'm looking more at our break being Dallas-Phoenix," Low said.

"That's 41 (actually 40) games. That's part of the year where we'll be able to have practice that means something, where we'll be on the road, and still going to be able to give guys a little bit of time to kick back and relax a little bit. That's the halfway point. To me, that is our halfway point."

After the Phoenix trip, the Rangers will leave the Eastern time zone once, for a game in Nashville, and play only one other Western team on the road—Columbus.

ROGER NEILSON, the ex-Rangers coach, used to tell a story about how difficult it is to play around Christmas time. Neilson says his junior team in Peterborough once had to play Christmas Eve. "We lost 11-0, and we were lucky to get the nothing," Neilson said.

JUST WHEN IT SEEMS the Rangers have seen their last Wayne Gretzky ceremony comes word that the Coyotes are planning a pre-game introduction ceremony of Gretzky as owner prior to the Rangers' visit January 4.

<hr>

WEDNESDAY, DECEMBER 27, 2000

RALEIGH, N.C.

Because Glen Sather was getting itchy to make a trade, because the Atlanta Thrashers were ahead of them in the standings, and because the next four games after tomorrow promise to be difficult if not impossible, tonight's game was more important than it should have been for the Rangers.

Now, after their 4-3 loss to the Carolina Hurricanes at the Entertainment and Sports Arena, tomorrow's game against the Thrashers has become enormous.

The Rangers, who have won just once in their last eight games and three times in their last 13, overcame a 3-0 deficit only to lose on a goal by Rob DiMaio with 4:09 left in regulation.

"Just losing games, I think, is concerning right now," Mark Messier said. "We've got to get some points. At the clip we're going right now, it's not going to be enough in the end.

"It's going to get nothing but tougher for us, too. You know, teams are starting to tighten up. Everybody's starting to get their teams set now, and we've got to match that."

After their "showdown" with the Thrashers (a point up with two games in hand), the 10th-place Rangers play Dallas twice, Phoenix and the Devils in their next four games. Gulp.

The Rangers again were betrayed by their special teams with a power play that went 0 for 5 and is now 0 for its last 18, and a penalty-killing group that allowed two goals on Carolina's first two chances. They were again betrayed by a defensive breakdown and a missed assignment late, as they were Saturday when a 2-1 lead late in the third turned into a 3-2 overtime loss to Nashville.

This time they had to battle back from a slow post-holiday-break start and a 3-0 deficit to tie it, only to see one point, maybe two, go up in smoke again.

DiMaio, traded by Sather over the summer with Darren Langdon for Sandy McCarthy, scored an uncontested goal as the Rangers stood and watched Glen Wesley's wide dump-in shot carom out to the side of the net. Martin Gelinas, who scored two goals earlier, fed it to the front, and DiMaio knocked it past goalie Vitali Yeremeyev, making his NHL debut in relief of Kirk McLean.

What made that goal extra frustrating was that Petr Nedved, playing with a sore groin that got worse in the third period, was off the ice having a skate repaired. Tim Taylor had to jump into Nedved's spot, ice cold after sitting almost the entire period, and DiMaio got away from Radek Dvorak, then Taylor, to score.

"We need to win." Brian Leetch said. "We've been letting things slide a little bit here. In back-to-back big games that we needed points in, and we wanted to win both of them, we didn't get the job done in the third, so we've got a real important game tomorrow."

The Rangers struggled in their first game back after a two-day holiday, and with two of their top players at well under 100 percent. League scoring leader Theo Fleury was a gametime decision because of a bad case of the stomach flu that has ripped through the Rangers locker room, and Nedved not only has the sore groin, but has lost three pounds from the same flu.

Starter Kirk McLean allowed a fluky goal just 2:59 into the game, a 50-footer by Jeff O'Neill that went up off McLean's blocker and floated slowly over his head and into the net.

The third goal not only made the hole bigger in the second, but it cost the Rangers Tomas Kloucek. Gelinas's deflection went in off Kloucek's right cheek. He had x-rays which were negative, and a cut under his right eye.

"The last two games, we're up 2-1 with two and a half minutes left and didn't get the win, and we're tied going into the third and don't come up with a point tonight," Leetch said. "We're just not getting the job done at key parts of games."

Which makes this a key part of the season, a season that is getting late quickly.

THE NHL'S HOLIDAY TRADE moratorium ended at midnight. The rumored trade of Carolina's Rod Brind'Amour to the Rangers isn't happening, especially since the Hurricanes want either Mike York or Petr Nedved instead of Manny Malhotra, and even Nedved might not get it done. Remember, the Hurricanes dealt Keith Primeau for Brind'Amour less than a year ago, so they aren't giving him up for prospects. Besides, Brind'Amour suffered a leg injury in the second period tonight and did not return.

On another front, L.A.'s Rob Blake has said he will not sign a new contract if he is traded, so don't look for the Rangers to be in the hunt to rent the free agent-to-be.

FIRST IT WAS THE Yankees-Mets Subway Series that took New York's attention away from the Rangers. Now it's the football Giants and their run to the Super Bowl.

The bandwagon is getting big, and one of the passengers is Michal Grosek, who learned to love football in Buffalo.

Grosek's favorite part, not surprisingly, is the tailgate parties, or as he calls them, "party tails."

"Fucking coooook out," Grosek said loudly, stretching his words in his thick Czech accent. "Drink beer. Yell! Fucking awesome!"

THURSDAY, DECEMBER 28, 2000

NEW YORK

Before tonight's crucial game against Atlanta, Valeri Kamensky came out into the hallway outside the locker room looking for Ron Low. It was getting close to 6 P.M., the time for the usual team meeting.

Kamensky found Low schmoozing in the hallway.

"Meeting?" Kamensky asked.

"No," Low said. Then he said to nobody in particular, "You'd think these guys would be fuckin' sick of my meetings by now."

With the threat of a major snowstorm forecast for the Eastern part of the country, the Rangers switched up their plans and chose to fly to Dallas tomorrow morning for their New Year's Eve game against the Stars.

NO MATTER HOW MUCH of the season the schedule claims to have remaining, this season is in danger of slipping through the Rangers' fragile hands, and very soon.

They now face the daunting task of having to at least slow their downhill snowball trip in the next four games, against some of the best opposition the NHL has to offer, including three games against the two teams that fought for the Stanley Cup in June.

It could be deemed ridiculous that the Rangers were playing such a crucial mid-season game with playoff implications against the Atlanta Thrashers.

It is certainly even more completely inconceivable that the Rangers could find a way to lose that game, on Garden ice, 4-1. The highest-scoring team in the NHL was nearly shut out in an important game by a team that is a year and a half old, by a team that is now over .500 for the first time in its brief history.

After one of their more pathetic technical performances of the season, the Rangers (the Thrashees?) have won just once in their last nine games and three times in their last 14. They are four games under .500 for the first time since last season's disgrace ended. And lest one forget, these last three losses have come at the Southern hands of Nashville, Carolina and now Atlanta.

Now, with this season threatening to get away, they face the big boys—Dallas twice, Phoenix and the Devils—in their next four games.

"It's going to be very difficult, where we're going," Low said. "Maybe that's a good thing. We're going to have some time on the road here with a hockey club that has a bad feeling about itself right now.

"They've played some really good hockey the last five or six games and not come away with anything, and that's discouraging. Maybe a little time on the road will do some good to them."

They need something, because they got a point (one of those OT loss points) against the Predators, and zip against the Hurricanes and the Thrashers.

"We haven't had a lot to hang our hats on the last couple of weeks," Mark Messier said. "Two games we needed to win desperately and never won, so obviously there's some cause for concern.

"Like I've said, the proof is in the pudding. We needed to win two games and didn't. You can analyze it any way you want."

When asked, Messier wouldn't say whether if he's satisfied with the level of acceptance of such results among his teammates.

"That's not for me to say publicly," Messier said. "If there is an issue, we address it as a team, not publicly."

But Brian Leetch said the problem isn't in the attitude, the acceptance, or the emotion.

"It's not the emotion," he said. "It's the execution. Having every part of your game going every night. I think our approach is OK, but our execution for the whole game hasn't been there for a while, really, since the San Jose game.

"There's a lot of season left, but you don't want to keep falling behind and have to put a huge streak together," Leetch said. "You want to keep within striking distance."

Low scoffed at the notion that all the trade rumors swirling had an effect on the team.

"Those excuses there . . . excuses are for losers," Low said. "This is the National Hockey League. Wake up. I mean, there's no way that's got any bearing on the way we're playing right now. Not a chance."

THE RANGERS ADDED some depth to their defense, but some more years to their aged roster, acquiring 36-year-old defenseman Alexei Gusarov from Colorado for a fifth-round pick in the June draft. Low said Gusarov is a "depth" guy, in other words, an insurance policy in case one of their current six gets hurt or slumps badly. Low insisted that 20-year-old Tomas Kloucek's ice time will not be effected by the addition of Gusarov, who is a good-skating puck-moving, defensive defenseman known as "Steady Eddie" by his former Colorado teammates. Gusarov arrived during the game.

Rangers assistant GM Don Maloney said that Sather is still burning the phone lines trying to make more deals.

SUNDAY, DECEMBER 31, 2000

DALLAS

Happy New Year? Hardly. Remember when everybody jumped on the hype about what a disaster Y2K was supposed to be. Well, the year 2000 turned out to be just that for the Rangers, who closed out the calendar year in perfect fashion, a humiliating 6-1 loss to the Dallas Stars at Reunion Arena.

The worst defense in the NHL (146 goals allowed in 39 games) had an abysmal night, as Joe Nieuwendyk joined the growing list of players to post hat tricks against the Rangers.

"I think a lot of guys have to have a reality check right now," furious coach Ron Low said.

"That was one of those efforts that I thought was borderline "no-try" by some people.

"I don't know if the effort was there and that really does bother me."

Asked if the team had quit, or if players had quit, Low refused to say "No."

"Jesus, I hope not," he would only say.

Low was incensed that on a couple of the Stars goals, the Rangers were caught in player changes. But the chances didn't result from poor changes. Rather, Low felt that players were changing in order to get off the ice during the scoring rushes, which is unacceptable.

One of those who changed during a Dallas rush was Theo Fleury.

Mark Messier's statement afterwards, in which he said almost nothing, was nonetheless revealing, after he was asked about the effort.

"You're asking me to talk about things I'm not going to talk about publicly," he said. "I don't care to vent my view on those things publicly.

"I don't think anybody can feel too good about this game or anything that's gone on the last couple of weeks."

Low had juggled his forward lines, and the result was only 15 shots on goal.

"Obviously the line changes didn't work,' Low said. "A lot of guys looked like they were pouting about them, or whatever."

AN ENORMOUS SNOWSTORM hit the Northeast and the middle of the country. Dallas, meanwhile, was hit by massive thunderstorms, which made travel to and from this game a nightmare. Several newspaper reporters never made it out of New York. Some got stuck an extra day in Dallas as the team flight managed to get to Phoenix.

TIM TAYLOR WAS ROCKED by Dallas' Grant Marshall and appeared to be severely injured. Taylor was said to have only suffered a bruised hip, and X-rays were negative. He will have an MRI in Phoenix.

WINGER STEFAN CHERNESKI, the Rangers' first-round pick in 1997 attempting to come back from two major operations and two other surgeries on a shattered kneecap suffered in 1998, announced his retirement in Hartford. Cherneski's disability insurance policy would be negated if he played 30 games, so after Game No. 29, with his comeback not going as well as he'd hoped, Cherneski was forced to retire in order to collect the $2 million compensation package.

In his final game, Hartford coach John Paddock let Cherneski play the entire last 1:45, which he did with tears in his eyes. At the horn he was surrounded and hugged by his teammates.

ALEXEI GUSAROV, age 36, made his Rangers debut. So who was scratched? Tomas Kloucek, age 20. What a surprise.

SATHER WAS AT HOME, spending Christmas week in LaQuinta, California. The Rangers' performance, however, would cut short his holiday.

NIGHT7MARE

We Are What We Are

SCOTTSDALE, ARIZ.

The Rangers spent New Year's Day making the trip from Dallas to Phoenix, through the wet Texas weather. When they arrived in the dry sun of the desert, they had the rest of the day to themselves, to relax, get some sun, some rest, some fun.

That would end today.

Prior to practice at the Coyotes' training facility, Ron Low skated all alone on the ice. He fooled around with a puck, flicking it toward the net. When Low had enough, he wound up a slapper and ripped it into the empty net.

It would be the last puck seen until the Rangers' practice was over.

For 45 minutes, Low skated them hard. First they sprinted, repeatedly, from goal line to goal line. A short break and a meeting in the corner of the rink was followed by sprints from sideboards to sideboards. Then Low put them through a defensive-zone coverage drill where all six players chased an imaginary puck. Low would point to a spot where the invisible puck was, and the players would have to react. During the

193

sprints, several players looked ready to puke. Rich Pilon chose a really bad time to break in new skates, and he was just limping around like a guy walking barefoot across hot coals. Pilon knew better than to try to stop skating, because he didn't want to give the appearance that he was bailing out in the punishment being doled by Low.

The Rangers had also gotten a message prior to practice. Glen Sather arrived earlier than expected from his home in La Quinta, California.

Before the puck-less practice began, Sather closed the locker room door and addressed the team. That's why Low was out on the ice alone prior to practice. First, though, Low went to the Phoenix coaches and arranged for an extra 15 minutes of ice time to make up for the time lost in Sather's meeting. Low wasn't going to cut it short.

So the Rangers got spanked and comforted at the same time.

"Just to reinforce the fact that we all care about them, and we want to try to get them out of this little slide and the only way they're going to do it is together and through self-discipline, the discipline of the team," Sather said about the talk and the team's 1-7-1-1 record in its last 10 games after Sunday's embarrassing 6-1 loss in Dallas. Sather called that game the second (an 8-2 loss in Toronto being the other) this season in which the Rangers didn't compete.

Low said the Toronto game was worse, but that he couldn't punish the Rangers because that time they played the next day.

"When I see something like that I try to analyze what the problem is and try to find a way to come up with a solution and solve it," Sather said. "I mean, there's no sense in getting highly emotional over it. I know it bothers everybody when you see stuff like that, but there's answers to things. It just doesn't do any good to yell and shout and scream and throw crap."

Sather said he sensed that this would happen at some point during the season, because the system he and Low favor requires discipline.

He added that he doesn't think there's much difference in the talent on his team and the talent on most other teams, and he agreed that one of the players who is really struggling is goalie Mike Richter.

"None of us are fooling ourselves saying that Mike has not performed the way he has performed," Sather said. "Mike is working at it and he's falling into the same category. I mean, he's trying like heck. He's working at it, but he's overcompensating. He's got to collect himself and be a little more disciplined. Stand up, play the position, control the rebounds, do your own job."

Sather said that the situation won't dictate if and when he makes a deal.

"Whenever a certain thing comes along that's going to help the team

I'm going to do it, but there are certain things we don't have control over right now. We just have to be patient, that's all."

He was referring to the frozen assets of the Coyotes, the Rangers' next opponent, who can't trade Keith Tkachuk, Jeremy Roenick, or Nikolai Khabibulin until the ownership is solved, now hopefully by February 15 (the scheduled Gretzky ceremony has been postponed until the ownership situation is resolved, so it won't happen when the Rangers visit).

Sather said "It's not (Gary) Bettman's place to get into this" when asked if the commissioner is going to speed up the process.

Low was speeding up the Rangers' aching legs yesterday.

"Well, yeah there's a purpose to it." he said "You can practice D-zone coverage, you can practice back-checking drills in practice, and obviously those things aren't setting home, so we can do this every day."

He appreciated Sather giving his speech, saying "it also carries weight" when such a top executive steps into the locker room.

Low was worried about some of the things that happened in Dallas, particularly the players changing repeatedly while Dallas was on the attack, in other words, bailing out of bad situations and leaving those coming onto the ice completely hung out to dry.

"There's no excuse for things like that," Low said. "Those kind of things are ridiculous.

"Those things, when they creep into your hockey club, that borders on selfish. I mean, two guys stepped onto the ice and got minuses on that play. That stuff starts happening to your hockey club, you're in deep shit.

"That team outplayed us in the hockey game and that's why they beat us. But what we did is ugly. Those things that we did in that hockey game are the stuff that causes you to lose and to keep losing worse. You have to take responsibility for your ice when you're on there, and delivering that problem to somebody else on the bench, that's a bad thing. You can't do that, and it happened on two goals . . . three actually."

Brian Leetch cracked that the Rangers couldn't find a puck for practice, saying "They were Phoenix's pucks and they didn't want us using them" but he appreciated the punishment practice as one well-warranted.

"Yeah, well 1-8-1," Leetch said. "The record speaks for itself. At times you need a kick in the butt as well as a pat on the back. The coaching staff has been tremendously positive and supportive and there's times when that's not working and you have to resort to these kinds of practices. What it really does is, as you skate, it gives guys time to think about what's going on . . . why you're doing this."

PHOENIX'S KEITH TKACHUK, who is expected to be traded as soon as the new owners are officially in place, stepped out of the Coyotes' locker room while the Rangers were practicing and pretended he didn't know which lockeroom he should be going into.

MANNY MALHOTRA, called up from Hartford to replace Tim Taylor, didn't make it through the snow in time for the punishment practice. He was to joined the team later in the day. Taylor was on crutches and had gotten a new set of x-rays on his subluxed hip. There was still no official word on the extent of the injury, however.

WEDNESDAY, JANUARY 3, 2001

SCOTTSDALE, ARIZ.

When the Rangers acquired 36-year-old defenseman Alexei Gusarov from Colorado last week, the automatic assumption was that he would take away ice time from the team's younger defensemen.

Indeed, in his first game as a Ranger in Dallas, Gusarov replaced 20-year-old Tomas Kloucek. Thursday against Phoenix, Kloucek is to be back in, but not in Gusarov's spot, but rather replacing Kim Johnsson, 24.

"I don't think he played very well (in Dallas)," Low said about Johnsson.

"He was minus-3, and I didn't think he played very well."

Low allowed that it goes back further than the Dallas game, as well, and the coaches seem to think that Johnsson needs to be stronger to compete with bigger forwards coming off the wall or driving to the net.

Johnsson said, "of course, you want to get stronger" but refused to agree that his strength has been a factor, or that he has been outmuscled.

Johnsson, in fact, said he didn't know why he was out of the lineup.

"I have no idea," he said. "No idea. They haven't told me anything."

He also didn't think his struggles have been any worse than anybody else's.

"I think the whole team has been playing bad," he said. "I think we can play a lot better than we have, and that includes me, of course. We have to step up now and play better if we want to start winning.

"I just have to play harder, like everybody else. That's the way it is."

THEO FLEURY LOST HIS HOLD on the NHL scoring lead when Colorado's Joe Sakic put up five points against Los Angeles Tuesday and moved a point ahead of Fleury at 55-54. Sakic is a good buddy of Fleury, not only from Fleury's short stay in Denver, but since they were junior hockey rivals.

In fact, Fleury pointed out, the one thing neither player has ever done is lead the NHL in scoring.

Fleury said that when they were playing in the Western Hockey League as juniors, in 1987–88, he and Sakic tied for that league's scoring crown. Fleury (Moose Jaw) and Sakic (Swift Current) each ended up with 160 points.

"He tied me in the last game, with 12 seconds left," Fleury said. "I was listening on the radio and I almost cried."

Fleury, should he remain a Ranger, could be a big asset in the Rangers' attempts to lure Sakic to New York as an unrestricted free agent next summer.

Fleury comes into tomorrow's game with a 14-game point streak (6-15-21) and was tied with Jaromir Jagr and Boston's Bill Guerin for the league-lead in goals with 23. Jagr (44 points) may make all the scoring races moot, now that he has his old sidekick, Mario Lemieux, back.

TIM TAYLOR'S INJURY turned out to be not his hip, but rather his upper groin.

The initial expectation is that Taylor will miss 2–3 weeks, but the high groin injury has been known to disable hockey players for lengthy periods.

MANNY MALHOTRA, who probably would have been recalled anyway, will play in Taylor's spot. Low was happy with Malhotra before his assignment to Hartford and said he needs Malhotra's energy in the lineup. "They want the energy and that's something I want to bring to the ice, so when I hear things like that I'm even more eager," Malhotra said.

THE RANGERS' DEFENSIVE WOES get deeper when they are behind and have to open up. Two telling stats: Rangers opponents have scored first in 23 of their first 39 games, and the Rangers have won only three of those; and they have been outscored 62-45 in third periods. That works out to 1.6 goals allowed per game in the third period alone. St. Louis, by comparison, has allowed 1.98 goals per game.

GOALIE VITALI YEREMEYEV'S groin strain wiped out what would have been his callup from Hartford and a start against the Coyotes.

THURSDAY, JANUARY 4, 2001

PHOENIX

Ron Low needed to be convinced.

It seemed his players all bought the message that came out of a meeting with Glen Sather on Tuesday. It seemed they had understood why they were punished in a grueling no-pucks practice after the meeting. And it seemed as if they knew, finally, about the defensive responsibility Low has been preaching during a high-tempo practice on Wednesday, when Low loudly barked orders and players jumped.

But Low wasn't ready to pronounce his team cured of its awful streak (1-7-1-1 in 10) or its dreadful New Year's Eve non-performance in Dallas, an uncompetitive 6-1 loss.

"We're going to know tonight," Low said after an upbeat morning skate in preparation for tonight's game against Phoenix at AmericaWest Arena. "You're asking me prematurely. I hope there's an effect on everybody.

"There was a certain amount of intensity at (Wednesday's) practice, which is certainly something we're looking for. The things that were worked on we had been working on and, how long does it take to sink in? We'll find out, I guess."

Low said that, with Gusarov around and the Rangers having seven relatively healthy defensemen, whichever six are playing best will play, although one of those six will always be Leetch.

Low added that "I'd like to win eight in a row with the same people in the lineup."

That would be different. First things being first, though, the Rangers needed to win one in a row.

They went into the game in 11th place in the East, behind such non-powers as Atlanta, Boston and Carolina, and just three points up on Tampa Bay. Among the teams in the West with better records than the Rangers are low-budget Calgary, the terrible Anaheim Mighty Ducks, a decaying Chicago team, and the expansion Minnesota Wild.

Low and Sather both insist that the Rangers' talent level is high enough to be a playoff team, and that the Rangers have enough players to play a defensively-smart game.

"If everybody's playing well, you have enough," Low said. "The problem is right now, a lot of guys up front aren't playing well, and that is a problem."

While their main and most obvious problem is team defense, Low rightfully defended the puck-pursuit system the Rangers use as opposed to the trap of the Wild, Atlanta, and so many other teams.

"I don't know," he said. "You look at the game in Carolina and say, OK, what was that? A 40-minute aberration? You look at the first period against Atlanta when they had one scoring chance. Did we change our system during any of those periods? The problem is, it's the same as any system. If you're playing a trap and one guy doesn't go where he's supposed to go in the trap system, it's easy as heck to break. The difference with the trap system is you always have three guys back.

"The systems, it doesn't really matter which you play. If you play a left wing lock and the left winger isn't back to lock, what happens? We had three guys caught behind the net three times (in Dallas), and believe me that's not our forecheck system. And when you're on a rush and throw the puck in the middle with no hope in hell of getting it to the person you're throwing it too, that's not our system either. Those are just stupid plays."

Low still need to be convinced that his players know that and understand it. And that it won't be tolerated any longer.

FOR ONE NIGHT, apparently, the lesson got through. It's too late, and the hole is getting too big, for the Rangers to be satisfied with anything but positive results.

But they played their best game in a long while, and did most things well. Yet they still lost, 3-1 to the Coyotes. And they weren't satisfied.

That's six losses (one in OT) in row for the Rangers, who have won once in their last 11 (1-8-1-1) and three times in their last 16 games. They are six under .500 for the first time this season, heading home for games against the Stanley Cup champion Devils and against the Cup finalist Dallas Stars.

The Rangers also stretched their winless streak to 10 games on the road (0-9-1). Their once-mighty power play went 0-for-7, and is in a 1-for-34 slide.

"I have a pretty positive feeling here after a lost game," Low said. "I guess that's how bad we are at this point in time. We were lower than a snake's belly, but you have to keep working at it and tonight they delivered work. We're going to have to build on it."

The Rangers were once again throttled by Phoenix goalie Sean Burke, who shut them out 2-0 at The Garden in November and gave the Phoenix/Winnipeg franchise its first season sweep of the Rangers since 1984–85.

The best you could say for the Rangers is that they were far better than they were New Year's Eve in Dallas, or in previous losses to Atlanta and Carolina, for that matter. A lot of Low's demands —in a week filled with punishment, back-patting, meetings and hard practices— were met.

"I thought it was as good as we've played in a while," Low said. "It was a sustained 60 minutes; it wasn't 10 or 20. We came out on the wrong end of the stick.

"There has to be some thought process about how we're going to play. We basically said we're going to be hard to play against, not nice to play against, and a lot of guys stepped up tonight. . . .

"Everybody paid a price. Everybody took the body, and we're not going to be able to play any other way. We have to play like that."

They hadn't in a while, maybe since a December 8 Garden win over Buffalo 12 games ago. They had stopped playing that way.

"We've gotten away from it," Leetch said, "from very small things we've had success with before—the third forward high, our (defensemen) being able to keep the puck in, the first forward preventing them from getting rushes at us.

"I liked our attitude, and I liked the way we played the game. We need wins right now, and it's disappointing now, 10 minutes after the game, but it was the right attitude and thought process going into it."

Rich Pilon and Sandy McCarthy had mean faces going, and games to match; McCarthy spending the night battling Phoenix tough guy Brad May, who returned from his 20-game suspension for clubbing Steve Heinze of Columbus in November. Radek Dvorak was firing the puck. Defensemen were clearing the front, and getting help from conscientious forwards.

Goalie Mike Richter played perhaps his best game of the season, and kept the Rangers in the game until Claude Lemieux scored an empty-net goal. Lemieux acted like an idiot after scoring the goal, and Richter called him a coward and an asshole, among other nice things.

"I think, when you're coming out of a slump, the first thing you have to do is start playing well," Richter said. "We haven't played well enough to deserve to win too many games. The first thing that has to change is your approach to the game, and we really did that tonight. If we had done this the last few games, we wouldn't be in this position."

THE RANGERS PLAYERS, Mark Messier said, never lost confidence in Richter.

"There's not another goaltender in the league who could have come back and done what he's done from a physical standpoint," the captain said. "He knows he's our guy. We all believe in Mike and Mike believes in himself. He won us a Cup and he knows how to get it done. I don't have any problems with him. I never doubted him for a second."

MESSIER WAS IN A CHIPPER mood at the morning skate, probably trying to keep his teammates loose and positive.

He came off the ice and turned the corner to head down the long hallway that leads to one of two visiting locker rooms which are very far apart. He turned back and saw a couple of reporters. He asked one, Bridget Wentworth of the Newark Star Ledger, to tell the other guys to get off the ice.

"That's not my job, Mess," Wentworth said.

"We've all got to do a little more if we're going to get out of this thing, Bridget," Messier said, his deep voice faking sincerity.

"If I do more, can you get me a raise?" she asked.

"This isn't about money, Bridget," Messier deadpanned.

BRAD BROWN WAS HIT CLEAN and hard by Keith Tkachuk and suffered a shoulder injury that left numbness in his left arm and had Brown scared about it afterwards.

SATURDAY, JANUARY 6, 2001

NEW YORK

The Devils' mastery of the Rangers is now at 21 regular-season games (14-0-7) after an afternoon 5-5 Garden tie, but it didn't have to be, and it should not have been.

The Rangers did enough things well, some of them exceptionally well, to finally beat the Devils for the first time since 1996–97. They also did enough things poorly, some of them unbelievably poorly enough, to lose the game.

So, really, this was no measuring stick at all of where the Rangers are at the mid-season point (16-22-2-1). Or, maybe, it is a measuring stick of exactly where they are, of why they have managed to lose so many points in so many ways.

Yes, yes, if they play as they did in Phoenix Thursday and again today, against the Atlantas and Bostons and Tampa Bays, they might be just fine. But they don't, and haven't, played that way nearly often enough, and they know it.

They are winless in seven (0-5-1-1), with one win in 12 and three in 17. Teams are passing them with ease.

They nearly blew the one point they got, too, when Theo Fleury took a questionable slashing penalty ("another penalty for working too hard," he repeated) and compounded it by throwing a tantrum that got him an additional minor and a misconduct in overtime.

This brought about a mental blunder by the Rangers' coaching staff which didn't cost them, but surely could have.

In overtimes, for the last two seasons, teams play 4-on-4 instead of 5-on-5. It opens things up, and with each team guaranteed a point when a game is tied at the end of regulation, OT has become wildly entertaining.

But with Fleury in the box, the Rangers were down to three skaters, to four for the Devils. Low figured this was a good time to check for an illegal stick. The Rangers knew they had Alexander Mogilny of the Devils dead to rights. But what Low didn't figure was that Fleury's second penalty would make Mogilny's penalty moot. It would offset the first Fleury penalty, and the Rangers would still be short-handed.

Worse, Low believed if he lost the challenge on Mogilny, it couldn't affect the Rangers' manpower, since teams can never have fewer than three skaters on the ice. What Low didn't know is that, in OT, when a team down to three against four takes another penalty, the opponent simply adds a skater. So the Devils, who would have the power play for the remainder of overtime anyway, could have had a two-man advantage if Mogilny's stick proved to be legal.

Low also said he was about to check the stick of the Devils' Patrik Elias, believing it to also be illegal, but that during the Mogilny measurement, Elias ran off the ice. You can't call a player on the bench for having an illegal stick.

Elias, afterwards, noted that about 80 percent of the Rangers also went scurrying for legal sticks at that point.

Anyway, Fleury, who has been in the penalty box four times during OT this season, hurt the Rangers more with his tantrum than with his slash.

The Rangers had excuses against a Devils team that is in Cup defense mode, unbeaten in nine (6-0-3) and had lost just three of its last 23. They were missing injured body-moving defensemen Rich Pilon (shoulder, hamstring, flu) and Brad Brown (shoulder). Their charter flight from Phoenix Friday turned into a nightmare (commercial travelers, including the group of newspaper reporters who had return trips equally bad or worse, surely won't sympathize). The team jet took some nine hours, with a lengthy feuling and de-icing pit-stop on the tarmac in Hartford.

The Devils, however, were beatable on this day. Martin Brodeur was beatable, and the Rangers blew leads of 3-1 early and 5-4 late, wasted Jan Hlavac's hat trick, and failed to win while just about every player was playing about as hard as he could.

"We're disappointed that the win got away," Low said. "I think our hockey club battled as hard as it could battle, and I'm pretty proud of the way they played after (the travel) situation. You know what? We'll live with the point. It could have been better. I know one thing.

"There's not a guy in there that didn't leave what he had on the table, and that's all I care about."

The results have to start coming in a hurry, and in bunches, though.

THE RANGERS GAVE UP a horrid short-handed goal to John Madden on a terrible giveaway by Valeri Kamensky for a 3-3 tie with 1:07 left in the first period. It was Kamensky, remember, who stopped skating on the short-handed goal Nashville scored to send that game into OT, where the Predators won, December 23. It has been Kamensky often lately and over the last two years, but Low said he's hoping that Kamensky will eventually provide the offense to counter-balance his shortcomings.

At any rate, the Garden faithful have completely turned on Kamensky, the bust of the 1999 free-agent signing spree.

THE RANGERS POWER PLAY was 0-for-4 and is now 1 for its last 38.

KEN DANEYKO OF THE DEVILS twisted his right knee in a fight with Manny Malhotra, who knocked him down with a heavy right in retaliation for a Daneyko high hit on Eric Lacroix. Sandy McCarthy also won two bouts against big Jim McKenzie.

RANGERS PROSPECT PAVEL BRENDL was the leading scorer at the World Junior championships in Moscow (4-6-10), as his Czech Republic team won the gold medal, and Jamie Lundmark led Canada (4-3-7).

SUNDAY, JANUARY 7, 2001

NEW YORK

The Rangers held their team skills competition today at the Garden. Every team has to have one of these silly exercises. The Rangers piggy-back theirs with a celebrity hockey game—movie stars and such against Rangers old-timers—known as SuperSkate, for the benefit of the Garden's children's charities and the Christopher Reeve Paralysis Foundation.

Celebs in the game included actors Cuba Gooding Jr., Billy Baldwin, Jason Priestlay, Denis Leary and Rick Moranis, and former New York athletes John McEnroe and Boomer Esiason.

But the skills competition is dangerous, especially for goalies. Mike Richter ripped a groin muscle in the breakaway competition in the early 1990s, and last year at the All-Star game, in the same competition, he tore his right anterior cruciate ligament on a breakaway by Mariusz Czerkawski of the Islanders. Trevor Kidd, then of Florida, also suffered a serious injury in a skills competition, and Pittsburgh superstar Jaromir Jagr had suffered groin pulls in these things.

These Rangers took no chances. They brought up goalie Bryce Wandler, who is maybe sixth on the organizational depth chart, from New Haven of the United League just for today's event.

Radek Dvorak didn't surprise anybody when he won the fastest-skater competition (when he was in Florida, people thought he was faster than Pavel Bure, but he couldn't go head-to-head with Bure because of a groin pull). Dvorak, however, might have pulled an upset when he won the hardest shot contest with a 97.3 miles-per-hour slapper. He also hit four-for-four targets in the shooting accuracy event.

SATHER CAN DENY IT all he wants—and he has—but there is too much evidence around the league, and too many people who will say so, that Theo Fleury has been shopped around.

And now we know why. Sather knows he can't trade Fleury because of his no-trade clause (with a window exception in July and August). The only way Sather can trade Fleury is to put him through waivers as he did in the Stephane Quintal "deal" with Chicago.

So Sather asked around the league if teams would be interested in Fleury, with the provision that the Rangers would pick up part of his salary. That gave Sather a handle on how many teams might actually be willing to claim Fleury on waivers, at full salary.

This may have been nothing more than a fact-finding exercise for Sather. He insists he doesn't want to trade Fleury, and it would be an enormous gamble for the Rangers to put him on waivers and face the possibility that a team (other than the one with which they're dealing) would claim him, thus having the Rangers lose one of the league's top scorers and one of their MVPs and get nothing in return.

MONDAY, JANUARY 8, 2001

NEW YORK

The last time the Rangers played the Dallas Stars, nine days ago, there was a reckoning throughout the organization.

Tonight's rematch was much more palatable, but it still was a loss for the reeling Rangers.

Their season starts or ends now. It can't get any more simple.

They have 40 games remaining, and the immediate schedule could not be any more friendly.

After their 2-1 loss to Stars and backup goalie Marty Turco (first-stringer Ed Belfour left the team in a squabble with coach Ken Hitchcock), another one of those "nice try" losses they've been piling up lately—the excuses are gone.

They couldn't beat up the lousy teams early in the year because they were getting used to each other, to new coaches, to a new system. It was work in progress, they said.

They couldn't handle a wicked stretch in November and early December that had them seemingly playing three games in four nights every week, with some nasty travel mixed in. Then they couldn't do a thing with this grueling four-game stretch in which they played Dallas twice, Phoenix and the Devils once each (0-3-1), despite playing some of the hardest hockey this team has played since 1997.

It might be difficult to keep on playing this way after getting so little in the form of results.

"We've got to," Mark Messier said, after going a seventh straight game without a point.

"There's no alternative. We don't have any other choices. We've just got to keep playing. We can't give into the situation. If we do that, then it's over. So we've got to hang tough. It's not going to last. We've got to continue to forge ahead. Like I said, there's no alternative."

The Rangers have run into the ills that most teams do when they're battling to get out of a slump.

"When you're going into a slump you usually win games you shouldn't because you're on a bit of a roll and you're getting the breaks and bounces and things are going your way," Messier said. "Once you get into a slide and (you're) getting out of it, everything goes against you.

"We're in that predicament right now, and we're responsible for getting ourselves into it. The same guys are going to be responsible for getting us out of it."

So here they are today, looking at the final 40 that includes one trip outside the Eastern time zone (to Nashville) and one other road game against the West (at expansion Columbus). After four days off, they play a second-half schedule that is loaded with mediocre opposition, and if they really want to make the playoffs for the first time in four years, that opportunity is still sitting there for them.

Here they are today, though, seven games under .500, winless in eight (0-6-1-1), with one win in their last 13 games and three in their last 18.

The Rangers have been saying since Phoenix that they now know what it's going to take, the style they will have to play. And if they play as they did in these last three games, they should be able to beat teams.

But it will be up to them to do it consistently enough to wipe out all the harm they have inflicted upon themselves since a 7-6 win over Los Angeles that was a precursor to this 18-game freefall. It will be up to them to not have a backslide.

"You can't," Low said. "I mean this is the way we have to play the game, It has to be at a high tempo, with a certain price to pay. Everybody's paying it right now, and it can't back up. It has to go in the opposite direction. We have to go harder if we can."

"If you look at the last three games, we played hard and played with some character," said Eric Lacroix, who had the Rangers' only goal, on a Manny Malhotra rebound. "You can't change anything. Even though we're not coming out on top, that's a process. Sometimes you have immediate results. Sometimes, like tonight, you don't come out on top. We got to win some games."

VALERI KAMENSKY WAS SCRATCHED with what the team and Low insist was a shoulder injury that first came to their attention at the skills competition Sunday. However, Kamensky thought as late as the morning skate that he would play. Kamensky was a strong candidate to be benched for his recent performances, but the injury—according to the Rangers—took the choice out of Low's hands.

MIKE RICHTER PASSED Gump Worsley as the Rangers' all-time leader in games played by a goalie (583).

WEDNESDAY, JANUARY 10, 2001

RYE, N.Y.

Another red flag went up regarding Richter's rebuilt left knee today. Richter had swelling in the knee and had to have fluid drained by Dr. Tony Maddalo.

Richter, who had not had the knee drained previously, said he was assured by Dr. Maddalo that there was no cause for concern, and that "he was surprised it wasn't like this earlier in the year.

"He assured me it's not damaged, it's just a repercussion from having it repaired," Richter said.

Richter also said that the fluid removed from the knee was thick, an indication that it had been there a long time. He had reconstructive surgery last April, after suffering the injury at the All-Star game skills competition in Toronto last February.

Richter did not skate today, and won't tomorrow, but he fully plans to practice Friday and be available to play in at least one of the weekend games (at Boston Saturday, against Minnesota Sunday), if not both. Low said that Richter will be reassessed and probably won't play both games.

Low hopes to have rookie Vitali Yeremeyev up for practice tomorrow. Yeremeyev has missed a week and a half with a groin injury at Hartford, but has been cleared to resume full practice. Yeremeyev could get a start this weekend for the Rangers.

The latest setback for Richter—who had to be placed on injured reserve for a week in December because of fatigue—comes just as his struggling game is starting to get in order.

Prior to the 2-1 loss to Dallas Monday, Richter had allowed four goals or more in 12 of 20 starts. Richter did allow a bad one that turned out to be the game-winning short-handed goal by Dallas' Shaun Van Allen Monday, but all in all, he has felt more comfortable the last three games even though the knee has been troublesome and swelling since just before Christmas.

"I thought the game in Phoenix was a huge step forward," Low said. "I thought, there's been a couple bad goals, and they've been the backhand variety, which, those will get you anyway. I think he's been positioned better, he hasn't been scrambling as much, he's been keeping pucks with him, there aren't as many rebounds. That's the biggest thing."

LOW CONTINUED TO INSIST that he thinks Mark Messier is playing "outstanding," despite a seven-game point drought, and he will try to find Messier some new linemates for the weekend. Messier skated with Theo Fleury and Mike York in practice today.

Low didn't like the way Michal Grosek looked on Messier's right, and Valeri Kamensky is still questionable due to a sore shoulder that, at the very least, kept him from being a healthy scratch Monday against Dallas. Low wants to return Kamensky to his natural left-wing side, and said he has 30 or 40 pieces of video he wants to go over with his troubled winger. "It's not too complicated, the things that we see, and they're things that should be really easy for him to correct."

Low whispered to a couple of reporters today an interesting question. Why, he wanted to know, is Kamensky under such media scrutiny while Adam Graves is struggling at least as badly, yet goes unscathed?

Low knew the answer, a two-parter: First, Graves hustles and plays his tail off even when the puck isn't going in for him, while Kamensky appears to be floating around without emotion. Second, Graves is just about the most popular, most respected athlete ever to wear the uniform. People who know Graves are always going to cut him some slack. Low just nodded his head. He knew the answer.

Low plans to spend most of tomorrow's practice working on the power play, which is in a 1-for-42 nosedive that has coincided with their eight-game winless streak. Low said the most important thing is that the Rangers' pointmen, Brian Leetch and Theo Fleury, have to get back to shooting the puck more. "If we score a power-play goal in any of the last three games, we win all three," Low said. "I think we do, anyway."

RYE, N.Y.

Get used to this. Tomorrow is the Rangers' most important game of the season to date, and because of the hole in which they've firmly planted themselves, there are going to be a lot of these over the last 40.

The Rangers play the Boston Bruins in a FleetCenter matinee. They play a team that, on paper, shouldn't be in the playoff picture. But the Rangers have let the Bruins and a bunch of other rag-tag outfits into the picture by going winless in eight, and by winning three of their last 18 games. So tomorrow, somehow, the Rangers are looking up at a seven-point gap between their spot in 11th place, and the Bruins in the eighth and final playoff berth.

Simply, this is a game the Rangers have to win. And they are turning to goalie Vitali Yeremeyev, in his first NHL start, to win it for them.

Yeremeyev, an AHL All-Star with Hartford, who made his NHL debut in relief of Kirk McLean in Carolina December 27 (one goal, 33 minutes, and took the loss), might even start both the game in Boston and the next night's Garden meeting with Minnesota.

Mike Richter skated today after having fluid drained from his left knee Wednesday, and plans to play Sunday, but if Yeremeyev performs well in Boston, he could start both. The Rangers need an option for Richter, who may have to have the knee drained periodically the rest of the season and they want to find out if Yeremeyev is that option.

"I guess we're at a time and place where we have to find some things out about some people in Hartford and whether they're good enough to help us or not," Low said.

The Rangers also go into this crucial game with Mark Messier hobbled. Nobody will say what it is, and Messier said it was just general stiffness, but he skipped practice to rest—even though the Rangers haven't had a game since Monday.

"Mess will be alright," Low insisted.

Messier, in a seven-game point drought, will get new linemates, Mike York and Theo Fleury. With York's move to the wing, Low said that called-up center Derek Armstrong will get a realistic chance to see if he can produce in the NHL for the first time—not on a fourth line, but with wingers Valeri Kamensky and Sandy McCarthy, and with a reasonable amount of ice time.

The Rangers, now done with the most difficult portion of their schedule, need to take advantage of weekends like this. Boston has been inching up by beating mostly mediocre opponents. Carolina, which is a point behind Boston and six up on the Rangers, has feasted lately on teams like Florida, the Islanders, Tampa Bay, Chicago, and, yes, the Rangers.

"These are huge games, no doubt," Low said. "People have to respond. For the first time, you could say without lying, we could have won the last three and we only got one point. So we have to figure out a way to get two points."

THE RANGERS HAD TO make another roster move to fully recall Yeremeyev, who was up from Hartford on a 48-hour practice recall. They tried to send useful winger Johan Witehall through waivers (rather than send down Manny Malhotra, the one forward who wouldn't need to go through waivers), and the gamble failed. Witehall, secretly waived Wednesday, was claimed by Montreal.

"I thought he was a pretty steady guy for us," Low said. "He did some good things, and we're in a situation where we wanted to look at some other people, and I really didn't feel like Manny should be sent back down; he's played really well. We had to find ways to get (Armstrong) up here."

BRAD BROWN'S LEFT SHOULDER is still bothering him, and he's out this weekend. Tim Taylor's abdominal/pelvic area has a tear, and his status won't be known for another two weeks or so. Rich Pilon, who has assorted injuries, is still questionable.

PETR NEDVED WAS ASKED if there were any lingering feelings about Joe Thornton, whom he high-sticked in the last game against Boston. Nedved incurred a three-game suspension. He just smiled and shook his head. "No," he said.

UPON ARRIVING IN BOSTON, the players went out to dinner, where they roasted their captain, Mark Messier, just six days shy of his 40th birthday.

SATURDAY, JANUARY 13, 2001

BOSTON

It's difficult to say which was more of an indictment of the Rangers. Was it that, to replace Witehall, they claimed winger Jeff Toms off waivers from, ugh, the dreadful Islanders? Was it that Glen Sather admitted he has spoken to free agent goalie Tom Barrasso, a surly character who has said he won't sign with any team unless he is sure to be their No. 1 goalie, and therefore isn't getting many offers?

Or was it simply, again, the way they played in a big game?

Yeah, that was probably it.

When they are sitting at home for a fourth consecutive April, watching 16 other teams play for the Stanley Cup, this will be one of the games that stands out for the Rangers.

Their 4-1 loss to Bruins at FleetCenter will be the poster game for all that has gone wrong, and it will be the point-of-no-return game if the Rangers fall short one more time.

You want rock bottom? How about a nine-game winless streak, matching the team's longest since 1989–90; tied only with last year's quit down the stretch? How about an 11-game road winless streak (0-10-1), matching the club's longest since 1963–64 (only three others in the team's 75-year history have been longer)? How about a power play that has gone 1 for 46, and been outscored by opposition penalty killers 4-1 during that stretch, including a short-handed goal in three straight games.

So Sather added Toms, a player not good enough for the Islanders, and is thinking about adding the personality of Barrasso, which ought to be like throwing a grenade into a fragile locker room right about now.

Be all that as it may, the part that is almost as bad as the on-ice effort for the Rangers is that they now sit nine points behind the Bruins, who hold the final playoff spot in the East. Nine points behind a team that should never, ever beat the Rangers in a game that matters. That is, of course, if the Rangers didn't insist on being out-worked and out-smarted by teams like the Bruins . . . or Atlanta, Nashville, Carolina, Anaheim and probably Minnesota tomorrow.

Low, who can't seem to get much more effort, or much more smarts than John Muckler got, was asked if he was stunned after the three hard-fought games prior to this one.

"Yeah, very much so," Low, who was quietly livid, said. "I was definitely expecting a lot different look from our hockey club than we had in the game. Not very nice to watch. If this would have been in the Garden it would have been scary."

People would have held their noses between booing.

"The attitude of this hockey club is unbelievable," Low added.

He was rightly shocked by the lack of physical play in such a big game, although he absolved Sandy McCarthy and Rich Pilon in that department. Any idea why that happens?

"No, I don't know why," Low said. "And we've been through it a million times. If we're not going to finish checks, people are going to walk through you pretty easy. They walked through us easy."

Poor Vitali Yeremeyev, the rookie goalie making his first NHL start, was the victim. He had no chance on any of the Boston goals, the first of which was a Bill Guerin toss from the wall that went in off Brian Leetch just 33 seconds into the game. That was a fluke, and the Rangers didn't quit right then and there.

The killer was Guerin's second (his 200th career goal). It came on a power play. Jason Allison had the puck behind the net. Sylvain Lefebvre tried to take the pass away. Guerin, not two feet from Lefebvre and Radek Dvorak, and not four feet from two other Rangers, wasn't touched as he knocked in the pass from Allison.

"Guerin standing two and a half feet out," Low lamented. "There's not much chance you're going to have on that one. We chose not to knock Guerin down, and that's what's missing in the hockey club right now, a physical element. We had it for three games and you can't let it slide away, especially walking into a game like this, with the importance on this game."

Dvorak sped in to beat Byron Dafoe 17 seconds into the second period, and it could have been a game. But at 4:24, Leetch lost his edge behind the net and fell during a Rangers power play. Brian Rolston picked up the loose puck and nobody—Dvorak was closest—paid attention to Mikko Eloranta in front. He made it 3-1. Eloranta would tack on another one off a Kim Johnsson turnover in the third for the first two-point game of his career.

This could not have been foreseen after the hearty efforts against Phoenix, the Devils and Dallas.

"I mean, there's some serious things that have to go on on this hockey club before we can ever get things turned around," Low said. ". . . I mean, if we would have gone out and played our asses off and lost the hockey game, that would have been acceptable. This was not."

"I just didn't think we played the same as our last couple of games when we had good jump and good attitude," Leetch added. "(Today) we were very stationary in the game, and we followed around a lot. That's not what we wanted, that's for sure."

Nor is this enormous canyon into which they've fallen, right in the back of the pack with the Tampa Bays and Montreals.

"If we're not upset with the effort that was there ... we just can't accept playing a couple of games and not getting results, then to come out and play the way we did, it's just not going to cut it," Theo Fleury said.

FLEURY CALLED IT A "great honor" to be elected a starter for the All-Star game for the first time in his career.

There are reasons Fleury hasn't been elected. For one thing, he is probably the player who is booed more than any other in every city he goes, and last year he was even hated in his own arena.

"I'm surprised they voted for me in New York," he said. "Last year I thought I changed my name to Lou. Plus, I'm probably the most hated man in hockey."

Fleury has given part of the credit for his turnaround to the new Kevlar stick he used. Fleury, before the game, noted that Manny Malhotra has bought into the Kevlar.

"That's like handing a five-year old a (machine gun)," Fleury said.

SATHER ADMITTED HAVING TALKS with Barrasso's agent, Steve Reich, about what Barrasso's interest is, and if he's been skating at all. "He was interested and he said he'd get back to me," Sather said. "We've gone halfway through the season and we've got to get some consistent goaltending and some consistent effort."

Barrasso wants $2 million, pro-rated, and earlier in the year said he won't go anywhere if he won't be the No. 1 goalie.

This is probably one of Sather's calculated little motivational maneuvers, designed to get Richter's attention. What Sather doesn't know about Richter is that he doesn't need tweaks like this. If anything, Richter likely would react negatively to such a move/threat.

Richter, who stayed back home and practiced with a bunch of college kids and goalie coach Sam St. Laurent, is the planned starter in goal tomorrow, and Yeremeyev is expected to go back to play in the AHL All-Star game.

Low said that Yeremeyev could be back in goal again soon.

"I definitely don't think he played his way off the hockey club tonight,"

MESSIER, ASKED HIS FEELINGS about the Bruins by a Boston radio reporter after the game, said "I wonder what everybody thinks about Mike Keenan now."

Keenan, who coached the 1994 Rangers to the Stanley Cup before bolting, was about to be run out of town the last time the Rangers visited. He also wanted to coach the Rangers last summer, but Sather wouldn't even consider him.

Keenan beamed with appreciation when notified of Messier's endorsement.

THE RANGERS HAVE MADE a habit of falling behind early, and Low is just sick of hearing about it. "You know what? We've been using that excuse all year," he said. "We've been using the excuse that we got down early and it's too hard to come back. You know what? At some point in time there's a gut check and we all have to have it as a hockey club. You look at the third goal, there's guys floating back into our zone. There's no urgency on the play whatsoever."

And on the pitiful power play:

"Our power play is being outworked by the opposition I think pretty regularly right now, and I don't think that's an acceptable principle either. I think, to play in the National Hockey League, and to play on the power play is a privilege, not a God-given right, and I think there should be a lot of guys who should be looking at themselves in the mirror and thinking about whether we're working hard enough to score goals."

NEW YORK

The order of importance is arguable. Did the Rangers need to win tonight more than they needed to get Mike Richter back where he has to be for them to have a chance at anything this season?

Whichever is more crucial, more urgent, the Rangers got both. They got a win that was not artistic, not terribly convincing, but it was a win. And they got a performance out of Richter that, knee-willing, might be the start of his resurrection back to "elite goalie" status.

Richter and the Rangers both got their first win of 2001, their first win since December 18, a 4-2 decision over the expansion Minnesota Wild at the Garden, snapping a nine-game winless streak for the Rangers and a six-game slump for the goalie.

"He's the reason we won," said Brian Leetch, who had two goals.

Richter's confidence has been tested lately. He not only had his reconstructed left knee drained Wednesday, but he then had to watch as a rookie (Vitali Yeremeyev), making his first NHL start, got the call in the season's most important game Saturday in Boston while Richter stayed behind and practiced. Then on top of everything, Richter found out that Sather had exploratory talks with unsigned free agent goalie Tom Barrasso.

None of that matters, said Low.

"You can have all the names you want and still, it comes down to he's our guy," Low said. "He has to be the guy that's going to carry us. That's a simple fact. You can write all the stuff you want in the papers about this and about that, but that really is irrelevant. Nothing has happened, and I don't think anything is going to happen, and Ricky knows he's going to be the guy that has to carry us."

If the knee can hold up, that is. If Low can find a balance of playing him and resting him. If he doesn't have to sit out too much time from fatigue or swelling or draining. Richter certainly doesn't need the distraction of Barrasso's name, or the name of available, unsigned Phoenix goalie Nikolai Khabibulin, while he's trying to get his head and his knee together.

"There's nothing you can do about it but play well," Richter said about the rumors and distractions. "I know what I'm capable of doing, and they know what I'm capable of doing."

"There's nothing we can do," Leetch said. "I feel bad when we're not winning and he's taking a lot of responsibility on himself," Leetch said. "We're all making mistakes. He takes it hard. He's the last guy in there and he's the one that feels he's responsible, but to see him play like he did tonight is great."

Richter made seven saves during a crucial Minnesota 5-on-3 at the end of the first period, some of them as he tumbled through the crease, legs toward the ceiling. It was vintage Richter, but a Richter that hasn't been seen a lot lately. They were big saves at a big, big juncture of a big game.

Just what the Rangers needed, and will need, starting with two games against Eastern powers Philadelphia and Toronto this week.

This was the first step a team has to take before taking a second step.

"I can't remember how to feel after a win," Low said. "I thought the guys battled really hard, and I thought Ricky was great. That 5-on-3 likely saved us . . . and the team fed off that. That was as good as I've seen in a long time from him. He was fantastic on the 5-on-3. He must have made six saves that were destined for the top corner, or a corner, and he did them with all parts of his body."

Leetch scored a pair, each assisted by Sandy McCarthy, who continues to be the team's most consistent forward in terms of performance and effort the last two weeks.

Just as Richter had been stuck two victories behind Eddie Giacomin's team record of 266 since December 18, Adam Graves hadn't scored a goal in the nine games since that December 18 win over Florida, and was stuck one goal short of 300 for his career.

Richter got one closer to Giacomin, and Graves got his 300th, off a set-up from Valeri "Booooo" Kamensky, with an assist from captain Mark Messier, who had been without a point for eight games.

Some streaks didn't end. The Rangers' power play continued to be a growing albatross, going 0-for-6, and it is now 1-for-52, even if they were ringing shots off posts all night.

"You know what?" Low asked. "You can say anything you want about being zero for whatever we were tonight. I thought I was in the Sistine Chapel (with all the ringing) out there. I mean, we must have hit a minimum of six goalposts or crossbars. It was ridiculous. And all of them were labeled shots that were an inch too high or an inch outside. I thought that's the best the power play's looked in a long time."

"We could have beat them 7-2," McCarthy said.

The score didn't matter. A win is a win, and this was win that, for both the team and its goalie, needs to be repeated often.

PRIOR TO THE GAME, Low was asked what he was going to do with his lineup.

He shook his head, grinned and said, "Mum's the word. Don't even ask me what I'm going to do, because I don't fuckin' know."

Low then turned and walked into his office.

AFTER THE GAME, Valeri Kamensky, who was booed all night, passed a bunch of reporters in the corridor.

"Fuck you," he barked quietly, a curse probably intended for John Dellapina of the Daily News, who wrote an honest but negative story about Kamensky a day earlier.

IT'S BEEN A TOUGH TIME for Kirk McLean. With Richter hurt, or being rested, he should be the natural selection to start in goal. But the Rangers went with an unproven goalie, Yeremeyev, in Boston, passing over the veteran McLean.

So after tonight's game, a bunch of the younger players were trying to convince McLean to come out with them, to cheer him up. As they pleaded, Manny Malhotra planted a playful kiss on McLean's cheek.

"At least he has soft lips," McLean said.

MESSIER HAD A CROWD around him after the game, including some of the Canadian writers who occasionally parachute in because of his presence, and that of Sather—and previously Wayne Gretzky.

The questions began about his 40th birthday. But Messier has a way of turning an interview in another direction when he wants to.

Asked what turning 40, on Thursday when the Rangers play Toronto, means, Messier blinked and said, "Nope, nothing, it doesn't mean a single thing to me."

He scowled and turned his head as if to say, "next question." And it was clear that the next question had to be about hockey, and not about his age.

MESSIER WAS PRESSED on the guarantee he made when he re-signed with the Rangers in July, that they would make the playoffs. He became a big agitated by the question, but said, "That's over and done with right now. I believe we will make the playoffs."

BIG MATT JOHNSON of Minnesota is quietly one of the most hated Rangers opponents. It was Johnson who, while with Los Angeles, sucker-punched defenseman Jeff Beukeboom from behind, causing the concussion that led to Beukeboom's ultimate retirement. When Darren Langdon was a Ranger, he'd fight Johnson at every opportunity thereafter. Tonight Johnson fought a game Rich Pilon, then was knocked from the game with a concussion by an unpenalized Michal Grosek elbow in the third period. These events were unrelated, obviously, since Pilon and Grosek were not Rangers when Beukeboom was active.

SYLVAIN LEFEBVRE was a healthy scratch, the first game he's missed as a Ranger.

MONDAY, JANUARY 15, 2001

RYE, N.Y.

Glen Sather was to be honored at tonight's AHL All-Star game in Wilkes-Barre. Sather, though, didn't show up, claiming to have a case of the flu.

RICHTER WAS TALKING about inevitably becoming the Rangers' all-time wins leader, breaking Eddie Giacomin's record with No. 267:
"I do love the organization and it's the place I started, and where I want to finish, in this uniform. I feel good about being here for a fair part of its history, so yeah, I do take pride in that. But I think what I take pride in is having this team have success. You know, it's been a difficult time for all of us the last month, and we haven't performed to our capabilities and haven't been getting wins. So it certainly feels a lot better to get ourselves back on track. The way I want to be part of history is success."

TUESDAY, JANUARY 16, 2001

NEW YORK

It would have been another awful loss. It would have been a fairly acceptable tie. The Rangers turned it into a badly needed victory.
They beat the Philadelphia Flyers 4-3 on Theo Fleury's goal in overtime at the Garden, coming from behind just to stay even with their chief rivals for the East's final playoff spot—Carolina and Boston each came from behind to win, as well—and to stretch their tiny win streak to two.

The Rangers, who had been 0-15 in games they trailed after two periods, got a huge night from Fleury, who put up four points and called it his best game as a Ranger; a big night from Brian Leetch, who was added to the All-Star team earlier and had two enormous assists; and they got Mike Richter a share of Eddie Giacomin's team record for career wins (266), despite Richter allowing a potentially disastrous goal late in the third period.

"The thing about it is, tonight we battled back and got him one," Low said. "He didn't have to be great. And we have to do that sometimes, too. We have to bail him out of situations that aren't pleasant, and tonight we did. . . . We have to make some games for him, some wins that he doesn't make the difference in."

The Rangers had fought out of a 2-0 hole built on goals by Rick Tocchet and Paul Ranheim 17 seconds apart in the second period. Tomas Kloucek scored his first NHL goal with 1:51 left in the period, and the Rangers—get this!—scored a power-play goal after a 1-for-52 dive. Radek Dvorak calmly put a Fleury rebound past goalie Roman Cechmanek to tie the game at 2-2 in the third.

Then came the big botch by Richter, who had been so good against Minnesota Sunday, and who has been through so much this season.

Eric Desjardins' long, soft wrist shot from along the wall at the right point, skidded past Richter on the far side with 6:56 remaining.

"I was expecting it a lot quicker than it came," Richter said. "I was putting it in the corner before it got there. I missed one. I completely missed one."

Immediately, Low said, Fleury jumped up on the bench and screamed, "Let's not even worry about it, we've got to go out and get a goal. We've battled this hard, we have to go out and get a goal."

Then he got one, with 1:52 to go. He kicked a Brian Leetch pass up to his stick and fired through Cechmanek, and they went to OT.

And 2:46 into sudden death, Valeri Kamensky, at the end of a long shift, saw Fleury open. His long pass was tipped by Mark Recchi, and Fleury had to reach behind him to play it. He broke in, got caught by Recchi, and as he was being hauuled down, Fleury shot. His momentum carried him right into the goalie—not that he would have tried to avoid him—and both players and the puck bowled into the net.

The Flyers and Cechmanek went nuts that the goal was allowed to count, but really Fleury did nothing illegal.

Richter had a share of the record, with Giacomin, who was his goalie coach when he broke in with the Rangers. A record that should have fallen a month ago is now one win away.

For Fleury, there had been a long wait, too. Despite his marvelous numbers (26 goals, 35 assists), he wasn't completely happy because of one thing.

"Finally, a big goal," said Fleury, who is always up on stats, and knew he had just one game-winner, also an OT number against the Islanders. "That's what's been bothering me most. They haven't been big goals. It's gone really well all season long. The one thing that's been lacking in my game is the timing of my goals. It was nice to contribute in that way tonight."

Big or not, though, where would the Rangers be without Fleury's goals, without Leetch's attack?

Now, if Richter does get righted, maybe the Rangers can really build something. As Low pointed out, the Boston debacle Saturday was their only bad game in the last six (2-3-1).

"It's starting," Low said. "You can throw the Boston game away, which I'd really like to. But it's starting. There's a lot of decent things happening. Defensive-zone coverage tonight I thought was likely better than we've been for a long time."

Sometimes the way a team wins can make a difference. A win like this can be a springboard.

"It's huge, just for your mental (state)," Low said. "You had every chance to quit and you didn't do it. So you take baby steps and try to keep building."

Still, it's the Rangers, and based on the last four years you don't jump to conclusions that one win will lead to another, or that any streak will lead to a successful season.

Maybe it's not over. Yet.

WEDNESDAY, JANUARY 17, 2001

RYE, N.Y.

Another day, more questions about Messier's birthday.

"It's no different today than last year or the year before," he said. "I really don't hold any significance to it."

The significance is that only Colorado's Ray Bourque and Detroit's Igor Larionov are still playing in the NHL past 40, and Messier—who has played more playoff games than anybody in history—is an old 40 based on his odometer.

Messier did point out that, when he came to the Rangers in 1991, coming off a knee injury the season before, there were those who believed he was out of gas at 31. Of course, he won the Hart Trophy as league MVP in 1991–92, and led the Rangers to the Stanley Cup in 1994.

"When I came to New York when I was 30, I was supposedly at the end of my career," he said. "I had heard about the concerns. I had hurt my knee the year before. But I was kind of thinking to myself, 'Jeez, I was 30 years old' and felt like I was fine. But if you allow yourself to let that seep into your consciousness, I think that could be a determining factor where guys do reach the end.

"I was kind of laughing to myself when I first came to New York. I just felt that I had all this experience and I was still a young man that had a lot left. But the only thing that can prove it is to go out and do it."

The Captain is back. Mark Messier returned to Broadway after being exiled to Vancouver in 1997.

Glen Sather, who brought Messier into the league with Edmonton in 1979, believes there's a lot left.

"Gordie Howe played when he was 50 (until he was 52)," Sather said. "I think if Mark wanted to play when he's 50, he could probably do it as well. If you have the desire and strength to play, what's the difference between 36 and 40, or for that matter, 40 and 46? If you want to play and you come to the building hungry every day, I think you can really do it."

THURSDAY, JANUARY 18, 2001

NEW YORK

Messier called them the "Blueblood Rangers."

Brian Leetch and Mike Richter have played every second of their careers with the Rangers, the team that drafted them. They have been through miserable times together, they were the two most valuable players when the team won its only Stanley Cup in the last 61 years.

Tonight they were fittingly tied together on an historic night at the Garden, Leetch scoring the winning goal with 26.8 seconds left in overtime to get Richter the franchise record for victories (267), breaking Eddie Giacomin's mark, in a 2-1 come-from-behind win over Toronto.

Richter won it dramatically, with some spectacular goaltending during two Toronto 5-on-3 power plays and with an enormous save on Mats Sundin's 2-on-none redirection moments before Leetch's winner. And he won it by allowing one goal to a potent team, only the Rangers' second victory this season (opening night in Atlanta) and only their third in the last two seasons (3-48-2) in which they scored two goals or fewer.

That's how a goalie wants to break a record. That the Rangers needed the victory so desperately made it more special for Richter.

"It does make you feel good," Richter said. "I've been fortunate to be with this organization for quite some time, so individual records will fall. Honestly, the first thing for me, right now, is we need wins for the team. That's great to look back on over the course of your career, but you don't really have time to do that when the season's going on.

"I'm very proud of it, and very happy and flattered and humbled to be part of it, but at the same time, we have a job to do right now. That's the one thing with this record that I felt comfortable with heading into the year. It's wins, and that's what the goaltender's job is all about."

Richter beat the goalie, Curtis Joseph, who nearly took his job in the summer of 1998, when both were free agents. Now Richter's got the record that belonged to Giacomin, one of two players whose retired uniform numbers hang in the Garden ceiling. And it should be safe for a long while (barring a return by John Vanbiesbrouck), because Kirk McLean has 11 wins as a Ranger, Vitali Yeremeyev, Jason LaBarbera and Johan Holmqvist none.

Another long-time teammate, Adam Graves, went on a frantic search to find the puck for Richter, who won three in a row on the homestand that put the Rangers in position to get back into the playoff hunt. They remained seven points behind Carolina, but those teams will meet in a home-and-home series next week, after the suddenly resurgent Rangers visit Montreal in two nights.

Oh, did we mention it was Messier's 40th birthday, and that the captain very nearly won it in OT himself, but missed the net with "one I wish I had back" off a Theo Fleury setup. Messier also nearly didn't make it through his 40th, because he had his left knee badly twisted in a collision with Garry Valk in the middle of third period.

Messier said that he felt tearing in the knee, but he was able to explain the injury in an interesting way. Messier said that, since it has been damaged before—it was a factor in the Rangers' trade discussions with Edmonton way back in 1991—the "elasticity" in the ligaments might have actually prevented a serious injury.

"I knew it was bad, so I just tried to get myself flat as quickly as possible," Messier said about being scissored by Valk. When Messier came out of the box, his knee buckled again, "I was feeling kind of rubbery there. Sometimes when you hurt it really bad, there's not a lot of pain because you tear the nerve endings, too."

Leetch also gave the Rangers a mighty scare when he fell over Petr Nedved and limped off with a hyperextended right knee. But he didn't miss a shift, either.

"Our team's very dangerous in overtime," Richter said. "We're a great transition team and I think that scares the other team in that, they better be certain when they get their rush that they either score or keep the puck in. That's in the back of their mind."

In OT, the Rangers were going for it, Low throwing three forwards and one defenseman over the boards repeatedly. Radek Dvorak whipped the puck from the right corner, and Leetch put a shot off the near-side post and in behind Joseph.

"That's why we keep Brian around," Richter laughed. "He has a way of doing those things. He one-times a shot like that, short-side, and off the post. It's ridiculous."

So were some of Richter's saves. So has been Richter's season of ups and downs, his rebuilt knee and his goals-against average swelling, his confidence all over the map. Low has said time and again, the Rangers will go nowhere without Richter, and this week they've taken a little step forward behind their goalie.

"It was a great game (by Richter)," Low said. "I thought he was solid all night, and it's a good way to become the winningest goaltender. There was nothing out there tonight that was ugly about his game. He played super."

In front of him, the Rangers have discovered a resiliency. Low was asked from where it came.

"I don't know but we sure have to find it, and we have to keep it," Low said. "We're in an awful dogfight right now, and if we lay down at any point in time we're going to get slaughtered here, and we know it. The Boston game was an indication of, if you don't go out and give it what you've got, you're not going to survive. Basically, that's what it's been. We need everybody. We need the whole works."

As for Messier's 40th, well, the Rangers just had to win.

"I didn't want to say this, but we planned this since the beginning of the year," Richter deadpanned. "Hopefully we'll win a couple more for his 41st and 42nd."

NEDVED WAS HIT in the eye by a puck during the game. Afterwards, among a gang of reporters, he was asked about it.

"Yeah, it kind of popped out and I put it back in," he said.

Then Rich Pilon emerged from the trainer's room with three more icepacks. The guy has to be close to the league record for icepacks.

RYE, N.Y.

If you look at it with true objectivity, the Rangers have been pretty good in 2001. Since the New Year's Eve debacle in Dallas, they have played six strong games in their last seven. Unfortunately for the Rangers, the one in which they played lousy was a crucial game, in Boston, and they were trounced by the Bruins.

Prior to that, they had run into some tough competition, getting only a tie against the Devils and competitive losses to Phoenix and Dallas. Now, after a 3-0 homestand that included back-to-back come-from-behind, overtime wins over Philadelphia and Toronto, the Rangers feel they are ready to be rewarded if they put in the same efforts.

"It was a pretty important homsetretch for us," Mark Messier said. "It was frustrating at times because we played some really solid games before this, and just haven't gotten results. We just tried to stay positive as we could and reinforce in each other the things we felt were important. It's nice to see us get some results."

They got results by finally paying attention to Low's cries for better defensive-zone play by the forwards. They got results by finally getting top-notch goaltending from Mike Richter. And they got results by doing what Messier has said they needed to learn to do—play the game without changing anything based on the score.

"I thought we really did an excellent job, being down 1-0," Messier said about Thursday's 2-1 OT win over the Leafs. "We didn't change our gameplan, didn't beat ourselves, which we've done a lot this year. We stayed just real committed to the gameplan we had. We feel that in close games we have guys that can make plays at the right times. In situations early in the year, we'd get too excited to try to get back in the game right away, which opened it up for the other teams, and sure enough we'd be down two or three goals instead of just waiting for that one shot.

"The big thing is we didn't beat ourselves, and that's going to be a big key for us the rest of the season."

It was also imperative, and not just for the sake of the standings, that the Rangers get some victories after failing to do so while their game was improving in the three games after New Year's Eve.

"Again, what reinforces everything is, ultimately, wins," Messier said.

"The last three wins have been really timely for the team with what's gone on. We're starting to see that we've just got to really be patient, remain composed, and not beat ourselves by becoming individualistic, steering away from the gameplan, especially when we get down, and becoming undisciplined. That's starting to pay off for us."

To continue to see payoffs, they will have to feast on a friendly schedule that starts with a game in Montreal tomorrow, and continues with a big home-and-home with eighth-place Carolina, seven points ahead of the Rangers.

"You learn from adversity and we'll be tougher to beat as we go on," Richter said. "The most important thing is the atmosphere is changing. You can feel it, and we'll get back into this thing. That's a great feeling."

SATURDAY, JANUARY 20, 2001

MONTREAL

The task at hand was simple: Win. The Rangers had to beat the Montreal Canadiens. Had to.

They had to beat the Habs, a sad-sack outfit when completely healthy, but almost unrecognizable with their lengthy injury list, to make their upcoming home-and-home with Carolina meaningful.

So what did the Rangers do? They blew a third-period lead built on two Jan Hlavac goals, and tied the Canadiens 2-2 at Molson Centre, stretching their road winless streak to 12 games (0-10-2), their longest since 1963–64.

Of course, this is why the Rangers are where they are, well out of the playoff race, behind such average teams as Carolina and Boston; why the Canadiens are only four points behind the Rangers.

Just as there are moral victories when you play your heart out and lose to a Dallas or tie the Devils, there are moral losses when you play hard enough to win, but don't, against an inferior opponent. This tie was one of those.

Messier, Petr Nedved, and Theo Fleury all theorized that, because the Rangers spent the last two games coming from behind (to win each in OT), they might have forgotten how to play with the lead.

"We might have been a little guilty of just trying to win it 2-1," Messier said. "We didn't really have much pressure in the latter parts of the game, through the second period and third period. It's the first time we've been sitting on a lead in a while. We left ourselves in a position where a bad bounce could hurt us and sure enough it did."

The bad bounce was actually a bad play. Richter, who had won three in a row on the homestand and had played strong after a fluke Sheldon

Souray shot went in off Brian Savage's skate 20 seconds into the game, went behind the net to play Patrik Poulin's dump-in. Richter whiffed on his clearing try, then couldn't stop Eric Landry from throwing it in front. Xavier Delisle, unchecked, shot it into the empty net for the tying goal with 9:58 left in the third.

"I couldn't get the puck off the boards," Richter said. "In that situation, I guess you have to pinch the guy off. I couldn't get him off the puck, couldn't get him with a hip check, and I'm pretty much a spectator at that point."

"If he doesn't fan on it, Leetch gets it and we're out of there," Low said. "It's a play he has to make. . . . I thought he was solid other than that."

The Rangers did finally cut into the lead of the Hurricanes, who lost today and are six points up heading into the home-and-home.

"We just got seven out of eight points this week, which is pretty good," Richter reminded.

The Rangers, 4-22-10 in their last 36 regular-season visits to Montreal, also had a chance to do two things they hadn't done since 1978-79: beat the Habs three times in one year, and beat them twice in Montreal. The last time they did either, John Davidson led the Rangers to the Stanley Cup finals against the Canadiens (the Rangers would also win Game 1 in Montreal, then lose four straight).

The Rangers lost one of their most dependable and consistent players when Mike York left the game with what the team called bruised ribs. York was knocked down by Arron Asham in the second period, perhaps by a cross-check. He said he was a little sore after the game, and he'll be reexamined today. The Rangers can't afford to be without York for their series with Carolina, or for any period of time, really.

Messier had a chance to un-tie it with 3:11 left in regulation, breaking 2-on-1 with Valeri Kamensky. Messier cut to the net and goalie Jose Theodore stopped and held his back-hand shot headed between the pads. Messier hasn't scored a goal in 12 games, linemates Kamensky (none in 14) and Adam Graves (one in 13) continue to struggle.

"No, I'm not (getting) frustrated at all," he said. "I'd rather be going the way we are and winning."

RALEIGH, N.C.

The Rangers head into a crucial home-and-home series against the Carolina Hurricanes tomorrow, perhaps without one of their most dependable forwards, and definitely without one of their mightily struggling forwards.

Mike York had his bruised left ribcage reexamined, and no serious damage was found, but he might miss the game. Kamensky, meanwhile, suffered a second recurrence of the bruised kidney that has twice sidelined him this season, and was placed on injured reserve. Kamensky returned home to New York while the team flew from Montreal to Raleigh.

York remains day to day with the bruised ribs suffered on a hit by Montreal's Arron Asham Saturday night. He hopes to test the injury in the morning skate today before making his decision.

"We'll see," said York's linemate Theo Fleury. "He's a tough kid."

Kamensky's reinjury of the kidney bruise he originally suffered Oct. 29, and which cost him two more games in early December, combined with York's injury, might give Rangers coach Ron Low reason to finally break up the slump-ridden Mark Messier line.

After York went down in the second period in Montreal, Low chose to keep Messier with Graves and Kamensky, and double-shifted Petr Nedved with York's linemates, Theo Fleury and Sandy McCarthy.

Messier mentioned that his line remaining together allowed the "team to be set up the best way." That could be read as a dig by the captain; in other words, the only reason those three are still together is that the other lines are playing too well to break up.

Low, of course, might simply keep Messier and Graves together, and plug in right winger Brad Smyth, called up from Hartford.

The Rangers, in Messier's words, "are playing much better defensively now, no question about it" but lately their offense has disappeared. They have scored two goals in each of the last two games, and the power play, which didn't get a single opportunity in Montreal, is 2-for-59.

HURRICANES CENTER RON FRANCIS tied Messier for fourth place on the all-time assists list Saturday with the 1,113th of his career.

Messier's goal drought isn't the worst of his career. That came during the 1993-94 season, when he went 23 games without a goal down the stretch, then wound up scoring a number of fairly important goals (see Game 6 vs. the Devils; and Game 7 of the Stanley Cup finals) in the playoffs.

LOW ON THE HOME-AND-HOME against the eighth-place Canes: "We're going in there on four games without a loss. The next two games are going to be huge for us. That's going to be building blocks right there. We have to go in and play our best. The outcome will be whatever it is, but if we play our best, we'll be satisfied."

The Hurricanes have built their six-point lead on the Rangers by feasting on the league's weaklings. In their 7-0-2 streak (which ended Saturday) they played Chicago, Tampa Bay, the Islanders, Florida (twice),

Anaheim, Montreal, and Boston. The only contender they saw during the streak was Colorado (a 2-2 home tie). In the 13 games before the streak, the Canes faced Florida, Atlanta, Calgary, Minnesota, Boston, the Islanders, Tampa Bay, the Rangers, and Columbus, plus contenders Philadelphia (twice), Ottawa, and Buffalo.

RALEIGH, N.C.

The Rangers have believed in two things. One, if they could tighten up defensively, they had enough offense to win games. Two, that the hideous loss in Boston 10 days ago was an aberration, a flat game, for which they could atone.

Well, so far they've done both. They played a defensively sound game tonight, and got mega offense from their MVP, Theo Fleury (goals No. 27 and 28, plus an assist) and from the line of Petr Nedved, Jan Hlavac, and Radek Dvorak (a cumulative three goals and four assists) in a 5-2 win over Carolina before a sea of empty red seats at the Entertainment and Sports Arena.

The win, which snapped the Rangers' 12-game road winless streak, and stretched their overall unbeaten streak to 4-0-1, only makes Wednesday's Garden rematch the next "biggest game of the season."

The win leaves the Rangers four points behind the eighth-place Hurricanes, and three behind Boston, which lost to Florida.

"That was a huge game for us, one we had to win," Low said. "And we hadn't won on the road in God knows how long and that's something we had to do if we're going to get back in this race. We're halfway done the job. We've got another big game coming up in New York."

Or, as Nedved said, "Winning tonight and not winning the next game doesn't help us a lot."

Ironically, Low broke up Fleury and Mike York, who had played together for most of the last season and a half, in an attempt to get more offense from Mark Messier. Yet Both of Fleury's goals came while he was playing with York, one during a line change, and one while killing a penalty. York was in the lineup despite bruised ribs he suffered Saturday in Montreal.

Fleury, the littlest guy in the NHL, is playing his biggest when the Rangers need it most. His first goal, set up by York and created by the distraction Hartford callup Brad Smyth was causing in front, put the Rangers up for good. His second, a short-hander with 39.8 seconds to go in the second period, set a team record for short-handed goals (a league-leading six) and knocked the will out of the Hurricanes.

"It's always nice to contribute offensively, especially when you're expected to," Fleury said. "I think the biggest reason why we've turned this thing around is we've only given up 10 goals in our last five games, and with the offensive guys we have in our room we're going to get two or three goals every night. It's a huge difference in why we've been able to put this little streak together."

Patience has become a virtue, too. The Rangers gave up the game's first goal for the 13th consecutive road game, and for the sixth time in the last seven overall.

The Rangers had more at stake than the Hurricanes, who are looking at the Southeast title (and the third seed) more than they're looking at the teams chasing them for eighth place. Perhaps the Rangers were edgy early on.

But they settled down.

Then Marek Malik's power-play shot sailed through Martin Gelinas's screen and past Richter, who never saw it, never moved.

Richter, however, was terrific the rest of the night. His resurgence has more than a little to do with the improved defense, and vice versa.

The Rangers' power play went 0-for-7, running its fade to 2 for 65, but while it won't get credit for it, their first goal was essentially a power-play goal. Just one second after the man-advantage ended, Dvorak tipped a Fleury shot past goalie Arturs Irbe in the middle of the second as the Rangers took over. Fleury's pair made it 3-1 entering the third, and though Carolina cut it to 3-2 on Rod Brind'Amour's tip, it wasn't because the Rangers were sitting back. They were attacking.

Hlavac, who has been a force in both ends lately, made a spectacular rush and cut-in off the wing to set up a goal by Nedved, who has been regularly assigned to play against the opposition's best line and has excelled in doing so.

Hlavac then scored his 20th goal of the season into an empty net.

"It's a huge two points," Dvorak said. "Huge."

"I think it was the biggest win of the year," Messier said. "No question about it."

FLEURY'S BEEN GETTING the same questions in every city over his comeback from a 15-goal season last year. But this one came with a new and honest answer.

"Do you think you're playing the best hockey of your career right now?" he was asked.

"Yeah, I'd have to say," he said.

Fleury had shared the club record of five short-handers in a season with Mark Messier, Mike Rogers, Mike Gartner and Don Maloney. Now he has the record to himself.

Fleury also pointed out that Hurricanes goalie Arturs Irbe, a little guy like himself, is "my favorite goalie; I must have scored 100 goals on him." They were arch-rivals when Fleury played in Calgary and Irbe in San Jose. There isn't an arena in North America where Fleury is more despised than in San Jose.

KAMENSKY UNDERWENT TESTS at Lenox Hill Hospital, and it was determined he had a hematoma (bruise) on his kidney, which has knocked him out of action three times this season. Kamensky is to be completely idle for a week, then reexamined.

York said his ribs were sore after the game, and that he felt twinges of pain at times when he twisted. He couldn't take faceoffs, but he said he was unaffected by a huge hit by Shane Willis in the third.

ONCE AGAIN, Messier said the team "sets up best" if he plays with Graves and Kamensky, because the Czechs play so well together and York and Fleury have so much chemistry. So he's taking the bullet of playing with two struggling wingers for the good of the team, rather than demanding help on the wings.

TUESDAY, JANUARY 23, 2001

RYE, N.Y.

If this five-game unbeaten streak does indeed carry the Rangers into the playoff race, and not turn out to be just a blip on the screen like the seven-game winning streak they posted on their way to oblivion last January, there will have been two turning points.

One in Phoenix, one in Boston.

The game in Phoenix was preceded by the embarrassing, effortless loss on New Year's Eve in Dallas. Rangers president/GM Glen Sather flew from his home in California to have a long talk with his team, to remind the players what was expected of them, and Ron Low skated them into the ice at a Scottsdale practice facility for almost an hour without pucks.

Since that practice and Sather's speech, the Rangers have played nine games, and eight of them have been pretty good. They had well-played, disciplined losses to Phoenix and Dallas, a tie against the Devils, a horrid loss in Boston, and now a 4-0-1 streak since then. That included Monday's 5-2 win in Carolina to open a home-and-home series with the Hurricanes, which concludes tomorrow at the Garden.

"Ever since Phoenix . . . we talked about a lot of things," Theo Fleury said. "The team started to come closer together. It doesn't matter what happens in the game, as long as we continue to play the way we want to play, which is keeping scoring chances against down, we know, if we do get our opportunities, we're going to score."

The Boston loss was the other turning point. Mark Messier continues to stick with his story from that day—that every team has a "flat game" now and then, and that it was "magnified" because the Rangers hadn't won in nine games at that point.

But, Messier allowed, "We felt bad about it, but we just had to hang onto the rope. We couldn't give into the situation. We felt slowly we could turn things around if we did certain things. Sure enough, it's starting to play out a bit the way we felt it would."

"That was a big game for us and it seems like we weren't ready to play that game," Petr Nedved said. "Obviously we heard about it, and we read about it, and we were embarrassed. I think as a team we took it personally."

So they went out and got nine of the next 10 points, leaving only one on the table in Montreal. If they win tomorrow, they're right back in the playoff picture.

"At the start of the year we were beating ourselves," Messier said. "We got away from that in the middle there, where we started to win some games, then got back into it where we were just taking ourselves out of the game. We were just beating ourselves. Our biggest opponent was ourselves."

Fleury has been a huge reason for the turnaround. So has Nedved and his linemates Radek Dvorak and Jan Hlavac, who now regularly play against the opposition's top line, and also contribute most of the Rangers' offense. Nedved said that the Czechmates are starting to get back the feeling they had in the second half of last year, when they were a dominant force, and that an increase in their ice time and responsibility has something to do with it.

But Fleury said there is another factor, and that is for the first time in two seasons, the Rangers feel like a team, and that began in Phoenix.

"All the teams that are ahead of us have been together two, three, four years," Fleury said. "They come to training camp, they already have the chemistry, they know the style of game they want to play. The last couple of years around here, we've had to build almost from scratch. Finally, things are starting to go our way."

BRIAN LEETCH DOESN'T THINK his shot is any harder now, even if it appears to be.

"I'm just shooting it a little more," he said. "I switched to the graphite blade last year and I found that made a difference, but I had the broken wrist. But I've had more chances to shoot it. I don't know what my shots were at this stage last season, but I'd guess I have a lot more."

Last year, Leetch had 55 shots in 21 games when he broke his wrist. He had 80 in the first 21 games this season, and 155 shots through 48 games.

NEW YORK

Time will tell which is worse news for the Rangers—that they lost the second game of their crucial home-and-home series with the Carolina Hurricanes, or that they reverted to some of the defensive-zone night-mares they'd been having during a nine-game winless streak last month.

Carolina regained its six-point lead on the Rangers in the race for the final playoff spot in the East with a 3-2 win at the Garden, a win in which the Hurricanes out-hit and out-smarted the Rangers, who lost for the first time in six games. Boston, which also won, is five points up on the Rangers.

At this point, the Rangers will have to recover quickly, because they play the Islanders in another of those "must win" games Friday, then finish the three games in four nights in Toronto Saturday. They cannot afford to fall any further back.

The Rangers had to play without center Mike York, whose ribcage was too sore for him to be in the lineup, even though he played Monday in Carolina. So, in this important game, the Rangers' third-line center was Jeff Toms, who less than two weeks ago was waived by the Islanders.

Not that Toms deserved any of the blame for this game. Hardly.

The Rangers' self-destruction in the second period had everything to do with what has gone wrong for four seasons (horrid defensive-zone coverage), and what has gone wrong for the last 35 days (a power play that was 2 for its last 69).

Low can't figure out the reason for the power play's ineptitude, but he is sure he knows why they were so bad in the defensive zone.

"Certainly," Low said. "No hits. From the 10-minute mark of the first period to the 10-minute mark of the second, I'm not sure we threw a body check of any kind. We were terrible in our own zone and not just in front of our own net but everywhere. We were soft and played every-thing at long reach instead of being in people's faces and they just walked all around us in the second period. It was awful to watch. I mean we were absolutely, except for Toms's line, I thought we were almost non-committed in our own zone. We didn't eliminate anybody."

There is time left, no doubt, and if the Rangers play as they did for eight of the previous nine games they still have a shot. But they keep making the hole deeper.

"Well you're going to find out later," Low said. "It's drastic right now. It looks drastic. We have to get back to playing hockey the way we played it. This is not the way we had to play to win the hockey game. It was very important tonight that we had to do that, and we didn't."

Let's face it, when Rich Pilon scores a goal, you pretty much have to win. Pilon scored his first goal in 246 games, the equivalent of three full seasons—his last coming as an Islander against Pittsburgh in 1996-97. Mark Messier was a Ranger, then, spent three seasons in Vancouver, and played half a season back with the Rangers between Pilon goals.

But Messier now has a goal-less streak 14 games longer than Pilon's. Messier also played another game where he looked his age, especially in the Rangers' end.

Still, the Rangers were up 1-0 and in good position because of Pilon's goal at 6:16 of the first.

In the second, Carolina got physical and the Rangers got sloppy. Just 1:24 in, Jeff O'Neill, the Canes' leading goal scorer, rang one off the left post on a power play. At 2:18, as a Carolina power play was coming to an end, Martin Gelinas somehow got in behind Tomas Kloucek and Alexei Gusarov and had time to fire three shots. Richter stopped two of them, and the right post stopped the third.

The Canes kept coming, and the Rangers allowed two goals in a span of 29 seconds to relinquish the lead.

"The lapse in the second period definitely hurt us," Pilon said. "We weren't as strong as we should have been. We weren't sticking and pinning."

"It doesn't take much to happen," Brian Leetch said. "But after one or two shifts, you need to shut it down and get it going the other way. It just got worse."

Low said that forwards Manny Malhotra and Eric Lacroix were guilty on the first goal by a wide-open Niclas Wallin, and that was their final shift of the night. Twenty nine seconds later Shane Willis pushed the puck out of the corner, sending Rod Brind'Amour to the net, a step ahead of Messier. Brind'Amour whiffed on his shot attempt, but Messier nudged the loose puck right to David Tanabe, who gave the Hurricanes the lead.

Then, at 14:13, the Rangers did it again.

Four of them surrounded a loose puck in the defensive zone, and the Hurricanes came up with it. Messier and Dvorak left the zone, and Brind'Amour found Gelinas in behind defensemen Alexei Gusarov and Sylvain Lefebvre. Gelinas had plenty of time to force Richter to open up, then put the puck between the goalie's skates to make it 3-1.

Brad Smyth's first goal as a Ranger cut it to 3-2 in the third. It was too late. "Tonight," Richter said, "we could say that we beat ourselves."

AMONG THOSE IN ATTENDANCE was St. Louis GM Larry Pleau, who would like to add a defenseman and—more specifically—a No. 1 goalie to his Blues, a real Cup contender if they get one.

PILON'S GOAL-LESS STREAK ("It's good to get that gorilla off my back; it was getting heavy," he said) was the longest active streak in the league. Now Ken Daneyko of the Devils (155 games) has the longest streak, although he scored in the Stanley Cup finals last June.

YORK WANTED TO PLAY.
"We could have likely played him tonight at big risk down the road, and I did not think that was going to be worth it in the end," Low said.

THURSDAY, JANUARY 25, 2001

RYE, N.Y.

In the beginning of the power-play nightmare for the Rangers, it was shrugged off as a cyclical thing. In the middle, it wasn't a major concern because they were generating chances. On Wednesday, the Rangers' power play became a real problem, one that hurt them profoundly.

The Rangers went 0-for-4 in a 3-2 loss to Carolina at the Garden, stretching their freefall to 2 for 69 over a 16-game stretch. It could have been the difference in the game, just as Radek Dvorak's goal in Carolina two nights earlier, although scored technically a second after a power play expired, was the impetus for that victory.

"The power play's hurt us for sure in some of the close games we've played lately," Mark Messier said. "We had a couple of opportunities when it was 1-0 to make it a two-goal lead and didn't, and we had a power play late in the game where we could have gotten ourselves a tie. So it's definitely hurt us."

The Rangers play the Islanders tomorrow at the Garden in another terribly important game, a game in which they cannot afford a letdown following their big series with Carolina, and the power play might rescue or doom them again. The last time the teams met, the Rangers scored three power-play goals, including Theo Fleury's game-winner in overtime of a 4-3 victory.

But it has gotten bad. It looks bad and feels bad.

"We didn't have very many (chances)," power-play quarterback Brian Leetch said about Wednesday. "We couldn't get it into the zone. They lined up across the blue line and we made some bad dumps, tried to carry it in. We had a few chances, but our time of possession in the zone was minimal.

"It didn't feel good. Some games you feel like you got some opportunities and you're moving it around, but (Wednesday) it wasn't good at all. There was a bad feeling out there with some of the plays we were making . . . our plays at the blue line and then not getting it in, or getting it over the line and one pass or one shot, and right back into our zone again."

Low has become exasperated. Much of the problem has been that Messier (no goals, two assists in his last 14 games), Graves and Kamensky have each slumped terribly. Low tried some changes Wednesday, using Sandy McCarthy, Michal Grosek, Brad Smyth, even moving Fleury from the point to the wing and replacing him with Kim Johnsson on the point.

"Hey, you know what, let's keep trying to find a way," Low said. "We didn't generate enough on it. The first couple of power plays we never had the puck in the zone. After we did get it in the zone, we did have some chances and didn't finish, but not enough."

THE PERFECT SCENARIO for the Rangers would have been a win Wednesday, and then a choice of which game this weekend to rest Mike Richter. With the loss Wednesday, the choice was made for the Rangers. Richter must start tomorrow, and they will take their chances with Kirk McLean (or at least that's the plan at the moment) in Toronto Saturday. Richter has started six in a row, and the Rangers can't risk having his left knee act up again because of overuse.

TIM TAYLOR'S HIGH GROIN muscle tear isn't getting any better, and he's expected to miss at least two more weeks. Taylor was injured New Year's Eve in Dallas, and he might be looking at a long-term injury or surgery.

FRIDAY, JANUARY 26, 2001

NEW YORK

Just when it looks like the Rangers are finally sick and tired of embarrassing themselves, they find a new way to do just that.

They did that during a well-deserved 3-2 loss to the Islanders at the Garden, and they did it again after the game by failing to act angry or annoyed at the way they played. They just accepted it, took it as a loss in which they failed to bury their chances and otherwise, they felt, they played all right.

Never mind that this was the worst team in the NHL, a team that had been 1-10-1 in its last 12, and hadn't won on the road since December 6;

a team with its No.1 goalie, John Vanbiesbrouck, on the bench because of back spasms that struck him earlier in the day.

The breakdowns weren't as massive as those against Carolina Wednesday. The entire game wasn't as awful as the one against Boston January 13. And the effort surely wasn't as pathetic as those in Dallas New Year's Eve, or that earlier 8-2 loss in Toronto (where, by the way, the Rangers have to play tomorrow, with sacrificial lamb Kirk McLean in goal).

But this loss might be the worst of the lot. This was bad.

"Yeah, I think it is," Low said. "And a tough one."

Low wasn't steamed as he was in the aforementioned debacles, though. Nor were many of his players.

A few spoke honestly, though.

"I think (the Islanders) is a better team than the record shows, but this is a team we have to beat and there's no excuse for not having two points," said Petr Nedved. "And the only reason we were in the game was (goalie Mike Richter)."

Rich Pilon, who left with a bruised foot and is questionable tomorrow, knows from the other side of this rivalry. He knows that the games against the Rangers make the Islanders' season.

"It's our season, too," Pilon said. "We need these two points tonight. These are games we've got to have if we want to make the playoffs."

Which is starting to look more and more like a dream. The Rangers' recent 4-0-1 streak looks as if it was a mirage, just like the seven-game winning streak the 1999–2000 Rangers had in January, en route to quitting down the stretch.

"We're not setting the tempo in our building like we did prior," Low said. "One of the things we refuse is to dump it in deep and get a forecheck going, which was really the only thing they had problems with tonight. Not nearly enough of it."

He added, "There's not enough from the big guys right now. We're stymied."

The Nedved line didn't score until 31.7 seconds remained. Theo Fleury didn't score. Brian Leetch didn't score. And Mark Messier, for the 15th straight game, didn't score and didn't play well enough in his own end to justify not scoring.

"It's a tough long grind," Low said about Messier. "I talked to him. I don't think he's tired. He feels really decent right now, he said, and he's going to keep going."

Low made a couple of interesting, if not questionable decisions, and one of them worked out for him. Low wanted to keep Jeff Toms in the lineup after a strong game Wednesday, and especially since Toms had been waived by the Islanders two weeks ago.

So Manny Malhotra, who didn't see the ice after being partly responsible for one Carolina goal Wednesday, was scratched instead of Michal Grosek or Eric Lacroix. It was a fairly moot point, because the fourth line rarely hit the ice, despite the Rangers playing the first of back-to-back games.

Low also wanted to have Dale Purinton's toughness in the lineup, so he scratched Sylvain Lefebvre instead of Alexei Gusarov, who had a second shaky game in a row.

But Low hit the jackpot with Toms late in the first period, after the Islanders had taken the 1-0 lead early. Pilon, another former Islander who was claimed on waivers by the Rangers, sent Toms up ice.

Toms went around defenseman Aris Brimanis, and cut wide against goalie Wade Flaherty, and scored on a wrap-around.

Eventually, Toms replaced Graves on Messier's left, as Graves sat on the bench.

"I thought Flaherty was real good, but I thought we were inept also," Low said.

The Islanders struck first on another classic Rangers breakdown in their own end. They were soft in front as Mariusz Czerkawski came down the slot and fired. Richter made a pad save but couldn't control the rebound. Brad Isbister crashed the net and somehow jarred the puck through Richter and into the net at 4:59.

In the third, after veteran referees Paul Devorski and Terry Gregson refused to give the Islanders a penalty shot they deserved, nevertheless put them on the power play. And at 7:50, Isbister dragged the puck to the high slot. Mike York tried to hook him, but couldn't (probably because of his sore ribcage) and with the two defensemen backing away, Isbister fired a shot over Richter's glove and under the crossbar for a 2-1 Islanders lead.

Isbister tipped a Czerkawski pass past Richter for the clincher late in the third, after the Rangers' power play failed again, running its streak to 2 for 74.

"It's killing us," Low said.

THE RANGERS HONORED Richter in a pre-game ceremony for breaking Eddie Giacomin's team record for career victories on January 18.

SANDY MCCARTHY REPEATEDLY tried to goad ex-Ranger Eric Cairns into a fight, even though Cairns had just returned from thumb surgery and therefore couldn't fight.

TORONTO

The problem isn't the teams in front of the Rangers. The problem is the Rangers themselves.

Their 3-1 loss to the Toronto Maple Leafs at Air Canada Centre, their third in a row, only dug their playoff hole deeper.

The problem with the Rangers, never mind their 1-10-2 record in the last 13 on the road, never mind that they're back to seven under .500 again, and nine points behind Boston, is the Rangers. They have managed to play pitifully against the pitiful teams and lose (or tie); to play mediocre hockey against mediocre or struggling teams (such as Toronto is at the moment) and lose; to play well against very good teams. And lose.

Now their players are all messed up, their lines are confused, their special teams stink, their stars are burned out. It spells big, big trouble, and it starts with the captain.

If what Mark Messier (no goals, two assists in 16 games) needs is rest, it doesn't appear to be coming, with the exception of the All-Star break next weekend. Both Low and Sather have spoken to Messier, and he—surprise, surprise—told them he feels fine and he wants to keep playing.

"I had dinner with him the other night and he said he felt great, said he felt strong," said Sather. "I think he's just going through one of those little periods of time where things aren't going for him. Mark's no different from anybody else. He needs positive reinforcement."

Sather is probably the one person in North America who has enough of Messier's respect to get him to sit down, or at least take on a lesser role. That is, if Sather, Messier, and Low feel that's the dilemma.

"I'm not interested in getting into this debate publicly," Sather said. "But I wouldn't even suggest it to him right now. We've got a stretch of games here that are very important to us. And if he's not doing the things to carry this team, somebody else needs to step forward. We can't put all the weight on Mark's shoulders every day. What's wrong with (Adam) Graves doing something, or somebody else stepping forward and scoring goals and doing the things they're paid to do? Petr Nedved's another guy who hasn't exactly burned it up the last couple of games. He's got to step forward. We can't keep passing it onto Mark all the time."

Low continued to grasp for other answers. He had Messier, again, playing on a line with minor-leaguer Brad Smyth and Jeff Toms, who was claimed from the Islanders on waivers. Jeff Toms. Jeff Toms!

Messier wasn't on the ice in the final minute with goalie Kirk McLean pulled for an extra skater—Low said it was a tough decision, but that Petr Nedved had been having success on faceoffs against Mats Sundin.

Low also put defensemen Sylvain Lefebvre and Brad Brown back into the lineup, one replacing injured Rich Pilon (who was still badly limping from the bruised foot he suffered Friday) and one replacing rookie Tomas Kloucek, who has struggled lately. For the second game in a row, Manny Malhotra was scratched, too. Graves can hardly be expected to "step forward" from the fourth line, where he was for the second game in a row.

The Rangers played a much, much better game than they had in the previous two, but this was a superior opponent to the Islanders and the Hurricanes. Low, Messier and just about anybody you could ask said that the Rangers simply couldn't score, or in the case of the Nedved line, which exasperates Low, wouldn't shoot the puck.

"I'm not really sure you benefit by sitting them," Low said. "You might have to."

Low wasn't shy about pointing fingers on the two crucial breakdowns on the Leafs' second and third goals. Smyth failed to pick up Darcy Tucker coming off the wall for the 2-0 goal, and Nedved turned away and let Tucker walk down the slot for the 3-1 goal after Theo Fleury had scored his 29th to make it 2-1.

Fleury, another Ranger who looks tired and overburdened, has been checked extra closely because of the failure of Messier's line to produce. The trickle-down has been felt throughout the lineup.

Last year at this time, the Rangers were a .500 team. Last year, though, there ultimately was frustration, resignation, then out-and-out quit.

"They're not going to quit," Low said. "The thing about it is, you can get frustrated all you want, but quitting is the last thing you're going to do. That's not in the equation at all. It can't be."

When Low finished addressing the media on the various shortcomings, mistakes and problems, he walked away muttering, "Fuckin' redundant."

SATHER IS IN A TOUGH SPOT with the Rangers on the outside of the playoff picture and just 31 games left. He wants to help the team, but he said he is unlikely to want to trade any of the future for help now.

"Any time you start trading people you're not entirely sure of, it can come back and bite you in the ass," he said. "But, if you get a sure thing that's going to get us in the playoffs and be solid for the next four or five years, that's a different situation. But those kinds of deals are not deals that involve one guy. Those are multiple-player deals, cleaning your entire organization out of depth and youth, and I'm certainly not going to do that."

Sather said he also considered having Brian Leetch skip the All-Star game, but decided against it because the game is "an honor" and the players "love it". Leetch just laughed at the suggestion that he might skip the All-Star game.

IN A STORY in the National Post of Canada, Sather expressed that he had second thoughts about taking the job, and accepted the responsibility for the shape of the team.

"I knew there was going to be a transition time," he said. "Personally, it's been tough."

About having pangs of regret, Sather said, "I think everybody goes through that. Buyer's remorse."

But Sather, for one of the first times, stood up to be counted on the organizational faults.

"You can't cop out on the responsibility, because this is my team now," Sather said. "Where we are in the standings is my responsibility. So I'm working my ass off to try and fix it."

Sather also claimed "I'm not making any more money here than I was in Edmonton," which flies in the face of every report of his seven-year contract with the Rangers, believed to start at $3 million per with potential to rise perhaps as high as $5 million per.

KEITH TKACHUK'S AVAILABILITY from Phoenix became more probable this week. During a locker room shout-down among Gretzky and anti-Gretzky factions in the Phoenix room, Tkachuk loudly and seriously told Claude Lemieux to shut up, and called him "Gretz's caddie."

MONDAY, JANUARY 29, 2001

NEW YORK

The vultures are circling the Rangers. These vultures wear suits, and while they are waiting to pick the Rangers' bones, they might actually be beneficial to the Rangers.

After a humiliating 7-2 loss to the Atlanta Thrashers at the Garden, there is no reason for Sather to wait before starts cleaning out his rancid roster, a roster that made one phony run at respectability earlier this month.

Since that 4-0-1 mirage, the Rangers have lost to Carolina at home, to the Islanders (1-10-1 in their previous 12), to struggling Toronto an now to the Thrashers —a team that hadn't won in 2001; and in fact hadn't won in 14 games since beating the Rangers at the Garden December 28.

The NHL can't help but serve up soft opponent after soft opponent, and the Rangers can't do a thing with them.

"You never hope to get this bad, and you never really think it's going to get this bad," Mark Messier said. "But we are what we are, we stand where we stand. No denying it or hiding it or trying to make excuses for where we're at. It's pretty evident."

And if the record hasn't hit rock bottom, the confidence has.

"I'd say you're looking at a hockey club that's gotten about as low as it could possibly get," Ron Low said. "I think the confidence level of everybody on the club is waning. . . . It's exasperating for everybody in there.

"You can see it with everybody, not just one or two guys. The confidence level, or the ability to even handle the puck, has almost fled the scene. To me it's a situation where somebody's got to do something big. It's going to have to come from inside that room. We're in it together and believe me, we're the only ones who can fix it. You can't fix it without going about it in a different manner."

The way to fix is might be to start tearing it down.

So Sather might be ready to start making deals with the vultures, teams willing to take anything of value off the Rangers' hands in return for some prospects, perhaps draft choices. In addition to the usual array of scouts, tonight's crowd included general managers Pierre Gauthier (Anaheim) and Ken Holland (Detroit). Vancouver's Brian Burke had planned to attend, too.

Gauthier needs help, and is looking to deal Teemu Selanne. Holland needs a goaltender (Mike Richter?). Burke is reportedly ready to trade defenseman Adrian Aucoin, and is also looking for goaltending help. Virtually every contender in the league wants veteran defensemen—Sylvain Lefebvre and Rich Pilon are certainly available—and most would welcome (and this is sacrilege to Rangers' fans) Adam Graves to their locker room.

It is also possible, if not probable, that Gauthier and Holland were looking at Donald Audette of the Thrashers, a prospective free agent whom Atlanta GM Don Waddell (also at the game) might trade before the March 13 deadline.

From a Rangers standpoint, though, why wait any longer? The Rangers, back to their season-low eight games under .500 and nine points out of a playoff spot, have 30 games left. It would be a miracle for this team to play eight over .500 the rest of the way, considering the Rangers haven't been more than two over .500 at any point in the last four seasons, and even if they got back to .500 (82 points), that probably is going to be well short.

These Rangers, like their predecessors from 1999-2000, are disgracing themselves again. This team hasn't quit like last year's team, but its performances just get progressively worse. As it does, its lineup gets uglier and uglier. Again, Messier skated with Jeff Toms and Michal

Grosek—unwanted this season by the Islanders and Chicago, respectively. If the idea is to lessen Messier's ice time, that's fine. He needs the rest. But it also appears that Low has little choice, having tried everything else to get offense from Messier.

While the Rangers should have enough top-level talent to get to the playoffs, they also seem to have a lot of fourth-line forwards and third-pair defensemen. Or worse.

Or, in Messier's words, they are what they are.

"I think our confidence has been on the fence all year," Messier said. "We were doing a lot of excellent things the first 35 games of the season and we still found ourselves barely at .500 or a few games under .500. The power play was first in the league, we had two guys in the top five in scoring and we were scoring four or five goals a game we could barely keep .500.

"Obviously the power play wasn't going to maintain that level and we weren't going to keep scoring four or five goals a game. So if we couldn't get a winning record at that point, obviously our confidence has been shaky all year. We've never put a real sustained streak together in order to get the confidence our team needs."

The Rangers' horrid special teams hit new lows. The Thrashers scored power-play goals that took 23 seconds and three seconds on the Rangers' first two penalties. Then they added a 4-on-4 goal, and it was 3-0 after one period (Frantisek Kaberle already had three points). In the second, they got one at even strength, and another short-handed against the Rangers' power play, now 3-for-80. It was 5-0 after two. When it got to 7-1 in the third, the half-empty Garden began a "Let's go Thrashers" chant.

It is inevitable now that these Rangers—who embarrased themsleves in Dallas New Year's Eve, who didn't show up for an enormous game in Boston, who allowed Montreal to come back to tie, who lost to the Islanders, and who allowed Atlanta's first victory of 2001—are going nowhere again.

The vultures know it. Sather knows it, too. It's just a matter of when he wants to throw in the towel.

PRIOR TO THE MORNING SKATE, Sather walked into the locker room and for 40 minutes, with the coaches not in the room, let the players have it.

He told the players that their "grace period" was over and that it's time to take responsibility for what was happening. He threatened one and all that going through waivers and being sent to Hartford was a real option, and added an "I'm serious. If they don't believe me they can just try me."

LOW WAS ANNOYED and puzzled. He was mad as hell about the way the Rangers let teams walk into the Garden and walk out with victories.

"It has to be back to the old way of playing here like we did at the start of the year," Low said. "Make it tough for people in our building, make it ugly from the first shift on. That's the only way we can fix the damn thing."

At the same time, he was trying to fix it himself, but hadn't a clue how.

"The whole key is, there has to be a positive feeling somehow or other come Wednesday night," he said. "I guess that's my job.

"We have to go out and refocus our whole system."

But it isn't only the system at this stage.

"There is a bad feeling in there right now," Low said, sneaking a look toward the locker room. "You can go in and say whatever you want. It doesn't change the feeling that's in there right now. It's something that has to be fixed within the room itself. Somebody's got to do something huge. And it can't be done by one guy. It's going to have to be a group effort and everybody following."

Asked, once again, if he feels there might be some quitting going on, Low snapped, "There's absolutely no chance that can be happening at this point in time.

"Sometimes it has to get worse to get better. That's the way it is. Sometimes you have to bottom right out before you can get things turned around and get going the other way."

AFTER LOW HAD SPOKEN and most of the players had quickly showered and left, Sather emerged from the coaches' room. He found himself in demand by the media. Sather quickly turned and headed down a hallway, chased by reporters.

Sather wouldn't stop. He only waved his arm angrily and barked, "I've got nothing to say."

TUESDAY, JANUARY 30, 2001

RYE, N.Y.

Sather apologized to the media for bolting in the angry moments after Monday's terrible loss to Atlanta.

"I was hotter than piss in a frying pan," Sather said.

Then he and Low threw out some numbers and some facts.

This wasn't that "fuzzy math." This was reality. The Rangers have 30 games left, and they're going to have to win a whole lot of them if they're going to get into the playoffs for the first time in four years.

And if Low doesn't get the requisite number of victories and points, he has faced another reality. That he might be fired as his predecessor, John Muckler was. However, Low noted, his demise will only be results-driven.

"One thing that is for sure here, if the coach doesn't win, sooner or later the coach gets fired," Low said. "That's an automatic. It doesn't matter what happened. There also is a thought process here that we're going to work at this thing and work it out. I mean, it's not going to happen because one guy's fighting against the other guy. I mean, that's for damn sure. This is going to be a thing where we try to work it out."

That was an obvious and direct reference to last year, when Muckler went down fighting with team president/GM Neil Smith, and the two men took each other down.

"It hasn't entered my mind, but I know what the scenarios are," Low continued. "I mean, that's life in the National Hockey League, as everybody knows. I don't think there's guarantees for anything. I don't think there should be guarantees for anything, either. In the end result you're going to get looked at and say, 'How did it all come out?' That's what's going to happen."

Sather wouldn't comment on Low's situation, and said he never has and never will make public comments about things such as that.

The math, though, is this. The Rangers, on a four-game losing streak, are 20-28-3-1 for 44 points, with 30 games remaining—one tomorrow against Montreal, followed by the All-Star break, followed by the final 29. They are going to have to win 20 more games, and get 40-plus points, out of the last 30 games.

Low was asked if he's crunched numbers yet.

"Too early, too early," Low started. "But I can guarantee you one thing right now: You're not going to get in unless you win 20 (of the last 30), I would say. You might with 19, but I doubt it. So I guess I lied and was doing a little math the last couple of days."

"I've done it a long time ago," Sather said. "I've been doing it since the first week. I don't think the math changed. I think you've got to have somewhere in the vicinity of 84, 85, 86 points to make it, depending on what happens. And there's enough games after the All-Star break to get things rolling again. It can't be a situation where we play two or three good games, then have four or five bad games. We've got to go seven, eight or nine good games and one bad game, then seven, eight nine."

Can it happen?

"It can if we get the goaltending," Sather said, adding that good goaltending can't be expected without much better defensive-zone play. But he was putting a large slice of the onus on Mike Richter.

Low is in a bad, bad spot because of some other underachieving. Adam

Graves had three goals in his last 37 games, and had been removed from the top line. Mark Messier has two assists and no goals in his last 17. And the list goes on.

The other reality, Sather said, is that changes will be made if results don't change.

"Those things aren't fictitious," he said. "Those things are reality in this business. If the team doesn't snap out of it, we've got to make changes. You can't just flounder along and have a veteran hockey team that's making mistakes."

Sather lamented that the assets he has to deal aren't many, excluding the top young prospects that he intends to hold onto unless a wonderful trade comes along.

"I'm not making any excuses," he said. "I knew what I was getting into when I got into this. There's no sense pointing fingers at the past regime or anything else. The situation is what we have here today, and that's what we've got to deal with."

The All-Star weekend will provide trading partners galore. Sather, though, said that the next few weeks will make his decisions more clear. The necessary deals change based on whether the Rangers fall completely out of contention or get back into it.

He said he wasn't tempted, during or immediately after the 7-2 embarrassment of a loss to Atlanta, to make an emotional trade.

"No, it's easy to do something drastic," Sather said. "It's difficult to not do something drastic. But is it logical to do something in a situation like that? No.

"No, I'm not going to wait it out. I'm going to keep doing whatever I can do to try to help us."

Asked if this regime, like the last one, overestimated the talent, Low said "I think this team can make the playoffs."

He had a chance to guarantee it as Giants coach Jim Fassel did just before his team made its run into the NFL playoffs a few months earlier, but only would say, "I told you what I think."

Low pointed to Vladimir Malakhov's season-ending knee injury, which he said dramatically changed the look of the team and how it played; and to Valeri Kamensky's recurring bruised kidney, because Low felt Kamensky was playing well before he got hurt and that his loss also hurt Messier.

"There's a lot of things that happened, and in the end result, it still isn't too damn late. And it isn't."

Sather sat on a couch in the players' lounge and conducted one of the few group discussions with reporters all season.

He explained why he didn't want to talk after the game.

"It's like you're saying to me last night when I'm walking out of the room, 'Have you got a minute? Have you got a minute?' Well, why do I want to stop and talk to you guys after a game like that? Why do you think coaches get 10 or 15 minutes to cool off after a game? Because you're going to say something, or you're going to react to something, and then you're going to be sorry. So you're better off to sit back and look at it for a little while, rather than overreact to it."

One of the writers, comfortable in Sather's relaxed manner to crack a joke, said, "But it's a great story if your head explodes."

"And it was close to it," Sather said. "I feel sorry for my poor wife."

"I get more frustrated than anybody, so I just know from the competitive nature I have that I'm better off to just wait a little while."

Then he went off in different directions while talking about work ethic, or lack thereof.

"You know, I can remember my dad retiring. He's a guy who worked hard his entire life. He was a carpenter. He built stores, he built some houses. It was an effort that he had to get up every day at 6 o'clock and go to work. Then when he got to 65, he retired like most guys. He laid on the couch for a year, and a year later he died of a heart attack. Guys get into the retirement mode. You have to do things you do well at. If you're a defensive defenseman, be a real solid defensive defenseman. We've talked about this since the first day of training camp."

Then he went back to the predicament at hand.

"I don't know how many times you guys have really put yourselves in my place and try to figure out the number of assets you have in this organization to try to improve it. Sit down sometime and try to figure that out.

"It's one thing to say, "What are you doing, sitting around doing nothing? You're not making a deal?'

"Look at my phone bill sometime."

WEDNESDAY, JANUARY 31, 2001

NEW YORK

One down, 19 to go.

If the Rangers' season began tonight, as Sather said it should, and if they do have to win 20 of their final 30 games, as Low predicted they would need to do to make the playoffs, well, this was a start.

You can't win 20 of 30 until you get the first one, after all. So the Rangers beat the Montreal Canadiens 4-2 at the Garden and they go into the much-needed All-Star break on a one-game winning streak instead of a five-game losing streak.

"As the saying goes," Mark Messier said with a laugh, "you're only as good as your last game."

They go to the break seven games under. .500 for the first 53 games, and they go in a measly nine points behind Boston, which holds down the final playoff berth in the East.

All of which is very bad, of course, unless the Rangers—a team that hasn't been more than two games over .500 at any time in the last four seasons—can rip off 19 more wins in the last 29 games, starting with Buffalo Tuesday night at the Garden.

Low thinks they can do it. We will see. But the Rangers don't want to think about 20 out of 30 or 19 out of 29.

"Nobody can ever look at the schedule and tell us how many games we have to win," Messier said. "That's self-defeating. All we needed to do is win tonight, and when we come back Tuesday, all we need to worry about is winning Tuesday. Everything else will take care of itself if we concentrate on the game at hand.

"If we start getting into how many games we need to win, and things don't go your way, then you're getting tighter and tighter as the season goes on. That's not a good way to approach it at all, from my experience."

The Rangers were carried offensively by the Czechmates line of Jan Hlavac (one goal, two assists), Petr Nedved (two goals, one assist), and Radek Dvorak (two assists) and a commitment to battling physically, to getting the puck in deep, and to protecting a lead in a fairly smart manner.

Lately, the Rangers' offense has been the Czechmates or nothing.

"That's definitely been going on this month," Low said. "We have to get some balance somewhere."

Nedved, for one, is tired of playing usless games down the stretch.

"We want to get back into the race," Nedved said. "It's no fun when you've got games left and you're not in the playoffs. We know that from last year. It's miserable."

So a victory, over a banged-up, mediocre, just sold, but playing well Canadiens team, was a good way to go into the break.

"I don't think you'd want to go into it and have five days of thinking about a five-game losing streak," Low said. "This makes it easier, but the whole key is going to have to be on the thought coming back, that what we did tonight is grind it out. That's the way we're going to have to play."

The Rangers played the first period as if their lives depended upon it, both physically and tight defensively. Early on Sandy McCarthy had a three-hit shift, popping Karl Dykhuis's helmet off on one of them; Adam Graves bowled over Eric Weinrich, and Messier hammered Sheldon Souray.

In the second, rookie defenseman Tomas Kloucek woke up the crowd with an open-ice pancake check on pest Eric Landry.

"At times we've played as well as anybody in the league," Messier said, a line that would become tiresome. "At times we've played as bad as anybody in the league. We need to find some consistency, and we need to find a little sense of urgency in every game, no matter who we're playing. Obviously, I think we play much better when we have a little fear in us."

There should be plenty of that over the final 29.

WINGER/CENTER JEFF ULMER, who played minor-league hockey for Low in Houston (IHL) last season, made his NHL debut on Messier's right wing. Ulmer had been called up to replace Mike York, but York decided to play despite his aching ribcage. After the game, Ulmer, Manny Malhotra and Tomas Kloucek were assigned to Hartford where they will be able to play during the All-Star break. Malhotra and Kloucek will surely be back.

Ulmer actually started, and therefore found himself standing on the blue line during the national anthem with Messier, Graves, Leetch and Rich Pilon.

"I was thinking about other people looking at me and thinking, 'I can't believe he's out there with those guys,' " Ulmer said. "I was thinking, "Wow, what am I doing on the blue line with these names?' It was great for my family and my friends to see that."

Before the game, Ulmer was working on his stick outside the locker room. Low popped out of the coaches' room, hands in pockets and said hello to Ulmer. Then, when he was out of earshot, Low mumbled, "I hope you can fuckin' play, kid."

YORK, WHO WAS NOT supposed to play, told Low he would play because he'd get five days to rest during the break. "He's a gutsy performer," Low said. "He's got old-time hockey written all over him."

WITH ONLY BRIAN LEETCH and Theo Fleury representing the Rangers at the All-Star game in Denver, the rest of the club is scattering for brief vacations. Low plans to go to Los Vegas.

But, he said, "I might change my fuckin mind the way my luck is going."

Speaking of luck, it took Low about an hour and 45 minutes to make the normally 40-minute drive from his home in Rye Brook to midtown Manhattan. Sometimes, traffic just happens in New York.

Broadcaster John Davidson, who also commutes from Westchester, suggested to Low that the train is a good alternative for getting into the city.

"No way," Low said. "Walt (Kyle) took the train once and it derailed. Took him two and a half fuckin' hours. No way I'm getting on the train."

NIGHT8MARE

Any Arsenic?

DENVER

All-Star weekend has often revolved around the Rangers for one reason or another.

In 1984, at the end of the Islanders dynasty, it was a Ranger, Don Maloney, who won the MVP on the Devils ice at the Meadowlands. In 1990, then-GM Neil Smith stole the show in Pittsburgh by pulling off the blockbuster trade for Los Angeles sniper Bernie Nicholls the day before the game.

In 1993, Mike Gartner not only won the first of his two "fastest skater" competitions, but he also had four goals and an assist to take the MVP car in Montreal.

The next season, the Rangers hosted the All-Star game at the Garden, placed four players—Mark Messier, Brian Leetch, Mike Richter, and Adam Graves—on the All-Star team, and Richter walked off with the MVP car by repeatedly stuffing Vancouver's Pavel Bure on breakaways, a precursor to the series-turning penalty shot by Bure in the Stanley Cup finals that June.

In 1996 in Boston, Messier and Pat Verbeek set up Bruins captain Ray Bourque for the winning goal with 38 seconds left.

In 1997, the storyline in San Jose was the reunion of Messier and Wayne Gretzky with the Rangers, and because of the impending retirement of Mario Lemieux, that mighty threesome was focal in the media's quest to find which young players would be the torch-bearers of the future.

The next season in Vancouver, after Messier's emotional divorce from the Rangers and signing with the Canucks the previous summer, he and Gretzky combined to perform some of their old Edmonton-days magic on the ice.

In 1999 at Tampa, Gretzky played his final All-Star game and walked away with the MVP award. Along the way, he did some recruiting of All-Star linemates Theo Fleury and Mark Recchi, both free-agents-to-be. Gretzky convinced Fleury, who signed with the Rangers the next summer. And Gretzky was honored at the 2000 game in his backyard, Toronto's brand new Air Canada Centre, while Messier played what may have been his final All-Star game, and while Richter suffered his season-wrecking knee injury at the skills competition.

So now came the 2001 All-Star weekend in Denver, with only Fleury and Leetch present. While neither was the mainbar, both were busy. Fleury was trying to convince his buddy Joe Sakic to bolt Colorado to join him in New York in July; and Leetch was doing likewise to defenseman Rob Blake of Los Angeles.

Fleury remembered back to 1999, when he and Gretzky and Recchi lit it up, and when Gretzky laid the groundwork for Fleury to forget his original plan to remain in the West as a free agent.

"I can't tell you," Fleury said when asked how things went with Sakic.

When pressed on the subject, Fleury would only say, "I had dinner with him (Saturday) night."

FLEURY, THOUGH, was having a great time being not only an All-Star, but also being considered one of the game's best players again.

"It's special, with what I went through last year," Fleury said. "That was a tough season all-around, so to be able to come back and be considered among the best players in the game again is very satisfying. I'm very proud of that. After last year, I never thought I'd be back in one of these (games).

"It was fun, and I think that's just the way I'm taking this whole year. I've always been a guy who's always smiling on the ice, having fun, and I didn't have a whole lot of fun last year, so I wanted to get back to that. I think I can even play better, and I'm going to have to play better for our team to make a run at the playoffs."

Fleury's first of two goals in the All-Star game was scored against Buffalo goalie Dominik Hasek, who has tortured the Rangers, and who will be the first goalie they see after the break, Tuesday at the Garden.

Fleury bumped into somebody and was credited with the only official hit on the post-game stat sheet, although nobody could remember it.

Fleury claimed the hit was legit. Fleury said he hit Edmonton's Janne Niinimaa in the third period. "Actually, I slew-footed him," Fleury said.

SOMEBODY HAS TO BE the worst player (besides the goalies) and today that might have been Leetch, who was minus-6 through two periods (which is where he finished). Defense partner Ed Jovanovski was minus-5.

"He even jumped off once, and I was on with Blake and they scored, and he started laughing when I came back to the bench." Leetch said. "We were making jokes in the third because everyone in the locker room knew. Our shift came up with three minutes left and I said, "See, coach (Joel Quenneville) is letting us play out of this. He trusts us.

"It was unbelievable. Every time we were out there. It didn't even have to be a breakaway. Just loose puck, and it was in the net."

Leetch, nevertheless, said "it was a blast" and that at one point he was so into watching the game that he forgot to go onto the ice to replace Scott Stevens. "I jumped on after about five seconds, but it's fun sitting there watching."

ALL-STAR MVP Bill Guerin was asked by a French-Canadian radio reporter if he could answer a question in French. "No," he said, "I'm from Massachusetts."

EX-RANGERS COACH Herb Brooks and Pat Quinn must have thought they were dreaming while watching the All-Star game.

The two best lines in the record-setting 14-12 win by the North American Stars over the World Stars will be at their disposal a year from now, when Brooks coaches the United States and Quinn coaches Canada in the Salt Lake City Olympic games.

"I told them, 'Well, it could be easy for Herb right there,'" Brian Leetch, a certain U.S. Olympian said after seeing Bill Guerin, Doug Weight and Tony Amonte combine for six goals and seven assists. Guerin, who won the fastest skater event in the skills competition Saturday, walked away with the truck as the game's MVP.

Quinn saw a pretty high-powered trio himself, in Canada's Joe Sakic-Theo Fleury-Paul Kariya line, which had two goals (both by Fleury) and seven points. The game broke by four the record for highest-scoring All-Star game (22 goals in 1993).

"It's pretty easy playing with those two guys," Fleury said. "There's a lot of speed, tremendous hockey sense, all three guys can score. It would be a great line, I think, for the Olympics. There's all the ingredients there for what you need in these one-game, showdown-type things."

Another North American line with Olympic implications had Mario Lemieux playing with Brett Hull.

"Now, if we could just get Mario to play with Brett on the U.S. team . . .," Leetch said.

Both have dual citizenship, but Hull will play for the U.S. and Super Mario, who scored a breakaway goal and had an assist in his comeback All-Star game, smiled and said, without hesitation, that he will play for Canada.

VANCOUVER'S ALL-STAR winger Markus Naslund not only shares the league lead with 31 goals (tied with Pavel Bure), but he has also become one of the top young captains in hockey. He learned from the best.

After the Canucks' final game last season, Mark Messier symbolically handed the captaincy to Naslund. Knowing his contract option wouldn't be exercised, Messier removed his uniform jersey, with the "C" on the front, for the last time, had it washed, then wrote a message on the back before handing it to Naslund.

"He handed me the jersey," Naslund said. "It was a great thing to do. It said, 'Thanks for all the support' and a few other things. It was probably one of the biggest moments of my career, having a living legend do something like that. I really enjoyed the relationship we developed from the time when he first got there. I was intimidated just by his presence. Then I got to know him on a personal level. It was a thrill."

Naslund was one of those rare mistakes by Pittsburgh GM Craig Patrick, traded to Vancouver for tough guy Alek Stojanov in 1996.

But Patrick has another All-Star who has bloomed this year in Alexei Kovalev, the ex-Ranger who never understood the object of the game when he was in New York, overhandling the puck, refusing to shoot, playing lengthy shifts, and missing assignments in the defensive zone despite immense skill.

He already has a career-high 27 goals, and he played in his first All-Star game.

"I've done a lot of good things this year, but I still think I can do more," Kovalev said. "But like I've said, I don't want to prove anything to anybody, I just want to prove to myself that I can be the player I want to be, my consistency, scoring goals, being a better player overall, defensively. I proved to myself I can be one of those players."

When asked if he had anything to prove to the Rangers, or to ex-

Rangers president/GM Neil Smith, who regularly chided Kovalev's inability to reach his potential, Kovalev said, "No, I'm not that kind of person.

"Actually, somebody asked me if I want to tell anything to Neil. Neil did a lot of good things for me. I wouldn't be on the New York Rangers when we won the Stanley Cup if Neil didn't keep me there, because Mike (Keenan) wanted to trade me, and Neil kept me there and I had a chance to win the Stanley Cup.

"But I'm not the kind of person who wants to tell somebody something. The only thing I've proved, I've proved to myself."

MONDAY, FEBRUARY 5, 2001

RYE, N.Y.

John MacLean was finally freed. Glen Sather found a taker and traded MacLean to Dallas, a team that has been to the finals two years in a row. How does a player not fit with the Rangers, but fit with one of the superpowers of the league?

Well, for one thing, better teams can better use role players, veterans to plug into key situations.

That doesn't change the way Sather treated MacLean throughout this ordeal.

MacLean was freezing his tail off, fishing on the Red River in Manitoba as his Moose team had an off-day fishing outing.

"I had my line in the water when I got the call," MacLean said. "I didn't catch squat and I didn't care."

He was back in the NHL. The Rangers got a conditional draft pick, based on how far Dallas goes in the playoffs and how much MacLean plays. It isn't likely to turn into anything substantial.

MacLean couldn't have helped this team? He's good on special teams, and the Rangers' special teams are awful. He's good in his own zone, where the Rangers are awful. He can score a bit at even strength, where they are awful.

"They just told me to come and be ready to play," MacLean said of his orders from Dallas. "I wasn't asking too many questions."

Now the question is, how does this mediocre team give away players who become regulars on much better teams? For MacLean, Mathieu Schneider, Stephane Quintal, Kevin Hatcher, and P.J. Stock, the Rangers have nothing to show but Michal Grosek, who is about to be waived, and Brad Brown, who is a fifth or sixth defenseman at best.

NEW YORK

Those two games-in-six nights stretches must be killers. Or maybe it's not easy to play with a tan.

Whatever the reason—and it appears that either Ron Low can't get through to them, or that Low's players aren't very smart—the well-rested, tanned Rangers returned from their All-Star break vacation, gave up two quick goals, fell behind 3-0 and got bombed by Buffalo, 6-3 at the Garden.

Low was again quietly livid afterwards. He invoked the team payroll. He suggested that his players are too comfortable. He was dumbfounded that his pleas to play a simple defensive-zone system have been ignored, if not defied.

He also was faced, in a tiny room, with Garden president Dave Checketts and Rangers president/GM Glen Sather. Low looks much like John Muckler looked at the end of his time here, and like Muckler's predecessor Colin Campbell looked at the end of his time—like a coach that can't get a response from his players, and can't figure out why.

"It surprises me, but I guess in a way it doesn't," Low said. "We've been into this situation 54 times now and we've done the same thing a lot of times. Being down 2-0 on plays we talked about an hour and a half before game time . . . I swear to God I must speak gobbledy-gook or something because it doesn't seem to be getting across and the message doesn't seem to be setting with anybody. I mean, it's time to be accountable, for everybody, as a unit, as a hockey club. The accountability doesn't seem to be there.

"And the other part of it is, I guess, that everybody knows if you make a mistake you're going back out the next shift because 'what are you going to do to me?' . . . The whole thing is, there has to be a gut check time within that room that says, 'I'm going to do something about it; I have to do something about it.' . . . I don't know if we threw a hit in the first 10-12 minutes again, and we talked about the last game and the reason we won the hockey game is we were really physical against their club. I don't know. I guess I must talk a different language."

The Rangers may be lacking in personnel, but mediocre players, even lousy players, can do simple things. These Rangers can't.

That is why they are 11 points out of a playoff spot. That is why they will need to win 19 of their final 28, or more, to make the playoffs, which almost surely isn't happening.

It is why the Rangers are behind expansion Minnesota, and barely holding off expansion Columbus in the overall standings.

"I don't know how you change it," Low said. "What am I going to do? Am I going to sit somebody down? . . . Am I going to drop to three defensemen. I mean, surely to Christ, with a $60 million payroll, there has to some accountability from inside the room, from guys who say, 'I have to be accountable.' You have to hold yourself accountable. It's time for everybody to realize that. Accountability comes from within.

"I mean, I could drop to one and a half lines . . . I know I can't do it and win. But then, I guess, if we're going to lose 6-3, I might as well. There were a lot of people who looked like they were still on vacation tonight."

Just 1:24 into the game, J.P. Dumont was unchecked by Alexei Gusarov and Jan Hlavac to beat Mike Richter. Just 1:13 later, Jay McKee got away from Sandy McCarthy for his first goal since last March, first in 53 games.

The mistakes kept coming. At one point in the middle of the period, Mark Messier threw the puck to the middle of the defensive zone, where Doug Gilmour happily picked it off and set up a shot by Chris Gratton. Messier followed that up with an unthinkable drop pass in front of his own net, which was also easily stolen. Finally, Messier carried the puck out of the zone after the lengthy shift, and the fans cheered him sarcastically.

The Rangers had two more chances to clear the puck before the Richard Smehlik goal that made it 3-0. They got back into it briefly. Petr Nedved beat Hasek 13 seconds after the goal and in the second, the Rangers' power play—and Messier—scored!

To put it in perspective, since Messier's last goal (19 games earlier) on December 20, McKee had scored, Rich Pilon had scored twice, Montreal goalie Jose Theodore had scored, and a guy in Pittsburgh, who was retired on that date, had come back to score 16 times (and once in the All-Star game).

The 3-2 score didn't last two minutes, because the Rangers' awful penalty killers gave it right back. Leetch and Gusarov ignored Stu Barnes, who put back a rebound.

It was pretty much over there. But late in the second, it got worse for the Rangers. First Vaclav Varada's leaping elbow knocked Pilon out of the game with a concussion. Then Messier, right on Dave Andreychuk's tail in front of the net, allowed Andreychuk to score and make it 5-2.

"The coaches have preached all year long what we need to do in the defensive zone and we continue to make mistake after mistake after mistake, and I guess that's what he's talking about, accountability," Theo Fleury said. "We know what we've got to do. You can't be the guy that makes the mistake."

"I think we've had enough meetings," Nedved said. "I think Ronnie was saying after the first period, we can go over Xs and Os for two hours before the game, and unless we go out and do the job, it doesn't really make a difference."

MESSIER BECAME THE 10th player in team history to score 200 goals as a Ranger.

PILON'S CONCUSSION wasn't at first diagnosed as such. But Pilon didn't remember skating back to the bench, and on his way home, as his wife drove, he became "carsick from the oncoming headlights."

WEDNESDAY, FEBRUARY 7, 2001

RYE, N.Y.

When the Rangers fall completely out of playoff contention (if they haven't already) and the housecleaning begins, one of the Rangers who might have enough trade value to bring back top prospects or draft picks is Mike Richter.

The league is loaded with contenders who need proven playoff goalies, and Richter, despite his struggles, is highly regarded, especially by St. Louis, whose GM, Larry Pleau, was Neil Smith's top assistant for most of the 1990s.

Richter understands this bit of reality, although he said his preferred goal would be to right the Rangers and to win here, rather than to be sent somewhere else where he might be able to win. He certainly doesn't hope to be dealt.

"I really, to be honest, I try not to think about it at all," he said. "It just takes away energy from what I'm supposed to be doing right now. When you get into situations like these, you ask yourself, 'What can I do to help the team as much as possible?' And that is, to do my job as well as I can. That's going to help the team as much as possible.

"I just find that, last year we were kind of facing the same situation and it really takes away from some of your responsibilities. To me it undermines my ability to play. If you start looking across the league, and looking at other teams, and who needs what; the idea of trying to get your allegiance to someone else while you're still playing for this team, to me, you can't do that and still be effective. So I try not to entertain it because it's not helping me. In fact, it's hurting me."

The list of potential Rangers veterans with reasonable trade value includes Petr Nedved, Adam Graves, Richter, Sylvain Lefebvre, and Rich Pilon, and it wouldn't be a surprise if any or all of them went by the March 13 deadline. The knee-jerks on the radio and elsewhere needed to be reminded constantly that Brian Leetch and Theo Fleury have no-trade clauses they will not waive.

WAY BACK IN SEPTEMBER, before a preseason game in Hartford against the Islanders, Ron Low was talking about what he had learned about his new team in training camp and the preseason.

He said the one thing he didn't know was whether his players worked hard enough in the defensive zone.

Now, 54 games and five months later, Low knows the answer. The Rangers don't work hard enough in their defensive zone.

So why did it take so long to figure out?

On Tuesday, following the mindless 6-3 loss to Buffalo, Low

The team's uneven play drove coach Ron Low to look for an "arsenic" button on the coffee machine.

said he can't come up with answers. Then he took a turn a coach rarely takes. He admitted that he's helpless because his players know he won't or can't bench them. That idea might have been planted in a post-game meeting with Checketts and Sather.

By admitting it, Low rendered himself more helpless. You can refute his claim that the reason he didn't play his fourth line more—and therefore one of his underachieving other lines less—was that he doesn't believe his fourth line could score and help get them back into that game.

However, there comes a time, especially at 6-3 against Dominik Hasek, that you throw in the towel for the sake of a lesson. If he had sat Mark Messier's line or Petr Nedved's line or Mike York's line and played Manny Malhotra's line every other shift—and in doing so, admitted his team wasn't going to win that game anyway—an overdue message would have been sent.

Instead, the only Rangers who ever get punished are Michal Grosek, Brad Brown, Sylvain Lefebvre, and Kim Johnsson. Oooooh. That must scare the heck out of the rest of the lazy folks on the roster. It's the same tactic John Muckler used so ineffectively for two and a half seasons. If your big guys are allowed to be untouchables, everybody will play like untouchables.

"You can sit people if you're going to get the desired result," Low said. "And, I'm sorry, right now we're in a playoff race . . . and if our top three lines aren't scoring goals, then we're in trouble."

Now they're in trouble anyway. They're done like dinner. The play-offs are a pipe dream. Any drastic step Low might take now isn't going to change that, but, of course, he cannot write off his team at this point without signing his own resignation papers. Perhaps Sather or Checketts should run the white flag up the pole and declare another rebuilding stage will start, so that Low can be freed of the "we can't punish anybody because we have to win tonight" way of thinking.

Today, Low tried another avenue of punishment. He put the Rangers through a practice, then a horridly long, exhausting skate, interrupted only by an obscenity-filled speech to the group at center ice. Then came a 45-minute bike ride. Low said he would like to have worked the Rangers 8 A.M.–5 P.M., let them know how that feels, since they won't work for three hours on a game night.

In his speech, Low repeatedly barked at the Rangers. "Muck's fuckin' gone. Neil's fuckin' gone. Who the fuck are you going to blame now?"

He challenged them, dared them, to take the blame upon themselves.

You know what? That might carry them through their next game, at Florida. It won't last, though. The Rangers have proven that out over 54 games. It never lasts.

And, by the way, you can rail all you want about how they're just not good enough, or too old, or whatever. But if these Rangers could have mustered the smarts and the effort to have won their last two home games against Atlanta, a home game against the Islanders, and a game in Boston when the Bruins were reeling last month, they'd be sitting here one point out of a playoff spot, instead of 11.

Low thinks they can make the playoffs, and he claims that his team has everything with the possible exception of the willingness or ability to dump the puck and go bang away to get it back. He noted that in their best games this season, the Rangers' hits totals have been in the 40s or 50s. He also pointed out that, in the first period Tuesday, the Rangers tried 10 passes up the middle of the defensive zone, each a cardinal sin. And that all 10 were picked off. That's not physical. That's mental. That's players who don't listen to the coach.

You can bet that none of those 10 were made by Malhotra or Eric Lacroix or Jeff Toms. You can bet that each of the 10 offenders went right back out for his next shift while Malhotra, Lacroix and Toms sat, while Grosek, Brown and Dale Purinton sat in street clothes. You can bet that if Malhotra or Grosek or Brown made a pass like that, he'd be sitting for a long, long time. But not Messier or Fleury or Graves or

Leetch. Low has let them become untouchable. They can't be punished.

It is the one thing the Rangers have learned this season.

LOW WENT FOR HIS customary cup of coffee before meeting with the press today. The coffee maker is a big complicated machine, with buttons for all types of flavors of coffee, tea, chocolate milk, etc.

"Any arsenic?" Low wondered. "I've been pressing these buttons every day."

ONE PLAYER WHO SHALL remain nameless is among the growing bunch who think, among other things, that Sather is coaching the team via walkie-talkie (when he is in attendance, that is) from his skybox, and that Low is "Sather's puppet," and that Messier has been a selective leader. The player said that Messier hasn't even spoken to him all season.

Then he pointed to the problems of Graves, still the team's soul. Graves drives to the net, the player said, and Messier and Kamensky won't give him the puck. Instead, when they dump it in, they expect Graves to go in and do the dirty work and get it back for them.

"They dump it in the corner and say, "Go get it,' " the player said. "Adam must want to say, 'Fuck you. You go get it.'"

AN UNHAPPY CAMPER, Michal Grosek, was placed on waivers today. The Rangers will send him to Hartford if he isn't claimed by another team in 48 hours.

MIKE RICHTER STILL STEAMS when blame is placed on Muckler and/or Smith. He is one of the few guys who accepts responsibility for what went on the last three seasons.

"If a player is going to let himself off the hook for that, then he's going to let himself off the hook for anything," Richter said. "If you don't have a personal responsibility as an individual to know when you're playing well and know whether you can help the team, then you're going to find an excuse one way or another.

"Muck was fired last year and to sit there and pretend that it was all his fault is a God damn joke."

FRIDAY, FEBRUARY 9, 2001

SUNRISE, FLA.

Manny Malhotra has been the centerpiece of the Rangers' rebuilding project for almost three years, and he still just 20 years old and barely NHL-ready.

But this season, for the first time since he was drafted in the first round in 1998, Malhotra is being treated as the gem he might yet turn out to be.

When then-Rangers coach John Muckler said about Malhotra the same things that Ron Low says today, Muckler made it sound like such a terrible negative. Muckler then treated the kid as an unwanted pest.

"Sometimes I think the media has Manny rated too high," Muckler said on the second day of training camp, 1999. "I thought that last year. I thought some of you people had him rated as a first-liner or second-liner. I see Manny as a solid third-line hockey player."

Then Muckler buried him.

Low sees the same type of future for Malhotra, but Low and his assistants, Ted Green and Walt Kyle, are seeing to it that Malhotra gets the teaching and the ice time he needs to progress, especially after Muckler cost Malhotra almost a full year of development.

"You know, there's so much emphasis put on guys that are high draft picks to be scorers or whatever," Low said. "You know what? If a guy winds up being a great fourth-line center, or a great third-line center, what's wrong with that? The National Hockey League doesn't have enough of those guys. I don't think Manny's ever going to score 30 goals. He might, because he's got the pace (speed) to do it and he's also got a helluva shot. But if he doesn't and he learns to be a checker and a really good one, they're valuable guys. Teams are looking all over the place for guys like that. The whole thing with him right now is to make sure he keeps progressing, and if he does that, then you're off to the races."

Although Malhotra was sent to Hartford a couple of times, one of those in a confused state when told to go down and learn to be a winger, Low has since nurtured the young center.

"Let's just say that in the last while he's progressed very well," Green said. "I don't know what he's done the last two years. I wasn't here. My read on him right now is he's one of the better skaters in the National Hockey League, and I think earlier in the year, after training camp, we asked him to be a little more aggressive because he's got good size. I think he's a young man who's willing to learn and apply himself.

"There was a time here in the last little while where he and I have had time to sit down and have some discussions about other players in the league who have made themselves a real good career by being great defensive people. I could name a few—Craig MacTavish, who played here, Guy Carbonneau, Bob Gainey, Dave Keon—those kind of guys made real good careers being really good role players."

Malhotra, in addition to being big (6-foot-2 and a rock solid 220 pounds), strong and fast, is mature and bright. He is a coach's dream. And he is appreciative of the treatment he's gotten this season.

"They're always very positive towards me and encouraging, so it's good to be in that environment, where coaches are behind you and supporting you and trying to help you learn the game," he said. Green regularly goes to the videotape with Malhotra, but not only are his mistakes pointed out, so are his good plays. Green tries to reinforce the things he's done well while correcting the mistakes. It sinks in.

Last season, Malhotra had to go back to junior hockey in order that the Rangers could send him to their minor-league affiliate in Hartford after the junior season ended. He saw the return to Guelph, Ontario as "regressing." Then he came to camp and the Rangers had four centers ahead of him on the depth chart.

After two stops in Hartford—where he could end up again, so his development can continue if his playing time here begins to slip—Malhotra's responsibility and the quality of his ice time (he averages 7:31 per game) have increased.

"Without a doubt, the biggest thing is the way he's playing in his own zone," Low said. "I mean, in training camp we were really questioning whether we were going to be able to play him as a center because in low coverage he lost his guy time after time after time. Even when he first came up he did a little bit of it, and Teddy took him back and showed him films almost every day, of each game that he's played, every mistake he's made and also the positive things he did. And he's been better and better every game. Obviously, I'd like to get him more ice time on a regular basis, but when he's been on the fourth line he's gone out and done some good things, created some energy with his shifts."

Considering what he's been through in his first three years as a pro, Malhotra is probably farther along than he should be, but not quite as far along as he could have been if treated properly.

"It's not the end of the world, obviously, but I want to be doing more and to have more responsibility," he said. "That's just the way I am. I want to be pushed more and I want to be challenged all the time. I realize it's going to take time, but that's just the way my mentality is. I want to be moving faster."

Now, finally, he is moving in the right direction.

WELL, NOW THE RANGERS have turned the corner. Or maybe not. And if they did, right around the corner is a speeding 18-wheeler.

The Rangers kept their fading playoff chances barely flickering with a 4-2 win over the Florida Panthers at National Car Rental Center, but now they have to play the Devils, the undisputed kings of the East and a team they haven't beaten in four regular seasons.

They will have to play the Devils without Mike York, who was knocked out of the game in the second period when body slammed by Florida's John Jakopin. York suffered what the team is calling a mild left shoulder separation, and is day to day—and nobody took exception to the hit.

But the Rangers will go into tomorrow's matinee with two wins in their last three games (and one disgusting defeat in between). They also won for the second time in their last 15 road games (2-11-2), and "closed" to within nine points of a playoff berth.

Or, as Low put it, "4½ games out." The Rangers know that, with 27 games to go and all that ground to make up on two teams, it's too daunting to look at the big picture.

"We've got no choice," said Petr Nedved, who scored twice, including an empty-netter. "We can feel sorry for ourselves and play the way we played against Buffalo (a 6-3 loss Tuesday) and play the rest of the 27 games and start looking for the summer, or we go out there and don't think about the end result and just take it one game at a time and see what we can do about it. Obviously the playoff spot doesn't look very optimistic right now, but there's enough games, still, that we can do something about it.

"I still think we have enough time, but you're not going to be able to do it the way we played against Buffalo."

Let's keep this victory in perspective. The Panthers came into the game with the third-worst record in the NHL, having won two in a row for only the second time all season long.

But the Rangers are in no position to be bickering about the quality of opponents, not after losing home games to the Islanders and Atlanta (twice) recently, not when their victory only assured them that they can't be passed in the standings by Columbus when they visit the Blue Jackets Monday.

Also to be taken for what it's worth is the Rangers' readiness to play at the start of the game, and their apparent heeding of Low's pleas to use their heads in the defensive zone. They did that, but they have done so before this year, only to lapse into the—in Low's words earlier in the season—chickens-without-heads defense.

"Ronnie got our attention as a group the last couple of days," said Messier, who scored a goal for the second game in a row. "We came in focused and played a really solid game, I thought."

So we will see if anything good comes of this, anything at all.

The Rangers, for the first time in 15 road games—dating all the way back to November 22—scored the game's first goal, then added another.

At 6:21, York banged in a power-play rebound of a shot by ex-Panther Radek Dvorak.

Just 2:19 later, Tomas Kloucek's pass sent Nedved into the Panthers' zone. The defense backed off, so Nedved got up on one foot and launched a wrist shot over Roberto Luongo's glove and under the crossbar for a 2-0 lead.

Meanwhile, Richter, whose performance is being weighed by scouts around the league, was solid, especially against his old pal Pavel Bure. The Russian Rocket came out of the game with a single assist to show for 26 shifts and five shots on goal. Guess that "Leetch-wing lock" thing that John Muckler tried last season wasn't really necessary.

"We'll see what happens," Low said.

WINGER MICHAL GROSEK cleared waivers and wasn't happy about it. He can now be sent to Hartford, although that move may not happen unless the Rangers need a roster spot for another recall. "I just don't get it," Grosek said. "... They told me wait, wait, you're going to play more during the year. I wait and wait, and my ice time went (down) and just stopped. They told me I'm bad defensively. I don't think I'm bad defensively."

Asked if welcomes a change of scenery, either in Hartford or via trade, Grosek said, "In this situation, of course. You hear, "You are a lazy piece of shit and you can do nothing good for this team. You have a bad attitude. I don't think it's fair."

Then in a reference to Sather's treatment of John MacLean, Grosek said he would report to Hartford if assigned.

"At least I'm going to play there," he said. "I hope so. Maybe they can scratch me there, too. Maybe Slats can send me to the East Coast League. You never know. He can do whatever he wants. At least I'm going to play somewhere. That's all I want."

Low disputes Grosek's claim that he hasn't had a chance. "I think he's had opportunities," Low said. "I think he's had quite a few of them, actually, and I don't know if we saw enough on a nightly basis. ... The next move is up to him, to play another game, play another period and see what the response is. If you like it, you carry on. If you don't, the next move is Hartford, obviously."

Low added that he's not sure if Grosek will actually get another shot with the Rangers.

NEW YORK

Theo Fleury still hasn't been involved in a Rangers victory over the Devils. Most Rangers haven't.

But Fleury sure makes the rivalry a lot more fun.

The impish pain-in-the-neck was right in the middle of things today in a terrific 1-1 Rangers-Devils tie at the Garden, which stretched their winless streak to 22 regular-season games (14-0-8).

Fleury, who normally drives Devils captain Scott Stevens batty, this time got into it a bit with Martin Brodeur, the Devils goalie.

First, though, Brodeur got involved with a few other Rangers. Mark Messier stepped near the crease, and Brodeur leaped at him, decking Messier with a shot to the face, and was assessed a penalty. Later, Brodeur would wallop rookie Jeff Ulmer. He would also chop, in a nasty upwards manner, between the legs of Adam Graves. In the imaginable discomfort that would cause, Graves slammed his legs shut and Brodeur's stick got stuck in Graves's crotch. Amazingly, Graves thus was assessed a holding-the-stick penalty.

"What's his stick doing there?" Graves repeatedly complained.

But, late in the second period, Fleury was serving coincidental minor penalties for roughing with Randy McKay, when teammate Radek Dvorak was called for slashing. When Fleury left the box, Messier whipped a pass around the boards and out of the zone, and Fleury caught up to it. He went around Scott Stevens, bored in on Brodeur, and missed his shot. But Fleury continued in and knocked Brodeur and the puck into the net for a short-handed goal and a 1-0 lead.

Fleury, who early in the game appeared to be hurt by an Alexander Mogilny slash to the hand, stood over the fallen Brodeur. Just about everybody watching figured Fleury was trash-talking Brodeur.

It turned out to be just the opposite.

"He was in a daze, looking at me. I was looking at him, at his (missing) teeth," Brodeur said, referring to the gaps in Fleury's grin. "He gets really wound up, and he was staring me down."

Brodeur, though, admitted that he started the exchange.

"I told him he was missing the net, and he was," Brodeur said. "I was the one who knocked it back in. I told him he got lucky."

What Brodeur actually claimed he said to Fleury was, "You lucky bugger. You fanned on that sucker."

Fleury verified that story.

"I said, 'Yeah, well, it still went in.' That's why I was laughing," Fleury said.

As he stepped away from Brodeur, Fleury pointed toward the penalty box, where Stevens was skating. But Fleury swore he wasn't taunting Stevens, either. Rather, he was pointing to Dvorak in the penalty box. Fleury said that, while the two were in the box together, Fleury told Dvorak he was going to score a short-hander when he got out.

The Devils got the tie when Turner Stevenson scored a goal during another Dvorak penalty.

Brodeur, who started his 48th consecutive game against the Rangers, wasn't happy that he allowed the Rangers to earn a point in the standings.

"No doubt about it," he said. "The last thing we want to do is give these guys any help," said Brodeur,

"We have no gifts to give anyone, especially these guys. In '94, they took (the Eastern finals against the Devils en route to the Stanley Cup), and we heard about it all year. I've been involved for a long time, and I don't like these guys."

COLUMBUS, OHIO

Glen Sather's plate is full, or at least it should be at this point. Maybe that is why he sounds a bit confused.

At the morning skate today, Sather was going on about the depth of the organization—one of his favorite gripes—and the mess that Neil Smith left him.

Smith "never should have traded Sundstrom," Sather said, about former Rangers winger Niklas Sundstrom. He added that he liked Dan Cloutier, the young goalie now in Tampa. What Sather apparently didn't know was that Smith traded Sundstrom and Cloutier in the draft-day deals that brought the organization the bonanza of prospects Pavel Brendl and Jamie Lundmark, plus Jan Hlavac, who is emerging as a solid NHL player. What he also didn't apparently know was that the Rangers stood to lose Cloutier in the next expansion draft if they had kept him.

Sather said that, in the summer of '99 free-agent shopping spree, "Neil was trying to save his job, which is understandable . . . but if he'd done his homework . . ."

His homework? One thing that could never be said about Smith was that he didn't do his homework. Never mind that of the six free agents signed, the one who is really killing them is Valeri Kamensky, who is the one Sather and Low seem to love so much that he is in the lineup whenever he's healthy. Theo Fleury is a bargain now. Defensemen Sylvain Lefebvre and Stephane Quintal are what they are, NHL defensemen, not superstars. Overpaid, yes, because that is how you get unrestricted free agents, by overpaying them. And the since-departed Quintal is better than Brad Brown, the player for whom he was traded (along with Grosek, who is headed for the minors). Kirk McLean is fine in his role as backup goalie. Tim Taylor was fine in his role as checking center, even if Low didn't use a checking line as just about every other coach does, until the injury that will have ended his season New Year's Eve.

And what about the lack of homework done by Sather in the whole Mathieu Schneider-Vladimir Malakhov mistake last summer? Sather never even spoke to Schneider, whom he could have had for relative chicken feed, maybe $2 million a year for two years. Instead, Sather threw $14 million at Malakhov, whose history suggests two things: Inconsistency and injuries. Malakhov wasn't healthy enough to show the inconsistency with the Rangers. He's missed virtually the whole year.

Meanwhile, Sather never bothered to try to sign gritty, rugged free agents Scott Thornton, who went to San Jose, or Dallas Drake, who went to St. Louis. Nor was he aware of the free agency of former Devils draft pick Mike Van Ryn, who was also signed by the Blues.

Homework? Now Sather will probably be trying to get Van Ryn out of St. Louis if and when he trades Richter there.

Sather also said that Graves's priorities have changed, and that it was understandable, because of all the personal tragedy he went through last season. Graves might have been negatively affected by the losses of his son and his dad, and perhaps his preparation for this season suffered. But his priorities changed? That's doubtful.

It sounds as if Graves is a goner at the trade deadline.

Meanwhile, Sather keeps claiming that all the Rangers need to do is be more accountable to one another and more consistent in their performances; and that they need to continue to bring in young guys who can push the older guys, especially those with "long-term deals." He's right when he says there isn't much on the farm team in Hartford, which won the AHL championship last year with a roster heavy on veteran minor-leaguers.

"You guys (the press) seem to think that you just wave a flag and say, 'We're going to fix it.' It takes time to fix it."

THIS IS WHAT YOU GET when you put a trapping expansion team, with a full house on home ice, up against a team that lost its legs to a schedule of three games in four days. Throw in a couple of referees who decide that, on this night, hooking is no longer a foul, and you get hideous hockey.

You also get exactly the kind of game the Rangers are going to have to grind out, the kind they didn't win nearly often enough over the first 56 games. They beat the Columbus Blue Jackets 4-3 at Nationwide Arena.

Make that, Richter beat the Blue Jackets, because the Rangers had no legs, and because their special teams continued to be absolutely horrid.

So the Rangers are 2-0-1 in their last three, 3-1-1 in five on the road, and eight points out of the playoffs with 25 games left and four days off before resuming play in Tampa Saturday. Of course, while they are off, Boston and Carolina play twice apiece, so the standings could look dramatically different by Saturday.

"It wasn't a very good game," said Leetch, one of many veteran Rangers who didn't have a very good one.

"It wasn't pretty out there," added Nedved, whose blocked shot and 3-on-1 setup led to Jan Hlavac's game-winner with 6:49 to go. "We didn't exactly play the way we wanted to for 60 minutes, but at this point in time we just want to take the two points and get out of here."

Leetch wrenched his back on Alex Selivanov's goal, wrenched it, he kidded, "looking back to see how Richter was doing."

Richter, now 18-2-7 in his career when he faces 40 or more shots, was doing it all, and he wasn't even supposed to play.

Richter talked Low into playing him on consecutive days. His reconstructed left knee, he and trainer Jim Ramsay felt, could withstand the workload because he had only played three times since January 31, and because the four days off would allow the training staff to deal with any swelling that might occur in the knee. That knee had also taken two pucks in the last two games, further complicating the swelling.

"He was outstanding," Low said. "He won the game for us tonight. He must have made, I would say, 15 great saves."

Richter's play surely was an eye-opener for the scouts from around the league watching him (St. Louis has been following the Rangers around).

But the rest of the players' tired performance had to be an attention-grabber for Low, who has gotten down to three lines lately, and faces seven more occasions when the Rangers will play three games in four nights.

"Mess didn't have much jump," Low said. "Theo didn't have much jump, Gravy, Petr's line didn't have much jump ... It's something we're likely going to have to monitor ice time. I think we're in a situation where you have to try to win hockey games, and that's going to have to happen. If we run out of gas, we run out of gas."

They nearly ran out tonight, and this would have been a disastrous non-win if they didn't get it.

Richter got it, so now the Rangers are on another one of those little runs, which Nedved called "a snowball."

"We're starting something going here," he added. "With only 25 games left in the season, we can't afford to be losing against a team like this, and that's taking nothing away from those guys."

Richter took it away from them.

SATHER AND LOW plan to speak tomorrow about Michal Grosek, who cleared waivers Friday and probably would have been sent to Hartford if not for the injury suffered by Mike York Friday night. But with Tony

Tuzzolino being recalled and playing the last two games in Grosek's spot, and with Jeff Ulmer getting the coaches' attention with his hard work in both ends of the rink, it appears Grosek is headed for the AHL.

SATHER WILL SURELY re-open trade talks with Wayne Gretzky once Gretzky officially takes over the Phoenix Coyotes, now expected tomorrow or the next day.

YORK, DESPITE A SEPARATED left shoulder, had his bags packed for the trip to Columbus.

"Unrealistically, of course," Low said, after telling York to stay home.

ONE RANGER WHO begged anonymity: "You want to know why there's so much fuckin' parity in this league? Because the referees ref the score. Every one of them refs the score."

TUESDAY, FEBRUARY 13, 2001

RYE, N.Y.

As expected, Grosek was sent to the minors today, and center Tim Taylor's season ended.

Grosek, who had not played since January 29, sitting out the last five games, had cleared waivers on Friday. With the energetic play of recall Jeff Ulmer, there was little chance that Grosek was going to get a chance to get into the lineup barring injuries.

So the Rangers assigned Grosek to Hartford. Grosek, who wore out his welcome in Buffalo last season and was traded to Chicago as part of the Doug Gilmour/J.P. Dumont deal, had been obtained by the Rangers in their shady waiver deal involving Stephane Quintal just before the season began.

Taylor's season ended with the decision to have surgery to repair the torn abdominal muscle he suffered New Year's Eve in Dallas. Taylor was hit by Grant Marshall, and hadn't played since. He attempted to resume skating two weeks ago, but the injury hadn't gotten any better, so Taylor will have surgery Friday at the Medical College of Pennsylvania at Hahnemann University.

RYE, N.Y.

Once in a while Ron Low, a truly nice guy, likes to get into it with reporters. Today Larry Brooks of the *Post* asked Low if Valeri Kamensky goes back into the lineup as soon as he's healthy. The underlying part of the question suggested that Kamensky might ruin the little roll the Rangers have going.

"It's the same question with Yorkie," Low said.

"Different players," answered Brooks.

"Same question," Low answered. "If we're winning. If we've gone three games in a row winning without Yorkie and we're winning, are you going to ask me the same question, 'Do you put him back in the lineup?' You obviously put players back in the lineup because they're supposedly your best players. That's why you do it, and they have to be your best players in order for you to win.

"Where are we going with this exactly? I think Val Kamensky did a helluva job moving over to the right side when he's been a left-sider his whole life, to play with Mark, because we really didn't have anybody to play with Mark. Theo was on fire the first half of the year, and scored 70 points, or whatever he got, playing with Yorkie. I mean, I don't know where you're going with this. I never said Val was coming back to go on Mark's line to begin with. I never said that. Maybe he is, maybe he's not. I don't know where we're going to go. I'd like to be able to get Val back on the left side somewhere, so he can play where he should be playing. I mean, it's irrelevant. He's not back in the lineup yet, he won't be back in the lineup for another week, and by then we could have three more injuries and we could be begging for a spot for Val. Who knows? I mean, who knows?"

Kamensky resumed skating today, but he won't step right back into the lineup until he's in game shape. "Last time," Low said, "he came back, being out 10 days, practiced twice and went out, and I don't think he was in good enough condition to be playing. We have to make sure he is this time, for him and for us."

NOW, BACK TO the nightmare.

Low said that the Columbus game "was frightening. The same things we've done prior, and we didn't get bit, or beat, because of Mike. We did a lot of awful things in that game. Really, Florida was awesome. We did a really good job there. We did an unbelievable job against Jersey in our own zone. We did a great job against Montreal, terrible against Buffalo.

So if you start looking at the rotations, we're ready for another really bad one. Well we can't have one right now. It's impossible. We have to be strong defensively the rest of the way, and our offense will take care of itself most nights."

Low was asked if his experience has been that he has to keep on top of this particular thing more than any other team you've ever seen?

"Yes, yes, it has," he said. "I don't know why, but for some reason we're not comfortable in our own zone and the things we have to do there. By now it should be an automatic. But it never seems to stay automatic for more than three games, and I don't know why. But it's also something that we as coaches can't let slide at any time, and it's going to keep being be drilled at least once or twice a week when we have practice time. It has to be a big part of the puzzle, or else we're not going to win."

Part of it is the discipline and patience against teams that trap. The Rangers can't force plays up the middle against teams like Columbus and Florida, certainly not against teams like the Devils.

"We've played against three in a row that trapped against us and we didn't go in the middle," Low said. "Then you're going back into the same thing. We didn't play a very good hockey game. We played like we were tired, yet when you're tired, if you do the simple things and keep it out of the middle it saves you so much work, coming back into your own zone and being in there, if you just keep it simple. And when you're tired, that's generally what you have to do to win."

The coach is also happy with the way Adam Graves has started to play lately.

"He's been playing tough, he's played hard, he's been working really hard in the corners, and likely deserves more than one puck to deflect off him into the net," Low said. "He's had some good scoring chances the last four or five games that haven't gone in, and he's been aggressive. Way more aggressive. I like what I've seen from him, actually, for about three weeks now. He hasn't been putting any numbers on the board but he's been way more physical, way more involved in the play, everywhere."

MAYBE IT'S JUST A coincidence that the Rangers are unbeaten in their last three games while five young players have either stepped into the lineup or had their roles increased.

Make that, it probably is just a coincidence, since the Rangers wouldn't have tied the Devils without Theo Fleury's short-handed goal, and wouldn't have beaten Columbus if not for the acrobatic goaltending of Mike Richter.

Still, the increased ice time given to the defense pair of rookie Tomas

Kloucek, 20, and sophomore Kim Johnsson, 24; the increased time and responsibility given to third-year pro Manny Malhotra, 20; and the Rangers debuts of wingers Jeff Ulmer, 23, and even Tony Tuzzolino, 25, have added some enthusiasm and gumption to the Rangers' roster.

Besides, if the Rangers are going to go down in flames, it's a lot better to have players who go down fighting. Ask the 18,200 (or the fraction thereof who show up) at the Garden if they'd rather see Ulmer battle for a loose puck or an older winger (we won't mention any names) decide the puck's not worth the trouble or the work to go get it.

Kloucek may be the only one of the five who has the potential to be a really top NHL player, although Malhotra's stock has also risen in the eyes of the current coaching staff.

Low said he's not surprised that Kloucek is the player he has been lately, because of his strength, skating, and ability to pivot.

"He's still only 20 years old, which is unbelievable," Low said. "For that age, he's got great composure. Since he's been back, he's been beaten a couple of times, and he just comes back to the bench and it doesn't faze him. It happens in games.

"He' s been banging people and they know they've been hit by him."

Johnsson had been scratched a couple of times, but he and Kloucek have been paired for the last five games (3-1-1), and they've instantly clicked. That pairing has also allowed Low to lighten up Brian Leetch's ice time, and helped the Rangers survive the loss of Rich Pilon (concussion).

Overall, it has been part of the tiny youth movement, with Ulmer making Michal Grosek expendable (he's in Hartford now) and Malhotra making the loss of Mike York (ribs, shoulder) almost bearable.

"Kim and Kloucek have played really well as a pair," Low said. "I think Manny has added a little bit of enthusiasm. Ulmer's the same as far as the forechecking end of it. Tuzzolino hasn't had enough shifts, but the ones he's had have been pretty exciting, down in the end zone and he's been banging.

"I guess stuff like that, you look at it, and you need more of it. You need more of it on a regular basis. I think if you can force the play in the other team's end a certain amount, at least you've got them on their heels instead of always being in our zone and fighting to get it out of thee. They've added something for sure. They've added some pace, some up-tempo and some speed."

Why did it take so long to add these ingredients? Well, the NHL's 23-man roster limit makes it difficult for such moves to be made. Unless players are put on injured reserve or sent to the minors, they take up roster space. Most veteran players have to clear waivers before being sent down. Plus nobody really knows how a young player will react to his first time in the big league.

"I don't know where you're going to find it," Low said, when asked if he would have liked to add the youthful enthusiasm earlier. "It's pretty much everybody from the American League here now as far as the guys who are of a younger nature and guys who have got that true pace. I mean (Derek Armstrong) is a guy down there who skates pretty well, but not a lot of body contact from him. (Brad Smyth) certainly doesn't have the speed you want."

Tuzzolino is back in Hartford, but could be recalled by Saturday if York isn't ready to go. And when York comes back, Malhotra might go back to Hartford because, as a fourth liner, he won't be getting much ice time. When Valeri Kamensky (bruised kidney) comes back next week, Ulmer, who has two goals and has been a pain in the neck to play against, might be going to Hartford, too.

But they have made those decisions difficult, and they have added some enthusiasm and entertainment value to an unenthusiastic, not very entertaining bunch.

FRIDAY, FEBRUARY 16, 2001

RYE, N.Y.

Low rubbed his hands together and tried to keep a straight face.

"The Czechs were fuckin' awesome in practice today," he said. "Petr (Nedved) was awesome. They were just great."

A few minutes later, he repeated the praise. This was an obvious comeback to stories, the latest in the *Post* this week, that he always criticizes Czechmates Nedved, Hlavac, and Dvorak, his most trusty offensive line, but never criticizes Messier, Graves, Kamensky, et al.

SATURDAY, FEBRUARY 17, 2001

TAMPA, FLA.

The Tampa Bay Lightning hasn't been on national television in more than three years. Tonight's game against the Rangers is on ESPN, and you'd think the city is hosting the Super Bowl again (as it did last month).

This morning, Tampa Bay's new coach John Tortorella—yes, the guy who replaced Muckler with four games left in last season, a no-win situation; and the guy who wasn't contacted by Sather about keeping the job; the guy Sather referred to as "Tortorelli"—was holding court in an auxiliary locker room. He's chatting with the small contingent of local media, a few New York reporters he knew well, Steve Levy and Brian Engblom of ESPN, Lightning TV analyst Bobby Taylor and MSG Network's Sam Rosen.

Tortorella was singing the praises of some of his young players, such as kid captain Vincent Lecavalier, and rookie of the year candidate Brad Richards.

Richards, the coach said, refuses to exercise his option when there are optional practices, so Tortorella had a sit-down with him to explain he didn't have to be there.

Engblom, a defensemen on the dynastic Canadiens teams of the late 1970s, chimed in with: "In Montreal we were taught that optional was Latin for "Be There.""

Taylor added that it was necessary for guys to skate back then, "for cleansing the systems of the guys who had been out all night the night before."

"That was your day, Chief," Tortorella said. "These guys can't even get into the bars."

To this day, "Tortorelli" hasn't spoken to Sather.

THE QUESTION WAS SIMPLE and pre-emptive. Sooner or later, somebody was going to ask Mark Messier, and the reporter figured this to be as good a time as anybody. After all, if somebody else asks it first, and Messier's answer is interesting one way or another, you're beaten on a big story for no other reason that your refusal to ask it.

So, for the first time, Messier was asked, "Will you definitely be back next season?"

Messier, who answers all kinds of difficult questions all the time, who never flinches, who likes to say he "stares down the barrel" and faces things head on, didn't like it one bit.

He got downright angry.

"Why are you asking me that?"

When it was explained that it was an inevitable question that had to be asked, Messier wasn't buying it.

"You must have some ulterior motive for asking me something like that," he said. "What's your point?"

Honestly, he was told, there is no motive. But, if he has decided to definitely come back, or to not come back, either way it's a story—a much bigger story if he's calling it quits. He is 40. At some point, he will stop playing. The question didn't infer that he was finished, or that he should retire, or that there was a reason why he shouldn't come back for at least one more season.

Still, Messier wasn't convinced.

"I'm shocked you asked me that," he said.

When he finally calmed down, he said, "You know me long enough to know that if I make a decision, everybody will find out about it at the same time."

Okay.

THEY MAY BE RUNNING in place at this point, but it's better than dropping completely out of the picture with 24 games to go.

The Rangers, behind Nedved's hat trick and the Czechmates' five-goal night, beat the Lightning 5-4 before an announced 20,154 at the Ice Palace, their fourth win since Low said it would take 20 wins, at least, to make the playoffs. The Rangers are 3-0-1 in their last four, and are eight points back—not quite dead yet.

The Rangers caught a bit of a break when, during their four-day break, Boston only picked up two of a possible four points, and Carolina gained only one of four.

"We just have to win our hockey games," Low said. "We can't worry about what's happening with the other two teams. It was great they both lost (Thursday), but we can't rely on that. We have to make sure we play our games and win. That's where we're going, every night."

"There's not much room for error," Messier added. "Every game we face right now is a potential four-point swing either way and we've just got to not get too caught up in watching the other teams and trying to figure out how many games we have to win or what we have to do. We really need to concentrate on our next game. We'd sure like to go 24-0 the rest of the way. It's unlikely, but we just want to give ourselves a chance like we did tonight and the last few games."

But the Rangers had to win, and as difficult as they made it—they blew a 2-0 lead early, let Tampa Bay cut it to one goal twice in the last 5:53 and had to face a barrage before the final buzzer—they won.

"We seem to want to make it tough for ourselves no matter what happens," Low said. "We needed to win the hockey game and in the end result we did. We didn't make it easy, but we won."

Jan Hlavac and Radek Dvorak each scored a goal, and the line combined for nine points, four by Nedved, who also has eight goals in seven games.

Low has, seemingly all season, been critical of the Czech line for their refusal to shoot the puck. Tonight, even, there were times when they could have put away the Lightning and didn't.

"Thank God they shot when they did because every time they did they seemed to score," Messier said. "They play a style of hockey that is not unlike how they've been brought up and how they've been taught. They really hang onto the puck and cycle, and they've been really good for a long time. The last little while, the whole line has really carried the team offensively. They've been outstanding. Tonight they were just great in both ends of the ice. They did it all for us tonight"

Nedved doesn't disagree that they need to shoot it more, or that Low's complaints weren't justified.

"Some of the games, sure, and I'm sure in some of those games we could have made a difference and we didn't," Nedved said. "We have to pick our chances. If it's there, we can pass it, but if it's 50-50 you might as well shoot it. Early in the season, I don't think we had as many chances as we had tonight, but there were a few games where there were chances and we came out of it with nothing, and that was frustrating for us."

Messier made an awful play on Matthew Barnaby's goal—Messier cracked his stick over the crossbar while Barnaby celebrated, and Low admitted that Messier "was asleep" on that play. Then Fredrik Modin beat Mike Richter on a wrap-around to tie it.

It took only 13 seconds for Hlavac to un-tie it, on a 1-against-3 break, and Dvorak made it 4-2 early in the third. Dvorak also survived a scary tumble into the boards at the buzzer with nothing but a bruised shoulder.

MIKE YORK TALKED his way back into the lineup, despite a separated left shoulder and a still-sore ribcage.

THE RANGERS SHARE a luxury jet with the NBA Knicks. It is a luxurious 737, with all seats the equivalent of first-class. Some of the rows face one another, some have tables for cards or meals. There is mahogany trim and new carpeting. There are TVs and VCRs and all kinds of comforts, not to mention specially-ordered food. Since the Knicks had the plane this day, the Rangers had to charter an aircraft that other teams use. This one isn't equipped, for example, to make it coast-to-coast without stopping twice for fuel. The Rangers' flight to Tampa hit headwinds and had to stop to refuel, making it a long trip. Nobody could feel sorry for the poor athletes, though. Most of the time they travel without worry, in first-class accommodations all the way. There are those, though, who don't have it as good as the Rangers. Ottawa, for instance, still travels commercial.

So do the writers, of course.

MONDAY, FEBRUARY 19, 2001

NEW YORK

Now Cablevision and Madison Square Garden will find out what they got when they hired Glen Sather to run the Rangers last summer.

Because today, in the first period of a 4-2 victory over the Chicago

Blackhawks, in a victory that ran the Rangers' unbeaten streak to five games and pulled them to within six points of a playoff spot, their season might have died. Unless Sather can save it, that is.

Mike Richter suffered a complete tear of the anterior cruciate ligament in his right knee just over a year after tearing the other ACL on an eerily similar play. Richter kicked out his right leg on a wide shot by Chicago's Steve Sullivan, and when his skate slammed into the goalpost the knee buckled. He was immediatelty taken for an MRI, which showed a complete tear. Team doctors Bart Nisonson and Tony Maddalo will perform major reconstructive surgery when the swelling subsides, probably in the next two or three weeks.

On February 5, 2000, at the All-Star game skills competition, Richter's left knee was wrecked when he shoved it into the goalpost trying to stop Mariusz Czerkawski of the Islanders.

It would come to light that Sather was working on, perhaps even had finalized, a deal that would have sent Richter to St. Louis, where GM Larry Pleau is desperate for a proven veteran goaltender for his contending Blues. Now that deal, or any deal involving Richter, is dead.

Richter left the ice crying, especially after he tried to put weight on the right knee and it gave way. He cried because he knew what it took to come back from the last reconstructive surgery—a six-month rehab, and three more months of constant therapy while he played.

Knowing that it took so long also makes it important that Sather finds a goalie who can carry the load at the start of next season, as well. Rookie Vitali Yeremeyev, who has struggled in the second half of the season in Hartford, was immediately called up.

Sather also immediately phoned Cliff Fletcher, who was named Wayne Gretzky's new GM in Phoenix, to talk about restricted free agent goalie Nikolai Khabibulin, whose agent, Jay Grossman, has spoken to Sather in recent months. Grossman indicated that he expects Khabibulin to either sign with Phoenix or to be traded relatively quickly now that Gretzky is in power.

"You're not going to pick up the phone and make a deal the first conversation you have," Sather said. "It takes time. It's been going on for about four or five months."

Khabibulin hasn't played NHL hockey in almost two seasons, spending last year in the International League with Long Beach while at a contract impasse with the Coyotes. He has been practicing all season this year, and could be ready in a few weeks if signed. Plus, he's only 28.

"He's a good goaltender," Sather said. "That doesn't mean you're going to make a deal for him."

The ramifications are complicated, too, because it was widely believed that the Rangers would trade Richter for prospects, with St. Louis the likely contender interested in a Cup-proven goalie and the Blues having heavily scouted the Rangers the last few weeks. Sather insisted that, not only did he not have a deal of Richter to St. Louis in the works, but that "Richter hasn't been offered to anyone as far as I know" and that, believe it or not, nobody had called about Richter's availability.

Sather added that there may be other options—and that one of those is not Tom Barrasso, whom Sather contacted earlier this season.

But Sather now has to do something quickly, or hope and pray that Kirk McLean, a forgotten man as Richter's backup for two seasons, can carry them into the playoffs starting Friday in Pittsburgh. Richter had just gotten back near the top of his game to keep them alive during their 4-0-1 streak.

The Rangers' playoff hopes were dashed for good when goalie Mike Richter went down with a torn ACL in his right knee against Chicago on February 19.

JIM MCISAAC, BRUCE BENNETT STUDIOS

"It hasn't sunk in yet, and it probably won't for a few days," Richter said upon returning to the Garden on crutches. "I guess you can feel a little sorry for yourself, but this is part of sports. You are going to have setbacks, injuries, things you have to overcome. No athlete is immune to it."

Richter said it's both frustrating and encouraging that he has experienced the lengthy rehab before—because he knows how difficult it is, but also that he can come all the way back from it. Last season, he played until the end of March despite the injury, and didn't have the surgery until April 5.

"I would rather not have the experience but I certainly know I can get through it and feel great and I've got a lot of years left," he said. "The sooner I get operated on, the sooner I can get therapy going."

The Rangers, to a man, admitted there was an emotional sag after Richter went down with 1:37 left in the first period of a 1-1 game. But McLean stepped in, made two difficult saves right off the bat, and helped them get re-focused on the game.

"I don't think there's another guy in the league that would have put in the time to keep his knee ready to play on a daily basis like he did," Mark Messier said. "It's basically a 24-hour job keeping the swelling out of it. There's not a lot of guys that would have put that effort into it. ... That's what makes him a champion.

"He was playing with a lot of heart and experience and grit, but nobody could tell me he was 100 percent coming back off an knee injury like that. He was getting the job done with a lot of heart and a lot of courage and that's why he's Mike Richter. He was just in tears. He knew what was wrong and he completely broke down. I think everybody was a little bit shaken up."

Sather said his heart dropped, too.

"It did for a few minutes," Sather said. "But the reality of it is, problems like this become challenges, so you have to find a way to solve them. There's no sense feeling sorry for yourself or feeling sorry for the team. We've got to find a way to work around it, and if we can't do that, we're not doing a very good job. You can't just throw your hands up and say 'It's over with; we're out of this thing now because we've lost our goaltender.' We've got to find a way to fix the problem."

RADEK DVORAK, Jan Hlavac and Petr Nedved scored the Rangers' first three goals yesterday, giving the Czechmates line nine straight goals over the last three games. Sandy McCarthy broke the streak with a spectacular goal coming out of the penalty box.

THE RANGERS BEAT the Blackhawks at home for the first time since March 11, 1992, going 0-5-1 in that span.

TUESDAY, FEBRUARY 20, 2001

RYE, N.Y.

The Rangers goalie in their first game without Richter is ... Yeremeyev.

Low went to Kirk McLean and asked him which game he'd rather start, Friday in Pittsburgh or Sunday in Philadelphia when the Rangers come back from a four-day break to play three in four nights.

McLean chose Philadelphia.

The goalie was in a tough spot, and Low knew that when he asked the question. McLean has just been pummeled by the Penguins throughout his career (5-14-1 record, 4.52 goals-against average and the 8-6 loss in Pittsburgh October 14, before Mario Lemieux's comeback). Against the Flyers, however, McLean was 10-8-3, 3.02).

Low knew the numbers, but he wanted to hear something different from McLean. He wanted to hear the veteran accept the challenge, to acknowledge the need to step up to the plate for his desperate teammates, and to want to face Pittsburgh.

He wanted a dishonest, honest answer.

So when McLean said Philadelphia, Low and Sather were both ticked off that they had to feed the rookie to Mario, Jaromir Jagr, red-hot ex-Ranger Alexei Kovalev and the dangerous Penguins.

Yeremeyev will be the fourth Rangers goalie to see action against Pittsburgh this season (joining McLean, Jason LaBarbera and Johan Holmqvist).

THURSDAY, FEBRUARY 22, 2001

RYE, N.Y.

Not that it means much to the Rangers, but there was still a buzz around their training facility when it was announced that the Colorado Avalanche just became prohibitive favorites to win the Stanley Cup by acquiring superstar defenseman Rob Blake from Los Angeles around after midnight last night.

Everybody's talking about it today. That and the Grammys. The old guys are glad Steely Dan won the best album of the year. The young guys have one question: Who is Steely Dan?

Mark Messier couldn't help but leap into the commotion.

"(Eric) Lindros is going to Colorado for (Jon) Klemm, (Dan) Hinote, and (Stephane) Yelle," Messier reported to anybody within earshot. "Don't forget where you heard it first."

Of course, he was just making it up, trying to get people to believe him.

Some think the acquisition of Blake might mean that the Avalanche will try to sign him before he gets to free agency in July. And if they do, that could mean the Avs don't have enough money to sign some of their other potential free agents, including one Joe Sakic, the favorite to win the Hart Trophy as league MVP.

Fleury claimed today that he gets a bonus if Sakic comes here, for his recruiting efforts.

"But I have to be here, too," he said, aware that, while he has a no-trade clause, it expires this summer, and that Sather has been offering him around the league.

RICH PILON IS READY to come back after that concussion. He could be a key guy against Pittsburgh. Then again, maybe not. Pilon has had success and failure (who hasn't?) against Jagr and Lemieux. In the 1992-93 playoffs, for example, Pilon and then- Islanders teammate Darius Kasparaitis were a defense pair that drove Jagr and Lemieux nuts with physical play, and a bit of chippiness, even after whistles. Those Islanders stunned the two-time defending Stanley Cup champion Penguins in a seven-game second-round playoff series.

But Pilon has had some rough nights against Jagr, in particular, as well, such as the 8-6 loss in Pittsburgh in October.

Pilon remembered one night with the Islanders where "we had about five or six shifts, and we were down 4-0 already."

He hesitated a moment.

"I think that's the night I slashed Mario and got suspended. That's how frustrated I was."

BOY, THE RANGERS ARE LUCKY. They are still mathematically alive only because Boston and Carolina are backing up in the standings, unable to put any finishing stretch together.

FRIDAY, FEBRUARY 23, 2001

PITTSBURGH

It couldn't have worked out any differently. The Pittsburgh Penguins' 6-4 romp over the Rangers at Mellon Arena actually was quite predictable.

What else could be expected when one of the worst defensive-zone teams in hockey meets perhaps the best offensive-zone team; when the league's worst road penalty-killing unit goes up against the most lethal power-play fivesome; and when a rookie goalie is thrown to the wolves as Vitali Yeremeyev was in the first game since Richter's season-ending knee injury.

Throw into the mix the fired-up ex-Ranger Alexei Kovalev, who has somehow figured out the game after all these years and become a dominant force. Kovalev scored three goals (giving him 39 for the season) and added two assists to end the Rangers' unbeaten streak at 4-0-1, and to shove them to nine points out of the playoffs with 22 games left.

"I think coming here he felt more relaxed," Leetch said about his former teammate of seven seasons. "He's always had the skills to put himself in position, or to put other people in a position (to score) and a lot of times he's held it too much, or waited. He's just learned the game and gained a lot of confidence in the last few years here."

"He's entering his peak years," added Messier, who was Kovalev's biggest supporter for five seasons. "He was just a baby when he was in New York. He's an incredibly gifted player, a big, strong kid. . . . He's matured as a person and matured as a player, and you combine that with his skill and talent and love of the game, and he's just a bona fide superstar. He's got my vote as the MVP of this league."

Heck, Mario Lemieux (one measly goal) was hardly even a factor in his first game against the Rangers since his comeback, playing with a sore back and hip.

But Kovalev's big night was just the start of the bad news for the Rangers, who began a brutally tough stretch of three games in four nights against three of the better teams in the East. They plan to go back to Kirk McLean in Philadelphia. And since the team has repeatedly shown little faith in McLean, this night may have been an alarm for Glen Sather to step up his efforts to get a goalie.

Not that it was Yeremeyev's fault, but he didn't look NHL ready. Then, Pittsburgh has done that to more seasoned goalies than this 25-year-old making his second NHL start, even if he said he wasn't nervous. On five of the goals, he had almost no chance.

"A couple of plays made by skilled players, very skilled players," Ron Low said. "There wasn't a whole lot Yeremeyev could have done."

"They have great players, so we have to respect that," said ex-Penguin Petr Nedved, who came back to New York in the Kovalev trade. "I don't want to say we gave them too much respect, but in a way I guess we did. A guy like Kovalev, he's a great player, but if you give him the opportunity like that, obviously he's too good a player not to score."

ANOTHER MAN DOWN. Defenseman Brad Brown blocked a shot, suffered a broken right foot and could be out for the rest of the season.

SANDY MCCARTHY pounded Krzysztof Oliwa during a second-period fight. LEETCH DID NOT START the Rangers' first power play, which probably hasn't happened since Mike Keenan was coach in 1994.

SUNDAY, FEBRUARY 25, 2001
PHILADELPHIA

The Rangers were 5:19 away from getting to overtime, which would have guaranteed them at least one point and a much-needed step ahead in their fading playoff race.

Then the thing that has killed them for two seasons got them again, and they took a step back. On a play from behind the net, where so much defensive-zone trouble has begun this season and last, Mark Recchi scored the goal that sent the Rangers to a 2-1 loss to the Philadelphia Flyers at First Union Center.

So the Rangers, who have lost twice in Pennsylvania in three nights, remained nine points behind Carolina, eight behind Boston, and took another game off the schedule. There are 21 left, and that doesn't appear to be nearly enough.

"It's one we're going to look back at and think we should have won, because we did a lot of things very well," Low said. "It's going to hurt. It's going to hurt big-time. We could have closed the gap a little bit tonight and we didn't do it."

Keith Primeau and Mark Greig worked the back boards against Mark Messier and Rich Pilon late in the third. Everything appeared to be under control. But the puck hopped momentarily off of Greig's stick, Brian Leetch went for the puck and left Recchi open for a moment. Greig one-handed it past Leetch and Recchi smacked it past McLean for the first Flyers lead of the night.

"We can't afford to give up any points, obviously," said McLean, who will start again tomorrow as the Rangers close their three games/four nights stretch against conference-leading Ottawa at the Garden. By next Sunday, they will have played five times in eight days, and since several of their older players didn't seem to have much jump tonight, it will be a real test to stay in the playoff race.

The Rangers also didn't fare too well in playing one of their most physical, aggressive games of the season, led by Tomas Kloucek, who twice pancaked behemoth Keith Primeau in the first Philadelphia appearance of his career.

Kim Johnsson left in the second with a twisted left knee, and while he insisted he's OK after the game, he might not play tonight. Pilon, who had a massive game in the hits department, suffered a subluxed rib, had it popped back in, found he was able to breathe again, and didn't miss a shift. Adam Graves, who scored the Rangers' only goal, hyperextended his left elbow and didn't miss a shift. Mike York lost half a tooth when he was hit by a puck and didn't miss a shift.

"The guys really battled," Pilon said. "We deserved a point."

Once again, the Rangers can say "If only we had played like this earlier in the season . . ." They wouldn't be in this dreadful position if they had. But they didn't.

"We're battling for our lives and we have to keep it going," Low said. "We just have to keep it going. Somehow we're going to have to find enough goals to win games when we get that kind of goaltending and that kind of defensive effort.

"It's going to be a struggle. We know it. We put ourselves in this predicament and we're the only people that can bail ourselves out of it."

Not if they don't find a way to win a lot of these games; games where they play smart defensively, and strong all over the ice. Surely there haven't been enough games like that this season.

"For most part of the game we were the better team," Petr Nedved said. "There were a lot of good things we did out there, but still the bottom line for us is we needed the game and we needed two points. It is frustrating. We did everything we needed to do tonight. We took the body, we drove to the net, we created a lot of chances for ourselves."

THE RANGERS CONTINUE to be heavily scouted. For the second road game in a row, Edmonton scout Dave Semenko watched. Detroit has also had Mark Howe following the Rangers, and he was accompanied tonight by Red Wings scout Dan Belisle. The Wings are believed to have interest in re-acquiring Adam Graves, while they always are in the market for veteran defensemen like Pilon and Sylvain Lefebvre.

For what it's worth, Sather had lunch Saturday with agent Don Meehan, who represents many players, including Buffalo's unsigned Mike Peca.

AS THEY HAD in the preseason, Dale Purinton tangled with his old junior hockey buddy Todd Fedoruk. This time, ESPN's Bill Clement explained the relationship, and showed video of Fedoruk's back, his name tattooed there across his shoulders, just as it is on his uniform. Purinton, who received the instigator penalty and a misconduct, didn't want his tattoo shown on TV.

MONDAY, FEBRUARY 26, 2001

NEW YORK

Another night, two more points that slipped away. The Rangers couldn't hold a one-goal lead they briefly had in the third period, then couldn't hold onto the one point a tie or an overtime loss would have brought.

Instead, they allowed two late goals and were beaten 3-2 by the Ottawa Senators at the Garden. Just a night earlier, they turned a 1-1 tie into a 2-1 loss. So, instead of gaining three points the last two nights, they gained none, and sit nine points out of a playoff spot with 20 games to go.

"We've been running out of time steadily," Ron Low said. "You had two golden opportunities to close (the gap)."

Unlike Sunday, when they couldn't get the next goal in a 1-1 game despite constant pressure against Philadelphia, the Rangers got the big goal in this game.

Sylvain Lefebvre's simple dump into the right corner created a chance as Valeri Kamensky beat Shane Hnidey to the puck and threw it in front.

Mike York snuck between two defenders and smacked the pass past goalie Patrick Lalime with 8:47 to go.

But the Rangers failed to hold that lead. Just 1:09 later, Todd White stepped out from behind the net, completely alone, to stuff his first goal of the season past Kirk McLean (39 saves) to tie it at 2-2.

And with 3:11 to go, Daniel Alfredsson was all by himself to bury an Alexei Yashin rebound for the winner.

Once again, Low said his team "couldn't have worked harder" especially in the third game in four nights, but, "when you have the lead you've got to be able to protect it better than that."

The Rangers continued a trend that has been the opposite of what they had become accustomed to the last two seasons. For the eighth consecutive game, they scored the game's first goal.

It came at 18:28 of the first, when another big hit by Tomas Kloucek (which is becoming customary) created a turnover. Kloucek knocked Mike Fisher off the puck at the defensive blue line, and Theo Fleury wheeled it into a breakaway pass for Mark Messier.

Messier took the pass at the offensive line, flew down the right wing, and put a one-legged snap up over the right shoulder of Senators goalie Patrick Lalime for his 20th of the season—the first time in three years that he's hit 20, and the 17th time in his career.

Messier, who moved past John Bucyk into fifth place on the all-time list for games played (1,541), had an earlier chance stolen by Lalime during a Rangers power play. Brian Leetch found Messier at the right post, and Lalime sprawled on the ice, dropping his stick in the process, and stuck up both arms to bat down Messier's not-high-enough shot.

THE NIKOLAI KHABIBULIN sweepstakes opened today when the Phoenix Coyotes made their choice of goalies. Wayne Gretzky's new team decided to keep Vezina Trophy candidate Sean Burke, and signed Burke to a three-year, $9 million contract extension with a no-trade clause.

In doing so, the Coyotes made it quite clear that they will trade Khabibulin, and since several Stanley Cup contenders (including St. Louis) are in the running, the deal will have to be done rather quickly. The trade deadline is March 13.

Almost immediately, Glen Sather had conversations with Khabibulin's agent, Jay Grossman, but he denied he spoke with Coyotes GM Cliff Fletcher. Sather said he spoke to Grossman about "generalities" regarding Khabibulin's contract. Khabibulin, 28, has not played an NHL game the last two seasons, and the best offer he received in that time was the same deal Burke signed.

"I know they're going to trade him eventually," Sather said. "Whether it's in the next three or four days or by the trade deadline, I don't know."

Grossman, who denied a wire service story that quoted him as saying the Rangers were the front-runners, said there are six teams seriously interested in Khabibulin, and he believes it could be done in a matter of three or four days.

Khabibulin will be looking for a four or five-year contract worth at least $4 million per. In addition to obtaining younger, lower-priced talent in the deal the cost-cutting Coyotes will want to shed some additional payroll. That's why the Rangers will be in the mix, since not many other teams, if any, will be willing to add Khabibulin's $4 million plus an additional $2 million or more in players Phoenix insists be in the deal.

One of those players is defenseman Keith Carney (who has three years and $7.4 million left on his contract after this season), but another might be defensman Teppo Numminen, who has three years, $15 million left on his deal. The Rangers are probably the only team that could take on an additional $8 million or more. The big question, though, is how much the Rangers will have to give up, and whether Gretzky will want both Pavel Brendl and Jamie Lundmark, or Mike York, in the deal. That assumes that Sather will be willing to part with any of his top prospects for the goalie he sees as a long-term successor to Mike Richter.

"It's a risk," Sather said. "Everything's a risk."

FLEURY HAS BEEN STRUGGLING lately. The puck isn't going in nearly as frequently as it had for the first 50 games, and he looks as if he's getting frustrated. He also is getting tired of hearing that Sather is shopping him, that Sather might try to put him through waivers to make a Stephane Quintal-type of under-the-table trade, and that Sather will ask (force) him to waive his no-trade clause.

Part of Fleury's different appearance is his smile, too. Fleury has had his trademark gap-toothed grin filled in with false teeth. It changes his whole face. He also had his hair frosted blonde.

As for his slump, Fleury blamed it partly on his stick manufacturer.

He complained that the manufacturer sent him the wrong sticks. The shafts on the new batch are too whippy, he said.

"It's like aiming a gun with the sight a bit off. You don't know where it's going to go."

THE PRE-GAME LOCKER ROOM is always booming music of some sort, but rarely, if ever before, has it been heavy rap. Today's selections came courtesty of NWA, and DMX, and while nobody was taking credit or blame, they had to have been the choices of one of the young guys.

It was difficult to imagine that Mark Messier, for one, was in there rockin' out; or that Alexei Gusarov brought in the CDs from home. Sure enough, while the rap was blaring, Messier was in the coaches' room. When he came back into the room, his voice was loud and clear: "OK, that's enough of that." And the rap went off quickly. Someone, for a brief moment, played a bar of Frank Sinatra's Strangers in the Night almost mocking Messier's age. Soon, though, DMX was going loud and strong again.

THE SCOUTS WERE out in force again, at least 15 of them, including Detroit's top two scouts for a second game in a row and Red Wings GM Ken Holland, presumably to see Adam Graves and perhaps Rich Pilon. St. Louis scout Alain Vigneault was also in the building, but he's been following Ottawa.

MIKE RICHTER WAS GETTING treatment in the training room off the locker room after the game, when he bumped into Mike York heading for the shower.
York: "How are you?"
Richter: "They made a mistake. I'm fine. I'll be at practice tomorrow."
Actually, his surgery is scheduled for March 9.

MESSIER ON PASSING John Bucyk for fifth on the all-time games played list: "If you hang around long enough, I guess you're going to get a few records."

THEN THERE WAS this Michal Grosek story out of Hartford. It seems the Wolf Pack was on a typical minor-league journey of three games in less than four days, with an 11-hour bus ride in the middle. Grosek tried to get the players to take a collection to raise $10,000 for a charter flight. You could just hear him saying, "Eleven hours in a bus; it's a fucking joke."
But apparently, Grosek started playing better after the trip,
"I think that 12-hour bus ride from St. John's got him back to thinking about life," Rangers assistant GM Don Maloney said.

WEDNESDAY, FEBRUARY 28, 2001
NEW YORK

As if the Rangers needed another disaster. With their season in shambles for the fourth year in a row, and still reeling from the season-ending injury to Richter, the Rangers learned late last night that leading scorer Theo Fleury has entered a substance abuse program.

Fleury, 32, voluntarily entered the in-patient treatment as part of the NHL and NHL Players Association's substance abuse and behavioral health program and will be under the guidance of Drs. Dave Lewis and Brian Shaw, the same doctors who tended to Fleury's friend, Kevin Stevens last season.

Stevens was arrested in January, 2000, on drug possession charges which were eventually plea bargained down.

Fleury's entry into the California-based program was not believed to be his first, and it apparently was not triggered by any legal troubles. The NHLPA did not say at what stage Fleury entered the program, but Stage Two is for violation of Stage One and carries a suspension without pay for at least six months. Fleury, according to the NHL and the NHLPA, will receive his full salary and benefits for the duration of his treatment, and will have no penalty imposed as long as he complies with the pre-scribed treatment and aftercare program.

Fleury reportedly had been drinking following Monday's 3-2 loss to Ottawa. The team did not practice the following day.

(Immediately, Sather banned off-days after home games, figuring they only invite temptation to party).

Friends said that Fleury has been having family problems, perhaps caused by his move from the west to New York (he lives just over the border in Connecticut). He has also had trouble dealing with being away from his teenaged son in Calgary.

But his life has been marked by substance abuse and obstacles. Fleury's father is a recovering alcoholic, and his mother battled an addiction to Valium. Fleury was the first person in his family to graduate from high school. He has also battled Crohn's Disease his entire life, he suffered a frightening 400-plus stitch cut under his right arm, a slash that did so much damage that for a while Fleury couldn't pick up coins; now he can, but he can't tell which coins they are by feel. He also played junior hockey for Graham James, who was convicted for abusing some of his players, including former NHL player Sheldon Kennedy.

"That part of it's pretty well documented," said Low, who is a long-time off-season friend and neighbor of Fleury. "It hasn't been the easiest of lives, and I'm sure there are some things in his past that need to be addressed. This is a situation where hopefully he gets it all cleared out. It's extremely important to Theo and to his family, at this point in time, that he gets everything squared away in his life. To me it's sad thing. The guy, as I've said, has been a consummate player for us all year. To have him gone, we're really going to miss him, but that's not the important thing. The important thing is that he does get everything straightened away. He's a great person, and I feel for the kid. I hope he does get everything fixed."

According to a *Sports Illustrated* story in December, Fleury acknowledged he "entered an NHL program that treats players for problems ranging from substance abuse to emotional trauma" last summer, but wouldn't explain why. There have been rumors that part of the reason Colorado did not attempt to re-sign him following the 1999 playoffs was his drinking after his acquisition from Calgary late that season. Fleury missed Game 5 of the Western Conference finals against Dallas with what was suspiciously termed "the flu."

Messier called Fleury's latest trouble "a relapse" and said the team was aware of the problems Fleury had in the past, but that it still caught him by surprise.

"When it happens, it does for sure," Messier said. "I don't think anybody can pick a time, or know when it's going to happen. I'd say it's something we've seen before, from not only hockey players, but from everybody. And I guess relapses aren't that uncommon from somebody trying to get himself straightened out. Again, it's something he's going to have to be aware of and battle for the rest of his life. That's the really tough part.

"There's always an awareness. We've had several meetings as a group, as a team, with the coaches and Glen, and everybody was aware of this situation and Theo himself made everyone aware of what he was going through, but it's just something that nobody could really control, other than the person himself. That's the unfortunate part. We all feel, perhaps, we could have prevented it or done more or seen something that was leading to it, but in the end you really can't and it's something he has to deal with himself. When he's in a group situation like this, we can give him support and things he needs, but it's just a terrible disease and I really hope he just gets himself straightened out."

Fleury's first season as a Ranger was a disaster on the ice, if not off. He scored just 15 goals last season, the worst of his career, during the first of a three-year free-agent contract worth $21 million with an option for a fourth year at $7 million.

Fleury also got a two-year no-trade clause with that contract, yet this year has had to deal with the well-publicized attempts by Sather to find out if there's a market for Fleury. His no-trade clause expires this summer.

Sather pledged the Rangers' support.

"The New York Rangers are here to support Theo through this tough time in his life and we're going to do anything we can to support him and his family, and we all hope he's going to recover from this problem and be back here to play for us as soon as possible," Sather said.

"I think we're all taken back. You know, it's a situation where you try to monitor and help players as best you can, but it gets back to the same thing. Every person has an individual choice to do what he wants to do, and sometimes we make the wrong choices in life."

Low said he's not concerned how Fleury's loss will affect the team.

"For me, this isn't about Ron Low and this isn't about the New York Rangers," he said. "This is about a kid who's pretty troubled. Don't worry about me. Let's worry about Theo for the time being and let's hope he does get everything straightened away. I think this is really important for him, for his wife and for his family."

After a 4-2 win over the Florida Panthers, a team having an even sorrier season than the Rangers, Low addressed Fleury's situation again.

"I think as an organization we're shocked and surprised by it," he said. "It's a tough situation. The thing that's really important right now is that Theo gets himself back in order. As an organization and as coach and as a personal friend of the guy, my prayers go out to him, to him and his family. It's a tough situation and one he's chosen to address in the right way.

"When they deem he's ready to come out, he comes out. I don't think there's a time frame on it."

Messier said that the news hit as if Fleury was a family member.

"In our world, wins and losses seem to be the most important thing and it is the most important thing for us from a professional standpoint," Messier added. "When something like this occurs it makes you realize there are some things that are more important than the game itself. There's not many things that are more important, but obviously something like this is more important and I think that's why we need to support him as a person, to give him the support he needs in order to get himself back."

No MATTER HOW BAD things have gotten for the Rangers, there are teams that are worse. Take the Florida Panthers, which the Rangers have done three times in three tries this season. With Fleury checking into a substance abuse program and an ever-growing injury list piled on top of the nearly-impossible task of flagging down two teams hopelessly ahead of them in the standings, the Rangers still managed to snap their three-game losing streak against the pathetic Panthers.

Of course, Florida might have the right idea—jockeying for position in the draft rather than chasing an unrealistic dream. The Rangers inched to within eight points of Boston and Carolina, two teams in a fight for the final playoff berth in the East.

The latest injury isn't considered serious—Rich Pilon didn't play due to a left hamstring pull—but the loss of Fleury certainly is.

The Rangers needed to win, of course, but they have needed to win almost every night for the last month, and the three losses in the past six days just about finished them off.

Yet, in the Panthers, they found a team that is just about mailing it in.

Kirk McLean, the ex-Panther who has been terrific in three starts since Richter's season-ending injury, lost his shutout bid on a Greg Adams goal at 8:24 of the third. That stretches the Rangers' remarkable streak of 165 games without a shutout, going back to February 26, 1999.

Low said he had a team meeting prior to the game to address Fleury's situation.

"We talked about adversity and overcoming it, and I thought Kirk was really good tonight. I thought he stood tall and made a lot of good saves in the third period. I thought a lot of guys stepped up."

One of those was rookie Tomas Kloucek, who keeps getting better and more physical at age 20. He was assigned to Pavel Bure, and repeatedly frustrated the Russian Rocket, who leads the NHL with 43 goals.

The Rangers struck first, for the ninth game in a row—a streak they haven't accomplished since their championship year in 1993-94—and it came on a power-play goal, and a milestone, Brian Leetch's 200th career goal.

Sandy McCarthy—Fleury's old pal from their Calgary days together—put a slapper past goalie Roberto Luongo in the second, and Petr Nedved made it 3-0. After the first of two goals by Adams, ex-Panther Radek Dvorak scored to make it 4-1.

AT LEAST ONE TEAM in the Nikolai Khabibulin sweepstakes has dispatched a top scout to watch the unsigned Phoenix goalie work out, and it is believed a trade for Khabibulin will be completed in a matter of days.

NIGH**9**MARE

Low Must Go

RYE, N.Y.

Whether he checked into a substance abuse program or not, Theo Fleury probably played his final game as a Ranger on Monday.

The Rangers and the Phoenix Coyotes did, indeed, have a deal worked out in which Fleury and a package of prospects were headed to the desert for power winger Keith Tkachuk and goalie Nikolai Khabibulin.

Fleury, despite his denials to the contrary in recent weeks, was expected to bow to Sather's pressure and waive his no-trade clause, because it gave him a choice.

Fleury's no-trade clause expires at the end of the season. Originally, it was believed the clause contained a window in which he could be dealt over the summer. In fact, once this season ends, Fleury no longer has the no-trade clause. The only clause still intact is that he can only be dealt to a Western Conference team, and that the fourth year, an option year, on his contract automatically kicks in if he is traded.

All-Star Theo Fleury's substance abuse suspension scuttled Glen Sather's mega-deal with Phoenix.

So Fleury had a choice. He could go to Phoenix, where he has a close friend in owner Wayne Gretzky, and get the extra year, at $7 million, added to his contract; or he could refuse to go to Phoenix and be at the mercy of Sather, who could wait until April 8, then trade him to any Western team that would make a deal.

A source insisted that Fleury had not yet been approached by Sather or asked to waive the no-trade clause; and that while the Rangers and Coyotes had a deal in place, it did not include both Jamie Lundmark and Pavel Brendl. One or the other would have been dealt, probably with defenseman Kim Johnsson and another player.

However, Sather has coveted Khabibulin all season; and both the goalie and Tkachuk are in their primes at age 28. Brendl and/or Lundmark are probably still a year or two away from being impact players in the NHL, and perhaps Sather doesn't believe he can wait that long.

With Fleury out of the picture for now, a chance to dramatically change the Rangers roster via a blockbuster is just about evaporated.

Sather did complete a lower-tier deal, sending energetic fourth-line winger Eric Lacroix, 28, to Ottawa for big (6-foot-3, 205-pounds) Colin Forbes, 25.

Sather also went to work with Phoenix GM Cliff Fletcher in an attempt to structure a different deal that would bring Khabibulin. Sather will have to work fast, though, because a number of other teams have deals on the table, and a trade of the unsigned goalie could be imminent.

One team sent its president to Phoenix Wednesday to watch Khabibulin work out, and at least one other team is willing to trade for Khabibulin now and worry about hammering out a new contract later. Tampa Bay is believed to be offering its first-round draft pick, which could be No. 1 overall, in a package to get Khabibulin.

So Sather, who should have no problem signing Khabibulin, will have to move quickly, and probably have to offer more than he wants to offer.

And Fleury might still figure into the deal as some sort of "future considerations" agreement to swap him over the summer, or whenever his in-patient treatment ends. That could allow the Coyotes to keep Tkachuk for their playoff run, then send him to New York in the offseason.

SATHER HAS TIES with Colin Forbes's family, thus perhaps, the impetus for the trade with Ottawa. Sather knows Forbes's family, and his grandfather, who recently passed away, and whom Sather called a "great guy" held the lease and managed Northlands Coliseum in Edmonton at one time, according to the GM.

FRIDAY, MARCH 2, 2001

NEW YORK

On March 12, the Rangers get to see the Pittsburgh Penguins for the last time this season, and that is about the best news the Rangers have had in weeks.

They have seen the Penguins four times this season, and even though Mario Lemieux has only been active in two of those games, the Rangers have been squashed each time. Pittsburgh has scored 25 goals in the four victories, and has beaten the Rangers six times in a row going back to last season after tonight's 7-5 Garden cakewalk.

"When we've played them, they've scored in bunches, or bundles," Low said.

The Rangers remained 10 points out of playoff contention despite Carolina's loss to the Devils and Boston's night off.

Lemieux had two goals and two assists in his first game at the Garden since 1997, and his first Garden appearance since Wayne Gretzky's retirement party in 1999. Lemieux has 56 goals and 124 points in 63 career regular-season games against the Rangers.

It was a wild, wild night, with unusual calls, explosions of goals, and a threat afterwards.

Taking last things first, Sandy McCarthy, who took two ridiculous penalties on which the Penguins scored goals, didn't like the fact that Pittsburgh's Krzysztof Oliwa taunted him as he went off the ice with a misconduct late in the third period. Actually, Oliwa tried to get McCarthy into a tussle a couple of times during the previous shift, and McCarthy didn't appear interested in fighting until Oliwa swung an elbow at Brian Leetch as he went to the bench. Then Oliwa did something that set off McCarthy, but the two never got at each other.

"He had his chance to drop his gloves and fight me and he wasn't big enough of a man to do it," McCarthy said. "And then he's talking to me after so . . . we play them again, and he knows what's going to happen when we play them again."

Oliwa, the ex-Devils strongman, smiled at those remarks.

"Oh, really?" he said. "I don't care what he says. ... Ask him how many times I asked him to fight. That's what he said? Do we play them again? Great. I can't wait."

Oliwa also opened his eyes wide and said, "Oooooh, I'm scared."

There was another comical moment. Darius Kasparaitis, who left Rangers in his wake all night, decked Radek Dvorak. Linemate Jan Hlavac came flying to his aid, left his feet, and missed as Kasparaitis ducked under him. Hlavac went flying, ass over tea-kettle. Still, Hlavac was called for a penalty, and during the delayed call, Nedved cross-checked Kasparaitis. So the Penguins had a two-minute, two-man power play, which, of course, was lethal. Jaromir Jagr, disinterested most of the night, scored an easy goal, then scored again to make it 6-3, and Super Mario scored on the late McCarthy penalty for a 7-3 lead.

"I thought charging was when you hit somebody with a check," Low said about the Hlavac penalty. "Obviously, I must have misread the rule book."

PITTSBURGH'S KEVIN STEVENS was, predictably, sympathetic toward the Rangers' Theo Fleury, his friend while the two were Rangers last season.

Last year, Stevens was in the NHL's substance abuse program, this year it's Fleury. Stevens said that Fleury is in for a long road. "I have to remind myself every day that I'm an alcoholic," Stevens said. "I could be a timebomb. ... It's something that has to be at the top of my list. I mean my family and hockey, they're great. But If I don't stay sober, none of that matters. I don't have anything.

"If he takes it one day at a time, Theo will be fine. But the work is never over. You can never say, I'll be fine, because that's when it bites you on the ass. If somebody says, 'You have to be sober 35 years or 50 years or until I die,' I can't fuckin' (think about) that. But I can stay sober tomorrow. If I look past that, I'll be in trouble. I'll be drinking again."

MARK MESSIER'S TWO GOALS moved him to within three points of Marcel Dionne (1,771) for third all-time, behind only Wayne Gretzky and Gordie Howe.

THE HOCKEY NEWS made an interesting discovery. THN noted that, while it might appear that Valeri Kamensky had pulled a disappearing act the last two seasons, the NHL Guide and Record Book for 2000-2001 had Kamensky listed not among the active players, but among the retirees. THN suggested that it might be "wishful thinking" on Glen Sather's part.

SATURDAY, MARCH 3, 2001
RYE, N.Y.

It turns out that, unannounced, Rangers winger Sandy McCarthy received his second abuse-of-officials game misconduct penalty Friday night, and is therefore automatically suspended from tomorrow's game in Nashville.

McCarthy was assessed a misconduct and a game misconduct when he tried to get at Pittsburgh's Krzysztof Oliwa, between the team's benches, late in the loss to the Penguins at the Garden, although it was never announced that the game misconduct was for abuse-of-officials. It turns out that McCarthy was also assessed an abuse-of-officials game misconduct January 29, while trying to get at Atlanta's Denny Lambert, so he will sit tomorrow.

Jason Doig, a tough defenseman, was recalled from Hartford to skate in McCarthy's spot on the wing.

THE RANGERS HOPE to beat the predicted snow blizzard by flying back to New York immediately following the game, but there already were serious doubts that the next night's Rangers-Islanders game at the Garden will be played as scheduled.

MEANWHILE, SATHER SKIPPED Nashville and went directly to his home in LaQuinta, California, where general managers meetings begin Monday. Sather will continue his efforts to out-bid Tampa Bay and others for Phoenix goalie Nikolai Khabibulin.

SUNDAY, MARCH 4, 2000
NASHVILLE

There have been many games this season that fit in that "one of the worst" category. Today was another.

"One of the worst we've played in a long time," Ron Low called a 5-2 loss to the Predators.

Now it appears that there is a resignation among the players, maybe not a surrender, but a realization that the playoffs are out of reach.

"It's a situation where you definitely see it sliding away, but it's not acceptable not to work," Low said. "You're paid for 82 games, and you have to go out and play as hard as you can. To not put up 100 percent can't be acceptable."

Mark Messier, who does this about once a year—usually at the low-point of the season—tried to skip out on the media. He was briskly walking away when a few reporters caught up to him. He was asked if he saw resignation.

"Every time we lose it's disappointing," he said. "The guys are hanging in there. I don't see (resignation)."

Then Messier turned and walked away.

"I understand it gets hard when you look at the standings, but you know what, you're playing," Low said. "You have to play, and you have to play them as hard as you can, and anything less than that is unacceptable. I thought we played hard against Pittsburgh. We got beat, but we played hard. But I'm not sure we played as hard as we have to today. It was a lot like every afternoon game we've had on the road this year. The same exact thing, like dopey. I don't think we played with any kind of passion."

Once again, the Rangers offense was decent, but stopped by a good performance by a goalie, this one being Mike Dunham, and once again their defense was awful.

"It's not what you score, it's what you give up," Low said. "Every time we scored a goal we gave one up right away and that's a bad sign. We didn't play well in our zone at all. We have to play solid. If we don't, we're going to get killed. We didn't play worth a damn. That's a concern."

THE RANGERS WERE HOPING to get out of town quickly after the matinee, and get home before the snow buried New York. But the NBA Knicks had the plane in Toronto, and they took their sweet time getting back, which delayed the plane from picking up the Rangers in Nashville. Sure enough, the storm closed Westchester Airport, and the Rangers had to sit on the runway for three hours in Nashville before finally getting clearance to take off. They risked getting back at all, and a potential postponement of tomorrow's game.

NEW YORK

The door had been ajar for a while. Today, Sather kicked it open with his first veteran-for-prospect trade, wheeling 36-year-old defenseman Alexei Gusarov to St. Louis for 22-year-old defenseman Peter Smrek.

Why not? Not only is his team done as far as the playoffs concerned, not only have deals involving Mike Richter and Theo Fleury been killed, but now Sather has also lost out on goalie Nikolai Khabibulin, who tonight was dealt from Phoenix to Tampa Bay four three prospects and a second-round pick.

Now, after Sunday's mailed-in loss in Nashville, it figures that a bunch more of these—or at least as many as Sather can make by the March 13 trade deadline—will follow. The Rangers were playing the Islanders in the basement battle of New York, but Sather was at GMs meetings in California, looking to make more now-for-later trades.

And it won't be easy. The Rangers are going to have to deal some good people, some good team guys, who haven't quit.

Adam Graves, a Rangers cornerstone and perhaps the most popular player in team history, is almost certainly headed for Detroit, although the Red Wings will probably have to do better than their offer of enigmatic 29-year-old winger Slava Kozlov.

Sather will surely try to find takers for defensemen Rich Pilon and Sylvain Lefebvre (who each might bring a decent prospect from a contender), and for Valeri Kamensky (who probably won't bring anything of value).

"I think we're in the mode of trying to acquire the best assets possible," Rangers assistant GM Don Maloney said.

"Again, I think we're in the market where, if we could find a premier young asset, that regardless we were going to make the deal," Maloney said, addressing, in particular, the team's deal of Gusarov-for-Smrek today. "That's why you haven't seen a lot of deals happen yet with Glen. We're looking to build long-term. Nobody's looking to make a short-term fix for a week or two."

That sounds as if it's fine with coach Ron Low, who knows the season is gone now.

"As long as we're going forward," Low said. "We're shifting into next year every day as this season's progressed."

Back in January, Sather said the Rangers would need to win 20 of their last 30 games to make the playoffs. They were 6-6-1 so far in that stretch going into tonight's game, with losses in five of their last six games, including Sunday's embarrassment.

Low knows the playoffs are gone, even if he can't say it. But he hopes to find a reason for his team to continue to play, rather than quit as they did on John Muckler last season.

"This is going to come down to a game-to-game situation where you have to play hard, and the standings are almost a non-existent thing right now," Low said. "It's the people in the dressing room that have got to work and to work hard."

AFTER A 5-2 LOSS to the Islanders, Mark Messier was asked—in a group setting this time—if he plans to still be around when the Rangers are ready to win again.

"There hasn't been any talk of retiring or anything like that," he said. "At my age now, it's always something that at the end of the year you think about, but I don't have any plans. My plan is to be here next year or the year after that, right now. Obviously, coming back here and being truthful, I certainly want to be here for the success I know the team is going to have in the next couple of years, so that's my plan right now. Obviously (he laughed) that's subject to change at any given hour or any given day, but that's kind of the plan right now."

Messier stammered uneasily through his answer to the question, though, as if he didn't want to say whether he would or wouldn't be back next season. A few weeks ago, faced with the same question, Messier refused to answer it at all and became agitated.

But he was up front when talking about the reality of the current Rangers' chances, even if he did guarantee a playoff berth last July.

"We're a team that's struggled and not in the playoff hunt, if you're going to be at all honest," Messier said, while talking about the likelihood that changes will be made before the deadline next Tuesday.

"I've been in this situation now," Messier said. "It's very similar to my first year in Vancouver, and unfortunately I've had too much experience in this particular situation, but it takes time to turn things around.

"In all honesty, from my experience, even my first time I came to New York and then going to Vancouver for those three years, to change the culture and to change the team, it takes, from my experience, at least three years. And I'm talking about three years to get yourself in position to be a really formidable force in the league (with) as good a chance as most teams to win a Stanley Cup. In all honesty, in a perfect world this year, obviously we weren't good enough to win a Stanley Cup."

Yet Messier doesn't think the Rangers have quit, even if it appears that they have, especially after their performances in back-to-back losses to Nashville and the Islanders, which punctuated their current 1-6 streak.

"We've played poorly at times, but there hasn't been a lack of effort or a lack of care," he said.

He and Low admitted it's difficult to play now that the goal has been removed, but Messier hopes the final 16 games can be used to build something for next year, much as his Canucks carried their strong final stretch of 1999–2000 into this season.

"It's going to be a tough test for all of us, because it's not easy playing at this time of year when, obviously, the playoffs are looking a long way away," Messier said. "That's what you play for in any particular year—the chance to win the Stanley Cup. So that's taken away, and so far off as it is now, it's going to be tough.

"As a group we're going to try to salvage something out of the season that's respectable and something that we can hang onto and try to go into next year with."

That's about all they can do now.

LOW PUT BOTH THUMBS up when asked about the trade his team completed. The Rangers had been scouting the St. Louis Blues' prospects for weeks, because they were discussing a trade for Mike Richter before his season ended with a knee injury.

High on the list of four of their pro scouts (a list that did not include virtually untouchable Barret Jackman) was Smrek, 22, who they managed to acquire from the Blues in exchange for struggling Gusarov. Straight up. The Rangers had gotten Gusarov from Colorado for a fifth-round pick back in December.

"He's offensive minded, can move the puck, good skater," Low said. "I watched him play one game; I just happened to be watching it, and he scored two goals, and he does have offensive abilities."

Low will watch the native of Slovakia practice the next few days, and determine if he's ready to play the rest of the season on the NHL roster, or in Hartford, but the Rangers feel they got a prospect with a lot of upside, basically for nothing, because the Blues are trying to win a Stanley Cup.

Smrek was a virtual unknown, and therefore undrafted as an 18-year-old. He then came over to play in the U.S. junior league, and opened enough eyes to be drafted in the second round by the Blues in 1999. He has also played a lot, for Worcester, against the Rangers' Hartford affilliate in the AHL.

"We've seen him a lot," said Don Maloney. "We liked him his draft year. He's a thick, solid defenseman, excellent skater, good balance. I think it's a terrific deal for us."

WHAT WASN'T TERRIFIC was the game. Rookie goalie Vitali Yeremeyev made his first Garden start, and was down 4-0 early in the second as the Islanders scored three goals in a span of 1:25. One of those came short-handed, the last two just 15 seconds apart. The Islanders were all charged up in the debut of interim coach Lorne Henning, who had replaced Low's best friend, Butch Goring, fired just a day earlier. Now the Rangers are 6-7-1 since Low figured they would need to win 20 of their last 30 games. If that math is right, the Rangers are going to have to go 14-2 or something like that, to make the playoffs. And they'd still need help.

TUESDAY, MARCH 6, 2001

RYE, N.Y.

If the Rangers were a ship, they would have already taken on too much water to stay afloat. The question remains how far they will sink.

But the captain, and the previous captain, aren't jumping off.

Mark Messier said Monday night, while conceding that the Rangers are no longer in the playoff race and that he knew it would probably take three years for them to be ready to win again, that he has no plans to retire after this season, or even after next season, the last on his two-year contract.

And Brian Leetch, who fought for a no-trade clause in his four-year contract, now has said he will remain a Ranger for the final two seasons on that deal, no matter how many veterans and long-time teammates Sather moves out in his rebuilding attempts.

Sather has already had trades for Mike Richter and Theo Fleury undone because their seasons ended prematurely (although either could be dealt over the summer or next season), and he is speaking to teams about a number of other veterans, including Adam Graves and Leetch's defense partner Rich Pilon.

"I certainly wouldn't want to think about anything until it happens, but the reason I (demanded then no-trade clause) a couple of years ago was because I want to be here in New York regardless," Leetch said. "I never thought we'd be where we are now, but this is my home and this is where I want to win and play well. It wouldn't change my feelings toward anything.

"It's something I feel, that it's one of the commitments that I've made, wanting to be here, to win here. It's something I would want to be here for."

THE RANGERS, and 500 of Madison Square Garden's employees, visit schools all over the metropolitan area as part of their Cheering for Children campaign. Today was the day for the visits, and everybody was assigned a school. Trouble was, traffic was absolutely snarled into New Jersey as the George Washington and Tappan Zee bridges had multiple lane closures for ice removal, so a number of the visitors never got to their intended schools.

What was worse for Sandy McCarthy was being stuck in a truck with Dale Purinton for several hours of barely-moving traffic, while Purinton described, in detail, how to skin a bear.

WEDNESDAY, MARCH 7, 2001

RYE, N.Y.

In the wake of his failure to obtain Khabibulin from Phoenix, Sather got another goalie at virtually no risk.

Sather claimed goalie Guy Hebert (pronounced GEE ay-BAIR) off waivers from Anaheim, with the agreement that, if the Rangers don't want him at the end of the season, he will be the Mighty Ducks' responsibility. In other words, Anaheim, not the Rangers, will have to pay the two-thirds of his $3.8 million salary for next season in order to buy him out.

Meanwhile, on another front, there are at least two teams interested in Adam Graves—Detroit and one other, possibly San Jose, Dallas or St. Louis—but the clause that will pay Graves a $1 million bonus if he's traded, and the two years (at $4 million per) remaining on his contract, seem to have cooled talks. The Rangers will want a lot in return if they have to pay a large chunk of Graves's contract, so the likelihood of Graves remaining a Ranger has increased.

Sather appears to have a bidding war going on at least one other veteran, defenseman Rich Pilon, who is scheduled to be an unrestricted free agent and therefore will cost almost nothing in terms of salary as a rent-a-player for a contender. Pittsburgh and Detroit are among those with interest in Pilon.

Hebert, 34, and in the worst season of his career, was placed on waivers Monday when the Mighty Ducks acquired goalie Steve Shields as part of the blockbuster Teemu Selanne trade with San Jose. Hebert had been displaced as Anaheim's No. 1 goalie by Jean-Sebastien Giguere.

"It was a situation where we get a relatively inexpensive look at a player who has been a pretty good goaltender in this league in the past," Rangers assistant GM Don Maloney said. "I don't think anybody's saying we solved all our problems, and certainly he's struggled this season, but maybe a change of scenery is what he needs."

Ron Low said he will look at Hebert in practice tomorrow, and Hebert might get the start in Washington the next night, or in Ottawa the following night.

The Rangers are desperate to find a short-term fill-in for Mike Richter, who undergoes major reconstructive right knee surgery in two days and shouldn't be expected to be at the top of his game until the middle of next season, based on his comeback from the same procedure on his left knee last April. Khabibulin, who went to Tampa Bay, would have been a long-term answer at age 28.

Clearly, the Rangers' coaching staff has little faith in backup Kirk McLean, and their top goaltending prospects—Vitali Yeremeyev, Johan Holmqvist and Jason LaBarbera—are not yet NHL ready. Yeremeyev has been rocked in his three starts, allowing 15 goals in losses to Boston, Pittsburgh and the Islanders. He was returned to Hartford.

Hebert has had a winning record in three of his previous five seasons, and the last two years had respectable goals-against averages of 2.42 and 2.51. This year, though, Hebert had slipped as badly as the team in front of him (sound familiar?), and was only 12-23-4 with a 3.12 goals-against average and a terrible .897 save percentage. Comparatively, Richter—on one healthy leg for most of the season, and behind the NHL's worst defensive team—had marks of 3.28 and .893.

<hr>

FRIDAY, MARCH 9, 2001

WASHINGTON, D.C.

Excuse Guy Hebert if he longs for the defense of the Mighty Ducks.

Hebert got a taste of what it's like to be in goal behind the NHL's worst defense, and while he was hardly stellar himself, it had to be a nightmare.

Hebert's Rangers debut was a 5-2 loss to the Washington Capitals at MCI Center, dropping the Rangers to a season-worst 10 games under .500, and just two off their pace of last season when they quit on John Muckler and then John Tortorella to finish 12 under .500. With 15 games remaining, they can easily limbo under that mark this season.

The Rangers allowed an opponent hat trick for the league-leading eighth time this season when Peter Bondra scored his 38th, 39th and 40th—two of those in a 26-second span of the third period—and Trent Whitfield scored his first NHL goal to add insult to insult.

Meanwhile, the Rangers got back into the periphery of the Eric Lindros saga, as the unsigned multi-concussioned center expanded the list of teams he for which he would agree to play, beyond Toronto. Lindros reportedly told Philadelphia GM Bobby Clarke that he would play for a number of other teams, although the non-contending Rangers were not on that list. It included Cup contenders Dallas, Detroit, St. Louis (which is said to immediatly have offered Pierre Turgeon, only to be turned down) and Washington.

That the Rangers are going nowhere, and that what they could realistically offer the Flyers wouldn't help them much in their playoff run, makes the Rangers the longest of long shots if Lindros is dealt by Tuesday's deadline anyway. But if he isn't, the Rangers could be back in the mix over the summer.

THE RANGERS TONIGHT did a lot of things a team out of the picture should be doing, including improving their draft position by losing. Low, in addition to starting Hebert and playing new young defenseman Peter Smrek , showcased recalled winger Michal Grosek, putting him on the right of fellow Czechs Jan Hlavac and Petr Nedved. Grosek played aggressively after his minor-league banishment, and scored a goal on the power play. Low also used the poised and promising Smrek on the point on the power play, and Manny Malhotra on the penalty kill.

Low also removed Radek Dvorak from Nedved's line and put him on the left of Messier and Valeri Kamensky, a move that seemed to energize Messier. For months, Messier has languished without a speedy sniper on his wing.

Hebert, on a tryout of sorts, hadn't played since a 4-3 loss to Washington as a Duck on February 9, a game in which Bondra scored twice.

"So, yeah, I don't like those guys right now," Hebert said.

He also got an apology from Brian Leetch, who was beaten badly by Bondra for one goal and screened Hebert on another.

Hebert became the seventh goalie to wear the Rangers uniform this season, and the sixth to play (only J.F. Labbe didn't see action), which are ridiculous numbers.

"I liked what I saw," Low said about Hebert, noting that at least two of the goals were screen shots and one was a rebound. "I thought he made some big saves."

Smrek, the 22-year-old, got his first NHL assist and was a bright spot.

"I thought Peter Smrek played a great hockey game," Low said. "I thought he was a huge plus. He moved the puck, made some great decisions, and one-on-one he was great inside his own end zone all night."

"It's so tough, coming into a new situation like this and new surroundings," Mark Messier said. "But he looks like a real heady player. He's got great legs, and obviously the upside, the potential is there."

OTTAWA, ONTARIO

You could tell it felt good. Just plain good. The Rangers are smart enough to know that their 3-2 come-from-behind win over Ottawa was completely meaningless to their season. But there is still a chunk of season left to go, and it had been unraveling for so long, that the Rangers just needed to win a game.

Their third win of the season in a game they trailed after two periods (3-24-0) snapped a four-game losing streak, and was their second in nine.

Hebert, making his second start in two games since coming off the waiver wire from Anaheim, got his first victory since December 17, and deserved it with some of the saves he made to keep it 2-1 for more than 24 minutes.

"Somebody in there said it's an ape off our backs, not a monkey," a relieved Low said. "It's been a long time."

Depending on how you look at it, it could have been a better weekend for the Rangers because the teams behind them picked up points, thus potentially improving the Rangers chances to move up in the June draft. If they can get into the bottom five, they'll have a chance to win the lottery and come away with the first pick. But since there are a few blue-chippers in the draft this year, the worse they do from now until Game 82, the better they can do at the draft table.

In the meantime, the chances of the Rangers doing anything significant by Tuesday's trade deadline appear to be very slim. Rich Pilon is their hottest commodity among the many veterans who would be available, and it's unlikely that Glen Sather will be moving any of his top prospects, or other coveted youngsters like Mike York or Kim Johnsson.

MARK MESSIER, who sprung Radek Dvorak for a breathtaking high-speed goal around Wade Redden and a 1-0 lead, first handed out some punishment and some signals. He cross-checked Karel Rachunek early on, then Ottawa captain Daniel Alfredsson. Then he took a double-minor when he took down 19-year-old rookie Martin Havlat, and, after Havlat retaliated, Messier repeatedly cross-checked him to the ice. Havlat scored on the ensuing power play, and again for the 2-1 lead.

But Low thought a message had been sent.

"He set a tone for the game," Low said, "even though I don't think you want him in a situation where he's in the box for four minutes. But he also said it wasn't going to be an easy game for them, and we weren't going to roll over and play dead, and that message was there all night."

"I just think we've got to compete and play hard and play to win," Messier said. "Like I said when things kind of unraveled for us, I'm looking for the leadership, not only from Glen and the coaching staff, but also from the veteran players on the team, to help out. I said it then, and I'll say it again, there's still a tremendous amount at stake for the team and for us as individuals and we need to compete every game."

That hasn't been happening lately, and it will be difficult to make it happen the last 14 games. At least now, they have something recent to hang on to. Something that at least felt good.

IN AN INTERVIEW with a Canadian TV station immediately after the game, Messier was asked what was going through his mind during the altercation with Havlat.

"I was thinking what else I could do to him," Messier said.

UNLESS A DEAL IS MADE tomorrow, the scouts from several NHL contenders will be watching Rangers defenseman Rich Pilon tomorrow night.

Several teams, notably Dallas and Detroit, have eyes for Pilon, who throughout his career has had some terrific nights against the Pittsburgh Penguins and Jaromir Jagr, and will be facing the NHL scoring leader (100 points) again at the Garden. A good performance will almost surely seal Pilon's fate by the Tuesday trade deadline, if it hasn't been sealed already.

Pilon, who turns 33 on April 30, and becomes an unrestricted free agent July 1, will accept whatever that fate may be.

"You know, any time your name's getting thrown around like a softball, or a hot potato, it gets stuck in the back of your mind and you find yourself waiting around," Pilon said. "If something happens, it's good, and if it doesn't happen, then it's, 'Well, why didn't it happen?' Does it mean the Rangers didn't want to get rid of me, or nobody wanted me?"

But Pilon would welcome a chance to win his first Stanley Cup, a chance to play in the playoffs for the first time since 1993, and for just the second time in his career. He would also welcome the chance to remain a Ranger.

"I'm okay with staying," he said. "I'm okay with wherever. Wherever I am, I am. I think I've been fortunate with the year I've had personally, but the difficult thing, the disappointing thing is the situation we're in right now with the team. Your goal at the start of the year is to make the playoffs and make a run for the Stanley Cup. I would have put a lot of money on us, that we wouldn't have been in this situation."

That situation has Glen Sather trying to deal veterans for young players, prospects or draft picks. He may not be able to deal much more than Pilon.

There has been interest from contenders in Adam Graves and Sylvain Lefebvre, but both have contracts that might make moving them impossible. Lefebvre also has a shoulder injury and may not play tomorrow.

"I think the basic thing there is, whatever happens is going to happen," Low said. "That's not in my control, and there's a lot of things that could happen. Lots of times at the deadline, nothing happens."

DALE PURINTON, the tattoo-covered tough guy who hunts bear, regularly applies moisturizer to his skin and face. If you press him on it long enough, he might admit that the moisturizer makes his skin tougher to cut during fights. But first he'll tell you how he just likes to put it on, or some dumb such explanation.

"No girl's going to want me," he said. "I'm too high maintenance."

MONDAY, MARCH 12, 2001

NEW YORK

Adam Graves skated off the ice, and didn't take one last look around the Garden.

"I didn't have to take it all in," he said, pointing to his heart. "It's all in here. It's close to me. Regardless of what tomorrow brings, nothing's going to change."

The trade itself might be minor. What the Rangers get for Graves, if they deal him by tomorrow's deadline won't come close to measuring what Graves has meant to the franchise for 10 seasons. The Rangers will be ripping out the organization's heart, trying to acquire a little piece of its future.

So important is the deadline, that Garden CEO Jim Dolan made a rare visit to the locker room following the Rangers' 3-3 tie with Pittsburgh tonight. Sather, who is still in the hunt for Keith Tkachuk and Mike Peca, and might have a big day today, called Graves into the coaches' office for a 15-minute post-game meeting in which it was spelled out to Graves that he might not be a Ranger by 3 P.M. the next day.

Suddenly there is more than one team (Detroit) interested in obtaining Graves, perhaps Dallas or San Jose, which has long coveted the Rangers' single-season goal-scoring record holder, or even Boston, where Mike Keenan would love to have the guy who scored 52 goals during their Cup-winning season together.

With a bit of an auction taking place on Sather's telephone, the likelihood of Graves, 32, being dealt for young players, prospects or draft picks increased considerably.

Graves will have next season, at $4 million, due on his contract, and any team that acquires him will have to either pick up his option for 2002-03 or hand out a $1 million bonus.

The Garden will have lost some of its luster, and its favorite son, though, if Graves departs.

Graves said Sather was honest with him, but Sather refused to comment on the meeting. But he seems to have come to terms with the possibility that he has played his final game as a Ranger.

"I would be totally dishonest if I said it hasn't crossed my mind, or hasn't consumed me at times," Graves said. "But that's part of the game, and I understand how the game works.

"I don't know. It seems everything in life happens, as much as it seems slow, it happens really fast. So, I don't know, to tell the truth. I really don't.

And when asked if he expects to be a Ranger at 3 p.m., Graves paused and slowly repeated. "I don't know. I don't know."

There was a quiet pall over the locker room, too, even after the raucous, wild-ending tie, in which the Rangers blew a 2-0 lead, fell behind 3-2, then got the point on Brian Leetch's goal with 1:52 left.

"I think, obviously, everybody knows how I feel about Adam, not only as a person, but also playing with him for so many years," Mark Messier said. "What he's meant to my career playing with him, winning a Stanley Cup in Edmonton, then coming here and winning a Stanley Cup. He bleeds Ranger blue.

"I don't know what the situation is, but it's going to be a tough loss if something does indeed happen. It'll be a sad day for all Ranger fans."

Rich Pilon is almost certain to go, with Detroit, Dallas, Pittsburgh and perhaps a few others interested in adding the gritty defensive defenseman to their playoff-bound lineups.

On another front, it appears that a number of teams are figuring they're out of the Tkachuk sweepstakes, which would then indicate that the Rangers are still in it. The Islanders are said to be making a serious pitch for the Coyotes winger, as well. The Rangers thought they had Tkachuk twice this season. One blockbuster was held up because Wayne Gretzky's ownership group in Phoenix was put on hold and team assets frozen; the other collapsed because a key part of the deal, Theo Fleury, went to rehab.

Reports are that Gretzky and Coyotes GM Cliff Fletcher are demanding two of the Rangers' Czechmates—Jan Hlavac and Radek Dvorak or Petr Nedved, and either Jamie Lundmark or Pavel Brendl. The Rangers would then get back Keith Carney and/or Travis Green, and maybe more in the package.

Sather also wants Mike Peca, the unsigned Buffalo center who hasn't played a game this season, but the chances of getting both Peca and Tkachuk are virtually nil. And, if Sather empties his prospects vault for either player, he won't be able to bid on Jaromir Jagr, who is expected to be dealt by Pittsburgh over the summer.

Eric Lindros, meanwhile, was in St. Louis today for a physical, and he could be traded to the Blues, with Tkachuk winding up in Philadelphia, tomorrow.

THE RANGERS, for a second game in a row, played a pesky, physical game. Sandy McCarthy made good on his promise after the last meeting to fight Krzysztof Oliwa—the two dropped their gloves on cue the first time they were on the ice together—and McCarthy won the decision. McCarthy played one of his better games of the season, and the crowd appreciated the effort.

A few minutes later, Dale Purinton jumped Bob Boughner, who earlier this season jumped Petr Nedved and broke Nedved's nose. Purinton was ejected from the game, and the Rangers killed off the five-minute Pittsburgh power play his penalty left them.

PRIOR TO THE GAME, both Sather and his Pittsburgh counterpart, Craig Patrick, were in the press room having dinner. Sather sidled up to Patrick, who developed a reputation for being vague in answering questions when he was the Rangers' GM in the early 1980s.

Sather: "Are you interested in trading Lemieux?"
Patrick: "Not at this time."

PITTSBURGH'S KEVIN STEVENS, when told about the $1 million Graves would get if he was traded and the option year of his contract were not exercised, said, "I'd be kicking the door down (demanding to be traded)."

AFTER JUST ABOUT everyone was gone, Low was asked if he expected much to happen at the deadline. "I hope so," Low said. Then he shook his head.

"We're going to lose some good team guys. I mean some really good team guys."

TUESDAY, MARCH 13, 2001

NEW YORK

Glen Sather's first NHL trade deadline as the Rangers president/GM turned up nothing at all, but that doesn't mean Sather wasn't in there swinging for the fences.

The Rangers were right in the talks for Phoenix's Keith Tkachuk, who wound up going to St. Louis for a package of young players, prospects and draft picks. In fact, Sather left the Garden Monday night thinking he had Tkachuk in his pocket. And when they couldn't get Tkachuk—and when Tkachuk's landing in St. Louis ruled out Eric Lindros going to the Blues, Sather was in the mix with Philadelphia for the big unsigned center.

Incidentally, Sather said, both Phoenix and Philadelphia wanted virtually the same package for Tkachuk and Lindros—believed to be Jan Hlavac and Radek Dvorak, or Mike York, plus prospects Jamie Lundmark or Pavel Brendl. The Tkachuk deal died, reportedly, when the Coyotes insisted Tomas Kloucek be included in addition to Lundmark or Brendl and Dvorak.

Sather offered Brendl and Petr Nedved to Philadelphia for Lindros, and was willing to go farther in terms of prospects. He became so preoccupied with Lindros that he was unable to complete anything else by the 3 p.m. deadline. Sather didn't even get down to talking money with Lindros and his representatives.

"It just seemed in the end it was best to hang onto all our assets and try to build internally so we've got a good, strong, young nucleus," Sather said, adding that there are plenty of free agents he will pursue (Joe Sakic, John LeClair, Rob Blake, etc.) this summer.

"I wasn't willing to sacrifice more of our future for an immediate cure."

He talked about his years in Edmonton, and how he fought off teams trying to get him to trade his young players, and how "a lot of times the deal you don't make turn out to be the best deals."

In addition to Lindros and Tkachuk, Sather tried to get Mike Peca out of Buffalo, but Sabres GM Darcy Regier stuck to his guns. Regier told Sather he "wasn't going to move him unless he got an offer that knocks his socks off" and today Peca is looking at not playing an NHL game this season, as is Lindros.

That doesn't mean, of course, that Lindros and Peca won't be Rangers targets in the summertime. First, though, Sather wants Lindros to want New York. When he dropped his Toronto-only demand last week, the Rangers weren't on the list of teams Lindros wanted to join.

"It's still a risky venture," Sather said. "There's still the possibility the next hit will be the last time he plays." Sather spoke to Blues GM Larry Pleau, who had Lindros medically and neurologically examined Monday in St. Louis, and said that Pleau received no assurances that Lindros would last "two months or five years."

Sather also revisited the possibility of acquiring goalie Nikolai Khabibulin, whose rights were traded from Phoenix to Tampa Bay this month, but who is still an unsigned Group II free agent. Khabibulin's representative, Jay Grossman, called Sather and said "the negotiations haven't gone anywhere."

Sather said he thought he had a realistic shot at Tkachuk, and that he felt he had a couple of other deals that could have happened.

One was Adam Graves, York and Rich Pilon to Washington for Andrei Nikolishin, Jan Bulis and Chris Simon, which reportedly broke down when Capitals GM George McPhee asked for Kloucek instead of Pilon. At least two other teams were interested in Pilon as of Monday night, but Sather said that after watching "two giveaways in the third period" those teams must have lost interest. It's hard to believe that a bad game would change a team's opinion on a player as heavily scouted as Pilon has been. Sather probably asked too much.

One team interested in Pilon was believed to be Dallas, which decided to obtain Grant Ledyard for next-to-nothing instead. Sather said there was no interest in Sylvain Lefebvre because "you can only trade players who are peforming well." Again, that's a statement that's difficult to believe. More likely, Sather wanted too much for him, or wasn't willing to pick up much of Lefebvre's remaining salary.

As for Graves, he only got a reprieve, and a remark Sather didn't need to make hurt him.

"Now I can breathe out," he said after a talk with Low, in which Low said Graves was going nowhere, prior to leaving the practice rink.

"Obviously I'm relieved, and just happy that it worked out the way it has."

But Sather indicated that, unless Graves's game picks up dramatically over the final 13 games, he might ask him to retire after the season.

"Adam's such a character guy, and he's been through so much (personal tragedy) the last 15 months, the last thing I wanted to happen to Adam is to tell him 'I want to retire you'," Sather said. "I don't want that to happen. He's the one guy that bleeds Ranger blue all the way through and he's been a terrific sports hero for the people of New York.

"But this is a game that has to march forward and we all get changes in our lives that happen to us. We've got to overcome them one way or another."

So Graves's days are obviously numbered. He's headed for an off-season trade or a buyout, at two-thirds of his remaining salary, by June 30.

"He's had some confidence problems," Sather said. "I hope that he gets over that and gets his game back together. He needs to start playing on the edge like we've seen him in the past."

Graves diplomatically said that retiring is "not my intention at this point" and admitted that it's been a constant struggle this season. He also reiterated that he believes he is capable of still playing at a high level.

Mark Messier was glad Graves stayed, too.

"There's been so much speculation the last little while, and Adam was aware of it," Messier said. "But he's been through a lot personally in the last couple of years, and this is one thing he didn't need for sure. So, from that standpoint, I'm happy he's here, obviously, as a friend and as a teammate."

But Sather left the foreboding warning that many of the changes which weren't made will be made in the off-season. At least he will have his entire cache of prospects and young players when the changes begin.

AT LEAST TWO GENERAL MANAGERS reportedly cut off talks with Sather today because of his arrogance and smugness in the negotiations. There is an ever-growing number of GMs who take great joy in beating Sather in a trade, and even take joy in dealing with other teams just to tick off the Rangers' GM.

WEDNESDAY, MARCH 14, 2001

BUFFALO, N.Y.

Frontier justice. The Rangers have had enough, and they're not going to take it any more. When they played Pittsburgh Monday, Sandy McCarthy settled a score with Krzysztof Oliwa for a personal matter and an elbow that missed Brian Leetch in an earlier game. Dale Purinton settled a score with Bob Boughner, who earlier in the season jumped Petr Nedved and broke his nose.

Tonight, it was Rich Pilon's turn. Obviously unwanted by the Rangers, and blamed, ridiculously, by Glen Sather for the bad game Monday which supposedly cost the Rangers a chance to trade him, Pilon got even with Vaclav Varada, and nobody had a problem with it on the Rangers' side.

Pilon jumped the Buffalo pest, Varada, an obvious act of vengeance during a 6-3 loss to the Sabres at HSBC Arena, a loss that helped the Rangers' draft position since several of the teams behind them were gaining points.

Back on February 6, Varada took a flying run at Pilon's head with an elbow/forearm and caused a concussion that knocked Pilon out for four games.

The first time the two were on the ice together tonight, Pilon made a beeline toward Varada, dropped his gloves and began punching the Sabres' agitator, who himself was just returning from a concussion. For his one-sided punchout, Pilon received an instigator minor penalty (by rules, he should have gotten a double-minor for instigating a fight while wearing a shield), a fighting major, a misconduct and a game misconduct.

Varada left the game, but returned before the end of the period.

Pilon admitted it was "for the elbow the last time we played" and that he "wanted (Varada) to drop the gloves, but he wouldn't drop them."

The result, besides a certain review by the league—ESPN had no replay of the incident, so Pilon might get off on that technicality, for which there is precedence—was a seven-minute power play for the Sabres, in a 1-1 game.

And Ron Low had no problem with it, except that he would have preferred Pilon to have stayed in the game a bit longer before getting his revenge.

"No, I don't," he said. "I don't. That was for the elbow a month and a half ago."

"Not one bit," agreed Mark Messier, who reached two major milestones. "He took a cheap shot the last time we played."

The Rangers killed off the entire seven minutes, two of which were erased when Buffalo's Alexei Zhitnik took a hooking penalty; just as they had killed off Purinton's five-minute penalty against Pittsburgh. Amazing as it seems, the Rangers' horrid penalty killing, which was a main cog in their drop out of the playoff race, managed to rise to the occasion both times.

But their penalty killing, and some shaky goaltending by Guy Hebert, undid them in the second, when Buffalo stretched a 2-1 lead to 4-1 on power-play goals by J.P. Dumont (his first of two) and Chris Gratton. Messier assisted on a Radek Dvorak goal, which moved him into a tie with Marcel Dionne for third on the all-time scoring list with 1,771 points, trailing only Wayne Gretzky and Gordie Howe. Messier also moved into a tie for fourth on the all-time games-played list with Alex Delvecchio (1,549).

"It all sees to be coming on at this point in my career," Messier said. "There are guys coming up behind me who are going to surpass me, so it's nice while it lasts, but I don't think it's going to last too long."

MIKE YORK KEEPS ON GOING, when there is no reason to do so. He suffered an 11-stitch gash above his right eye when he collided with McCarthy's helmet. York returned, wearing a visor.

THE NHL'S TRADE DEADLINE is a misnomer of sorts, because the only actual deadline was for acquiring players who would be eligible to be on playoff rosters.

Since the Rangers aren't going anywhere, and since three of the players in whom they have varying degrees of interest don't figure to be involved in the playoffs either, deals could still be done.

Sather said he could and still might be able to make a trade.

Sather said that he won't call Nikolai Khabibulin's agent, Jay Grossman, or Tampa Bay GM Rick Dudley, but he'll listen if they call him. Tampa Bay acquired the goalie from Phoenix earlier this month, but did so without agreeing to a contract, and the sides haven't come close to getting one done since the trade was completed. So Khabibulin, still technically a restricted free agent to whom Sather can talk without breaking tampering rules, could possibly be had.

The other two players Sather tried to get at the deadline were Eric Lindros of Philadelphia and Mike Peca of Buffalo, who apparently will not play an NHL game this season unless they're dealt. Now, though, the Flyers and Sabres can't get anything in return that will help them in this season's playoffs, so they'd be better off waiting for the summertime.

The deadline also was one for the AHL playoff rosters, so the Rangers made paper transactions on Tuesday, assigning, momentarily, Tomas Kloucek, Manny Malhotra, Peter Smrek and Mike Mottau to Hartford so they'll be eligible to join the Wolf Pack for the postseason.

FRIDAY, MARCH 16, 2001

RYE, N.Y.

The Rangers better play these final 12 games as if their jobs are at stake.

That is the message Glen Sather delivered when he addressed the Rangers before they headed to Philadelphia for tomorrow's game.

"I told them today that if I see these guys are going to give up and quit, I'm going to send them home," Sather said. "If you're not going to put in 100 percent every game, then don't bother coming here because we're not going to accept that.

"We've got some big games coming up against some pretty tough teams, so I don't want anybody to have the attitude that, let's just go through the motions and get the year over with. We're going to play these games and we're going to play them to win."

Sather said he was supportive in his talk, and that he understood the atmosphere which descends on a team once it realizes the playoffs are out of reach.

"In the end, it amounts to playing for the pride of the sweater and for your job," Sather said. "There are a lot of young guys here that are playing for their jobs. There are a lot of old guys here that are playing for their jobs as well.

"Every job is up for grabs as far as I'm concerned. Nobody has got a lock on a position."

Last season, the Rangers went 1-11-2 in their final 12 games. Everybody got fired.

"I'm not going to let that happen," Sather promised.

PHILADELPHIA

The third-leading scorer in NHL history, a first-ballot Hall of Famer, started his NHL career the exact same way Manny Malhotra is getting his start—finally.

Mark Messier, the Rangers captain, started 22 years ago by playing out of position, on left wing, with then-Edmonton captain Ron Chipperfield as his center.

Today in a competitive but meaningless St. Patrick's Day 2-1 loss to the Philadelphia Flyers at First Union Center, Low used Malhotra for the entire game as Messier's left winger, an experiment that began in the third period in Buffalo Wednesday.

The line on Malhotra's day: 22 shifts, 15:38 of ice time, an assist on the Rangers' only goal (by Radek Dvorak), killed penalties, and saw his first power-play shifts since his rookie season. Those are numbers that are not normal, for those who haven't followed the tale of misuse Malhotra had to endure the first two years of his career.

This, more than anything, is why the Rangers wanted Messier back in New York. There is no better player to have bring along a kid like Malhotra at this stage.

"I remember myself coming into the league," Messier said. "I came in as a center and played two or three years on the wing, just to get a little less responsibility, to get in there and do some things without being so responsible down low. Really, it just frees him up to just play the game a little bit more. That's what he needs, to get out there and play the game without all the things that go with playing center.

"I think it's a great move to keep him there for the rest of the year and let him play some hockey and get him excited about next year. He's a great kid, a very special kid, who really wants to play. Physically, he's so gifted. He just needs to play some minutes. That's a real positive for the team, to have a kid that can skate like that. The same for (Peter) Smrek."

Smrek was back on defense after a rib injury cost him two games, and Low went with seven defensemen for the first time this season, so that Dale Purinton's fists would be available if needed. Smrek played regular shifts on both special teams, threw his body around, and made another big impression.

"I thought Smrek was outstanding," Low said. "He did all kinds of really good things out there. We played him on the power play every chance we got, and I thought he played a really good game. I thought he played tough and aggressive, also."

After much of a crowd had dispersed, Low exclaimed, "That kid's going to be a player."

So, the Rangers hope, will be Malhotra. Low saw him as a winger at the end of training camp, and while Malhotra wasn't happy with that news after playing center throughout camp, it might be his ticket to regular minutes, especially with Messier, Petr Nedved, Mike York, Tim Taylor, and, eventually, Jamie Lundmark in the middle.

"I liked Manny on the wing, a lot," Low said. "I thought he did some good things. Him and Dvorak made a heckuva play to spring Mess late in the third. He also added some jump there. He added lots of get-up-and-go.

"He looks like a winger to me. The thing about Manny, what he's got is great outside speed which he doesn't get to use in the middle. He doesn't have to handle the puck nearly as much there. If he gets outside he shoots. He's a big, strong kid that can fly, and to me, outside speed is his forte, and I think it's a good chance to use it when he's on the wing."

Low noted that, had Tim Taylor not gone down on New Year's Eve, Malhotra might have spent the entire season getting his needed minutes in Hartford.

Malhotra said he feels more comfortable at center, only because he's always played there, and that he's gained tons of confidence this season, at either position.

"That was Ronnie's original plan at the beginning of the year, and being given the opportunity I want to show that I can play that position," he said. "I'll play wherever he wants me to play."

What better place than on Messier's left wing, just as Messier started out on Chipperfield's left before Malhotra was born?

(In case you wondered, the right wing on the Chipperfield-Messier line in 1979 was Bill "Cowboy" Flett.)

"I'm trying to help him out a little bit," Messier said. "It's been a tough go for Manny and I really want to instill some confidence going into the summer. I think he's only going to get better over the next 10-12 games. Just trying to help him out with a little tip here and there but don't clutter him up with too much stuff."

GUY HEBERT HAD TO leave the game after two periods when he aggravated a groin injury he believes is the result of his inactivity in Anaheim. Forgotten Kirk McLean played the scoreless third.

LOW SAID THAT THE youth movement will continue as long as the young guys play well. He plans to use Mike Mottau on defense against Washington.

NEW YORK

Mark Messier is right in the middle of it. Right in the middle of the Rangers' rebuilding process, at age 40. Right in the middle of his own renaissance of sorts.

He is both feeding, and feeding off of the 20-somethings that Low has sprinkled into the team's lineup.

Messier scored a short-handed goal and a short-handed assist, moved into sole possession of third place on the NHL's all-time scoring list, and generally looked as if his young, high-speed linemates had lit a new fire under him in a 6-3 Garden win over the Washington Capitals.

Low said what he believes has happened, in addition to young players like Messier's left winger, Manny Malhotra, and defensemen Tomas Kloucek, Peter Smrek, and Mike Mottau getting newfound ice time, is that Messier has thrived on speed.

His right winger for the last six games, Radek Dvorak, is one of the league's best skaters, and Malhotra flies, too.

"Well, Devo, since he's been there, he's done everything," Low said. "His outside speed, which was likely what was missing all year with Mark, and he's added a whole bunch of jump back into the big guy."

In order to get Dvorak on Messier's right, Low had to do something he wished he'd done a while ago.

"I think what I should have done earlier is break up the Czech line and put Dvorak with Messier, which I thought about a couple of times," Low said. "The Czech line was playing so well, it was hard to do. In retrospect, it likely would have helped our hockey club a lot better.

"It's been a tough process with Mark this year. He played 15-18 games with AHL players (including Jeff Toms and Brad Smyth) on his right and left side and never once did he complain. In fact, a couple times I suggested breaking up that other line and he said, "No, leave me with the kids; I'll play with whoever.' That's the way Mark is."

Messier, who passed Marcel Dionne, now has 1,773 points, trailing only Wayne Gretzky (2,857) and Gordie Howe (1,850).

"It's surprising to me, coming into the league scoring one goal my first year in the WHA," Messier said. "I never really considered myself a pure goal scorer or a pure point getter. But obviously it's the longevity that's enabled me to be in this position, and obviously a lot of great people around me. But, when I look at it myself, I'm still trying to figure out why I'm sitting there, or how I'm sitting there."

In another sense, he is perfect where he is, the teacher, the guardian, for the young kids. And Messier is perfectly okay with it. He loves the speed.

"Just speed itself is something that can get you out of a lot of trouble, can create a lot of offense and is good defensively," he said. "The game is always, from where I've played and as long as I've played, speed kills everything. I know Glen (Sather) really is a big believer in speed. When you can get to the puck, get to loose pucks, create speed through the neutral zone, that's always a big factor in successful teams. I know Glen's a big believer in that, and I know this team will definitely get faster as we go along.

"Sometimes the best fix is right under your nose if you give it an opportunity."

Low was thrilled with the three young defensemen, with Mike Mottau joining the youth parade.

"I think what's happened with us, you put a guy like Smrek in there, and he can find open people. He moves the puck to them. He has a really low panic level. He's been outstanding. He's got good puck sense, away from it and with it, which is really hard to find in young guys. He and Kloucek are long range people for us, and I mean long range."

Like, for the next decade or so? Like, the future of the Rangers' defense?

"I would say definitely," Low said. "You're looking at three young guys that can move the puck. The physical part of it, Smrek and Kloucek are adept at playing it. Mike, I imagine, is going to have an issue with size, but if he learns to play positionally, which he's done in Hartford, is in the same category."

Mottau made a terrific play to set up fellow Boston College alum Brian Leetch for the goal that turned out to be the winner, and the last allowed by all-world goalie Olaf Kolzig, who was pulled after one period, down 4-1. Malhotra also assisted on that goal. Dvorak's speed set up Messier's short-handed goal, and another by Dvorak himself, who outraced goalie Craig Billington to a Messier pass and swept it into the empty net.

The Czechs (Petr Nedved and Jan Hlavac, with Michal Grosek in Dvorak's spot) accounted for three goals themselves, one by another young defenseman, Kim Johnsson.

And while all this is happening, the 18,200 who buy tickets each night, or a fraction thereof who actually show up, have a reason to be optimistic even as the season slowly fritters away ... and a 40-year-old is in the middle of it all.

AMID ALL THE QUESTIONS about Messier's place among the top three scorers of all time—he has never been comfortable considering himself a pure scorer or point getter, because his game is so much more complex and complete than most scorers—came the one about the World Hockey Association.

Somebody noted to Messier than all three of the NHL's top career scorers went through the WHA. Messier didn't hesitate to note that it was purely coincidence. He and Gretzky spent one season, as 17-year-old kids, in the WHA; and Howe jumped to the WHA as an old man at the end of his NHL career, before returning to the NHL when the Hartford Whalers were among the surviving WHA teams to merge into the NHL.

So Messier wasn't going to just go along with the notion that the WHA was responsible for the success of the three all-time greats.

"It was a great breeding ground," he smirked. "A great breeding ground for Gordie Howe. A great developmental league, huh?"

LEETCH HAS A FRIEND who is an assistant coach at B.C. and therefore he and Mike Mottau already have a relationship. They have been in touch for three years. "He's got no problem coming to me to ask me about certain plays. It reminds me of when I was first here. He's an American kid, and he knows a lot about my career, obviously, so it's been a lot of fun."

So when did he stop calling you Mr. Leetch?

"A few years ago. I had to have a beer with him, though."

Mottau called the play on which he set up Leetch for the goal, "An old B.C. play that's handed down from generation to generation."

<hr>

TUESDAY, MARCH 20, 2001

RYE, N.Y.

If the Rangers can do what the Devils just did, and win their last 11 games in a row, maybe they can make the playoffs.

But since that's not going to happen by any stretch of anybody's craziest imagination, tomorrow's game against the Devils at Continental Arena could be the best chance for the Rangers to do something meaningful this season.

The Rangers look to end two streaks: The Devils' team-record 11-game winning streak, and the Devils' 22-game unbeaten streak (14-0-8) in regular-season games against the Rangers.

(And, if the Rangers fail to do both, they could get another crack at the Devils' streaks March 31, in a game that would potentially be the league-record tying 17th straight win for the Devils, matching the 1992-93 Pittsburgh mark).

Since that is still 11 days and six more Devils wins away, tomorrow's game is the one that matters.

For the Rangers, this is their best chance, too. The Devils return from a five-game road trip, and everyone in hockey knows that the first game back from a trip of three games or more is always hellish on the home team's legs.

The Rangers are also playing well, energized by their recent turn toward rebuilding with young legs and fresh faces. In their last five games, all against playoff-bound teams, the Rangers have gone 2-2-1 with wins over Ottawa and Washington, a tie with Pittsburgh, a competitive 2-1 loss in Philadelphia and a downright poorly-played 6-3 loss in Buffalo.

The Rangers have been in all three games against the Devils this season (0-1-2). They had Garden ties of 5-5 (which they led 3-1 in the first and 5-4 with 1:30 left) and 1-1 (which they led 1-0 in the third). And in a 5-2 loss at the Meadowlands, the score was 1-1 in the third when Messier suffered a nerve injury in his leg and had to leave, in the Devils' playoff nemesis' first visit as a Ranger since 1997.

After that game, Messier was quick to remind the celebrating Devils that, while they had the streak, they had lost three times to Messier and the Rangers in three playoff tries.

Now Messier is more low-key, more complimentary, and more realistic about where the two clubs stand.

"You're looking at two franchises (going) in two different directions," he said. "The Rangers have really struggled the last five years, and (the Devils) have really kind of molded themselves into a bona fide powerhouse right through the franchise, not only for the Devils but their farm system. (GM Lou) Lamoriello has done a heckuva job keeping the team together and putting important pieces in.

"We're trying to build ourselves right now. So it's really two contrasting teams. Having said that, I don't think for us right now, whether it's the Devils or their streak (matters). We've got to play all these guys next year, and it's all going to be the same players, so you never really want to give an inch no matter what your situation is. Although we're out of the playoffs, we still want to go in there and compete hard and show that we're not going to give up under any circumstances. If we can turn that into a win, great. If not, the first thing we want to do is compete and play as hard as we can. Whether we can come up with a good enough effort to beat the Devils right now is secondary to going in there and competing hard, playing hard."

The next 11 days will be more feet-wetting for the many rookies now in the Rangers' lineup—defensemen Peter Smrek, Mike Mottau, Tomas Kloucek, and Dale Purinton—plus young veterans like Manny Malhotra, 20, who is Messier's new left winger.

"Wins are important now," Brian Leetch said. "It would be great for some of those (young) guys—we've got four games (in the next 11 days) against the Devils and Islanders—and it would be great for them to get involved in those type of games. With us maybe sliding out of the playoffs, that type of atmosphere would be great for everyone."

Messier also noted that the Rangers are now doing what the Devils have historically done by tossing young players in with the veterans, and that it's made the game enjoyable for him.

"For me to play with Manny right now is kind of fun, too," he said. "It's fun to see him enjoying himself playing the game, getting opportunities, knowing he's going to be able to play if he makes a mistake, playing the power play.

"To me, that's always an important part of any team, no matter whether you're a team like the Devils that's been so successful the last few years. You've always got to incorporate younger guys, and I think it's really important to have the right leadership from all the players and the coaching staff and management to really bring those kids along. I think that's a really important part for this team, starting now, for going into next year."

LOW ISN'T HAPPY about the talk that not only can the Rangers be the Devils' 12th consecutive victim, but also that the Rangers would be win No. 17 in a row for the Devils on March 31, tying the NHL record for consecutive victories held by Pittsburgh in 1993.

"You read the articles from the papers over there and they're basically saying that this is a blur in the middle of the path to their run of 18 wins in a row. Basically, they aren't giving us much respect. If you don't beat somebody enough times, you don't really think they're anything but a bump in the road, and we've got to go out there and be bigger than a bump."

That was also the message Low tried to plant in his players. Ah, the disrespected underdog motivation strategy.

EAST RUTHERFORD, N.J.

The dirty dozen, and the filthy 23.

The Devils stretched their two streaks to 12 and 23 with a 4-0 victory over the Rangers at Continental Arena.

With the victory—in Martin Brodeur's 50th career shutout—the

Stanley Cup champs have won a club-record 12 in a row and maintained their lead in the Eastern Conference standings over Ottawa.

And they stretched their mastery over the Rangers to 23 regular-season games (15-0-8), since January 7, 1997, which was also the last season in which the Rangers made the playoffs.

Given the difficulties the first game back from a five-game trip might present, it was probably beneficial to the Devils that their first opponent was the Rangers, and the natural anti-blahs the rivalry brings.

If the Devils can continue their winning streak, the Rangers will be potential victim No. 17 in a row, which is the league record.

What the Rangers did accomplish was the clinching of their fourth consecutive losing season, the ninth in a row for Glen Sather, and the sixth in six seasons as an NHL coach for Ron Low. They can be mathematically eliminated by the weekend.

While most of the Rangers gave the Devils their due props, Low was crazy with the lack of effort and the disregard for the game plan by the forwards, as the Rangers produced just 11 shots on goal.

"We talked about not putting the puck in the middle of the rink against this hockey club, and we must have done it 50 times," Low said. "There was no penetration on the walls, nothing on the outsides. ... I think the walls are maybe a little too tough to go down."

Low felt the Devils were ripe for an upset, if the Rangers cared enough to do enough.

"You've got a hockey club that came in here and they were supposedly dead tired from a long road trip and we, I thought, laid back," Low said. "We didn't play with anything near the emotion I thought we would have to have, or motion.

"It's a simple thing. You haven't won in 22 games, and to me, if there was a time you could end the streak it would be right here tonight, just from the whole thing that's happened here, their traveling yesterday, and I don't think there was enough competitiveness from our hockey club."

The Devils broke open a scoreless game with two goals in a span of 1:32 of the second period, and that pretty much clinched that both streaks would stay alive.

At 13:44, Devils goalie Martin Brodeur kicked out a bad-angle shot by Mark Messier, and the Devils countered. Sergei Brylin carried the puck out up the left side and cut to the middle in the Rangers zone. Brylin dumped it off to his left, to Scott Gomez, who quickly moved it to Alexander Mogilny in the middle. Mogilny immediately fired, but his shot appeared to hit Rangers defenseman Brian Leetch. The puck changed direction and speed, and fooled goalie Kirk McLean for Mogiliny's 35th goal and a 1-0 Devils lead.

The Rangers, who have been decidedly more aggressive lately, wanted to do more of the same, and their defensemen did. Rich Pilon took a couple of runs at Devils, and Tomas Kloucek knocked around Devils stars Patrik Elias and Petr Sykora, and had to answer the bell for his first two NHL fights—against Randy McKay and Colin White, who appeared to have broken his nose in the exchange.

The elbow that led to the McKay fight, however, turned into a Devils power play, and that turned into a 2-0 lead. Jason Arnott, at the top of the power-play umbrella, slapped an end-over-end shot through a crowd created by Bobby Holik, and past McLean's glove at 15:16.

A series of spats broke out in the third, around the Kloucek-White incident, and the Devils added a goal by Scott Stevens during the ensuing 4-on-4, and another by Arnott during a subsequent 5-on-3.

Sather, who was being verbally harassed in his press box seat by a large Meadowlands regular, simply laughed and trotted out an infamous old line from one-time Devils coach Jim Schoenfeld, telling the guy to "have a donut." The fan pointed to the zero on the scoreboard as his donut.

"Just trying to get the rivalry going," said Sather, 0-2-2 with the Rangers against the Devils.

SATURDAY, MARCH 24, 2001

NEW YORK

It's officially over for the Rangers now, although their pathetic showing in a 6-0 loss to Detroit at the Garden and the mathematical elimination it brought really doesn't change what was long known.

The Rangers didn't need such a severe punctuation when the end arrived. They didn't need to learn any more about themselves than they already knew.

And Ron Low really didn't need to invoke the name of the guy he succeeded, the guy who was fired nearly a year ago, a day after being clobbered in the same fashion by the same Detroit team for a second game in a row.

Because what Low did was admit that all that he did as coach this year failed. He blamed the players, who deserve to be blamed, but he also sounded as if he was saying that he didn't do a better job than John Muckler did, that he was unable to get his players to play the way he wanted them to play.

"Believe me, (I knew) this was not going to be a cakewalk," Low said. "You knew that coming in. These last two games you likely really got a true feeling, I did these last two games, of what Muck and I talked about this summer. There's a certain element of being disappointed in the fact that you work as hard as you can in preparation for games, and (it) would get wasted. I mean, we talked about being physical, otherwise they were going to run roughshod over us, and in my estimation, two guys (Mike York and Sandy McCarthy) got the message.

"I don't know. I just don't get it. . . . Too many people are going in different directions."

Down being the main direction.

"Surely," Low said, "you don't just get signed to come to the Rangers to retire. If that's the case, then it's really bogus."

Here is what the Rangers accomplished. They were eliminated earlier than they had been in any of Muckler's three disasters. They ran the combined score of their last two games to 10-0, and the cumulative score of their last three meetings with Detroit to 20-2. They hit the 40-loss mark for the second year in a row, and with eight games left they have a good shot to break the team record of 44 losses (1984–85). They allowed a season-high 47 shots on poor goalies Guy Hebert and Kirk McLean.

And, that, Mark Messier said, could have been worse.

"Thank goodness Scotty (Bowman) had enough sympathy and class to call the dogs off in the third period," he said of the Detroit coach. "It could have been 10 or more (goals)."

Messier, Brian Leetch, Adam Graves, and the injured Mike Richter have now all missed the playoffs for four years in a row, Messier's last three with Vancouver.

"It's very disappointing," Messier said. "I've been fortunate to have some good success in my career, and now to have four years in a row, it's getting a little bit tiresome, I'd have to say."

Low is tired, too. He's tired of trying to explain why he hasn't gotten through to his team all year; hasn't gotten them to play consistently physical, to pay attention in the defensive zone, to avoid throwing pucks in the middle of the ice. And game after game, he cries the same cries. Once he wondered if he was speaking "gobbledy-gook."

He has no answers, just as Muckler had no answers.

And like Muckler, today he started to hear the "Low Must Go" chant.

"I guess I can implore upon them all I want that quitting is not acceptable, and I guess at this point in time they can tell me it doesn't make any difference, seeing as we're officially out of the playoffs," Low said.

"I don't know if it's any more frustrating for me than any of the fans that sat in the stands and watched it, or for the front office. It's frustrating to watch. You have to have a certain feeling of pride in being a New York

Ranger, and I don't know if there's enough of it there. I don't know if there's enough of it. I mean, we can't go out night after night after night and have Mark be the guy that's going to lead the physical end of it.

"I don't know if there's enough care, or if it's such a bad mix that it doesn't make any difference how much they care, it's just not going to happen. I don't know. To me, it's frustrating to watch it. . . . It's not nice to watch. You feel helpless back there. It's a bad feeling in the gut and I'm not sure enough of them have that same feeling after the game is over."

Messier doesn't think the Rangers have thrown in the towel, but rather that they don't belong on the same sheet of ice as teams like the Red Wings.

"It's a different class," he said. "Just a completely different ballpark and level (from) what we're playing at, and it showed from the (opening) faceoff to the end of the game. No comparisons to our two teams in any area. The bottom line is, two different leagues of teams out there, and that is the brutal reality of it. I hate to be that honest, but that's where we're at right now, and if anything, I think it serves as a good lesson for our young guys of how far we have to go to even be close to competing for anything.

"I think that sometimes when you're beaten that badly it can look worse than it is. We weren't able to contain them, we weren't able to generate anything in the neutral zone, we weren't able to move the puck. On top of that, fear or lack of confidence, and all of that, can look like a lack of effort. Do I think we played as hard as we have this year? No I don't. But I think there are a lot of things that go in to a team not playing hard. We were just completely overmatched. Detroit took everything we had to offer and we didn't have an answer for them, so when you look at it, it might look like a lack of effort."

But Messier pointed out that there is still something left to play for, and he didn't mean pride. He meant jobs.

"If I was a young guy starting out, I'd be making good use of these games to establish myself as a player in this league," he said.

THE RANGERS GAVE OUT their end-of-season awards before the game, and, as their 75th season nears an end, had a post-game reception attended by some of the old-time former Rangers.

"I don't know how these guys are going to go up into that room afterwards and sit with those guys from the alumni, all those great players who played here, and can even be satisfied sitting with them," Low said.

SANDY MCCARTHY, who probably had the best season of his career, and who provided protection even if he didn't always look interested in fighting, was the winner of the Steven McDonald Extra Effort award and the car that goes with it. The award, named for a New York City policeman paralyzed in the line of duty, had been in the stranglehold of Adam Graves.

THE LAST TWO TIMES the Olympics were played on U.S. soil, the American hockey team has come away with the gold. Of course, the USA will have gone 22 years without a medal of any kind when the Olympics are played in Salt Lake City next February.

The first step toward building a team that can extend the first streak and end the second streak, were taken when U.S. general manager Craig Patrick selected the first 10 NHL players to be on his roster in 2002 today.

The 10 were defenseman Brian Leetch of the Rangers and forwards Keith Tkachuk (St. Louis), Tony Amonte (Chicago), Chris Drury (Colorado), Bill Guerin (Boston), Brett Hull (Dallas), John LeClair (Philadelphia), Mike Modano (Dallas), Jeremy Roenick (Phoenix), and Doug Weight (Edmonton).

The rest of the team doesn't need to be selected until December 22.

"We feel we have great depth at all positions," Patrick, the Pittsburgh Penguins GM, and the assistant coach of the 1980 Miracle On Ice team, said. We feel right now that our strength is our forwards because we have a number of players that are in the prime of their careers. We have a number of questions in goal and on defense."

The biggest question was on crutches at the Garden. Two-time Olympic goalie Mike Richter, who won the World Cup for the U.S. in 1996 and was the No. 1 goalie in the American's disappointing non-medal performance in Nagano in 1998, had major reconstructive knee surgery earlier this month. He has informed coach Herb Brooks (the Lake Placid miracle coach, and the coach of the 2002 team) that he plans to be ready physically, and at the top of his game, in time for the Salt Lake games.

If Richter can't go, the No. 1 job will probably go to Mike Dunham of Nashville, and the backup goalies spots will be up for grabs.

Patrick said he chose LeClair, despite a back injury, surgery and a subsequent infection that has kept him out of all but eight of the Flyers games before yesterday, because "you can't exclude him, in our opinion.

"We feel that he should be a part of this team today that the other eight forwards are. We feel he will be healthy enough to play and he should be part of this team at this point."

The U.S. has a lot to prove on and off the ice. In Nagano, not only did the U.S. fail to medal, but some players trashed the team's living quarters. Nobody has yet owned up to the vandalism.

"Certainly, what happened in Nagano on and off the ice, we dealt with," said Leetch, who will play in his third Olympics. "We were disappointed in what happened there. We're excited about this year. I don't think it's something that, because you play well or do something different this time, it changes anything about Nagano. What happened there happened, and this is a new opportunity for the Team USA and for all the players that are going to be a part of it."

There was also some kidding that the players will wear nametags when they get together next February, because the NHL will only shut down for 12 days. That means the teams will have exactly one day of practice together before the tournament begins.

NEW YORK

Radek Dvorak, Mark Messier, and Tomas Kloucek threw three big hits in bang, bang, bang fashion in the first period of the Rangers' game against Boston at the Garden. In the second period it escalated not only into more hits, but also into a mean, snarly game.

This wasn't completely unique for the Rangers, it was just too rare.

The Rangers lost again, 3-2 to the Bruins, to fall to a season-worst 13 games under .500 and match last season's 41-loss total with seven games remaining. Boston closed to within two points of eighth-place Carolina.

But the decision had nothing to do with a lack of physical play. Not this time.

It is one of Low's major peeves with his team, that it didn't play a hitting game on any kind of consist basis this year, and Low is now trying to come to terms with why they didn't. Were they unwilling? Unable? Was it the not in the players' wills or hearts? Or was it not in their bones and muscles?

"There has to be some changes on this hockey club," Low said.

On Saturday afternoon, after his club was mathematically eliminated and physically obliterated by Detroit, Low first moaned about the lack of consistent hitting. Tonight he took it a few steps further.

"I've seen our hockey club play physical for a certain amount of time, and for one or two games in a row, and I don't think it's capable," he said. "I think we have people here that aren't going to finish checks on a nightly basis.

"I don't know if they're built that way. I guess (Mike) York's a perfect example. He wears himself down doing what you ask. You have to look. I think Mike Grosek is a physcal player and hitter. Does he do it on a nightly basis? Yeah, he does if you prod him to do it. Jan Hlavac is not the kind of guy who wants to go out and take the body.

"But if you look across the street at Jersey, at (Petr) Sykora and (Patrik) Elias, you say, 'They're not big guys'. But they've bought into a system that says, 'We have to be physical'. Look at Colorado. How big are their forwards? They don't have a lot of big guys, other than (Scott) Parker. But they finish their checks. They go out and do it on a nightly basis. Your culture has to say that that's the way it's going to be, and there has to be a certain amount of peer pressure from inside the hockey club that says that's the way it's going to be, also."

But how does it start? How does a coach, an organization, or other players, instill this in a bunch of players that don't necessarily like to play that way?

"A couple of ways, I guess," Low said. "You take people's ice time away that don't do it. You build a system that has guys play it in the minors, that says, 'If you play like this, you're going to make it to Jersey and when you get there you're going to play the same kind of system there.' I don't know how you do it. I think it's a built-in thing. There has to be a certain amount of pride in doing it. A lot of time it's a dirty job, not a nice job, but it's something that has to be system built, and it's got to start from the very basics, the roots of your organization, right to the top part."

Low hasn't taken away ice time, and hasn't gotten results. Meanwhile, down the hall last night was a coach who wanted the job Low got last summer, but wasn't seriously considered. Mike Keenan, though, had the Bruins still in playoff contention, and the option on his contract belongs to the Bruins, who might turn him free again this summer.

Interestingly, Keenan was summoned by his old pal, Messier, for a lengthy pre-game pow-wow in a room between the teams' locker rooms.

When asked if there were things he could have done differently, Low repeated that he wished he had put Dvorak on Messier's line earlier, to give the captain the speedy linemate he lacked. He couldn't think of much else, when given the opportunity to second-guess himself.

He was asked about playing Mike Richter too much, and he had a legitimate response when asked if his team might have had different results if it had gotten NHL-caliber goaltending all year.

"We didn't have it, so I don't know," Low said. "But we knew we weren't going to get it. We were surprised as hell the way he played at the start when he first came back. He was great, then he hit what I knew was coming, which was the wall. At that period of time, that's when (the media) said 'he's tired, he shouldn't be playing.' That is when he should be playing. He has to play himself through that, or else he's not going to get there. . . . You have to play your way through it, otherwise it's not going to get better."

The Rangers got no better this year. They took what Low called a step forward in integrating some young legs into the regular lineup. But again, their inconsistent performance has them playing meaningless games these last two weeks.

NEW YORK

This is what it has come down to for the Rangers. They are playing a home-and-home series with the archrival Islanders and all that's at stake is the inaugural Pat LaFontaine Trophy, a charitable undertaking co-sponsored by the teams' owners.

The Rangers are also still vying for a drop down to the bottom four in the standings and a chance to win the draft lottery and steal the No.1 overall pick from the Islanders.

But the Rangers got back into the LaFontaine hunt and fell further away from the No. 1 draft pick by beating the Islanders 4-2 at the Garden.

The Rangers snapped a three-game losing streak, and the Islanders' three-game winning streak at the Garden.

And this is what the rivalry has come to. Islanders GM Mike Milbury sat peacefully in the stands throughout the game. Imagine!

The rematch and the final meeting of the season is tomorrow at Nassau Coliseum, and the Islanders hold a five points to four lead in the series (LaFontaine was actually at the game to present the award). The Rangers have just one home game left among the six still on their schedule, next Wednesday against Carolina.

The Rangers played this game as they did Sunday's against Boston—with a snarl. They were physical, and angrily so, from the start. The Islanders' Steve Webb ran over rookie Mike Mottau early in the game, and the Rangers set their sights on revenge. Dale Purinton jumped Webb in the second period, took six minutes worth of penalties, and the Rangers again killed the whole thing. Purinton and Webb later squared off and Purinton won a two-fisted decision.

But it wasn't just about Purinton and Webb. This was a rugged game, and 19 power plays were awarded.

"That charge by Webb likely woke us up," Ron Low said. "After that it was a pretty intense hockey game. Richie (Pilon) had one of his better games. Boy, he really finished every check he had, and a lot of guys did.

"I imagine it's going to be much the same tomorrow night."

The Rangers killed the six-minute disadvantage and a long 5-on-3, and belied their status as the worst penalty killers in the NHL.

"Dale did the right thing," Pilon, the ex-Islander, said. "You kill off penalties like that."

"It was good tonight," added Mark Messier. "We had guys doing down in front of shots, a lot of blocked shots, and Guy (Hebert) made the saves when they got one through."

The Rangers took the lead early, continued to pound away, and stretched the lead to 3-0 by the middle of the second period.

The second goal was perhaps a glimpse of the future. Brian Leetch flipped the puck out of the zone, and Manny Malhotra chipped it past Branislav Mezei, then sped around him.

Malhotra moved up the left wing, and stepped into a slap shot that whistled past goalie Chris Terreri on the far side. It was a showcase of the 20-year-old's speed and sense and shot, and it came, ironically, on the one-year anniversary of coach John Muckler's firing.

"I think he's learning to play that position, and tonight was perfect evidence of what he can do there," Low said. "He can get the puck and he can really rip it. He got outside and he shot it. He did a lot of good things tonight. He was very physical, really, really physical in the penalty-killing part of it. He did a great job there, too. He's improving every day and it's good to see. He's done a pretty good job there (on wing).

"We put him with Mark for a reason. We want to see how well he's going to respond to the challenge. He wanted more of an active role on the hockey club, and a higher level, and he's responded pretty well. He's definitely making steps, very good ones, too. The things he showed tonight, he's been showing signs of it. Tonight he handled the puck better than he has in any of the games so far. I'm sure it comes down to confidence with him."

Low reiterated that he sees Malhotra's future on the wing, not in the middle.

"No doubt in my mind," he said. "I think the evidence is right there tonight. He went down the wing and blasted the puck, and he can do that and do it very well. He's also a better checker or forechecker from the wing because you can dump it in his corner and he's going to get there most times."

ABC-TV HAS BAILED out of televising next Saturday's Rangers season finale in Florida. Since ABC has exclusive rights to the time slot, and since the game can't be moved due to arena scheduling, MSG Network will air the game on a tape-delayed basis that night. Imagine. The network doesn't want the New York City market, and the Rangers won't be on live television. How far they have fallen.

UNIONDALE, N.Y.

There has been very little left to salvage for the Rangers these last weeks. One of the remaining little goals was the inaugural Pat LaFontaine Trophy, which was won when they beat the Islanders 6-4 on Radek Dvorak's four goals, to sweep a home-and-home series.

The next remaining goal would be Saturday at the Meadowlands, where the Rangers will try to put on a better show than the no-show they staged when they visited March 21, a one-sided 4-0 loss that stretched their regular-season winless streak to 23 against the Devils.

Winning the LaFontaine trophy means that the Rangers' charities—NYR SKATE and the Lustgarten Foundation for Pancreatic Cancer Research—will receive the $100,000 ponied up by the two teams' ownership groups. An additional donation will go to LaFontaine's charity, Hockey's All-Star Kids for children's hospitals.

When captain Mark Messier received the trophy from LaFontaine, he brought it into the locker room, where there was a mock celebration. The hardware then went into the laundry bin to be carted back to the Garden.

Dvorak's four-goal explosion, which included a short-hander and an empty-netter, gave him 29 goals for the season as the Rangers flaunted the speed of their recently-formed line of Dvorak, Manny Malhotra, and Messier.

"I think he's getting used to playing with me a bit and trusting me that he can spring for the goals and I'm going to find him," said Messier, whom Dvorak compared to a quarterback.

"He's just starting to figure it out like all young guys do. With experience, he knows when to use his speed, he plays both ends of the ice really well, he's very conscientious defensively, an excellent penalty killer. I think he's learned a lot this year."

Ron Low said that Messier constantly reminds Dvorak that he's "one of the fastest skaters in North America" and that he believes Dvorak "can easily be a 35-goal scorer."

First, Dvorak wants to hit 30, which he considers a big accomplishment.

"To score 30 at this time means something," he said. "I always felt I could score 30 or 25. But I didn't get to 30 yet, so let's wait."

The Rangers played a third straight game in which they initiated most of the considerable body contact (let's see if they can do it again tomorrow), led by Rich Pilon, who was a monster on defense. Pilon, the ex-

Islander and almost certainly an ex-Ranger in five more games, killed several penalties by himself, simply because Islanders puck carriers were coughing up the puck as they came over the line for fear of Pilon charging at them. To the Islanders' delight, Pilon left the game after the second period with a hamstring pull.

BUFFALO HAS HAD a scout at each of the last two games, which is odd in that the Sabres don't play the Islanders or Rangers the rest of the season. Obviously, both southern New York teams are interested in Western New York's unsigned Mike Peca, and would have to be willing to give up young talent to get him this off-season.

AT LEAST THREE RANGERS plan to play in the World Championships in Germany after the season. Kim Johnsson will play for Sweden and Jan Hlavac and Radek Dvorak will represent the Czech Republic. Several others may be asked to play, including Mike York (USA) who hasn't decided if his banged-up body can handle the additional hockey.

The World Championships is a misnomer because, first of all, the best teams in the world are competing for the Stanley Cup when the tournament is held every spring. Also, because NHL players are eligible, it becomes a tournament filled with players whose teams didn't make the playoffs, or got knocked out early. It's sort of a consolation event for NHL players.

DALE PURINTON SHAVED the big, furry moustache he'd grown, which had become something of a conversation piece, especially since moustaches are now rarities in the NHL.

Purinton claimed he grew it so that, when the people who create those realistic video games drew up the "Dale Purinton" guy, he'd be easy to pick out because of the moustache.

That was one of the many reasons Purinton said he sprouted this ugly thing on his upper lip. One of the others was that "The chicks dig it."

Now it's gone.

"Some of my friends had been calling me, telling me to put some mousse or something in there because it looked like a cactus," Purinton said.

SATURDAY, MARCH 31, 2001

EAST RUTHERFORD, N.J.—

For four years, not only did the Rangers have to suffer through the embarrassment of being unable to beat the Devils even once, but they also

330 NIGHTMARE ON 33RD STREET

had to live with Bobby Holik and Scott Stevens, et al., leaving them like roadkill on the ice.

So today, while the Rangers were celebrating their tiny, little streak-snapping 4-3 victory over the Devils at Continental Arena, it was almost ridiculous, nearly hilarious, that gigantic Jason Arnott was down the hallway accusing the Rangers of playing dirty.

Imagine, the big, bad Rangers bullying the Devils? Maybe in Ron Low's dreams.

But they did beat the Devils for the first time in 24 regular-season meetings (1-15-8), for the first time since January 12, 1997, and now they have a three-game winning streak. The Devils, who lost for the second time in 17 games, remained a point behind Ottawa for the Eastern lead.

Arnott was steamed about an incident that occurred late in a rugged second period, with the Rangers up 3-1 thanks to Guy Hebert's best goaltending as a Ranger. Half a minute earlier, Petr Nedved had an angry exchange with Stevens (hard to imagine that was part of some great intimidation scheme by the Rangers), and Stevens was still making gestures and yacking at Nedved in the penalty box.

Stevens put his forefinger and thumb in the "L" shape on his forehead, the international symbol for "loser". Nedved was simply nodding toward the infuriated hot-headed Devils captain, telling him something like, "I'm not going to fight you, but if you come near me, you'll get my stick."

Now rookie defenseman Mike Mottau was mixing it up with Devils sniper Patrik Elias in front of the net. Mottau, who is probably the smaller of the two non-brutes, and Elias wound up dropping the gloves and throwing punches. Arnott jumped in and began punching Mottau, by then pinned at the bottom of a pile. And Mark Messier literally leaped, like a linebacker at the goal line, and tackled Arnott from behind. Arnott took one too many punches for Messier's liking, and the captain bloodied Arnott with an uppercut. Both were ejected from the game, Arnott in obvious rage.

"I thought it was a really cheap shot, and whether it was Mark Messier or anybody else, I wouldn't have felt any different about it," he said.

Arnott, understandably, felt the rough stuff against Elias, in particular, began in the last meeting. Tomas Kloucek sent Elias flying with an elbow in that game, and it is part of Arnott's job to protect his linemate.

"It started last game," he said. "They're out of the playoffs and going after Patty, and we've got to stand up for each other. I didn't think it was fair when they went after Patty."

But Mottau, as a goon?

He laughed at the accusation. But Mottau was glad Messier was there for him.

"It makes me feel good that not only a teammate, but the captain, is willing to back you up when you need it, especially a guy like Mess."

Brian Leetch, who was right there, said Messier twice told Arnott to stop punching the prone and helpless Mottau before stepping in.

Sandy McCarthy, who is known more for his fists than his soft hands, scored a beauty of a goal as the Rangers played a Devils-like third period, protecting the lead and countering the Devils' gambles.

Petr Nedved gave the Rangers the lead with his 32nd goal on a power play, and Adam Graves (who scored the winning OT goal in the Rangers' last win of any kind over the Devils, in Game 5 of their 1997 playoff series) scored his first in 17 games to make it 2-0.

The Rangers just wanted to get rid of the streak. Graves called it a "point of embarrassment."

Leetch said, "It's just been a long four years. It's not like we've been fighting them for first or second place and haven't been able to beat them. We've been grinding every year, and this is just another part of what has grown into four long years. We've had ups and downs, more downs, through these years. So it's not like we're sailing along and just thinking, 'Why can't we beat the Devils?' We've got other things going on, too."

The Rangers treated this as a big game, and Low called it "huge" and there was some ridiculous talk about this victory making the Rangers season.

"If it is," Devils goalie Martin Brodeur said, "it's a sad thing."

Low talked to the players before the game, and convinced them that, if they went out and gave it all they've got and lost, they'd live with it. But also that they couldn't live with giving less than everything they had left.

Right now, they've got four games left, having played four rugged games, following Low's harsh criticism after the 4-0 loss to the Devils and the elimination loss to Detroit.

Which leads one to wonder where the Rangers might be if they'd played this way more often.

"You can leave that to wonder all you want," Low said. "We didn't."

It's Time
to Get the Gun out

SUNDAY, APRIL 1, 2001

ATLANTA

Probably the brightest spot of this entire dark season was snuffed out today. Rookie defenseman Tomas Kloucek, the 21-year-old who leaped to the top of the Rangers' prospects list and looked like he will be a cornerstone for years to come, wrecked his left knee. Kloucek not only is finished for this season, but for the early portion of next season, at the very least.

After four victories in five days, the Rangers should have been happy leaving Atlanta. Instead, they left shellshocked.

Their mood was wiped out when, during a 4-2 win over the Thrashers at Philips Arena, Kloucek suffered a torn anterior cruciate ligament and a torn medial collateral ligament as well when he hit Atlanta's Ray Ferraro and his left leg whipped awkwardly into the boards.

Kloucek will need major reconstructive surgery, which normally carries a 5-6-month rehabilitation period, but he will probably have to wait 4-6 weeks until the MCL heals itself before he can undergo the ACL surgery. Otherwise he won't have the strength to rehab the knee properly.

Kloucek should be ready to play by November, at the earliest, but may not be 100 percent until later in the season. His is the third torn ACL the Rangers have endured this season (Vladimir Malakhov and Mike Richter being the others), and the injury occurred eerily close to the exact spot where Malakhov suffered his injury on opening night in the same arena.

"It's depressing," Kloucek said. "It's a nightmare."

The Rangers were already without veteran defensemen Rich Pilon (hamstring) and Sylvain Lefebvre (shoulder sprain), and playing a second game in two days with four rookie defensemen, one sophomore, and one veteran, Brian Leetch.

"It made me sick when I found out," Leetch said. "He's worked so hard this year to get to the point where he is right now, where he's such a big part of our team."

Kloucek's punishing style made him an instant hit on a team that didn't have nearly enough physical players.

"It's just a terrible break for the kid, unbelievable," Mark Messier said. "Just seeing him play the way he has, the way he's coming along and then to have that happen is just a terrible break for him.

"I look around the league at guys who have had the same thing and once he has the operation he might come back and play next year, but it takes a good year to really recover."

RADEK DVORAK REACHED his goal when he scored his career-high 30th into an empty net.

MONDAY, APRIL 2, 2001

RYE, N.Y.

There is but one blue box remaining on the schedule, one more home game for these dreadful Rangers.

And while there will be plenty of empty Garden seats on Wednesday, when the Carolina Hurricanes close the curtain on New York City hockey for the season, those of the 18,200 who have purchased tickets will have an opportunity to do and see something special.

They will get to thank Adam Graves. And say goodbye to Adam Graves. And tell Glen Sather, Dave Checketts and Jim Dolan what they think of Adam Graves.

Barring some unforeseen change of mind and heart, Wednesday will be Graves's last game as a Ranger at the Garden. He knows the possibility is there, even the probability. He said this week that he's trying to not think about it, that he's trying to keep only the great memories and positive thoughts in his head, even as he is consumed with getting his own game back together again.

He knows that Sather tried to trade him at the deadline, had a deal with Washington worked out before it fell apart. He knows that Sather isn't going to have a $4 million third- or fourth-line left winger or center on his team.

Of course, Sather doesn't have to treat Cablevision's money as if it's coming out of his own pocket, either, but that's the way he is. For, on sheer value to the team, to the young players, to the organization, to the community, Graves is worth keeping around. He can play on anybody's third or fourth line, in any worst-case scenario,

Adam Graves, an inspiration on and off the ice, playing in his final season as a Ranger.

and when Sather buys him out, between the end of this season and July 1, for two-thirds of that salary (paid out over two years), Graves will hook up with a better team than the Rangers and play effectively in that role.

It made more sense to trade Graves at the deadline, and get something in return. But to let him go for free—when he can contribute something to the team and still play right where he's been the last few weeks, on the third line—simply because he's making too much money, well, that's Sather's way.

Right or wrong as that move may be, Graves is one of the most popular athletes ever to grace New York sports, one of the most giving, caring people ever, period. He was also the team MVP in 1993-94, when he scored a team record 52 goals and kicked the ghosts out of the Garden.

Anybody else would sound corny when they say what Graves says, that "nobody has ever worn the red, white and blue more proudly" and this at a time when the organization has claimed there isn't nearly enough darned pride left on the team.

Graves was voted the Rangers fan club's winner of the Ceil Saidel Memorial Award (for dedication to the organization on and off the ice) for the seventh year in a row last week. He has won the Steven McDonald "extra effort" award five times. He has won every award there is for his service to the community and charitable endeavors.

And even as his game has escaped him, his determination and try has never been questioned.

When Neil Smith traded for Mark Messier, he said, "Whenever he leaves here . . . he'll leave us with something we didn't have before he arrived. We'll be a better organization for having had him. He will put something into the Rangers logo that you won't be able to see. ... You will sit here and say there is something dramatically different about this team."

Smith could have easily been talking about Graves.

It is rare, indeed, when you get to say "goodbye and thank you" to a player before he walks out the door. The folks at the Garden may never again get to say it to a player and a person like Graves.

RON LOW SAID "it will be an expensive summer" around here. He didn't mean expensive in terms of signing expensive players, although there will be attempts to reel in a big name or two. He was talking about buyouts, probably of Valeri Kamensky and Sylvain Lefebvre (another guy who will end up producing for a team far better than the Rangers), maybe Tim Taylor, too.

Sather will also not re-sign Rich Pilon, who is another of the few, the rare, Rangers who left it all on the ice this season. Granted, it's time to get younger, and letting Pilon go might make room for a younger guy to get more ice time next season. But there will be times next season, to be sure, when the Rangers will wish they had a solid, physical, combative veteran defenseman. And they will wish they had kept Pilon, who could have been retained for a reasonable salary.

It would also be a good bet that Petr Nedved won't be a training camp—either having been traded or lowballed in contract talks by Sather—and that Theo Fleury will be traded over the summer or early next season, and that Mike Richter will be dealt as soon as he's healthy and playing well at some point next season.

WEDNESDAY, APRIL 4, 2001

NEW YORK

The circus was in town, so the odor at the Garden was even more pungent than usual.

There were 20 Rangers in the lineup for a 3-1 loss to the Carolina Hurricanes, the final game at the Garden this season. For many of them, it was their last.

"This team isn't going to sit still," Mark Messier said, "and it's important for this franchise to start to grow again. It's been a tough four years here."

The first step will be shedding salary and age, and the two most obvious shed-ees of any import are Adam Graves, who is expected to be bought out in the off-season, and Rich Pilon, who will be an unrestricted free agent the Rangers probably won't pursue.

So a game which was gigantic for the Hurricanes—still tied with Boston for the final playoff spot with two games to go, and holding the tiebreaker with two more victories—was a good-bye of sorts for many Rangers.

Unfortunately, the Garden was only half-filled, and of those who came, many were non-regulars. Therefore, while the crowd was warm and cordial to Graves—there were a few signs in the stands and they got to cheer when Graves was singled out repeatedly on the over-ice scoreboard screen—it was nowhere near what one might expect from Rangers fans.

The Rangers also endured yet another season-ending injury as Jan Hlavac collided with Craig Adams in the third. Hlavac suffered a Grade 2 sprain of his left medial collateral ligament and, while it shouldn't affect him for next season, he obviously won't play in the remaining two games. Hlavac said he was "very sad right now" because he was looking forward to representing the Czech Republic in the World Championships. The Rangers have already lost Vladimir Malakhov, Tim Taylor, Mike Richter, Theo Fleury, Tomas Kloucek, Sylvain Lefebvre (shoulder), Brad Brown, and now Hlavac to season-ending injuries.

Pilon played a mammoth game on defense in his first game back from a hamstring injury. Pilon was ferocious in the hitting department in his audition for a job, here or elsewhere this summer. At one point, he sent Ron Francis into a mid-air cartwheel with an open-ice hit, and Pilon never stopped throwing bodies around.

Both Messier and Brian Leetch, normally Pilon's defense partner, called him "a warrior."

"We have two games left, and you play for the jersey," Pilon said. "You play for the Rangers. You play for pride. We're athletes and losing's no fun. But I think I've kind of proven already that I played hard all year.

"With Glen (Sather) here and Mark and everybody, this team's going to turn things around. This is not going to happen again next year, for sure, and if I have an opportunity to sign here next year, I'll definitely jump on it."

Pilon played his 67th game, after playing more than 54 just once in the last eight years, and because of the top condition in which he reported to camp, he was able to pile up minutes and play some of the best hockey of his career.

"This is the best year I've probably had in the last five," he said. "Playing with Leetch has been a huge positive with me. ... I can look in the mirror and say I worked my butt off. It's tough. You've got the frog in your throat because of the situation, just standing out there, and you know it's the last game here and it might be my last game. That's brutal. But I left it out on the table."

Graves has done so for 10 years, but he won't speculate. He only would say, "I don't live in a fog" meaning he's aware of the possibilities. He was told outright the night before the trade deadline that he might be dealt, and he very nearly was (to Washington, among others).

"Regardless of what, I've been very, very fortunate to have been part of this organization for the last 10 seasons," he said.

He would love to stay. He doesn't plan to retire. So Sather will have to buy him out, or pay a chunk of his salary if he can find a trade.

"Everyone knows what a quality person he is," Brian Leetch said, "And I don't think there's any team that wouldn't benefit from having him on the team."

Yet another guy whose future is in doubt is goalie Guy Hebert, who played a second stellar game in a row. He has probably earned a chance to make the team next year, but he may not get that chance if it means the Rangers are on the hook for his $3.8 million salary.

TODAY WAS THE DAY the Rangers took their annual team photograph. So they practiced at the Garden this morning, got into their game uniforms, and posed at center ice in rows.

Adam Graves, like many others, had a new crisp haircut for the photo. Sandy McCarthy shaved his trademark fu manchu. He has rarely been seen without some menacing, dark facial hair.

"I've been kind of getting sick of it," he said. "I've been tasting last night's supper in there."

Even the injured players dressed up, but Theo Fleury couldn't be there, since he's still in rehab.

John Rosasco, the team's public relations director who is just about the same height as Fleury, donned the No. 14 jersey and stood in for Theo for the team picture. Later, thanks to computerized art, Fleury's head will be digitally superimposed. The Rangers did the same thing with Bill Berg a few years ago.

In fact, in the 1950s there was one season where the team was too cheap to take a new team photo. Instead, they took the photo from the year before, and cut and pasted heads of the new guys over the heads of the departed guys. It was a really amateur job before days of photo technology.

THURSDAY, APRIL 5, 2001

TAMPA, FLA.

The Rangers and Madison Square Garden brought Messier back to New York for a few reasons. One of those was an abject failure. Messier came back to get the Rangers back into the playoffs.

He guaranteed they would make it, and they didn't. Messier could hardly be blamed for that.

As everyone knows by now, though, Messier's value to a team is certainly not only measured in Ws, Ls, Ts or OLs. It's certainly not measured in goals (23 coming into today's game), assists (43), games played (it'll be all 82 if he makes it through Saturday's game at Florida!) or plus/minus (minus-24, among the worst in the league).

Messier's real value was going to be how he helped change a losing culture, how he helped bring along the young players in the rebuilding process, how he carried himself as an example. Simply, most obviously, how this greatest of leaders led.

So, on the verge of playing all 82 for only the second time in his glorious 22-year NHL career, Messier will be back next season, when he turns 41, and can and will still be the valuable hub of the Rangers team, despite published reports around the continent that he will retire in the off-season.

Look no further than how hard they have played since elimination, compared to the quit-like-dogs act they pulled in each of the previous two seasons.

Low pointed out that Messier told his teammates, in Low's words: "We can't get beat, or beat up, going down the stretch. I mean, we're out of it, but that's besides the point. We have to show some pride and go out and play as hard as we can."

"And, you know," Low said, "it's rubbed off on a lot of people. That ugly two games we had against Detroit and New Jersey, thank God we've played well since and they're forgotten. We've played hard and with a purpose, and he's been a big part of that."

Messier doesn't want the credit. To him, it was only a natural thought process.

"I think it's important that, first of all, that we didn't give up on each other," he said. "I know there's a lot of talk about playoff positioning, and standings and draft picks and all that. But when you're in a team, in the dressing room, your responsibility is to play the best you can and to win every game. Anything other than your best is not acceptable. It's not good enough.

"I think a lot of the players here are gaining a lot of respect for each other the way we've handled this situation this year, the way we've handled the adversity, and that is going to go great lengths when we go to training camp and we have these experiences to fall back on. No matter what happens, we've got to stay united and responsible to each other, and those are some of the things I've been talking about. We can start to see that some of the chemistry of the team has changed. I think the players themselves have played better, more as a team, and we've done it all through an amazing amount of injuries. So, having said that, I think it's exciting that some of these things are happening for next year."

As he spoke outside the visitors locker room to a small group of reporters, following a 4-3 overtime win over Tampa Bay at the Ice Palace, the team bus was being held for him. When Messier is speaking like this, from the heart, nobody is going to rush him, not the P.R. department, not the coaches, certainly not teammates.

Messier allowed that, with the success he has had in his career (six Cups, the NHL record for playoff games played, and only one non-playoff season until 1998) have made it more difficult for him to miss the playoffs four years in a row.

Physically, Glen Sather said, Messier could still play for years, maybe to age 45; and Messier says the off-season work it would require is not a problem because he is hungry to compete.

"Individual records are something I'll never play for," Messier said. "I'll never play just to break a record or to set a record. That's never been what I've felt was important to me as a person or a player. I was brought into the league, into an environment where everything was predicated on what the team did. I think because of that, I've had success, and because of that, it has extended my career. I guess it's always a question mark, because you don't see a lot of guys playing as long as I have; you don't see a lot of guys playing at my age.

"I know if I want to play, I have no problem competing at a level where I can contribute to a team that's going to be successful. So, at this time it's just year to year. Other than that, I'm not staying in the game to pass Gordie Howe (for second all-time in points) or to get games played. The thing that's always been important to me is winning championships, and if I'm playing it's because I want to win another championship."

IT'S NOT AN ENVIABLE POSITION. Goalie Guy Hebert has done a commendable job since coming to New York, but it really wouldn't have mattered if he had won every game and thrown a hatful of shutouts.

Hebert was good again in beating the Lightning 4-3 on Manny Malhotra's overtime goal, a game defined only by its place as the second-to-last game of this miserable season.

Hebert's chances of being a Ranger when the summer ends are about the same as a snowball's chance here in Tampa. The key number being 3.8, as in the millions of dollars remaining on the one year left on Hebert's contract.

The Rangers have an agreement with Anaheim, from whom they claimed Hebert on waivers March 7. At the end of this season, if the Rangers don't want him, Anaheim is on the hook for the last year of his contract, or is responsible for buying him out at two-thirds of that salary.

Hebert insisted that he doesn't know from whom he will be drawing paychecks after this season, only that he knows he is being paid by the Rangers at the moment and that he has the one year left on his contract.

Either way, though, Hebert isn't going to get $3.8 million to play for the Rangers next season, even if he has impressed his coach by going out night after night on a tender groin and battling. Hebert had a three-game winning streak last week, punctuated by his 38-save, winless-streak-snapping 4-3 win in New Jersey, and he had another strong outing in a 3-1 loss to Carolina Wednesday.

"He's played really well," Low said. "He's had likely two off nights, and both of those games he was very tender. But other than that he's been sound. Awfully sound. He's played very well."

Low was asked if Hebert has made a case for himself to remain a Ranger next season?

"Oh, definitely. I think he has," Low said.

But it certainly doesn't sound like Low's boss thinks he has.

"I think he's played OK," Sather said. "I wouldn't say he's been outstanding, but he hasn't been here very long and he hadn't played in a while, so I think he's done a good job for us."

"Let's wait until the season's over. The season's not finished yet, and I'm not going to tell you what I'm going to do anyway, until we do it."

Asked if a decision could be based on Hebert's performance, Sather simply said, "It's more complicated than that."

But Sather has gone on record saying he doesn't think the Rangers can trust one of their rookie goalies to carry the load until Mike Richter is healthy at some point next season, and in fact Sather tried to trade Richter before he went down with season-ending knee surgery. He will probably try to trade Richter again if and when he gets his value back up.

Sather also tried to obtain the guy who was pretty solid in goal for the Lightning tonight, Nikolai Khabibulin. Sather and Low obviously don't have much faith in backup Kirk McLean, either.

So Sather has to make a move for a No. 1 goalie this summer, and in a TV interview Wednesday he said he has a plan of attack. He wouldn't even hint what that might be.

THE RANGERS LEAD the NHL with 16 short-handed goals this season, and while that number has been largely driven by Theo Fleury, it's worth noting that the Rangers had only 11 short-handed goals in the three seasons Messier spent with the Vancouver Canucks.

THE RANGERS ENDURED another gigantic scare in this parade of season-ending injuries when Peter Smrek went down after a knee-on-knee collision with Tampa Bay's Alex Kharitonov in the first period. After limping off, Smrek returned to the game a few minutes later.

"I'm sitting there going, 'Are you fuckin' kidding me?' Low said. "Fortunately, it's just a charley horse."

DESPITE THE WIN, the Rangers continued to turn over the puck in the neutral zone, trying to go up the middle

"It's time to get the gun out," said Low, who is just exasperated by such things at this point.

IF SATHER DOES buy out Adam Graves, this will be one question worth asking: If Graves was making, say, $1 million instead of $4 million, would he still be a Ranger? If the answer to that is yes, then Graves should not have been sent packing. MSG's considerable money should not all of a sudden be such an issue with such an important franchise player. Simple as that. If Graves is valuable to the team, the franchise, the community, the city at one price, he is just as valuable at another price. End of argument.

SATURDAY, APRIL 7, 2001

SUNRISE, FLA.

The Rangers never gave up, they just gave up too much too often.

As the sun set in Sunrise on the Rangers' fourth consecutive non-playoff, losing season, they lost 3-0 to the Florida Panthers in a game too familiar.

The Rangers allowed two goals in a span of 17 seconds and another 1:09 later, and minimally improved their draft position. They will finish 10th from the bottom of the NHL's standings (33-43-5-1), and will have a 2.1 percent chance of winning the draft lottery, which would move them up four spots to sixth. If a team with a worse record than the Rangers wins the lottery, the Rangers will draft 10th.

All of which seemed moot in the litter of this season, which was far better after the Rangers' mathematical elimination than it was before, because of the incorporation of youth into the lineup.

"I think they played hard down the stretch, which is what I wanted to see, and nobody quit," Ron Low said. "There's definitely been some steps forward, although it might not look like it in the standings. I think there's a lot of young guys here that contributed quite a bit down the stretch."

But Low is an honest fellow, sometimes brutally so, and he knows nobody will be fooled by the effort the Rangers put forth after it no longer counted. There are major steps that need to be taken to get the franchise where it should be, and that ought to make for a busy, expensive (in terms of signing free agents, and also buyouts) summer.

"Definitely," Low said. "I don't think any time you miss the playoffs by 12-15 points, you're looking at it (any way) other than saying you're not good enough, and you've got to do some changes on the hockey club."

Nor would he deny that the current team should have been better than it was, that there was an undeniable level of underachievement.

"I'll tell you what," Low said. "I think there were some circumstances on this hockey club that likely predicated where we are in the end. Losing Ricky (Mike Richter) in the end was devastating, and Theo (Fleury) within a week after that. I mean, those were likely two of your most relied-on guys, and Ricky was never Ricky until the last month before (the injury). So, did we underachieve? I think, yeah, we did. Is there a reason for some of it? Yeah, there's definitely some reasons.

"We went out and spent $4 million on (Vladimir Malakhov) and got a grand total of three games. He was a guy that we were going to rely on heavily. You don't replace those things in your lineup. And there's not enough depth, I don't think, in the organization, to cover those things up. There isn't."

There will be changes, and some it might be selling long-term for short-term, which is dangerous in that such an approach in the past has been a reason for where the Rangers are today.

There are a number of players who have played their final games as Rangers. Valeri Kamensky, who was awful but certainly doesn't deserve the load of blame he endured, will probably be bought out immediately. Sylvain Lefebvre might be bought out, too, and goalie Kirk McLean's a goner.

In recent days, Glen Sather has praised the way Adam Graves has played since moving to center on a checking line. Perhaps he is wavering on his idea of buying out Graves; or perhaps he's trying to soften the blow he dealt when he first said a month ago that he might have "to retire Adam Graves".

Goalie Guy Hebert almost certainly won't be back, not at $3.8 million. Rich Pilon, an unrestricted free agent, most surely will sign elsewhere without an offer from the Rangers. Petr Nedved, a restricted free agent, could be facing a nasty negotiation, and might be traded.

Sather tried to trade Richter and Fleury before they went down for the season, and there's no reason to think his plan will be to deal them again if and when they're healthy. But Sather also tried to trade some of his top prospects—Pavel Brendl, Jamie Lundmark, even terrific sophomore center Mike York—at the deadline, in deals that fell apart for Keith Tkachuk and Nikolai Khabibulin, and in a big deal with Washington.

Then there's the Jaromir Jagr factor. If Pittsburgh's NHL scoring leader is available—and he will be—there is no price too high in terms of prospects, young players or money.

Who will be back for sure? Mark Messier and Brian Leetch (no-trade clause) and injured Tomas Kloucek and Malakhov. Probables: Radek Dvorak, York, Jan Hlavac, Nedved, Kim Johnsson, Dale Purinton, Manny Malhotra, Sandy McCarthy, Peter Smrek, Mike Mottau, Brad Brown. Maybe: Richter, Fleury, Michal Grosek, Colin Forbes, Tim Taylor.

A lot of those names depend on which new names Sather acquires. If Sakic comes, York or Nedved are expendable. If Graves stays as a checking center, what happens to Taylor? And how much do you have to give up for Jagr?

Further, Sather has ideas about a No. 1 goalie, and next year is an option on Dominik Hasek's contract in Buffalo, so he might be unrestricted, too.

MANNY MALHOTRA, Mike Mottau and Peter Smrek will go to Hartford tomorrow to play in the AHL playoffs. Call-up Derek Armstrong went back today. Armstrong, the AHL MVP, was given a choice to stay and play in the last two games, or to go back to Hartford where he led the AHL scoring race by one point. He chose to stay, and will play in the season finale at Hartford tomorrow to go for the scoring title.

AS HE GOT OUT of an elevator from the press box, Sather sighed, "Well, I'm glad that's over with."

We Need Help Everywhere

RYE, N.Y.

Breakup Day is usually an interesting day. It normally isn't scheduled in advance, because the 16 teams that make the playoffs don't know when they'll be eliminated. Some of the teams that go down to the wire don't know if they will be in the playoffs.

But when you're out of it as long as the Rangers have been out of it, Breakup Day can be put on the schedule in pen.

Another thing that playoff teams normally do is leave a day between their last game and Breakup Day so that the players can go out and tie one on. Honestly. And there have been plenty of Breakup Days when players are hung over and still reeking of alcohol.

These Rangers were wide-eyed and sober.

The Rangers arrived home from Florida last night, and this morning they were packing their things, taking final physical exams, and having their exit interviews with coach Ron Low and president/GM Glen Sather. A lot of them won't be back here next season and know it. And a lot of what they had to say had been said for weeks, so unlike other years, reporters weren't terribly interested in interviewing players. Messier talked about how the injuries to Malakhov and Richter and the Fleury episode cut down their chances to compete for the playoff berth he guaranteed last July. Leetch spoke of the disappointment of this fourth consecutive non-playoff year.

But the words of Sather, on this day, would be the ones that counted.

Sather, late in the day, plopped down on a couch in the lounge outside the locker room and was surrounded by reporters. He tried to smile an easy smile, but he looked edgy and as if he didn't really want to be there.

Sather was smug, but he was also adversarial and contentious. He would answer only those questions he wanted to answer, and then only as far as he wanted to answer them.

"Well, I think we changed the attitude," Sather said. "There was never any of the internal bickering that I guess was here before. Now, I wasn't part of that so I only know what people told me. And maybe you guys don't think we changed (the attitude) but there hasn't been any internal bickering."

Okay, maybe the bickering had been mostly eliminated. But what about what went wrong, and how to fix it?

Instead, there were contradictions. You looked. You listened. You tried to figure out which way they're going.

And you come up with nothing and everything.

Where they're headed, nobody seems to know. Not even Sather, for the next six years or so, the man in charge of that department, if there ever is such a department at Madison Square Garden.

Are the Rangers rebuilding? Yep. You bet. Do they have to make major changes to be playoff contenders again?

"Yeah, I think there will be some significant changes," Sather said. "I can't think of one area where we don't (have a) need. We need help everywhere."

He later said he wants to add "speed, size and strength" as if there's a team anywhere that wouldn't love to add those three attributes. He said the best way to fill holes in an organization is through free agency, provided you sign the right type of people.

Sather was asked if it is possible to continue the flow of young players into the lineup, and at the same time build a team that can compete, can get to the playoffs.

"I can't give you a guarantee that any course of action is going to be the right one," he said. "I think one of the biggest problems that happened here is that there wasn't the flow of young kids coming in. The young kids keep the old guys going, and every year there has to be some transition of new people, new blood, new ideas. That's always easier said than done."

Neil Smith was rebuilding, too. He missed the playoffs and got fired a year ago. Sather came in and declared that anything less than the playoffs was unacceptable.

Well, he missed the playoffs, too. Yet he was rebuilding, too.

Sather was asked whether he thinks the Rangers' needs are greatest among front line players, among third- and fourth-line types.

"All of the above," he said, adding later: "I don't think it needs a total makeover."

Again, though, comes this feeling from the organization that, if things had broken right—a lot of things, from both of Richter's knees to Fleury's life—they were good enough to be in the playoffs this season. Certainly, if you saw them play Carolina last week, it's virtually impossible to say Carolina has better personnel.

"I thought that, the year that Fleury was having, and when Richter started to get on a roll, yeah, I thought we had a real good shot at (the playoffs)," Sather said. "There was a period there of about 10 days that everything started to fall apart, just before the trade deadline."

It fell apart. Now Sather has to figure out how to put it back together, and how much has to be put together and how much to tear apart. One immediate problem is that his buyouts of veterans, beginning as early as today, has to be completed by June 30. The next day, free agency begins. So there will be players gone, before he really knows what new players he will be able to get.

Then there's the same old question. Do you go after a Joe Sakic, a John LeClair, a Rob Blake? How about a gritty guy like Detroit's Martin Lapointe or Buffalo's Michael Peca; or a franchise goalie like Dominik Hasek, sure to be available; or even the often-concussed Eric Lindros?

Will any of them come to this four-year shipwreck? Would any big-name signing be another big, expensive Band-Aid? Could any such signing be a disaster? Might a Lapointe come to New York for lots of dollars and therefore be expected to be a star rather than a grinder? Might Jaromir Jagr be had for a whole handful of top young players, and come to New York and start sulking?

Can any of these questions ever be answered ahead of time?

These Rangers might simply be better off this year to say, "You know what? We're going to continue what we started these last few weeks, let the Peter Smreks and Manny Malhotras have their growing pains, and let them all grow up together. We might lose 40 games again next year, but it will be a progressive season for the franchise. And if they go down playing hard, people will understand."

Sather knows the Rangers' most legitimate excuse this season was that they had top-level goaltending for about a month, just before Richter went down. He will try to get a No. 1 goalie, since Richter won't be 100 percent at any time near the start of the season.

Who knows? Maybe a No. 1 goalie could have masked a lot of the other problems, and gotten the Rangers to the playoffs. Maybe the goals-against average wouldn't have been so pitiful, despite the short-comings of the forwards in the defensive and neutral zones. Maybe the penalty killing wouldn't have been so embarrassingly bad.

But it seems like that type of simple trouble-shooting isn't in the plans. It seems like the Rangers want to make major moves, gigantic overhauls, without a specific direction.

It seems as if the rebuilding will continue, but so will the quest for a playoff spot and ultimately a championship.

It seems as if trying to do all those things at once is doomed to fail. Again.

SATHER DID AGREE that Messier suffered in the middle part of the season because he needed a rest.

"I'm not sure how you do that," said Sather, who could have ordered Messier to take a break, but never did. "We asked him if he wanted some time off this year and he didn't. He sure isn't going to volunteer."

Sather also said he was "blindsided" by the Fleury incident and that he felt he should have found a way to "anticipate what was going on."

And when asked if buyouts make more sense this summer than last summer, when Sather joined the organization, he said "I really don't think you can walk into an organization and start buying people out until you've given them the full opportunity to do what they have to do."

The follow-up question was "Is a season enough?"

"I think it's a pretty good opportunity," Sather said, before abruptly ending the interview session.

TUESDAY, APRIL 10, 2001

NEW YORK

Three days after their final loss, the Rangers lost again. The Atlanta Thrashers won the NHL's entry-draft lottery, stealing the No. 1 overall pick in the June 23 draft from the Islanders. The Thrashers, who were to select third before winning the lottery, leaped over the Islanders and Tampa Bay, which will now have the second and third selections, respectively.

All the other teams remained in their original order, including the Rangers, who will choose 10th.

IN AN UNRELATED MATTER, Rick Curran, the agent for goalie Kirk McLean, who is to be a free agent July 1, has been told by Glen Sather that McLean will not be returning to the Rangers.

Curran, who also represents Adam Graves, said he has not yet discussed Graves's status with Sather. Last month Sather indicated he might buy out the final season of Graves's contract.

WEDNESDAY, APRIL 18, 2001

HARTFORD, CONN.

Even when things go right for the Rangers, they have a way of going wrong.

On Monday night, the Rangers' top two prospects were eliminated from their junior league playoffs, and therefore headed to Hartford, where they could begin their professional careers with the Rangers' farm club in the AHL playoffs.

Pavel Brendl's Calgary Hitmen were ousted in six games by Red Deer, and Jamie Lundmark's Seattle Thunderbirds were swept by Spokane.

It was to be, depending on the success the defending AHL champ Wolf Pack would have, a six-week introduction to pro hockey and an early audition for the two players in Hartford.

Well, as Brendl and Lundmark made their way from Western Canada to Connecticut, the unexpected happened. Hartford was upset by Providence in a decisive Game 5 tonight, the defending champs out in the first round of the playoffs.

So the pro debuts of Lundmark and Brendl will have to wait until next season.

A ROUNDUP OF EX-RANGERS who are/were in the playoffs while the Rangers teed it up:

James Patrick (Buffalo), Darren Langdon, Rob DiMaio and Kevin Hatcher (Carolina), Sergei Zubov, Mike Keane, John MacLean and Grant Ledyard (Dallas), Pat Verbeek (Detroit), Doug Weight and Todd Marchant (Edmonton), Luc Robitaille, Mathieu Schneider, Mattias Norstrom, Ian Laperriere and Aaron Miller (Los Angeles), John Vanbiesbrouck and Sergei Nemchinov (Devils), Rob Zamuner and Eric Lacroix (Ottawa), Jody Hull and P.J. Stock (Philadelphia), Alexei Kovalev and Kevin Stevens (Pittsburgh), Niklas Sundstrom, Stephane Matteau, Todd Harvey and Tony Granato (San Jose), Mike Eastwood, Alexei Gusarov and Jeff Finley (St. Louis), Tie Domi and Glenn Healy (Toronto), Dan Cloutier (Vancouver), Ulf Dahlen (Washington).

And coaches Lindy Ruff (Buffalo), Craig MacTavish (Edmonton), assistant coaches Roger Neilson (Ottawa), Mark Hardy (Los Angeles), Keith Acton (Toronto), Charlie Huddy (Edmonton), Bill Moores (Edmonton), Bobby Carpenter (Devils), Steve Weeks (Carolina); and GMs Larry Pleau (St. Louis), George McPhee (Washington), Kevin Lowe (Edmonton) and Craig Patrick (Pittsburgh).

CRAIG PATRICK HAS PULLED another rabbit out of his hat. Pittsburgh needed a goalie for the playoffs and everybody, Penguins players included, had a good laugh when the GM came up with Johan Hedberg in a minor trade. Well, Hedberg has turned out to be better than good enough for the Penguins as the No. 1 goalie in the playoffs. Is there a better GM in hockey, outside of Lou Lamoriello, than Patrick? And what are all these scouts doing if a guy like Hedberg is wasting away on the Manitoba Moose of the IHL? Could he not have been a better, longer-term answer for the Rangers than Guy Hebert?

TUESDAY, MAY 15, 2001

NEW YORK

Like a bolt of lightning out of nowhere, Dave Checketts resigned as Madison Square Garden's president and CEO. His Rangers missed the playoffs for a fourth year in a row. His Knicks were knocked out in a first-round upset by the Toronto Raptors, who had never won a playoff series before.

Checketts took over the Rangers, remember, after their Stanley Cup victory in 1994. So his seven seasons in the hockey business were fairly unsuccessful. Not only did they include the four non-playoff years, but Checketts was front and center in the Mark Messier-bashing after helping to force out Messier in 1997, which backfired badly.

Checketts was also instrumental in the 1996 signing of Wayne Gretzky, a high-profile acquisition that never lived up to its billing.

Checketts also had a big hand in the free-agent spending spree in 1999, when the Rangers signed Theo Fleury, Valeri Kamensky, Sylvain Lefebvre, Stephane Quintal, Tim Taylor, and Kirk McLean during their Checketts-approved rebuilding process.

Checketts lauded then-Rangers president/GM Neil Smith's work, saying "I can't imagine a GM ever having a better summer than Neil did" then fired Smith in March of that season, when it all went wrong.

And when it was time to replace Smith, Checketts search went only as far as one man—Glen Sather, who was signed to a contract that could run as long as seven years, and who also failed miserably in his first season.

Checketts always made money at the Garden. Checketts brought back big-time boxing. He was, reportedly, a wonderful leader of Radio City Music Hall, a Cablevision/Garden property. He was even discussing with his boss, Jim Dolan, a contract extension. However, it was believed that the extension would be for Checketts to remain in charge of the "other" Garden toys, and no longer the Knicks and Rangers.

In short, as a hockey man, Checketts's record wasn't very good.

Despite that, the word that Checketts was forced out of the World's Most Overrated Arena might be the worst news possible for anybody who cares about the Rangers.

Just when Rangers fans think it can't possibly get any worse than the last four years, it has gotten worse.

Jim Dolan is now the hands-on, soon-to-be-very involved manager of the Garden's two teams. Who knows how good or bad Dolan is at running his dad's legal cable monopoly, or what his track record is with The Wiz stores? You would imagine that, under his watch and the watch of Checketts, the Garden has made tons of money. Certainly, MSG Network has maintained a level of excellence, and Fox Sports New York, with MSG Network holding its hand, has improved dramatically, especially compared to the old SportsChannel (remember that?), although the network was on the verge of losing the Yankees.

But Dolan is not a hockey guy. He rarely is seen at games, and when he is, it's usually because all hell is breaking loose. His points of reference are 1) that he befriended Wayne Gretzky while trying to talk Gretzky out of retirement, and 2) that, on the recommendation of NHL commissioner Gary Bettman and probably Gretzky, he and Checketts hired Sather.

Dolan's influence was so strong that Checketts signed Sather to a contract that is orbits out of whack when compared to contracts of other general managers. Sather's deal is believed to be for seven seasons, and with options and bonuses could reach $5 million per year.

The next highest-paid GM in the NHL is believed to be either Brian Burke of Vancouver or Pierre Lacroix of Colorado, at around $1.2 million. Lou Lamoriello of the Devils was a part-owner and hit the lottery when the team was sold, but his salary is in line with other GMs, and most of the top GMs in the league make $800,000 to $1 million per year.

The spending on Sather is not out of character for Dolan, who also, upon failing to convince The Great One to stick around in 1999, walked into the locker room and promised the players that the Rangers would be spending ridiculous amounts of cash on free agents that summer. We all know how that worked out.

Okay, so money isn't really a concern for MSG or the Rangers. Fine.

Dolan's takeover of power, though, means more spending, and that could mean an end to the rebuilding steps, even a reversal of the movement toward bringing in young players.

Not that Sather is completely sold on that movement. He tried to trade a whole bunch of his top prospects at the deadline in March, in attempts to bring Keith Tkachuk or Eric Lindros to New York.

So there's no reason to think the Rangers won't be big-time players in the free-agent market this summer (that is where they will miss the recruiting savvy of Checketts, and where their success might hinge on the willingness of Sather to realize he's not in Edmonton anymore).

If the Rangers sign a Joe Sakic or a John LeClair or an Alexander Mogilny or a Martin Lapointe, the focus is going to start to change, and expectations are about to do an about-face.

When the expectations rise, though, you can bet that Pavel Brendl and Jamie Lundmark and Manny Malhotra and Radek Dvorak will be flying out of town in trades designed for instant gratification. If the Rangers get off to a slow start, Dolan may pressure Sather to make deals to get them going. And if they get off to a strong start, Dolan and Sather might try to pump them up to instant contender status by sacrificing the young.

With Checketts gone, Sather's power doesn't change much. Ultimately, he will still be responsible for all decisions and, so far, he hasn't shown that he knows which direction he will go—Win Now! or patience toward the future. Now, though, Dolan's influence goes right to Sather, and not through Checketts.

This could be a nightmare.

MURRAY MURDOCH, the last survivor of the original Rangers team in 1926-27, died this week at age 96 in South Carolina. Murdoch, who was the oldest living Ranger, was also a distant relative of Mark Messier.

Murdoch was honored by the Rangers in 1990, on the 50th anniversary of the 1940 Stanley Cup championship team. Although Murdoch was no longer a Ranger in 1940, he won Stanley Cups with the Rangers in 1927 and 1933. Then-Rangers GM Neil Smith awarded Murdoch a Stanley Cup ring from 1933, at which time rings had not yet become traditional. That's how things used to work at the Garden.

SATURDAY, JUNE 23, 2001

SUNRISE, FLA.

In the very building in which their season ended, the Rangers started to retool at the NHL draft. Glen Sather's big plan was to draft a goalie in the first round, and he got one, Dan Blackburn, who is expected to be a good one, but at age 18, shouldn't be nearly ready to help for a number of years.

The big news on draft day, rather, was of the imminent trade of Adam Graves, the team's heart and soul.

Graves was at his mother's house in Windsor, Ontario, watching the draft on TV, when he heard the swirling rumors.

Sather also spoke at the draft to Philadelphia GM Bobby Clarke about Eric Lindros, who sat out the entire season unsigned and unwanted; to Buffalo GM Darcy Regier about Dominik Hasek, whose $9 million contract option for next season makes him an almost-definite ex-Sabre; and to Edmonton GM Kevin Lowe about ex-Ranger Doug Weight, whose pending free agency next season makes him a sure ex-Oiler.

The selection of Blackburn with the 10th pick doesn't say much about the Rangers' faith in minor-league goalies Johan Holmqvist and Vitali Yeremeyev, who had been considered among their top prospects in recent years, or Jason LaBarbera, who was signed last summer.

With Mike Richter coming off a second serious knee operation, the Rangers need help short-term and long-term, and Blackburn is very long-term.

Sather, who knew the Alberta-born Blackburn from his days in Edmonton, still needs a goalie or two. Neither Kirk McLean or Guy Hebert will be back next season, and Richter may not be 100 percent until late in the season. Richter may also be traded, since Sather had a deal in the works with St. Louis when Richter tore his left knee late last season.

SUNDAY, JUNE 24, 2001

SUNRISE, FLA.

A big piece of the Rangers organization was ripped away today, as Sather completed the deal of Adam Graves to the San Jose Sharks for a pair of prospects.

It was more a matter of when, than if or where. So Graves was ready for the call he got from Sather, who had seriously considered buying him out if unable to make a deal.

That he knew it was coming didn't make it any easier for Graves, who scored a team-record 52 goals in the greatest season in franchise history, 1993-94; who scored a huge goal in Game 7 of the Stanley Cup finals, and who refused credit for the Cup-winning goal given to Mark Messier, even though Graves appeared to have scored it.

"I'm letting it sink in right now," Graves said by phone from Windsor, Ontario. "I don't think you can ever totally prepare yourself for it, but I understood it was a distinct possibility."

As it turns out, the Rangers will foot two-thirds of the $4 million Graves will earn on the final year of his contract next season, and the Sharks will be responsible for the $1 million bonus Graves's contract called for in the event of a trade.

"I guess I have two trains of thought, the first being that the last 10 years have been absolutely tremendous," said Graves, 33, who was signed as a free agent from Edmonton in the summer of 1991. "I have nothing but great memories of being on the ice, in the dressing room, within the organization, and also in the city, in the area, with all the people we've met and all the friends we have made. It's been just a great experience for my family.

"Second, as much as this is part of the game, you always wonder about where you're going. I've heard nothing but great things about the San Jose organization, and I'm looking forward to the challenge."

Graves refused to buy the organizational line that he needs a change of scenery after his disappointing 10-goal season in 2000–01. That would hint of an excuse, and typically he wanted none of that.

"You have to evaluate yourself and hold yourself to your own expectations," he said. "A lot of this is preparation, and I've begun my preparation, not only physically but mentally. I'm going to work as hard as I can to earn the respect of my new teammates."

Graves insisted since last March, when he was nearly dealt at the deadline, that he can still play at a high level.

"Yes, most definitely," he said. "If I felt any differently, I would say so. But I feel I can."

Since Sather had planned on ridding the Rangers of Graves' salary since mid-season, he did well to get two 24-year-old players—Mikael Samuelsson, a center/winger who had 78 points in 66 games for San Jose's Kentucky affiliate last season; and enormous (6-5, 235) defenseman Christian Gosselin.

Sather said he felt Samuelsson would "slide" right into the Rangers' lineup last season, which may be a stretch. The AHL is no proving ground— the Rangers' Derek Armstrong was AHL MVP and scoring leader, and their Brad Smyth led the league with 50 goals, but neither is considered a top candidate for an NHL job, or perhaps even a new contract.

Sather praised Graves for what he has meant to the franchise, and to the city, but said he thinks Graves needs a change of scenery. Sather added he doesn't feel Graves is finished.

"Sometimes you have to make some painful decisions and go on with life," Sather said. "Dealing with Adam over the years, in two cities, he's probably one of the classiest guys I have dealt with. There isn't anybody finer in the game.

"I just hope this is the right decision for Adam and for the Rangers."

Graves was a Santa Claus when it came to charitable endeavors, the list far too long to mention here. He won every possible award for his off-ice work, both on a league-wide and a New York-area basis. Last week he won the Masterton Trophy for perseverance and dedication, mainly for getting through last season after the losses of his infant son, and his father and idol within several months of one another.

Now this.

"That's part of life," Graves said. "Everything happens for a reason, and I'm excited. I'm looking to contribute. They've got an excellent hockey team. I just want to let things come naturally.

"No one can ever take away the 10 years I had in New York."

SATHER DID INDEED offer Petr Nedved and Pavel Brendl to Philadelphia for Eric Lindros prior to the draft. The deal never got anywhere because Sather wants Lindros to say he wants to be a Ranger; then they have to hammer out a new contract. But it isn't dead.

The Rangers, at the moment, appear to be the only team in the Jaromir Jagr sale in Pittsburgh; so until there's a bidding war, they don't expect Jagr to go anywhere.

FRIDAY, JUNE 29, 2001

NEW YORK

Midnight tomorrow is the deadline at which the Rangers' ever-changing roster might significantly begin changing further.

It is the deadline for buying out contracts at two-thirds salary, and both left winger Valeri Kamensky and center Tim Taylor are almost certain to be bought out at that time, unless the Rangers can find a trade for either player. A third buyout candidate, defenseman Sylvain Lefebvre, had shoulder surgery, and is therefore ineligible to be bought out. Players who are bought out become unrestricted free agents.

Among the top names scheduled to become totally unrestricted are Joe Sakic, Rob Blake and Patrick Roy of Colorado, Martin Lapointe of Detroit, Pierre Turgeon of St. Louis, Brett Hull of Dallas, Alex Mogilny of the Devils, Rich Pilon of the Rangers and many more. Jeremy Roenick was removed from the market when he got permission from Phoenix to sign with Philadelphia prior to the free-agency period.

Restricted free agents, such as Petr Nedved and Manny Malhotra of the Rangers, must also receive offers of 10 percent raises over last season in order for teams to retain rights to match any other offers they receive, or to get compensation from any other team signing them. Nedved has already received a qualifying offer.

Meanwhile, the Rangers made a minor-league trade, obtaining tough defenseman Sean Gagnon, 27, from Ottawa for little-used defenseman Jason Doig, 24, and winger Jeff Ulmer, 24.

NEW YORK

Glen Sather has done relatively well considering he was willing to give away so many of his veteran players for nothing.

As expected, Sather bought out winger and the bust of the Rangers' 1999 free-agent signing spree, Valeri Kamensky for two-thirds of the remaining two guaranteed years and $8 million due on his contract.

Kamensky, who scored 27 goals and was mostly injured while collecting $9 million of Cablevision's money the last two seasons, became an unrestricted free agent at midnight. There are expected to be several teams interested in signing him at a greatly reduced price.

Sather, who managed to get two young players for Adam Graves, did the same today when he dealt buyout candidate Tim Taylor to Tampa Bay. In return for reuniting Taylor with former Rangers coach John Tortorella, the Rangers got back left wingers Nils Ekman, 25 and huge, tough Kyle Freadrich, 22. The smallish (5-11, 175) Ekman had nine goals and 20 points in 43 games with the Lightning last season. Freadrich's key stats are 6-foot-7, 260 pounds, and hundreds of penalty minutes in the minors and the NHL the last two seasons.

In dumping Taylor, Kamensky, and Kirk McLean, only two players remain from the Dirty Half Dozen of the summer of 1999—Theo Fleury, who could still be traded this summer, and Sylvain Lefebvre, whom the Rangers were forced to keep because he underwent shoulder surgery Friday. A fourth, Stephane Quintal, was sent to Chicago in the October waiver deal that brought Michal Grosek and Brad Brown to the Rangers.

The rugged Brown, 25, likely became an ex-Ranger, too. The Rangers decided to let him turn unrestricted free agent rather than offer him the $880,000 necessary to keep his rights. It is possible, though not likely, that Sather could sign him for a lower price.

Sather did extend qualifying offers to all his other potential restricted free agents: Petr Nedved, Manny Malhotra, Jan Hlavac, Sandy McCarthy, and Kim Johnsson. The Rangers will therefore have the right to match any unlikely offer they might get from another team, or the right to compensation.

The Rangers, who have already waived and/or released goalies McLean and Guy Hebert, and are not expected to pursue unrestricted Rich Pilon, are trimming their minor-league payroll as well.

With the free-agent market opening tomorrow, Sather was not out on the road as Dave Checketts and Neil Smith were when the bell rang in 1999. He is expected to be a player in the attractive market, but not one who loads his shopping cart to the brim.

SUNDAY, JULY 1, 2001

NEW YORK

The first day of NHL free agency produced a flurry of activity, and two things happened.

One, the four best teams in hockey—the Western Conference super-powers—all made loads of noise that will reverberate down the stretch and through the playoffs next season. Two, Rangers Glen Sather was quickly shut out of most of the players he coveted, but may have moved inches closer to landing Jaromir Jagr or Eric Lindros.

The Rangers never even got a crack at free agents Joe Sakic, Rob Blake, and Patrick Roy, all of whom re-signed with Stanley Cup champ Colorado before the free agency bell rang at midnight.

They never got close to obtaining goalie Dominik Hasek, who was dealt from Buffalo to Detroit.

They missed out on Doug Weight, who was traded from Edmonton to St. Louis.

They didn't land Pierre Turgeon, who signed with Dallas for five years, $32.5 million.

And they even got beat to low-profile free agents like Bob Boughner, who was close to signing with Calgary. Instead the Rangers wound up signing limited, recycled defensemen Dave Karpa, 30, from Carolina and Igor Ulanov, 31, from Edmonton, which might make you wonder why they chose not to simply keep Rich Pilon and Brad Brown.

The Rangers—get this—have interest in Los Angeles' Mathieu Schneider, whom Sather let walk away last summer, a decision he later regretted.

So, is this summer better than the supposedly disastrous summer of 1999 so far?

The Turgeon signing may or may not knock out the Stars as the Rangers' chief rival for Jagr, who has two years and $20.7 million remaining on a contract that likely will be extended before he is traded from Pittsburgh. While Jagr has said it's not necessary for his contract to be reworked, any team giving up the kind of assets it will take to pry Jagr from the Penguins will surely want him signed long term.

Dallas owner Tom Hicks—best known for the $252 million Alex Rodriguez contract with his baseball club in Texas—had promised to spend big money this summer in order to get the Stars back to the top. Turgeon's salary simply replaces that of Brett Hull, who was not re-upped, so Hicks and the Stars are likely still in the Jagr hunt. They also signed role players Rob DiMaio and their own Kirk Muller.

Dallas and Detroit were also among the lead teams in the Lindros derby— such as it is—but the Red Wings' addition of Hasek (and signing him for three years, $24 million) may conclude their big-dollar spending.

It remains to be seen if Lindros will add the Rangers to the list of teams to which he'd accept a trade; and/or if another team, such as Los Angeles, gets involved with Jagr.

Meanwhile, Detroit's big acquisition might make Chris Osgood available, and the Rangers need a proven goaltender. While Osgood has faltered at times during the playoffs, he has won a Stanley Cup and, at 28, he could be a long-term answer for the Rangers. At worst, Osgood would give the Rangers far better goaltending than they have had since Mike Richter's first major knee injury in February, 2000.

Sooner or later—probably sooner—Sather is going to have to stop talking and hoping, and start doing and spending. His payroll, with all the buyout deals done, is down in the $40 millions, and he reportedly has permission to go much higher. He also may still shed Theo Fleury's salary ($6.5 million and $7 million the next two seasons) in a trade this summer, since his no-trade clause has elapsed.

MONDAY, JULY 2, 2001
NEW YORK

Glen Sather played the free-agent game with fiscal responsibility, which could be commended or condemned, since his Rangers swept up only the crumbs when the first two days were over.

Sather saw Martin Lapointe sign today with Boston—a team no closer to playoff contention than the Rangers—for mind-blowing money, $5 million per year.

That is just too much, Sather and others in the league believe, but sometimes in order to get the most wanted free agents, you need to go much higher than reason warrants.

"When the numbers started to get a little crazy we kind of backed out of it," Sather said.

He said he was "shocked" at the first day's activities, which included the re-signing of Colorado's three jewels of the potential free-agent market (Joe Sakic, Rob Blake, and Patrick Roy) hours before the market opened; plus the signing of Pierre Turgeon and the trades of Dominik Hasek and Doug Weight before the Rangers could get involved. He said he was stunned, also, at the speed of the signings and the dollar amounts.

"Yeah, I think that all of the above kind of shocked me," he said. "I'm surprised that the guys in Colorado opted to stay there as quickly as they did. But understanding that they won the Stanley Cup, it probably makes a lot of sense that they want to stay together, and try to repeat it. They certainly got some pretty good deals. Some of the other free-agent signing surprised me a little bit, the amount of money they paid them and the length of contracts they got into.

"If you look back at the historical signings of Group III (unrestricted) free agents, you'll find that a lot of guys haven't done too well in that market. I think that the real trick is smart shopping. I know that all of us see players differently, and all of us are trying to fulfill different needs, but I really want to leave some spots open for young guys on this team."

Sather, who signed defensemen Dave Karpa and Igor Ulanov Sunday, after being beaten to Bob Boughner (Calgary) and Sean O'Donnell (Boston), said he might have interest in guys like Brett Hull and Alex Mogilny if the terms and money are right. They aren't likely to be right, though, with Toronto reportedly interested in Mogilny. Sather said he heard another of his targets, Mathieu Schneider, was on the verge of re-signing in Los Angeles.

Sather's main focus remains Jaromir Jagr, who certainly won't come cheaply. Sather mentioned, by the way, that the Sakic, et al., signings established the "ceiling" on salaries at around $10 million. If Jagr negotiates an extension, though, he might demand $12 million or more.

"It really hasn't changed," Sather said about the Jagr situation in Pittsburgh. "I had some conversations with Craig (Patrick), and of course read the comments that Jagr has made about how he would like to come here, but at this stage it's still speculation, so I really don't have anything more to say about it than that."

Sather added that he expects Detroit to make goalie Chris Osgood available because of Hasek's arrival, but that the Rangers' interest will depend on what they would have to give up to get him.

He also said he thinks the Rangers are better today than they were a year ago at this time.

"I suppose the other point of this whole thing is that we didn't get locked into any real long-term contracts that were going to be a problem for us in the future," he said.

That may be a case of searching for a positive.

NEW YORK

What had been Glen Sather's infatuation now has a chance to become reality.

For better or worse, Philadelphia's troubled Eric Lindros has added the Rangers to the list of teams to which he'd agree to be traded.

Lindros and Sather, who has publicly been intrigued by the possibility of adding the dangerously risky center to his team, spoke at length last Thursday and Friday.

Lindros finally said he would play with his boyhood idol, Mark Messier, and knows he has to revive his career—after the Flyers let him sit out the entire 2000-01 season—if he wants to represent Canada in the 2002 Olympics.

In March, Lindros' wish list included only St. Louis, Dallas, Washington and Toronto.

Sather, painted into a corner by his inability to land any of his prime targeted free agents, may now have to decide if he will pursue Lindros, 28, or Jaromir Jagr. Even Cablevision probably can't afford both. Those two players, plus the goalie the Rangers will require if they want to get anywhere near the playoff race, remain Sather's only chance to dramatically alter his roster this summer.

There are several complicated steps involved in the Lindros chase. One, the Rangers will have to come up with a trade offer better than reasonably good offers made by the Leafs and Blues last season. Better, most likely, than the ridiculous offer of Petr Nedved and Pavel Brendl, which Sather made prior to, and at, the NHL draft.

Flyers GM Bobby Clarke has said he would let Lindros sit out another season, or even three more (until he is eligible for unrestricted free agency at 31), but indicated he might now be willing to accept draft picks and prospects since the 100-point Flyers have replaced Lindros with free agent Jeremy Roenick.

Two, the Rangers will have to reach an agreement on a contract with the restricted free agent, who turned down Philadelphia's $8.5 million offer last summer.

Three, Lindros will have to pass a ton of medical tests because of the six concussions he has suffered, including three serious head injuries at the end of 1999–2000. Sather has to be convinced he's not giving up assets for a player who might play one shift before being forced to retire.

Would Sather be willing to part with Theo Fleury for Lindros? Probably. Would he give up top prospects Pavel Brendl or Jamie Lundmark, players he is desperately trying to keep out of any potential Jagr trade with Pittsburgh?

Sather also spoke to Clarke about a Brian Leetch-for-Lindros swap, knowing that Leetch has a no-trade clause he won't waive.

As for Jagr, it doesn't appear any deal is imminent. There are at least four teams involved to varying degrees, although Dallas apparently is out. The Kings, who sought Jagr in 1997, are believed to be one of the top contenders, along with the Rangers and perhaps San Jose.

Penguins GM Craig Patrick, in no hurry, has talked to Sather about Brendl, Lundmark, Mike York and Radek Dvorak, and been rebuffed on all four. Sather has offered Jan Hlavac and Kim Johnsson.

Obviously, that package will not get it done.

WEDNESDAY, JULY 11, 2001

NEW YORK

The Rangers' summer of 1999 will always be infamous for the team's overindulgence in the free-agent market.

The summer of 2001 has become quite the opposite. This is the summer where the Rangers continually came up empty, their feeble swing-and-miss on Jaromir Jagr punctuating the entire famine.

Sather's refusal to negotiate further than his original offer of Jan Hlavac, Kim Johnsson and goalie Johan Holmqvist cost him a chance to get the premier offensive player in the league, the player who has led the league in scoring four years in a row, and probably the one player who could have put the starving Rangers into the playoffs for the first time in five years.

Instead, Jagr wound up in Washington today for three 20-year-old prospects and future considerations.

Sather, in Boston for a celebrity golf event with buddy Harry Sinden, said he was called by Pittsburgh counterpart Craig Patrick and notified of the deal. Sather asked Patrick if "it was too late to change the offer" but was told the deal was done.

So Sather, who might now put his foot on the pedal in the questionable chase for accident-waiting-to-happen Eric Lindros—Sather said he will take a couple of days before deciding his next move—will go into next season with a team not nearly as good as the team that missed the playoffs so badly last season.

The Rangers now apparently will not be in the hunt for free agent Brett Hull, who wanted to play with Jagr in New York, or at least he did according to his agent, who happens to also be Jagr's agent. Hull may join Jagr in Washington.

Patrick insisted all along that there were other teams involved, and obviously there were. The fact that the Rangers were the only team negotiating with Jagr's agent Mike Barnett on a contract extension was misperceived as the Rangers being the only team dealing with Patrick.

So Patrick, who, according to a source with knowledge of the situation, couldn't even get Sather to discuss Mike York in the package, and who wanted Radek Dvorak instead of Hlavac, and one of the Rangers' top two prospects, Jamie Lundmark or Pavel Brendl, turned to Washington GM George McPhee. A Rangers' source said that the offer was Hlavac, Johnsson and a third changing component, either an NHL player or one of the prospects.

The Capitals, looking to spend a ton of money on free agents (Jeremy Roenick, Joe Sakic and others went before the Caps could get involved), hit the jackpot.

Sather said he thought the negotiating back-and-forth was still ongoing with Patrick, and that he felt his offer was better than what McPhee traded.

"I was trying to make as good an offer as we could, but I didn't want to decimate the team in the future," Sather said. "You want your team to be able to grow internally. It didn't work out. I wasn't willing to give it all away."

The cost in prospects was steep. Washington cleared its cupboard in giving up centers Kris Beech and Michael Sivek plus defenseman Ross Lupaschuk.

All three were chosen in the same 1999 draft in which the Rangers plucked Brendl fourth and Lundmark ninth, but only Beech is considered the A-level prospect Brendl and Lundmark are. Beech went seventh overall and played his junior hockey as Brendl's center at Calgary (WHL). Sivek and Lupaschuk were taken with the first and sixth picks in the second round.

There has been the theory that the talks between Sather and Lindros the last two weeks were a cooked-up ruse to try to force the hands of Pittsburgh (with the Rangers) and other suitors interested in Lindros.

Now, desperate and unable to make a single move to improve his floundering franchise, Sather may have to give up a chunk of the team's future to get Lindros.

FOR THE DECADE of the 1990s, the Rangers were mocked as being Edmonton East. Their thirst for obtaining any and all of Edmonton's aging stars resulted in a Stanley Cup and a baring of the cupboard of young prospects and players.

Now the Rangers are again Edmonton East. Only this time they are the Oilers in that they have become a small market team. The Rangers can't/won't get star players here. They can't/won't because one man, the former GM of the Edmonton Oilers, who hasn't had a winning season in nine years, can't/won't spend the money or take the steps necessary to complete big-time trades.

Sather blew it on Jagr. Simple as that. First he blew it on every free agent he wanted, because Sather won't pay players more than he thinks they're worth. Well, that is how unrestricted free agency works. You get UFAs by overpaying them.

For two summers now, Sather has sat back and watched. His Rangers needed beef and grit, but Sather would rather do nothing that to over-bid for gritty, beefy guys like Dallas Drake and Scott Thornton last sum-mer, or Martin Lapointe this summer. Lapointe was just too expensive, Sather felt.

Yeah, there comes a point where it's just too much money, but the last place to reach that point is MSG, where Cablevision prints money.

Sather seems intent on doing things the opposite way of Neil Smith, his predecessor who was booted out of town after a failed series of moves he made in 1999. That's fine, too. Except that Smith knew that there was a way to rebuild and to try to keep your team competitive at the same time—and that was through free agency.

He lost Wayne Gretzky in 1999, then had to deal Dan Cloutier, Niklas Sundstrom and Marc Savard off his roster to get Jamie Lundmark, Pavel Brendl and Jan Hlavac. So he had holes to fill, and he did it with Jim Dolan's checkbook. It didn't work. The only thing it cost the Rangers was money.

Sather came in and said, through his actions, that everything here before him was wrong, from coaches to players to scouts. So every free agent the Rangers had was let go, last year and this year. That includes Mathieu Schneider, whom Sather didn't even investigate. And it includes Rich Pilon, who played his heart out this year (and signed with St. Louis). They were wrong just because they weren't his.

Meanwhile, Sather signed career underachiever Vladimir Malakhov, who was grossly overpaid even though nobody else was bidding; and this year's beauties, Dave Karpa and Igor Ulanov, neither of whom is as good as Pilon or the unwanted Brad Brown.

As for Jagr, Sather played smug tough-guy, which may have worked in the 1980s when he was dealing from strength, but won't work when he's dealing off the bottom of the pile. He dared Craig Patrick to trade Jagr elsewhere, and Patrick did.

There are those who laud Sather for holding onto Brendl and Lundmark, and perhaps Tomas Kloucek and others, instead of sweetening his original offer of Hlavac and Kim Johnsson. That the Rangers held onto their top prospects is admirable, except that Sather has offered them around everywhere else—for Keith Tkachuk and Nikolai Khabibulin; for Eric Lindros. So he has kept Brendl almost by accident.

And if there is one player on this planet for whom you include Brendl, it is Jagr, despite his baggage. Jagr automatically gets the Rangers into the playoffs. Jagr, at 29, is still here when they are ready to contend again. So why not?

Brett Hull made no sense then, and makes absolutely no sense now. His 25 goals, even if he gets 35, don't improve the team, don't make his teammates better.

Jagr would have.

Guaranteed, Jagr would be a Ranger today if Smith was still the GM, or if Dave Checketts was running the Garden. They understood this isn't Edmonton.

It's funny, too, how those who battered Smith because he wouldn't give up his prospects for Pavel Bure, praise Sather for not giving them up for Jagr, a player in a different stratosphere.

Now Sather will turn to his last chance to make noise, the guy with whom he's been infatuated for all of his 13 months in office, Eric Lindros. Sather offered Petr Nedved and Brendl for Lindros previously; and is said to have offered a lot more at the trade deadline.

For all and any of those offers, he probably would have been fired if he didn't have complete autonomy at the Garden for six more years. How do you offer up Brendl for Lindros but not for Jagr? How? And how did Bobby Clarke, the Flyers GM, turn it down?

If Sather gives up anything of value off his roster—even unwanted Theo Fleury—he is tempting a total disaster. Lindros's career is on a shift-by-shift meter which is ticking every time he goes onto the ice. Besides, the first thing the Rangers need is a goalie, not a headache.

Everybody knows it. You would think Sather knows, too.

FOR SATHER, the timing of the Jagr deal could not have been worse, either. It came the day after the major-league baseball All-Star game, so there were no baseball games played. Thus baseball-crazed New York became a hockey town for a day. On WFAN, the city's all-sports radio station, Sather was absolutely destroyed by callers and hosts alike. He was further roasted for being out playing golf—he was actually en route—while the deal went down. In other words, the perception was that Sather was asleep at the switch.

The hits kept on coming for the Rangers and Sather, whose most positive moments came when A) it was announced that training camp for the coming season would be held at Madison Square Garden (free admission) as a gesture of reaching out to disgruntled fans; B) Sather's trip to Calgary to attend Theo Fleury's charity golf tournament and support his troubled winger; and C) the acquisitions of some young players, including those he got for Adam Graves and Tim Taylor, as well as 21-year-old signees Barrett Heisten, a winger, Matt Kinch, a defenseman, and 25-year-old goalie Scott Meyer.

But Sather made some other questionable deals, signing soon-to-be-32 Zdeno Ciger, a winger who spent the last five years playing in his native Slovakia. He is skilled but soft, and you have to wonder why a team would spend $3.5 million over two years for a guy like that, while letting an important leader like Graves take a hike.

Ciger, listed at 6-1, 190 pounds, plays much smaller than that, and he will be taking up a roster spot that might better be used to bring along Manny Malhotra, Pavel Brendl or even another Sather acquisition, underachiever Michal Grosek.

There were other bits of news, too. Kamensky signed with Dallas as a free agent. Brad Brown, whom the Rangers could easily have kept for a 10 percent raise, signed with Minnesota.

Malhotra was forced to sign his qualifying offer, since he had no bargaining leverage based on his numbers over three mostly wasted seasons. Derek Armstrong, the AHL's leading scorer last year, has signed to play in Switzerland rather than return to the Hartford Wolf Pack.

Sather lost more scouts, too. When he took over last June, he learned that the scouts had clauses in their contracts which said, if they weren't terminated in June, they would automatically be extended for the following year. So Sather immediately terminated them last summer, so that this summer he would be able to clean some of them out. Sather lost Martin Madden to Montreal last summer, then dropped the respected Darwin Bennett and Dick Todd this summer. Kevin McDonald also left the organization, to join St. Louis. Sather also canned strength and conditioning coach Scott Livingston, and before the summer was out, he fired long-time team doctor Bart Nisonson, probably for operating on Sylvain Lefebvre's shoulder and thus preventing Sather from buying out Lefebvre's contract.

FLEURY COMPLETED his substance-abuse rehab in Southern California, then hid out in New Mexico with new team strength coach Mark Puttenvink, who has worked in the past with players in rehab. Puttenvink had Fleury in top shape, the player and the team said.

Fleury, 33, then went to Calgary to host his charity golf event for Crohn's Disease, from which he suffers, and to face the media for the first time since his season ended in February.

"I don't think about the past anymore," Fleury said. "Today is all I have.

"There was never a thought in my mind that I would not be back. I basically have the tools to deal with situations that used to perplex me."

Fleury is prohibited by his doctors and the program from discussing his specific troubles or his treatment process. He was looking forward to going home—which has always been the hockey rink.

"I always felt joy, I always felt happiness, I always felt complete when I was on the ice," Fleury said. "The hockey rink has always been my happy place where I felt really comfortable."

Sather sat with Fleury as he spoke.

"This is not something where you spend four or five months changing your lifestyle," Sather said. "He's going to have to fight until someone sticks him in the ground 50 years from now."

MIKE RICHTER BEGAN SKATING a month before camp, for which he expects to be ready to participate. Richter, who returned from his left knee reconstruction in late October last season, should be back earlier than that from his right knee surgery, which was less complicated, and a month earlier.

It had come full circle, from Richter's baby steps last September, to these new baby steps in August.

Asked if he was concerned about Sather trying to trade him in March, or trying to bring in another goalie for the coming season, Richter became defiant.

"For me that aspect is secondary to getting myself healthy," Richter said. "The only way I'm going to make a contribution to the team is if I'm 100 percent. And when I feel I'm 100 percent, in my opinion, it doesn't matter who they bring in; I'll beat him out."

Getting healthy is all that matters at the moment. Richter's place on the U.S. Olympic team is being kept warm, too, in the event he gets back to his old form at some point in the early going. Richter noted that he was playing "some of the best hockey" of his career when he tore the left ACL at the 2000 All-Star game skills competition in Toronto, and was reaching his peak again when he ripped the right ACL.

He said the therapy on the right knee has also helped the left knee, which, he claimed, is stronger than it has ever been. He also said that his first time on skates he felt stabile and strong, as opposed to the first time back last year, when he was wobbly. He has had an extra month, this time, having had the surgery in March instead of April.

Richter was asked if he expects to remain a Ranger for the final year of his contract (he is to make $6 million) this season.

"Yeah, I expect to be in a lot of ways, but certainly I can't have those expectations so rigid that your shattered if it doesn't work," he said. "There's a zillion things that can come up that compromise anybody's design. That design, Slats (Sather) can change in a heartbeat, depending on who gets hurt or how we're doing.

"The most important thing for me is to play well. It's what you're paid to do, and it's how I'm going to help this organization and how I'm going to help my chances of staying in this organization and staying in this league."

He insisted he was not hurt, nor will he be, by trade rumors.

"Big deal, so there were trade talks last year," he said. "What am I going to cry about it? I mean, he'd be nuts if he didn't think about trading every single guy on the team at one point. If my ego's so fragile that I can't be considered in trade rumors, well, I shouldn't be in the freakin' locker room."

That was an apt description of the place it was these past 12 months, even these past four years. The freakin' locker room.

THE SUMMER WAS GOING absolutely nowhere when Sather finally made his enormous splash on August 20. That was the day he landed his big fish, Eric Lindros. The news of the trade, which sent Brendl (and all of his 20-year-old potential), Jan Hlavac, Kim Johnsson, and a third-round draft pick to Philadelphia, had leaked more than a week earlier, and Sather took another public beating in New York City and its environs.

RISK? WHAT RISK?

According to Sather and his newest superstar center, there's not a worry in the world about the blockbuster trade finished off on Aug. 20.

The Rangers finally obtained Eric Lindros and all of his potential, along with all of his baggage, both physical and personal, for two young players, a top prospect and a draft pick, not to mention anywhere from $3 million to $38 million.

But, if you listened to Sather or Lindros that day, this wasn't a gamble. Not at all.

"No, I don't think it's very risky," Sather said. "I think that someone that's had a concussion before, it's probably easier for him to get another concussion. But (Lindros) and his family feel very comfortable about this. He wants to play and the doctors approved him to play a long time ago."

Lindros was cleared to play last November, to be exact, after suffering the sixth concussion of his career (all in a 27-month span) on a frightening hit by New Jersey Devils captain Scott Stevens in Game 7 of the 2000 Eastern Conference finals.

But he hadn't played because A) he turned down Philadelphia's contract offer in the summer of 2000; and B) the Flyers were unable to trade his rights because Lindros had a short list of teams to which he'd agree to be traded.

But when potential deals with Toronto and St. Louis fell apart last season, Lindros expanded his list to include the Rangers in June.

So Sather, who coveted Lindros since becoming the Rangers' boss only a week after Lindros' last concussion, finally completed a deal with his counterpart, Philadelphia GM Bobby Clarke.

The Rangers traded winger Jan Hlavac, a 28-goal scorer last season, defenseman Kim Johnsson, top prospect Pavel Brendl, a sniper of a left winger, and a third-round draft pick for the rights to Lindros.

They then signed Lindros to a complex four-year contract that somewhat protect the team in the event that Lindros suffers another major head injury. Lindros's guaranteed base salary for 2000-01 is about $3 million. However, if he plays the first 50 games of the season without a catastrophe, that salary goes up to a reported $9.5 million. Should Lindros suffer a concussion that costs him 12 months of playing time prior to the 50th game, however, the Rangers owe him nothing more, and the Flyers owe the Rangers a first-round pick in 2002, and a return of their third-round pick.

The last three years of the contract, should Lindros stay relatively healthy this season, will carry a base salary of about $9.5 million per. Each season, though, is reportedly at the club's option, except for the final year, which is a mutual option. The most Lindros, 28, could cost the Rangers in terms of money is about $38 million.

What he might cost them in players is arguable, so much so that the skeptical New York fans were largely up in arms over the acquisition of a player who is not only scorned, but also considered damaged goods.

If Lindros is healthy, as he claims to be, and can return to being the power center and one of the league's top-10 impact players, then it won't matter a lick what Brendl—who has the potential to be a big-time goal-scorer or a bust with no work ethic—turns out to be. It won't matter if Hlavac develops into a 35-goal, two-way force on the wing.

But if Lindros follows the footsteps of Pat LaFontaine, Jeff Beukeboom, Geoff Courntall or even his own brother, Brett; or of NFL stars Troy Aikman, Steve Young and Al Toon, just to name a few, the Rangers will have given up way too much.

If Lindros goes down for good, as LaFontaine did upon returning to the NHL as a Ranger after 67 games in 1997-98, the Rangers will have given up two legitimate NHL players and one of their top two prospects, off an organizational depth chart that is hardly deep enough to absorb such a blow.

The difference between Lindros and the historic line of athletes who have never been the same, or who have been forced to retirement by repeated concussions, he said, is that he has had 15 months off to heal.

"I've been symptom free for 15, 16 months now," Lindros said. "Other players haven't had that opportunity to heal."

If it were that simple, though, wouldn't doctors prescribe long layoffs for athletes with multiple concussions? If it were that simple, why did Lindros want to play last November through March?

Lindros said that was the difference between himself and his brother, Brett, who retired from the Islanders at age 20, and called the comparison, "apples and oranges."

Sather said he completely bought the stamp of approval from the group of doctors who gave Lindros the go-ahead to play last November, and who reexamined Lindros prior to the trade's completion.

Sather showed his typical old-school feelings, or his lack of enlightenment on the subject of concussions when he said, "You get a headache today, you've got a concussion."

Less than two days later, Sather had lost out on his bid to sign free-agent winger Brett Hull, who agreed to a two-year contract with the Detroit Red Wings.

By then, the anti-Lindros sentiment in New York had cooled a bit.

Lindros repeatedly said he was "fired up" to be back in the NHL, and 24 hours after the announcement he was on the ice at Rye Playland, the Rangers' practice facility, to skate with a group that included Brian Leetch, Mike Richter and a bunch of young prospective Rangers.

"I understand there's probably some skepticism because of the concussions," Lindros said, "so we're just going to have to win them over."

Lindros also got the blessing of the Rangers captain, and his boyhood idol, Marl Messier.

Messier called Lindros the "prototype New York hockey player — he's a tough player, he plays hard every night, he's physical."

Messier then added that "I just see it as a great match for New York.

"I don't look at it as being a tough decision when you can add a player like Eric Lindros to a team. Unfortunately, you don't get a player like Eric Lindros, at 28 years old at the peak of his career, for free."

He wasn't free.

Asked if the cost for Lindros is a departure from his rebuild-with-youth philosophy he has espoused for almost a year, Sather said, "It's absolutely not. This is part of the long-range project to build this organization.

"Sometimes you get a young asset who just doesn't seem to be turning out to be what you expected. So you make the deal. You parlay one thing into another. But it doesn't mean that your attitude has changed toward young players. You've got to build through youth."

Sather insisted that he first "replenished the assets" by his early-summer signings and trades for young players like Barrett Heisten and Mikael Samuelsson.

Sather also insisted that his failure to get Jaromir Jagr had no bearing on his willingness or the necessity to make the Lindros trade. He said the same package would not have gotten Jagr, although that package was not ever offered. Jagr, though, is much more of a sure thing — an unquestionable superstar in his prime, who could have been around for the next eight or 10 years.

Reportedly, Sather's final offer was Johnsson, Hlavac and goalie Johan Holmqvist, while the Penguins wanted those three and another prospect—but not Brendl. Still, one source insisted that had Brendl been in the deal, Jagr would be a Ranger today.

"YOU CAN BE A LION maybe once in your life," Sather said. "If you don't make this deal, you're a mouse forever."

Sather's behind was clearly on the coals.

But, in a sentence that told of just how powerful Sather had become in the organization, Garden boss Jim Dolan said he didn't even know about the Lindros trade until he read the breaking news in newspapers.

So here they went again. The Rangers were having their annual major news conference, announcing the latest savior, the latest big change.

And yet nothing ever seems to change at the self-proclaimed World's Most Famous Arena. Nothing changes for a team that has won one Stanley Cup in 61 seasons.